Plantation Ente...

in Colonial South Carolina

...cs of History
...reaks down
...nder theory

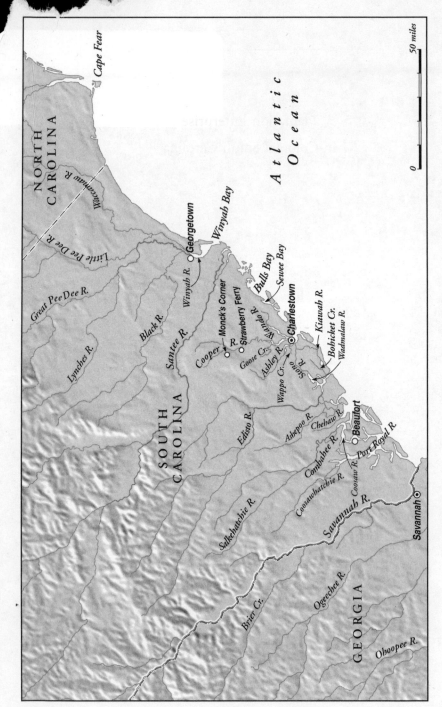

The South Carolina Lowcountry. Map by Philip A. Schwartzberg.

Plantation Enterprise
in Colonial South Carolina

S. Max Edelson

Harvard University Press
Cambridge, Massachusetts
London, England

First Harvard University Press paperback edition, 2011

Library of Congress Cataloging-in-Publication Data

Edelson, S. Max.
Plantation enterprise in colonial South Carolina / S. Max Edelson.
p. cm.
Includes bibliographical references and index.
ISBN 978-0-674-02303-1 (cloth: alk. paper)
ISBN 978-0-674-06022-7 (pbk.)
1. South Carolina—History—Colonial period, ca. 1600–1775.
2. Plantation life—South Carolina—History—17th century.
3. Plantation life—South Carolina—History—18th century.
4. Rice farmers—South Carolina—History.   5. South Carolina—
Social life and customs.   6. Slavery—South Carolina—History.
7. Landscape—Social aspects—South Carolina—History.
8. Human ecology—South Carolina—History.   9. Human
geography—South Carolina—History.   10. South Carolina—
Environmental conditions.   I. Title.
F272.E34   2006
975.7'02—dc22   2006043539

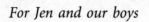

For Jen and our boys

Contents

Illustrations and Tables

Acknowledgments

I am grateful to Jack P. Greene for his advice and encouragement, and especially for the example he sets as a scholar and intellectual. It was a privilege to have been a part of the Colonial British American History Research Seminar, the community of early Americanists he assembled at the Johns Hopkins University. Michael P. Johnson's enthusiasm for this project from its inception has been invaluable. I relied on many other scholars and colleagues in writing this book. Some contributed insights and advice that I have tried to incorporate into these pages. Others have provided references or drafts of their own works-in-progress, or have engaged me in rewarding conversations and e-mail exchanges. Among them are Ira Berlin, Matti Bunzl, Vernon Burton, Judith A. Carney, Benjamin Carp, Peter A. Coclanis, Clare Crowston, Adam Davis, Trudy Eden, Emma Hart, Karen Ordahl Kupperman, James La Fleur, Olga Linares, Russell R. Menard, Sidney W. Mintz, Alex Moore, Philip D. Morgan, Norris Nash, Robert Olwell, Stephan Palmié, Jonathan Poston, David Roediger, the late George C. Rogers Jr., Richard Ross, David B. Ryden, David S. Shields, Michael Tadman, Adam Tooze, Robert M. Weir, Peter H. Wood, and Natalie Zacek. I offer special thanks to April Hatfield, Nils Jacobsen, Fred Jaher, Mike Johnson, and Bradford Wood for reading and critiquing a draft of the manuscript in its entirety.

My research would have been impossible without the assistance of librarians and archivists at the South Carolina Historical Society, the South Caroliniana Library at the University of South Carolina, the Special Collections Room at the College of Charleston's Robert Scott Small Library, the Southern Historical Collection at the University of North Carolina, and the Special Collections Room at Duke University's William R. Perkins

Library. Charles H. Lesser was especially generous with his time and advice at the South Carolina Department of Archives and History in Columbia. The Department of History at the Johns Hopkins University provided generous support in the form of a William and Lois Diamond Fellowship, a Southern History Research Fellowship, and a Mellon Foundation Sawyer Fellowship. An American Historical Association Albert J. Beveridge Research Grant and a John E. Rovensky Fellowship in Business and Economic History from the University of Illinois Foundation funded initial research for this book. The Liberty Fund's 2002 colloquium on South Carolina politics during the Revolutionary era offered a remarkable forum for reading and discussion that shaped its conclusion. At the University of Illinois at Urbana–Champaign (UIUC), course releases provided by an Illinois Program for Research in the Humanities (IPRH) Faculty Fellowship and a Mellon Foundation Faculty Fellowship gave me the time to complete additional research and revise it for publication. A grant from the UIUC Research Board supported the production of maps and other images.

My editor, Joyce Seltzer, offered excellent guidance to help bring this work to press. Philip Schwartzberg of Meridian Mapping produced the maps. Two able graduate student research assistants helped compile the materials that made this book's statistical analysis possible. At the College of Charleston, Charles Phillips Jr. copied more than 1,000 memorials of land titles and entered data from them into a computer database. Bryan Nicholson identified, copied, and logged at least as many newspaper advertisements at the University of Illinois. Mary Stuart, head of the University of Illinois History, Philosophy, and Newspaper Library, helped secure important books and primary source materials. For many years I have depended on Brad Edmondson and Steven Helland for their friendship. For their support and encouragement I also thank my parents, Bob and Fran Edelson, as well as Gerry Seedyke, Elizabeth Pugh, and Bill Seedyke. This book is dedicated, with love, to Jen Edelson and our sons, Will, Leo, and Ben.

A Note on the Text

The characterizations and conclusions in this book rely on the statistical analysis of data drawn from land records, plantation advertisements, account books, and other sources. I describe my key findings in the text and offer further details about methods and results in the notes. Those who wish to review more comprehensive summaries of this data can turn to the tables gathered in the appendix. I have included citations to books and articles in the notes that provide broader statistical overviews of demography, economy, and society in colonial South Carolina. In citing plantations and tracts of land advertised in the *South-Carolina Gazette,* I have included the last name of the "subscriber," the person who placed the advertisement, along with the date of publication to identify specific advertisements within an issue of the newspaper. Throughout the text I refer to the capital and port city of South Carolina as "Charlestown," which remained the most common spelling until its incorporation as "Charleston" in 1783. Unless specifically indicated, all monetary values are given in South Carolina currency. In the period 1725–1775, £100 sterling was worth approximately £700 S.C. On the value of colonial currency, see John J. McCusker, *Money and Exchange in Europe and America, 1600–1775: A Handbook* (Chapel Hill: University of North Carolina Press, 1978), table 5.2.

Plantation Enterprise
in Colonial South Carolina

Introduction

During the unsettled Revolutionary War years, more than one South Carolina planter opened his Bible to the same place to express a desire for tranquility and retreat. Looking forward to a time when swords would be beaten into plowshares, Henry Laurens sought nothing more than to "plant & Cultivate my Vine & my Fig Tree" and "Sit quietly under them."[1] He packed a good measure of self-delusion into this pious sentiment. For more than a century after the establishment of English Carolina in 1670, planters were loath to sit still. From Charlestown outward into the surrounding countryside, they initiated an expansive process of colonization that transformed what they saw as a swampy wilderness into a cultivated landscape of rice fields. This drive to bring land into agricultural order scattered slaves and settlers across a vast coastal plain. With this dispersion came deeper integration. Watercraft and wagons linked plantations to the colony's port and capital and, through it, brought even the most distant outposts into networks of exchange that spanned the Atlantic world.

Planters inhabited a colonial world defined by movement across a landscape in the throes of change. One of the colony's wealthiest men before British forces invaded the Carolina Lowcountry, Laurens had owned "Eight fine Plantations" and kept more than 300 people enslaved to work them. But even so, he recalled, "I did not think I had too much Land." He found a way to market for profit everything that his slaves could be forced to make, including the corn they grew for their own rations. Only when he surveyed his "impoverished and almost ruined" estate at the war's end did he convince himself that he had "abundantly more Land than one Man ought to hold."[2] Disowning a life's work spent enlarging the geographic reach of planting, Laurens dreamt of retirement and set-

1

tled into a diminished vision of the plantation as a refuge from the wider world.

Before the war disrupted its expansion, planting was an economic, cultural, and imperial enterprise that set South Carolina apart as it set it in motion. Colonial planters can be called by many names. They were settlers who established dominion over American land and masters who enforced a brutal work discipline on African slaves to make it pay. In all of their endeavors, however, they were colonists who saw each of their individual plantations as an enterprise that contributed to the transformation of an American wilderness into a settled, British place. With slaves bearing axes and surveyors equipped with compass and chain, colonists advanced across the coastal plain, adding "House to House & laying Field to Field" as they claimed more land. They integrated new territory into Britain's transatlantic empire as they extended the geographic scope of plantation agriculture.[3]

Occupying, cultivating, and inhabiting land was Britain's defining strength as a colonizing society in the new world.[4] Across eastern North America and along the island archipelagos of the Caribbean Sea, colonists established distinctive regional cultures by developing agricultural land. Environmental difference refracted British America into an array of colonial places perhaps even more powerfully than specific European backgrounds, religious convictions, and political systems framed to guide the establishment of new societies. From modest seventeenth-century beginnings within grim, fortified outposts, surging populations laid claim to new lands, extending the practical reach of British hegemony along coastlines, up rivers, and into interiors throughout the eighteenth century. Variations in climate, soil, and topography distinguished regions from one another by delimiting what each could produce to eat and to sell. The strategies colonists put in place to sustain life and export commodities from these lands magnified natural variations into distinctive economic cultures.

During the first half of the seventeenth century, "plantation" conveyed two distinct ideas, that of colonial occupation, on the one hand, and entrepreneurial agriculture, on the other. Within England the term referred to those enterprising farms that served London its fruits and flowers. Any newly settled place could also merit the title, which survived in the name of the institution in charge of American administration, the Board of Trade and Plantations. As colonists and slaves populated plantation America, these distinct meanings coalesced. After 1700 the commonplace definition of plantation was a privately owned domain within tropical or subtropical America that was geared relentlessly toward the transatlantic marketplace. So novel was this new meaning in the early eighteenth century that one writer had to define "plantations (for so we call our farms)" as something familiar and yet still exotic, owned by someone who resembled a distant relative of the "Country Farmer, which we call there Planters."[5] In warm-weather colonies such as South Carolina, where reproducing the signature features of English material culture, such as wheat crops and tilled fields, proved difficult, this process of adaptation was marked by stark departures from conventional practice and initiated significant changes in behavior and identity within transplanted European societies. Even within British plantation America, despite a shared commitment to African slavery and plantation agriculture, the Chesapeake, the West Indies, and the Carolina Lowcountry traveled separate paths through this process of environmental and economic articulation. Their economies took shape around the specific demands of tobacco, sugar, and rice as staple crops, each of which encouraged particular ways of cultivating land, organizing slave labor, and marketing commodities.

This redefined plantation was a vehicle for the territorial extension of empire, more so because it could be tailored to suit the diverse environments of each of plantation America's three major regions. From the moment colonists imagined cultivating this territory south of Virginia and north of Florida, ideas about its natural potential shifted, as did the agricultural methods put in place to raise food, animals, and commodities. Planters in eighteenth-century South Carolina established a highly adaptive economic culture that was open to unfamiliar techniques and committed to agricultural innovation in the face of environmental extremes. Although Carolina's founders, the Lords Proprietors, attempted to enforce a vision of orderly village settlements, the first planters refused to be bound by either the schemes of social superiors or the narrow reproduction of European agricultural precedents. They moved into Cusabo Indian country, enlarging a pale of English settlement that traced the watercourses of a few lowcountry rivers. Their corn-and-cattle enterprises served markets of consumption in the Caribbean and aspired to a plantation form that featured large slave labor forces, the intensive development of land, and the production of a lucrative staple commodity modeled by Barbados sugar planters who helped settle the new colony during its first decades.

In pursuit of a clearer picture of the Carolina Lowcountry's system of racial slavery, historians have seen its plantations as stages on which dramas of repression, resistance, and negotiation between masters and slaves were played out. From the perspective of black endeavor in early South Carolina, plantations were frontier outposts built with African expertise and a flexible task labor system. As communities peopled by the transatlantic slave trade, they were societies defined by ethnic pluralism. Despite the rigors of slavery, plantations in which blacks outnumbered whites by more than ten to one became preserves for the development of an autonomous African American culture.[6] Plantations also bore the marks of South Carolina's deepening economic, intellectual, and political integration within the Atlantic world. As sites of production bound to transatlantic markets, they were specialized capital investments in a vanguard form of international commerce. The wealthiest among the planter elite made them into laboratories for sophisticated agricultural methods that could shore up their credentials as participants in a modernizing world. As tensions escalated between officials and colonists in the 1760s, plantations became kingdoms in microcosm in which rulers and subjects struggled to define the terms of legitimate authority.[7] Each of these views has privileged its own image of the plantation, holding it in place as the context in which to cast other kinds of change into sharper relief.

My approach describes the plantation itself as a dynamic instrument of colonization and economic development. By tracking the ways in which plantation agriculture changed across time and space, we can see the creation of a new-world society as it took form. At the heart of this process was the creation of an economic culture that featured an intensive engagement with the natural environment and a willingness to adapt market agriculture to its constraints and opportunities. In their entrepreneurial sensibilities, as well as their devotion to production for the market, planters were early modern capitalists. Their plantation businesses were a form of enterprise, although they centered on slavery rather than free labor, and in the long term, industrial manufacturing proved to be more influential than plantation agriculture in shaping the evolution of the modern, global economy.[8] Against the idea that plantations were connected to, but were not constituted by, the rise of European capitalism, I argue that the imperatives of commerce shaped the evolution of

South Carolina plantations internally, as well as in their external relationship to the Atlantic economy. Lowcountry colonists were calculative participants in long-distance exchange who restructured plantation production, labor, management, and organization in their drive to amass wealth.

This quest for increased productivity and profits directed how planters planted, but it did not determine their behaviors entirely. This book describes how plantations changed over time and across space and assesses these changes in cultural terms. All who came to the Lowcountry—founders and settlers, masters and slaves, overseers and merchants—staked out a place on the land to find a purchase for their own interests and desires. By paying attention to the perceptions, practices, and experiences by which these actors made sense of their participation within this plantation society, I seek to describe South Carolina's distinctive economic culture, as well as its economic development. Planters managed their enterprises as independent "firms," but saw themselves as part of a collective planter class with its own standards, history, and customs. As they worked to reconcile the several roles they played—as settlers, masters, and colonists—their membership in a community committed to extending dominion across the lowcountry landscape provided a context in which they could claim coherent identities.

planters gained coherent ids thru their roles as masters & colonizers

South Carolina colonists realized four critical environmental adaptations that shaped the evolution of their plantation economy. First, seventeenth-century settlers adapted a British model for valuing and using land to create the first plantations. Although their hardscrabble settlements diverged from the model of an ideal English farmstead, they secured the means of subsistence and an early foothold in Atlantic exchange that entrenched a permanent English presence in the region. Second, as they learned to grow rice in cleared swamps around the turn of the eighteenth century, colonists turned a foreign crop into a lucrative staple commodity by adapting the strategies of "improved" British husbandry to its culture. Planting onetime wastelands with rice intensified South Carolina's participation in the Atlantic economy, gave rise to a unique task labor system, and wrenched slaves into a new plantation regime with violence. Third, in response to the Lowcountry's volatile climate, planters shaped land and commanded water to secure their staple crop from the elements. Technical innovations in irrigation and rice processing, and the addition of indigo as a second staple crop, transformed the mid-

4 environ. adaptations

eighteenth-century rice plantation into a more productive and reliable vehicle for colonizing new lands and building family fortunes. Fourth, as they settled slaves across the extent of the Lowcountry's vast coastal plain after midcentury, colonists shaped the region into contrasting zones for production and consumption. As planters became wealthier, they retreated to the long-settled environs of Charlestown and its hinterland to enjoy the material comforts of living in an increasingly anglicized world. The slaves and overseers who made this refinement possible with their labor lived in a crude and productive frontier, far from the colonial metropolis.

The cultivation of rice set South Carolina apart from other transplanted British societies in America because it created a highly divergent landscape. Colonists fitted the crop to the Lowcountry by putting slaves to work in swamps, a shift in agricultural practice that meant leaving British standards far behind. "Swamp" was an obscure English land term before colonists dusted it off to describe the Southeast's "Moorish Grounds." Because "Low Land" in the Lowcountry resembled a waterlogged forest, dense with vegetation, familiar terms such as "morass" and "fen" did not do justice to its rank fertility.[9] Although South Carolina's swamps bristled with cypress and tupelo trees, the first settlers avoided them as incapable of cultivation. Instead, they cleared tracts of oak and hickory land, claiming scarce plots of good arable soil that traced the contours of riversides in "narrow Streaks, between Pineland and Swamps."[10] Those who had come to Carolina to claim their portions of a temperate agricultural paradise found themselves surrounded by wastelands that, by traditional English standards, ranked as close to worthless for commercial farming.

The rise of the rice economy after 1700 turned this familiar hierarchy of land values on its head. By midcentury Governor James Glen could celebrate the fact that the "Country abounds every where with large Swamps," which slaves had "cleared, opened, and sweetened by Culture."[11] Far "from being waste land," a newcomer reported with surprise in 1736, swamps were now regarded as "equal to our best Lands in England."[12] In waves of expansive eighteenth-century plantation building, colonists deployed growing slave workforces to clear, embank, and irrigate riverside swamps. Planting the wastelands brought colonists into a sustained engagement with the specific dynamics of the lowcountry environment. It also divorced the plantation landscape from the model of the English countryside, forcing planters to imagine the productive possibilities of land in new ways.

Planters cultivated new identities as they transformed this landscape. As they amassed lands and settled slaves on them across the Lowcountry, plantations changed from discrete places of residence and authority into distended ventures that were scattered across space and managed from a distance. Developing multiple sites for agriculture and integrating them into interdependent enterprises accelerated the colonization of the Lowcountry, especially after 1750. But as the scale and organization of plantation enterprises changed, so did the roles of their owners as masters and colonists. Unlike the Chesapeake, whose towns never grew into cities, the Lowcountry's dispersed plantations funneled commodities to Charlestown, turning it into one of colonial British America's largest urban places. Instead of leaving for England, as did prominent Caribbean sugar planters, those in South Carolina generally remained in the province, but took up residence in their growing provincial metropolis. "Many of these planters live not upon their plantations," observed a visitor at the end of the century, "but go, from time to time, to visit them; and have overseers constantly resident upon them."[13] Planting became an activity that was initiated from the city and enacted in the countryside. Although some plantations were literally islands, none were beyond these circuits of exchange. Even the most remote outpost was connected—by coasting schooners, wagons, and flatboats—to direct communication with the colony's dominant Atlantic port. The notion that plantations were "self-contained communities run by a resident patriarch" has fixed on rural great houses and family graveyards as emblems of "identities predicated upon a deep sense of place."[14] The shifting geography of plantation settlement in South Carolina was not a fertile ground in which to nurture the kind of insularity that, for other planters in other colonial places, perhaps, came with the direct mastery of land and people on isolated tracts. With their holdings spread far and wide, members of this the planter elite imagined a range for their ambitions as extensive as the Lowcountry itself, from North Carolina's Lower Cape Fear to British East Florida and into the vast backcountry interior.

White plantation culture celebrated agricultural expertise. Mastering the techniques that adapted the land for agriculture stood at the core of planters' self-conceptions as colonists. The first invitations to leave England "to be a planter" in seventeenth-century Carolina had come at a moment of social disruption that put the very idea of fixed social categories under new pressures. "Plantership" began as a new-world calling that stressed individual character over inherited rank as the key to acquiring land, wealth, and independence. As colonists gained expertise in making exotic plants grow in a "Strange Country," they entered into Atlantic trade as concerned with staking claims to desirable social identities as they were with reaping profits.[15] South Carolina planters, always sensitive to how they were viewed from London, worked to show the value of their colony to Britain's mercantile and territorial empire. British merchants, it seemed at times, failed to credit their commodities for what they were really worth. When British agricultural writers dismissed their prized swamps as "Dismals" and ridiculed their pinelands as infertile "barrens," planters claimed a defensive pride in the hard-won experience by which they had learned to convert wastelands into productive fields.[16] When imperial officials put forward plans to colonize new southeastern lands that excluded their model of plantation slavery, planters critiqued these schemes as impractical. In these transatlantic encounters, they saw their characters, accomplishments, and expertise held up for valuation. Although their society departed from British standards, planters made the case that these differences were necessary adaptations to the Lowcountry's unique environment. The practices they had developed to lay claim to the land, despite their recent vintage, could be considered place-defining customs that should command respect rather than derision. From the vantage of Charlestown, a place where the plantation countryside opened onto currents of transatlantic exchange, colonists conceived of South Carolina as a viable provincial society within the larger Anglo-Atlantic world.

As planters acquired the trappings of gentility, they took on the sensibilities of merchants, applying commercial strategies to integrate their scattered plantations and hold proxies and dependents to account. Their identities as provincial elites seemed to draw from two very different cultural models. One was the head of a gentry household, perhaps best represented by their planter counterparts in tidewater Virginia who were known for the elaborate ways in which they displayed their authority through dress, architecture, and a ritualized culture of hospitality toward other white men.[17] The other was the persona of the striving man of trade, who put the demands of commerce at the center of his social world, mixing the prosaic concerns of business into public and private life. Lord Adam Gordon noted this hybrid social character on a visit to Charlestown in the mid-1760s. His lowcountry hosts lived up to their paradoxical reputations as "courteous" yet "affable," as "hospitable and attentive to

Strangers" as they were "clever in business."[18] In this regard, they aspired to become a "polite and commercial" people, more like Britain's rising class of traders, professionals, and new landowners than its landed aristocracy.[19] When South Carolina planters traveled abroad, encountering stiff formality in the company of fellow elites from the Chesapeake to the British Isles, they took stock of the distinctive identities they had cultivated along with barrels of rice and casks of indigo.[20]

This portrait of planters in engagement with nature, economy, and culture offers new perspectives on slavery's role in the development of plantation America. This history of a colonial society built around adaptive responses to volatile change suggests that plantation societies and the elites who led them had secured a purchase on American land that was not easily dislodged. In contrast to a vision of plantation slavery as a social relic, progressively undermined by the forces of modernity, this story of the colonization of the South Carolina Lowcountry suggests how firmly plantation societies were entrenched and how capable they were of reproduction outward in space and into the future. Although masters claimed absolute possession of slaves as property, historians have undermined such claims during the past three decades by tracing "continuities with Africa, reassessing 'the weapons of the weak,' cataloging acts of resistance, searching out signs of unbroken cultural strength, and applauding forms of family life that endured through enslavement."[21] This focus on resistance to domination has represented plantation societies in terms of their instabilities. A by-product of this appreciation of African American agency is the figure of the "anxious" planter, immobilized by fears of insurrection and desperate to keep the ideological contradictions on which his authority supposedly rested—as planter, master, and patriarch—from coming undone. As historians dismantled the caricature of the cowering Sambo, they also redrew the figure of the planter against the grain of his own idealized self-image. Their stories of black resilience have cast planters as characters in a satire of thwarted mastery, their desires for absolute dominion always undermined by those they claimed to own.

Those who seek signs of vulnerability need not look far beneath the surface of the documentary record to find them. Descriptions of plantation enterprise contained in letter books, published accounts, and government records can be made to yield a catalogue of disorders that suggests a brittle system under sustained assault by bad seasons, unruly

slaves, and volatile markets. At the same time, the statistical record of the
eighteenth-century economy shows a rapid rise in the value of exports,
strong gains in white per capita wealth, increasing agricultural productivity, and sustained territorial expansion. Throughout the colonial period
and into the nineteenth century, plantation slavery was the driving force
behind South Carolina's surging growth.[22] These two perspectives on the
lowcountry plantation economy—one that privileges the shock of contingent events, and the other that describes a long-term advance—need
to be reconciled. Early modern critics stigmatized American planters as
a class of new-world tyrants, a debased aristocracy characterized by vul-
garity, idleness, and violence. This negative portrayal of planter character
has been joined to the idea that plantation societies, because they were
built on the crumbling foundation of a system of labor and social organization deemed archaic, began falling apart almost as soon as they were
put in place. By this logic, acts of resistance not only demonstrated the
humanity of the enslaved at the moment, but also introduced permanent
fissures into slave societies that progressively undermined their growth
and stability. Understanding slavery as a pathological social condition in
this way gains moral clarity about its evils at the price of underestimating
its flexibility in the face of destabilizing change.

In 1739 slaves rose up at Stono River, killing more than twenty colonists. Although this was the last slave rebellion attempted in colonial
South Carolina, enslaved people continued to burn, steal, and run away
in ways that threatened white rule. In response to the violence at Stono,
South Carolina legislators framed the repressive Negro Act of 1740
around the idealized figure of the immobilized slave, whose every step
beyond the plantation was to be authorized by a master. In practice,
placing the colony's dispersed black majority under such restraint was
never more than a prescriptive fantasy. South Carolina possessed the territorial extent of a mainland colony along with the skewed demography
of a West Indian sugar island. Slaves passed between wild and cultivated
spaces; they journeyed by road and river between town and countryside,
slipping in and out of the glare of white scrutiny.[23] Although whites sometimes saw the movements of this numerically dominant population as a
menace to their security, they also set an increasing minority of their
slaves in motion, tasking them with specialized jobs, from boatman to
itinerant carpenter, required to link their plantations together as integrated enterprises that could be managed from town. Moments of violent

resistance punctuated the history of slavery in colonial South Carolina. The everyday engagement of enslaved workers with the shifting order of economic life, however, played out across a long-term process of plantation settlement. Some slaves struggled to protect customary practices that currents of productive change eroded. Others exploited new work opportunities that these changes offered. Colonists and slaves maneuvered for advantage as the very shape and extent of plantations changed over time and across space.

Far more effectively than has been recognized, colonists stabilized slavery as a means of settling the Lowcountry. The agricultural innovations they introduced in rice production, for example, undermined the effectiveness of the task labor system, long seen by historians as a crucial point of leverage used by the enslaved to limit planters' demands for work. Although they found ways to counter and contain slaves' bids for more control over their lives and labor, they did not believe in the legal fiction that slaves were mere chattel. South Carolina masters saw slaves as the motive force behind landscape change. George Ogilvie waxed lyrical about the "shelter of the vine and the figtree" that he claimed his "own hands had planted and reared" on Myrtle Grove Plantation. It is unlikely that Ogilvie actually dirtied his hands with such hard labor. The common figure of speech by which an individual field worker was represented was the "taskable hand." John Martin bragged that with sixty slaves "about me to do what I order," he could plant more than 100 acres with rice. Martin's slaves also grew actual, rather than metaphorical, grapes and figs in his "Garden & Vineyard" on the banks of the Winyah River.[24] In practical terms, a plantation was less a physical place than it was a process of settling slaves on the land and forcing them to develop it.

In their financial reckonings, planters put slaves at the center of their calculations as a special kind of animating capital "stock." Settling "good working Hand[s]" on the land transformed it into a viable estate that was capable of generating a reliable annual return. Land "without Slaves" languished as an investment.[25] The image of slaves at work on the land lodged deep in planters' imaginations when they described this capacity to effect landscape change. One went so far as to visualize the scale of a hurricane's destruction as if "a thousand negroes [had] been employed for a whole day in cutting down . . . trees." Directing so many slave hands gave planters the ability to change the land and profit from it on a massive scale. Despite the everyday dissonance of slave resistance, "nothing [was] so much coveted as the pleasure of possessi[ng] many Slaves."[26] From within the expanding plantation landscape that slave work made possible, planters saw slavery in the service of colonization that improved the Lowcountry more than it reproduced disorder within it. Only after the disorders of the War for Independence did the idea of slavery as a long-term liability to South Carolina's economic and territorial growth take root to tarnish this confidence in slavery as a means of settling the Lowcountry.

These dynamics of extensive settlement, agricultural innovation, and economic integration circulate as central themes in the history of Henry Laurens's plantation enterprise, perhaps the best-documented plantation business in colonial British America. Despite moments of pessimism, planters saw their colony before 1776 as part of plantation America, a prosperous and expanding zone for enterprise that stretched from the Caribbean to the Chesapeake. The destruction visited on the Lowcountry during the war disrupted this confidence that they had acquired over the course of a century spent adapting agriculture to nature. Once committed to a vision of unlimited expansion, Laurens and his fellow planters saw the colonial period end on a collective note of loss despite the American victory. Whatever their preindependence politics, planters faced the American Revolution as a painful cultural break. In the generation before the war, rising incomes allowed them to emulate British material culture, demonstrate their value to empire, and stake claims as standard-bearers of a viable provincial culture. At this moment when their desires for metropolitan recognition seemed close to realization, the war cut them off from the British transatlantic community that had long given their pursuits meaning. They were forced to turn away from the cultural currency of Atlantic exchange and toward an uncertain future tied to the task of reproducing plantation society within an emerging continental South.

— 1 —

Laying Claim to the Land

English Carolina began as a landscape of possibility. Its official boundaries extended across continental North America and terminated at the coastline of a distant western sea. Constrained only by lines of latitude that focused the ambitions of its founders to the south of Virginia, a 1663 royal grant carved out the northern reaches of Spanish Florida as a space for innovative agricultural dominion. When North Carolina settlers received their own colonial governor in 1712, "Carolina" vanished as a meaningful title for this vast grant of American territory,[1] but this division was already a matter of administrative semantics. By this time the environmental promise of Carolina had been realized in racial, social, and economic terms with the creation of a plantation society in the South Carolina Lowcountry. By the early eighteenth century, with its enslaved African majority, its freshwater swamps cleared for rice fields, and its port city teeming with transatlantic commercial traffic, the colony embarked on a developmental course whose orientation had been set by seventeenth-century encounters. As colonists fortified Charlestown and took up lands along nearby rivers in the 1670s, 1680s, and 1690s, Native Americans, enslaved Africans, English founders, and European planters each attempted to set a course for the colony's future by fixing people on the land in different ways. In this multicultural contest over the shape of an emerging plantation landscape, the planters' vision prevailed because of their practical command of land and an early willingness to absorb lessons from those they displaced, enslaved, and overthrew to plant it.

The transformation of "Carolina," the prospective colony, into a market-driven, expansionistic plantation society in South Carolina was a contested process. Unrealistic expectations for what the English settlement of the region would mean were challenged not only by environmental realities, but especially by the divergent landscape visions of several groups, each of which claimed the Lowcountry as its own. The founding Lords Proprietors attempted to impose a vision of a progressive, corporatist polity in South Carolina. Coastal Indians worked to establish the English within Cusabo country as interdependent partners in a defensive strategic alliance. African slaves worked in wastes and wilderness to control their own material culture and domestic economies, creating plantations within plantations. Exposed to diverse models for harnessing Carolina's natural abundance, its European settlers ran roughshod over each of these landscape visions. As they asserted a planters' landscape, they laid the foundations of an economic culture that was highly adaptive to changing circumstances and new knowledge. At the same time, this culture was tightly focused on the goal of establishing the plantation as a private domain for authority and enterprise.

Early colonizers saw Carolina as an environmental Eden prepared by nature to become an outpost of the surging Atlantic economy. A latecomer to England's North American empire, it was a space that seemed equipped by climate, soil, and water to make its founders' fantasies of extensive settlement a self-fulfilling prophecy. Situated geographically between plantation America's tobacco colonies and sugar islands, the colony's inchoate abundance was a riddle that improved agriculture could solve by yielding a commodity matched to its promise. As they classified the land with the categories of English farming, settlers saw new-world abundance as a force to be harnessed for profit. Early colonizers understood the environment as a surrogate capable of nurturing the world's exotic produce. Through experiments in husbandry, according to the logic of its promoters, Carolina would find its lucrative and defining staple, luring European immigrants to take up lands within the grant's vast extent to profit from its production. Until rice became that wished-for staple at the turn of the eighteenth century, settlers settled for new versions of old-world farms. Their corn-and-cattle plantations, though scarcely recognizable to those who tilled the soil with plow and ox, made use of familiar English land types and retained a productive focus on grain and livestock. The pursuit of new commodities and the replication of English agriculture were two models for making use of the Lowcountry's natural abundance. These programs for adaptive cultivation intertwined to form a distinctive plantation culture in the American Southeast.

The 1663 grant's continental claim to the land reveals a grasping arrogance, common to European colonial endeavor in North America generally, that far surpassed the material reach of early colonists. By 1700, after three decades in the Lowcountry, plantations still largely clustered along the banks of a few rivers near Charlestown, leaving mapmakers to their imaginations as they depicted Carolina's interior, still a space of Indian hegemony only beginning to be eroded by European enterprise. Confined to a narrow zone of settlement encouraged by Native American guides, planters took up scarce upland tracts surrounded by wetlands they denigrated as wastes. At stake in this early phase of colonizing the Lowcountry was the direction that the plantation economy would take into the eighteenth century. Would the English live among coastal tribes, affiliated through agriculture and interest to serve as a military counterweight to the menacing power of external adversaries? Would plantation society reproduce itself as a series of productive agricultural enclaves, guided by the enlightened example of an entrepreneurial class of landlords? Would settlers detach themselves from any collective plan for their settlement and disperse in search of "good land" on which to build newworld versions of English farmsteads? A planters' landscape prevailed in South Carolina because colonists became agricultural omnivores. They pursued the founders' hopes for exotic export commodities, but on their own terms. They learned from Indian and African subsistence strategies, but subordinated non-European crops to the task of reconstituting English market farms in subtropical America. As agricultural agents with direct experience in adapting American land to European agriculture, planters claimed special environmental authority to grow Carolina.

[handwritten margin note: adapted Ind Afr. practices but prioritized Eng-style commercial ag]

Interpreting Signs of Abundance

The recipients of this vast grant of American territory, the eight Lords Proprietors of Carolina, were men of high rank and extensive experience at the leading edge of early modern commerce. This background distinguished them as a group of especially capable colonizers. Two among them, Sir William Berkeley and Sir John Colleton, had stakes, respectively, in Virginia and Barbados, English America's leading plantation colonies. Others were committed to programs of economic and social "improve-

[handwritten margin note: Wm Berkeley]

ment," especially the Proprietors' guiding force, Anthony Ashley Cooper, Lord Ashley, soon to be named the first Earl of Shaftesbury.[2] As they preoccupied themselves with framing a government, society, and economy that would succeed at planting a self-perpetuating English community in the region where others had failed, they sought to draw settlers to populate their colony with visions of natural abundance, climatic temperance, and individual prosperity.

As writers in the service of the Lords Proprietors published "prospects" of coastal Carolina from the mid-1660s, they meditated on the origins and promise of abundance that was everywhere on vibrant display. A careful reading of the land predicted its capacity to yield commodities and sustain transplanted European society through transatlantic commerce. Ashley feared that early explorers would find gold and that news of extractable wealth would inspire Carolina's first settlers to "forsake their Plantation" and strike out for the interior "in Search of Gold and Silver." To avert the collapse of this nascent plantation colony and to ensure that settlers would become planters rather than prospectors, he directed his agent in Indian country to report the discovery of any mines in code, calling "gold always Antimony and Silver Iron."[3] Early writers looked for signs that lowcountry land possessed powers of generation as potentially lucrative as deposits of precious metals. Their sightings of impossibly large and sweet fruits, teeming populations of animals, and, particularly, stands of monumental trees fixed the "fearful novelty" of the new world in old-world contexts.[4] Just as gold gave its luster to new-world land in the sixteenth century, reports of flourishing flora and fauna were signs of abundance for the late seventeenth century. Promotional tracts saturated the senses, situating the reader within an intended landscape in which every physical and social desire could be satisfied by what the land produced.

Taking stock of this English literature of colonial promotion, John Dryden mocked the many "penny-scribes" who were paid to "inform the nation / How well men thrive in this or that plantation."[5] Although such tracts reveal little about actual settlers' first engagements with nature, they present a honed psychological profile of the prospective planter. He was a figure (invariably male) who desired and yet feared the physical, social, and economic transformations that transplantation to the new world would initiate. A view of the natural world percolated from learned circles to inform broad popular understandings of a nature abstracted into the elemental components (earth, air, and water) that generated and sustained life. Theories matched the workings of unseen soil and invisible atmosphere with empirical observation of natural phenomena to explain the mechanics of Carolina's abundance.[6] Promoters, eager to populate English colonial ventures, "described a pleasant and fertile Countrey, abounding in health and pleasure, and with all things necessary for the sustenance of mankind." They held up Carolina so that the prospective planter would be "ravisht with Admiration" in terms that might just as easily have been applied to the landscapes of New England, Virginia, and Barbados at the beginning of the seventeenth century. So commonplace were declarations of the "Salubrity of Air," the "Fertility of Soyl," and other "Luxuriant and Indulgent Blessings of Nature" that satirists could scarcely resist puncturing such effusive praise for new-world nature by placing it on a pedestal of derision. Ned Ward's *Trip to Jamaica* (1698), for example, distinguished the island as the "Dunghill of the Universe," whose breezes stank of "*Sulphorous Vapours*" and whose "*Sharp* and *Crabbed*" fruits that tasted more like a "*Curse*" than a "*Blessing*" sprang from its soil.[7]

Following Ward, we might be tempted to write off more than a dozen publications that presented lowcountry nature to prospective planters between 1664 and 1707, a formative half century framed by the initial Charlestown settlement and the South Carolina plantation economy's decisive orientation toward rice production. Given the unspoken realities of early deaths from infectious diseases, hostile Indians, and a climate liable to hurricanes and droughts, these accounts can seem like deceptions designed to lure the gullible to a false paradise. To view such descriptions of the natural world as mere propaganda underestimates the degree to which, by the late seventeenth century, prospective planters demanded more than beguiling visions of Carolina as an "American Canaan, a Land that flows with Milk and Honey."[8] Aware that they possessed no monopoly on information about America, writers preempted the skepticism of an audience "apt to doubt the truth." They knew that their readers had become jaded by the "far fetched fancys," since shown to be false, that gave new-world nature the power to generate prosperity without toil.[9] Visions of frigid New England winters, stultifying Caribbean heat, and early deaths along Virginia's sickly riversides mingled in their minds with images of prosperous farms and lucrative plantations. Descriptions of trees, fruits, and animals offered material evidence for promotional claims about nature. These signs of abundance sought to reconcile specific fears and desires about what awaited them in Carolina. This recently claimed English region was made to seem more temperate, and therefore less dangerous, than previously settled colonies to its north and south. Its continental expanse of land was so vast and so framed to generate agricultural windfalls that even the indolent might escape poverty. Promoters offered a vision of Carolina as an exotic facsimile of England, enhanced and opened for colonial occupation.

The first planters expected to find, concealed beneath the canopies of coastal forests, "good large convenient tracts of land" and "rich ground" in abundance. Around 1700 England's rural landscape maintained a rough balance among three basic types of land. About a third was arable land, prepared by the plow to stand at the center of most farming systems as the most valuable sort, groomed and fertilized to yield crops of wheat, barley, and other cereals for the market. Another third was pasture (on which livestock grazed) and meadow (from which hay was mown for feed) that served as an indispensable adjunct to grain growing, especially by the late sixteenth century, when farmers began pasturing cattle on arable fields to restore them between cycles of cultivation. Leaving aside woods, roadways, parks, and lakes, the remaining third of the English countryside was regarded as waste, uncultivated land set outside the scope of commercial agriculture because of its rockiness, infertility, or liability to flooding.[10] These views of Carolina land stressed that beneath its potential for exotic production was a familiar foundation for husbandry. Abundant farming land and expansive grazing ranges predominated, with only a smattering of wastelands to mar the scene.

In the vicinity of Port Royal, where the "Lands are laden with large tall Oaks," William Hilton identified "good Soyl, covered with black Mold." At Ashley River a "competence of timber" burdened land of "a light blackish mould," much of which was "fitt and ready to plant."[11] While England's improving farmers struggled to enhance the productivity of their marginal lands, Carolina's settlers could take advantage of "good land enough for millions of people to li[v]e and worke on" already perfected by nature. "[M]ellow" in appearance and "soapy" to the touch, these deep deposits of "black Earth" scattered "generally all over the Countrey" were "just like the fine Mould of our well order'd Gardens."[12] The prudent reader had cause to doubt Robert Ferguson's claim that just as fruit trees in the "*Gardens* in *Asia,* and *Europe*" replanted their progeny without human assistance, "every Field" in Carolina "is replenish't with

Corn." Comparing Carolina's hardwood soils with English gardens balanced the allure of an exotic landscape with the comforts of a familiar one. This association gave prospective planters a credible analogue with which to imagine the agricultural potential of lowcountry land. Before colonization shifted the meaning of the term, the English "planter" cultivated fertilized fields along commercialized waterways to provide urban consumers with high-margin produce, such as fruits, vegetables, and flowers. Its vast forests testified to the fertility and extent of arable land in Carolina. Land so rich, its promoters asserted, gave the colony a gardenlike capability of producing "any thing as well as most part[s] of the Indies" as well as "every thing . . . that will grow in any Parts of Europe." "There is nothing which they have put into the Earth," claimed John Ogilby, "that through any defect in the Soil, hath fail'd to prosper."[13]

Alongside "Soil which contrives and nourishes any thing," the presence of vast "pastorable Savanas" completed the prospect of establishing enhanced English farmsteads in America. Just as they depicted Carolina's tree-covered lands as potential gardens, promotional writers tempted prospective planters with visions of "choice pasturage" that nature, rather than painstaking labor, had readied for imported livestock herds. Beyond the marshy wastelands of the coastline, Robert Sandford and his party exulted when their journey inland "opened to our viewe soe excellent a Country both for Wood, land and Meadows as gave singular satisfaction to all my Company." One "Meadow," "clothed with a [f]ine grasse" and "adorned with yeallow flowers," extended across more than 1,000 acres. Most described such tracts as savannas, opting for an obscure land term that had entered English by way of Spanish, and Spanish by way of Carib, to name these uniquely American "grassy Plains" that seemed too vast and lush to be contained by a term as gentle and familiar as "meadow." In England farmers planted and tended grasslands to keep them producing hay; in Carolina, whose "flourishing Savana's" were "crowded with Deer," nature had prepared spaces "little or nothing inferiour to our *English* Meadows," ready to support "large and stately Herds" of English cattle.[14] Such paeans to the land's fertility made a case for Carolina's environmental allure in the conventional terms of English husbandry. By detecting rich arable soils and ready-made pastures, landscape interpreters invited the prospective planter to see, as they did, the outlines of a familiar agricultural topography within the rough abundance of the land's dense vegetative cover.

Nature favored planters, Carolina's advocates alleged, by changing the *headrights*

relationship of the factors of production in its farming economy. Colonists claimed headright grants of at least 50 acres for themselves and for each free and enslaved dependent when they arrived. By buying hundreds of additional acres at a small charge, they expanded their farmsteads into vast landholdings. But a "Rational man will certainly inquire, 'when I have Land, what shall I doe with it?' " An ironclad law of agricultural economics insisted that gains in productivity had to be purchased with investments in labor. The Lowcountry's soils and seasons seemed to relax this severe logic, enforcing in its place a new "law of plenty, extended to the utmost limits of sanity."[15] An "Ox is raised at almost as little expense in Carolina, as a hen is in England," asserted Samuel Wilson in 1682. Instead of taking pains to gather hay for their cattle, "nature of her self" provided free-roaming livestock with winter fodder. A new planter could watch his animals "multiply infinitely" as he devoted "his hands, and strength" to cultivating commodities for export. Wild groves and untended orchards "thrive[d] to a Miracle," yielding so many large, delicious peaches that planters let them fall to the ground to feed their pigs. Eighteenth-century writers provided schedules of the costs and returns of a new plantation that made the case for Carolina with pragmatic calculation. This more explicitly financial appeal to prospective planters, however, rested on the same core claim: that the land's abundance and temperance guaranteed farming fortunes.[16]

Claims for the fertility of land—that it was arable, "pastorable," and prolific—presented Carolina as an ideal place for English husbandry, supplied by nature with the two critical prerequisites for the transplantation of English crops and animals: "dry plantable Land" and "firme Meadow or pasture Land." Claims for the floridity of the climate moved in the opposite rhetorical direction, from displaying the environment's capacities for production in familiar terms to laying before the prospective planter exotic delights of consumption that awaited his arrival. Demonstrating the suitability of English agriculture in Carolina spoke to concerns of the head, but promoters promised that the physical, sensual experience of inhabiting the land would also satisfy "all that the Heart of Man can wish." Immersing oneself in this environment opened the body and mind to "Pleasures," "Sweets," and "Felicities" that ranged across the senses.[17] "It would ra[v]ish a man to heare in a morning the various notes and the chanting Harmonious sound" that vast flocks of songbirds "soe delicately warble forth in the Aire." "[O]doriferous and fragrant" groves of

"Pine, Cedar, and Cypress," "pleasantly green all the year," gratified both sight and scent. So did the constant blossoming of roses, which "sprout up so plentifully, in every Plantation, that the Planters themselves are thinking therewith to make Fences."[18] When writers touched on novel environmental dangers, such as rattlesnakes and alligators, they did so to quiet fears of nature's threats to English bodies. Far from appearing as a hostile wilderness, sublime in its unpredictable power, Carolina's "Woods may rather be called a Garden."[19]

Massive hardwood trees testified to the land's coarse vitality, but its abundance of "excellent *Fruits*" and medicinal herbs revealed the climate to be a temperate force for measured growth. New England's "extream and violent Colds" killed off frost-sensitive citrus and stone fruits, while the "violent Heats" of perpetual Caribbean summers deranged the reproductive process.[20] Heat, the "great catalyst of variety" in early modern understandings of generation, was never "so predominant" in Carolina as to "suffocate the air," but instead invited "everything to vegetate with admirable success." The profusion of fruits that flourished "up and down the Woods" included grapes, limes, apricots, strawberries, plums, and "ten thousand more plants, herbs, fruits th[a]n I know," wrote one early official.[21] Gentle winters followed by resurgent springs made the "Fruits Bud and Blossom in their distinct Seasons," adapting the "Country to the production of all the Grains and Fruits of *England*" in addition to those native exotics that thrived "without Culture." A recurring image of thin coatings of ice dissolved instantly by the "least blast of the sunn" illustrated this climate's benevolent temperance compared with the "inconstancy of the Weather" in other English colonies.[22]

Along with fruits "which do serve to satisfie Hunger, or provoke it," temperate Carolina was a natural pharmacy for medicinal plants that promised to "correct the Humours of Mens Bodies." English physician John Peachi promoted Carolina "cassiny" as a "temperate herb" effective at allaying the "violent Fermentation" of smallpox infection. Breathing the air quickened the digestion, and a draught from its "Rivers of running Water" purged the urine.[23] Every delicate wild fruit that gratified the palate, every transplanted English crop that flourished in its soil, and every natural cure that rebalanced the vital fluids was a sign that showed Carolina to be compatible with English constitutions. Such harmony between bodies and the environment in the "most amiable Country of the Universe" suggested an earthly "*Paradise*" or the promised land of "Canaan." Few failed to identify the colony as occupying the "Northernmost part of the spacious and pleasant Province of Florida," a region "stretch't out on a Bed of Roses so famous and so much celebrated by all the Spanish pens." The "settlement of an English plantation in that goodly land of Florida," a long-standing object of English envy over Spain's command of lush tropical territories, connected the colonization of Carolina to a national mission to displace an imperial and religious rival. Spanish explorers had conducted abortive "running searches" for precious metals and failed to realize the land's potential for commercial agriculture for which it seemed preordained, forfeiting any reasonable claim to it.[24] England's industrious planters, by contrast, were prepared to exploit the environmental promise of this neglected paradise.

The English Pilot placed the Charlestown settlement "exactly in the Lat[itude] of 32° 45'." Any reader with a smattering of geographic knowledge recognized that Carolina occupied a climatic golden mean halfway between the equator (0°) and the arctic circle (66.5°) at the "very Center of the habitable Part of the Northern Hemisphere." Early modern theories of climate, based on Aristotelian cosmography, divided the globe into the uninhabitable Frigid Zone, the "scortching" Torrid Zone, and the ideal Temperate Zone, "universally allowed to be the best for the Production of all the Necessaries and Conveniencies of Life." Situated between extreme environments on the "Warmer side of the Temperate Zone," Carolina's "florid temperament" was believed to be "destinated to sanity, by reason of an equality of Heat, and Cold so cotempered together[,] that neither predominates."[25] If this band of latitude was traced along the northern edge of the Tropic of Cancer eastward, from the new world to the old, the colony lay "parallel with Jerusalem" and therefore shared its "Climate and Temperature." Following the precedents of "Aleppo, Smyrna[,] China, [and] Antioch," the acknowledged "gardens of the world," uncultivated Carolina claimed an old-world pedigree of agricultural prosperity by virtue of its latitude, shared by "all the best Countries in the Universe." Its fertile soil and temperate climate would "produce anything, which those Countryes doe, were the seeds brought into it."[26] An extension of Protestant dominion in America, the colony was pictured as an environmental Promised Land.

Carolina's promoters advertised it as a place that offered the settler both "pleasure and profit." This stock phrase of early modern English didactic writing, which appeared in the subtitles of scores of seventeenth-century publications, had particular relevance for environmental claims about production and consumption in the new colony.[27] Advocating "profitable pleasure" reconciled the two sides of the colonial imagination, one devoted to work and the other to play. Such claims pointed to the gains (from the material to the spiritual) to be had in enjoying novelty and investing in refined material lives.[28] By promising "great *Pleasure* and *Profit*" to the prospective planter, material concerns about the risks and rewards of plantation settlement were brought into the realm of cultural desire. For the middling readers of late seventeenth- and early eighteenth-century promotional tracts, experiences of consumption provided an important frame of reference for what such pleasure, play, and leisure might mean. With increasing appetites, they purchased goods to emulate elite material life, fortify the body with medicinal exotics, and create rituals of consuming and serving that increased demand for products from England's colonial periphery, such as West Indian sugar and Chesapeake tobacco, and those imported through the global reach of its maritime commerce, such as Chinese tea and Indian calicos. By associating Carolina with the places in both the old and new worlds from which these sought-after articles of consumption originated, writers invited the prospective planter to imagine himself (this was a gendered discourse that showcased male desire) not only as a producer who stood to profit from the burgeoning demand for new commodities, but also as a consumer immersed in an exotic locale. During the eighteenth century colonists advertised their plantations for sale as places of "pleasure and profit." This long-standing motto of South Carolina's economic culture defined the plantation as a place to inhabit as much as it was the means of generating returns from the land.

When it came to selling the environmental promise of Carolina, promotional writers pointed to powers of generation potent enough to fulfill a heady mix of desires for possession, wealth, and consumption, yet argued that these were restrained enough to do no violence to transplanted English bodies. The developmental journey that these texts mapped out, from admiring trees as emblems of the land's potential to cutting them down to settle plantations, demanded that the prospective planter set himself in motion to complete it, leaving behind the static role of reader and taking on the work of carving out versions of English farms from Carolina's wild landscape. They lured the settler with two images of transformation. Plantations would change the landscape from a place of wild

improving the land would result in refinement of the land of the planter

generation into a place of refined cultivation. As the primary agent of colonization, the planter himself would take on new sensibilities, new capabilities, and new identities—would himself be remade and refined as he harnessed nature's abundance for profit.[29]

Anglo-Indian Environmental Encounters

Native Americans mediated colonists' initial encounters with the Carolina landscape. English settlers found in Indian fields signs that agriculture was possible in this environment. In 1670, when a Charlestown-bound sloop from Barbados stopped for wood and water at "St. Katherina" in present-day Georgia, Indians traded corn, leeks, and onions, among other goods, the products of "bra[v]e plantations with . . . 100 working Indians." Whether centralized in such large-scale farms or, like the "Plantations" of the Santees, "lying scattering here and there, for a great many Miles," Indian agriculture established the worth of the land for production but registered no claims to its ongoing possession by Native American farmers that English colonizers believed they were bound to respect. When Lord Ashley's agent "marked 12000 acres of Land" for his personal use, he did so "upon the first Indian plant[ation]" on the western side of the Ashley River.[30] In the eyes of English colonizers, the sight of "fields of Maiz greenly flourishing" targeted a space for future English plantations on the sites of present Indian plantations. From a Native American perspective, the wild turkeys, peaches, tobacco, corn, peas, and pumpkins they gave to settlers were tokens of amity that initiated friendly diplomatic overtures. English recipients understood these offerings as proof that the land that produced them was worth coveting for commercial agriculture. When a group of Indians arrived in Charlestown in 1672, the very "furniture" they carried on their journey, including "Mulberrie Cakes and dies of divers sorts," came under intense scrutiny, and, more than anything these visitors said or intimated, the things they brought led some to "tak[e] up the scent of better land" from which they came. Like canaries in the coal mine that was Carolina's possibly dangerous climate, the sight of "Strong," "Lusty," and "well shaped" Indian bodies and the presence of "many very Aged amongst them" proved that the "Ayr is clear and sweet" and the "Country very pleasant and delightful."[31]

Saw Ind agri knew the land was fertile

Robert Sandford reconnoitered the Carolina Lowcountry in 1666. His Indian guides led his party across terrains that answered his every expectation for good land. The wetlands that so evidently dominated this landscape in the eighteenth century appeared as marginal features to Sandford. He noted favorably of one place: "Noe Swamps, noe Sandy land." This Anglo-Indian band traversed some "plashy corners of marshes," and in a sojourn deeper into the interior, Sandford found "water standing everywhere," the result, he thought, of a recent rainfall rather than a "signe of constant swampishness." As an early land prospector determined to show the viability of English agriculture in the region, Sandford took little notice of Carolina's swamps and other wastelands and instead sought out analogues for arable uplands and natural pastures. His Indian guides, who literally carried the white explorers over swamps that obstructed views of pastures ("not inferiour to any I have seene in England"), as well as tracts of "dry plantable Land," possessed their own motivations for showing explorers land the English deemed good and steering them away from land they deemed bad. Indian guides recognized English expectations for the environment and used their influence, knowledge, and example to encourage Sandford and other early explorers and settlers to find the idealized landscape that they had come to colonize.[32]

Coastal South Carolina Indians used what they knew of English expectations for the land to encourage them to settle in their midst. By the late seventeenth century the eighteen independent tribes that made up the Cusabo people were isolated, vulnerable, and in decline. They were prey to the French, Spanish, and Native Americans allied to them from the mid-sixteenth century, but their numbers were reduced most drastically by smallpox infections introduced by Europeans. When English colonizers arrived in 1670, the Cusabos were under intense assault by Westo Indians from the south. These coastal tribes concentrated their populations in summerhouses surrounded by cornfields and within easy reach of fishing grounds and oyster beds. When these food sources faded, they assembled into smaller bands and traveled as far as fifty miles into their interior for the rest of the year. Before the arrival of Europeans, their country's location between the two waterways, the Santee and the Savannah rivers, that reached deep inland from the Altantic coast, took advantage of the Lowcountry's marshy topography for security. A landscape of interconnecting swamps and meandering rivers, difficult to navigate for outsiders, had once served as a natural buffer between these small tribes and their adversaries. By drawing colonists to what would become Charlestown, the Cusabos imagined shoring up their lowcountry lands as a refuge from outside threats.[33]

They made an environmental case for the Charlestown settlement site that betrayed an awareness of English expectations for the natural world. First, they encouraged the Carolina colonists to disband their initial Clarendon settlement of several hundred colonists in the Cape Fear region (on the southeast coast of present-day North Carolina) and replant the colony to the south. The "cassique"[34] of the Kiawah Indians had visited Clarendon on a trading mission that gave him a firsthand view of the grim conditions its inhabitants faced. He and other "principal Indians" who represented coastal tribes approached Sandford, sent from Clarendon to scout the southern coast in 1666, about the prospects of the first English colony in Carolina. They "knewe wee were in actuall warre with the Natives att Clarendon," he reported, and "frequently discoursed with us concerning the warr." Highlighting Clarendon's distress, these cassiques repeated the same argument, that "the [Cape Fear] Natives were noughts, their land Sandy and barren, [and] their Country sickly." If the English were to resettle "amongst them," however, they would "finde the Contrary to all their Evills, and never any occasion of discharging our Gunns but in merriment and for pastime."

Sandford saw these coastal leaders competing with one another "concerning us and our Friendship," with each "jealous of the other" to secure a new settlement in their midst. That each should importune him in turn puzzled Sandford, because all were supposedly "allyed." As John Ogilby explained these encounters, the "several little Kingdoms strove with all the Arts and Arguments they could use, each of them to draw the *English* to Plant in their Dominions, by commending the richness of their Soil, conveniency of their Rivers, the healthiness of their Countrye, the disparagement of their Neighbors, and whatever else they judg'd might allure the *English* to their Neighborhood."[35] Their schemes offered Ogilby the chance to picture Carolina's Indians in disparaging terms, as self-interested flatterers whose cunning was rendered comic rather than treacherous by the repetition of patently incompatible claims. Neither considered that these Indian leaders spoke from the same script as part of a general attempt to draw the English to a point of their choosing on the southeastern coast.

Some Native American leaders appear to have orchestrated their appeals to English scouts and settlers to encourage a specific site for settlement. The second phase of an Indian strategy of engagement with Carolina's colonizers diverted them from their intended destination at Port Royal and directed them instead to take up land among one of their own, the Kiawahs. Accounts of Port Royal, a place of previous French and Spanish occupation, had circulated among English readers as an ideal colonial beachhead within the fabled land of Florida.[36] In addition to bearing the imprimatur of rival imperial powers, Port Royal ("which by the Spaniards is called *St. Ellens*" or St. Helena) was also outfitted with a deep harbor sheltered by surrounding sea islands. A group of Barbadians, disappointed with the location of the Clarendon settlement, commissioned William Hilton to investigate Port Royal in 1663. As Clarendon settlers struggled to survive on the Cape Fear coast, the Proprietors commissioned Sandford's 1666 expedition to promote "the designe of the Southerne settlement" that was likewise focused on Port Royal.[37] When Sandford anchored at the entrance of the Edisto River, he realized that he had missed the "the River w[hich] Hilton was in" that led to Port Royal by some miles. There he encountered the two critical interlocutors who served as his advisors, the cassiques of the Kiawahs and Edistos. The Kiawah leader's presence among the Edistos to greet Sandford was fortuitous, but perhaps not entirely coincidental, just as an earlier appearance at Clarendon for the explicit purpose of trade had allowed him to lay the groundwork for future diplomacy with the English. The cassique of Kiawha "was very earnest with" Sandford "to goe w[ith] my Vessell thither [to Kiawah,] assuring mee a broad deep entrance and promising a large welcome and plentiful entertainm[ent] and trade." The explorer demurred, telling him: "I must first goe to Port Royall and that in my retourne I would see his Country." To ensure that he made good on this promise, the cassique joined Sandford, serving as his pilot and intermediary with other Indian leaders and then leading the English expedition to "see the Country of Kywaha," where he "undertooke to bee my Guide."

During Sandford's brief excursion to Kiawah, the site of present-day Charleston located about fifty miles to the northeast of Port Royal, he deemed it an "Excellent Country," based on the "Commendacon the Indian[s] give itt," and he named one of its rivers the Ashley in honor of Proprietor Anthony Ashley Cooper.[38] Despite the efforts of the cassique of Kiawah, the Proprietors persisted in their "Port Royall desine," equipping three ships with settlers and supplies bound for the southern sea islands. Although storms waylaid the *Port Royal* and *The Three Brothers,* the more than 100 settler-passengers aboard the *Carolina* made land some eighty miles to the northeast of Port Royal in March 1670, where Sewee Indians "stroaked [u]s on the shoulders with their hands saying Bony

Conraro Angles," a pidgin phrase that expressed a posture of friendliness as it betrayed Indian expectations for their arrival. Their Sewee hosts discouraged the expedition's "business to S[t.] Helena." They informed the English that the "Westoes [were] a rangeing sort of people reputed to be . . . Man eaters" and that they had recently "ruinated that place." Two days later the cassique of Kiawah reappeared in Sewee country to guide the English to Port Royal. When they arrived, this "[v]ery Ingenious Indian & a great Linguist in this Maine" probably translated the comments of aggrieved Port Royal Indians interviewed to confirm the news of Westo attacks near this intended settlement site. Their only direct communication with the English was the phrase "Hiddy doddy Comorado Angles Westoe Skorrye (which is as much as to say) English [v]ery good friends Westoes are nought." The Kiawah leader also convinced the *Carolina*'s crew that a group of Indians spotted on shore bearing a flag of truce "were eyther Spanish Indians or those that we call westows," and he, or perhaps another of his countrymen, went out to meet them, an encounter that ended in gunfire and a hasty retreat. Unnerved by the plight of local Indians and the sight of seemingly hostile Indians, the settlers dispatched a sloop to "Kayawah to veiwe that Land soe much Commended by the Casseeka," whose crew reported that the "Lande was more fit to Plant in th[a]n S[t.] Helena" on their return.[39] With Governor William Sayle "adhearing for Kayahaw" and the majority convinced of a "better convenience" there, "those that Inclyned for Port royall were looked upon straingley soe thus wee came to Kawayah." When *The Three Brothers* arrived at Port Royal two months later, the Edisto leader Shadoo, who had accompanied William Hilton to Barbados seven years earlier, informed this second contingent of English colonists that the crew and passengers aboard the *Carolina* "had been at Port royall & were now at Keyawah," where he offered to take them the next day.[40]

Coastal Indians appeared as translators, navigators, and landscape guides at critical junctures in the establishment of English Carolina. With tales of Westo savagery to the south and warnings that the northern coast of present-day South Carolina was "Hiddeskeh, [that] is to say sickly," they intervened in attempts to settle Port Royal and steered English colonists to Kiawah.[41] Stigmatizing the Westos as cannibals was a tactic of alliance building reminiscent of Caribbean Tainos' first encounter with Columbus, but defining the Westos as dangerous enemies did not exaggerate the threat they posed to coastal peoples. A confederation of Iro-

quoians displaced by Anglo-Indian conflicts in Virginia, the Westos, reported Stephen Bull in 1670, "strike a great feare" among "our
neighbouring Indians." Armed by Virginia traders with "guns & powder
& shott," the Westos came upon the Cusabos every harvest, "destroy[ing]
all by killinge" and "Caryinge away their Corne & Children" not to "eat
them," as he was told, but to sell such captives as slaves. Inviting the
English to Kiawah/Ashley River placed a powerful military ally close to
the geographic center of Cusabo summer camps. In addition to selling
settlers "Provisions att very reasonable rates," the Indians around Charlestown took an active "notice of our necessities" and "almost daylie bringe
one thinge or another," aid that prevented "extreme hardshipps" in early
Carolina of the kind endured by Virginia settlers some sixty years earlier.
In return, they expected protection from the Westos and urged the English to offensive military action. William Owen argued that if the English
failed to mount a campaign to the south "and shoote, as they call it,"
then "we shall hazard our reputacions among our owne Indians." By
setting up the English as resident guardians who promised to search out
and attack their enemies in the distant southern interior, the Cusabos
stood between the English and the Westos, retaining the power to define
them as bloodthirsty cannibals. They "reckon themselves safe," observed
Owen, "when they have us amongst them."[42]

Urging a settlement at Ashley River also worked to forestall the possibility that the English, although welcomed as "great friends," might yet
become dangerous adversaries. Port Royal offered access to three nearby
rivers (the Savannah, Combahee, and Edisto) that reached at least fifty
miles into the interior. An English colony at Port Royal would be well
positioned at the southern edge of Cusabo lands to initiate independent
contact with the Westos and forge relations with the Cherokees further
inland. The network of smaller, obstructed waterways that emptied into
Kiawah's harbor, by contrast, extended less than thirty miles from the
Charlestown peninsula in any direction. Throughout mainland North
America English explorers searched for river headwaters to evaluate the
strategic situation of coastal settlements. Second in importance only to
securing a "safe, commodious and spacious" harbor, commanding a river
that was "deep and navigable above 100 miles up" positioned colonial
outposts to expand into new territories and engage in diplomacy and war
with neighboring Indians from positions of geographic strength. The settlers who came to Kiawah anticipated that the Ashley was one of these

"great Navigable *Rivers*," only to make the disheartening discovery that it was "not to be soe big as at first imagined." When they searched for its source, they found that the river "spent itt selfe in a marsh" some "20 or 30 miles upwards." They wanted a river that could serve as a vector for the expansion of English influence into the Carolina interior, but they found themselves confined to a fortified compound along a mere "arme of the sea."[43]

The settlers gave reasons for "deserting Port Royall" that echoed the panick with which local Indians described the Westo threat and the danger of Yamassee incursions supported by the Spanish at St. Augustine. Colonists justified this departure from the Proprietors' plan by noting that the "greate pointe in this designe is securietie." Along the southern bank of the Ashley, the colonists had "pitcht on a point defended by [th]e maine ri[v]er" and surrounded by an "inaccessible Marshe," a site they further reinforced with an encircling palisade. During their first few years at Kiawah, they adopted the geopolitical worldview of the Cusabo tribes that surrounded Charlestown and accepted the defensive posture against invaders that it called for.[44] If Kiawah, Edisto, and Sewee leaders feared that an English colony at Port Royal might use the Savannah River as an independent corridor of communication with the Westos, then their concerns were prescient. Even as official Joseph Dalton reported that no other site along the coast surpassed the Ashley River "for security," he eyed the Savannah ("called by the Indians Westoe bou signifying the enemies River"), whose "vast length" "runns in fresh water into the Maine backwards of us" and which "may prove of great advantage to this settlement." A short-lived colony of Scottish Presbyterians at Port Royal, settled in 1684 and burned to the ground by Spanish and Indian forces two years later, revealed an ongoing British interest in establishing a presence at this strategic crossroads of the southern frontier.[45]

In 1674 the Westos took the initiative to bypass the Cusabos and contacted the English directly. A party of "strange Indians" arrived at Ashley's private plantation, where they seemed "very unwilling to stay [the] night," and invited the colony's most important Indian negotiator, Henry Woodward, on an overland journey back to the banks of the Savannah River. Traveling far beyond the "head of Ashley River," Woodward described the "fertile banks of this spatious river" that the first settlers had passed up when they chose Kiawah over Port Royal. Using the code devised to conceal gold from Carolina settlers, Woodward spied "a sparkling substance like Antimony" clinging to the soles of his guides' moccasins. At the Westo town the assembled population displayed its arms, deerskins, and "young Indian Slaves." Although Woodward had mastered several Indian languages, he could not understand the Westos until they communicated "their desire for friendship, & comerse," by means of barter, drawings, and other "signs."[46]

The Anglo-Westo agreements that followed from this diplomatic mission made Charlestown a major port of embarkation for deerskins and captured slaves, many seized in Spanish-allied Indian communities. This Proprietary trade monopoly also left the coastal Cusabos at the mercy of Westo raiders. Successive English trade alliances with the Westos, the Savannahs, and the Yamassees, each an aggressor against neighboring Indians and each based around the Savannah River, ended in bloody wars of extermination when relations with the English soured.[47] In the last of these conflicts, the Yamassee War of 1715, many coastal Indians stood by their English allies against a devastating invasion that killed hundreds and threatened Charlestown. Despite the efforts of "all those Petty Cassekas" to set themselves up as Carolina's gatekeepers to Indian America, the English soon viewed the Cusabos as weak and innocuous neighbors. They expected those they named "Settlement Indians" to live "peaceably and quietly" beyond the pale of their expanding plantation settlements. After 1751 there is no documentary record that any of the Cusabo tribes existed as corporate entities within lowcountry South Carolina.[48]

Drawing the English to the Ashley River was a successful tactic in a losing effort to gain security from the expansion of English influence in the colonial Southeast. The resolve of the Cusabos to nurture the settlement at Kiawah during its first years in the early 1670s, however, shaped the material life and domestic economy of South Carolina plantations into the eighteenth century. In sharp contrast to the hostilities that erupted when early Virginia colonists strained the hospitality of the Powhatans, Charlestown's neighbors were unstinting in their efforts to avert a "starving time" in early Carolina. Despite the promises of easy subsistence in promotional literature, settlers found that the "Country afford[s] us nothing." Under the burden of an "Extreme wan[t] of Provisions," Stephen Bull traveled among the Cusabos "to Get some Corn from the Indians." As he went "from one place to another," they "showed great joy that wee are Setled amongst them" and sent him back with maize. For the better part of three years settlers were "forced to live upon the

Indians," who "furnished us beyond our [e]xpectations."[49] Native American farmers supplemented this steady flow of food supplies with instruction. Indians, perhaps those who lived in the "village" just beyond Charlestown's fortifications, worked alongside servants, slaves, and settlers, "assisting them to clear and plant their land" and modeling agricultural methods as they provided temporary and voluntary labor. In addition to helping planters "to fall Timber, to plant Corn, and to gather in their Crop," Indians offered their services as hired hunters and pilots. Women performed much of the work of cultivation in Indian fields and predominated among the Native American slaves recorded in early estate inventories, a presence that suggests that this transfer of agricultural knowledge continued with coerced labor.[50] As for the "proper season to plant Corne & Beanes & Pease you will be informed by [th]e Natives," instructed the Proprietors. The early settlers could take comfort after their first crop withered for want of rain during the summer of 1671 because "the Indians say such droughts are [not] usual."[51]

Two years later Governor Joseph West hoped that "we shall never fear wanting Indian corne againe" and that the settlers' experiences of deprivation would teach them "to be better Husbands." But what sort of farmers had they learned to become? If the Proprietors shipped over cattle, West argued, then they "might fall upon English Husbandry." For the time being, the settlers farmed and ate more like Indians. They mastered the techniques of slash-and-burn agriculture, featuring mixed crops of beans and maize, and soon were harvesting crops "of pease and corne from the same ground." Because girdling trees and then firing the fields left them strewn with stumps, the iron hoes imported as Indian trade goods proved far more useful than English plows as settlers struggled to "provid[e] for [the] belly" before "makeing any Comodity."[52] The Proprietors accepted this early emulation of Native American agriculture as a preliminary adaptation undertaken to guarantee sheer physical survival in a newly planted colony. They envisioned that a more refined landscape of carefully tilled fields yielding wheat for the table and exotic commodities for export would soon follow.

The environmental lessons of the Cusabos, however, proved an enduring legacy as the practices of the early plantation economy diverged from the Proprietary ideal. Native American names for officially renamed rivers lingered in settlers' everyday usage, a reflection that they oriented themselves in Carolina by the benchmarks of an Indian sense of geography. When Governor West signed a 1670 letter to England from "Albemarle point at Kyawah," Ashley replied with a rebuke: "that you may not hereafter mistake the name of the place you are in, you are to take notice that the River was by Captain Sandford long since named Ashley River, and is still to be called soe, and the Towne you are now planted on we have named and you are to call Charles Towne."[53] Elsewhere in the Lowcountry Indian geographic terms resisted anglicization, populating South Carolina maps with the names of the Pee Dee, Sampit, Santee, Sewee, Wando, Kiawah, Bohicket, Edisto, Ashepoo, and Combahee long after infectious diseases, slave raids, and advancing plantation settlement had depopulated these riversides of their namesakes. By the mid-eighteenth century, "dispersed up and down" the coastal South Carolina countryside stood "Lands that have been cleared by the Indians, and now remain just as they have left them." These "large Indian old Fields" marked the latter-day absence of the Cusabos as much as they recalled an earlier, influential presence.[54]

Carolina as a Project of Improvement

Early English accounts of Carolina certified the land's potential and held out images of that promise realized in a prosperous plantation settlement. But how would a "savage" land populated by Indians be transformed into a refined landscape occupied by industrious planters? These writings passed over the details of its development as if the powers of generation they observed in its soil and climate guaranteed that an English society implanted in Carolina would flourish by the same organic logic. Promotional praise for land held the idea that Carolina was capable of replicating English agriculture in tension with the idea that it would feature distinctive commodities. Promoters assured settlers that a familiar material life could be cobbled together from its natural resources, but also that colonial tables would sag under the weight of exotic delicacies. As they asserted physical control over this landscape, English colonists used this uneasy equipoise between exotic and familiar aspects of the lowcountry environment to come to terms with it psychologically.

Carolina's founders, the Lords Proprietors, sought to reconcile these divergent expectations by linking the colony's fortunes to a vast project of improvement under their direction. Although Anthony Ashley Cooper never set foot in a place he called his "Darling," he imposed a detailed scheme for its expansion that extended the concerns for economic innovation and social reform of England's "Age of Projects" to America. Like those who came to Carolina to plant, Ashley owned land and expected to profit from a "private plantation." He also conceived of the province as a whole as "the Plantation," a single community of endeavor in which all settlers were concerned, but over which a cadre of elite landowners and government officials would preside. He asserted a Proprietary prerogative to direct the ways in which settlers took up and made use of lowcountry land as the single most important factor in achieving the progressive vision of security, prosperity, and civility he anticipated.[55]

English economic projects in the sixteenth and seventeenth centuries put forward plans to manufacture or cultivate goods for consumption characterized by a "stream of invention and experimentation." In the realm of agriculture, projecting initiatives focused on lucrative crops such as fruits, vegetables, and plants (especially those for making and coloring textiles) destined for industrial uses. By the mid-seventeenth century the influence of these new productions transformed the structure of the English economy, spreading throughout the kingdom, enhancing opportunities for employment, and offering farming families access to cash with which to purchase consumer goods that were themselves made cheaper and more available through the cumulative efforts of projectors, as these agricultural and industrial entrepreneurs were called. Many of the commodities paraded before the ambitions and appetites of prospective planters in promotional tracts—among them wine, silk, linen, tobacco, oranges, medicinal plants, and a range of dyestuffs—first came to the attention of English farmers as desirable articles of domestic production and consumption. Atlantic colonies, beginning with sixteenth-century Ireland, possessed special appeal for the merchants who had absorbed the ethos of improvement and played influential roles in financing overseas settlement and organizing commerce to and from newly colonized lands.[56]

Beyond the commodities it promised to provide for the home market, the Proprietors betrayed their vision of Carolina as a project of improvement by emulating English examples. English entrepreneurs looked abroad for "models of economic advancement" and courted European refugees who knew how to make cloth and drain fens, among other skills. The Proprietors likewise sought to procure the seeds of valuable plants and "men Skilled in the management of them," particularly persecuted French Protestants recruited for their silk- and wine-making abilities. Just

*props wanted
to settle in
commercial
towns*

as the followers of Samuel Hartlib, a noted seventeenth-century disseminator of scientific ideas and writings, planted their English gardens with potential commodities to prove the commercial viability of new crops, the Proprietors established an experimental garden on the Ashley River to make a "full experiment of what [the] country will produce best."[57] Ashley's plan to found an ordered society in Carolina mirrored the assertions of English innovators that schemes for industrial and agricultural improvement would alleviate English social ills that came from unemployment and inefficient production. With the leverage that came with the Proprietors' control of lowcountry land, he insisted that settlers congregate in village enclaves along navigable rivers, a plan that echoed English plans to seat new commercial towns along England's waterways.[58]

The proponents of projects in England and Carolina viewed commerce as a double-edged sword. Without the oversight of enlightened economic actors, the unorganized pursuit of self-interest threatened to disband communities, dispersing an impoverished underclass away from productive work and down an irrecoverable spiral of crime and poverty. The social agenda of English projects promised to constrain economic individualism, rationalize economic life, and confront the specter of social decay with new opportunities for work. As John Evelyn argued in *Sylva* (1664), the ideal agents at the helm of economic development were great landowners steeped in humanist learning.[59] We "ayme not att the profit of merchants," the Proprietors lectured the governor and Council in 1674, but rather "the incouragement of landlords."[60] They proposed that two-fifths of all land be reserved for themselves and for the newly minted aristocrats they were authorized to ennoble to enjoy in vast tracts. These provisions of Carolina's Fundamental Constitutions were designed to populate the Lowcountry with men who would command social inferiors through the power they wielded in government and by example as agricultural innovators.

When the Proprietors expected to see the "fruition of our desired Lande," however, was more influenced by the imperatives of commerce than Ashley was prepared to admit. They relished the mantle of benevolent directors committed to nurture Carolina for the benefit of its inhabitants, as well as to strengthen England's social, economic, and imperial position in the Atlantic world. Along with a wealth of political and colonial experience, these eight well-connected elites each contributed at least £775 sterling, small fortunes in the late seventeenth century, for which they expected a return. As costs mounted, settlers evaded quitrent payments, and expected commodity exports failed to materialize, the Proprietors betrayed the impatience of shareholders in a joint-stock company when they were each forced to contribute an additional £100 sterling per year to sustain the colony. Pressed for additional funds and supplies, they brooded that the "Country was not worth having at that rate." Given the prolific qualities of the land, only the idleness of the colonists explained why staples had not yet been exported to "turn to account for in our trade." "[N]ew settlements are like young scions," cautioned Barbadian Nicholas Blake; they "must have time to root and grow and in seven years will bring fruit." The Proprietors sought to realize profits "suitable" to their "great expences" within their lifetimes. Adopting a time horizon for financial returns better suited to a transatlantic trading venture than a colonial settlement, they expected to turn a profit, at the latest, after "tenn or twel[v]e years."[61]

Fundamental Constitutions

Once immigrants came to Carolina to claim its land, Ashley must have believed, they would gladly inhabit the ideal society the Proprietors outlined in their proposed Fundamental Constitutions and obey its rules for occupying the Lowcountry. Ashley described his dream of joining settlers together in villages in language that celebrated social, economic, and political order. He hoped that a society rooted in rural communities and made wealthy by Charlestown's access to the Atlantic economy might present planters with a vision of development that they would willingly embrace. Taking stock of the political upheaval, religious discord, and disruptive commercialization that destabilized seventeenth-century English society, Ashley intended to structure American colonization, especially the energetic acquisitiveness of its planters, for the benefit of Carolina as a collective enterprise.[62] His scheme sought to counter dispersion by forcing planters to settle in towns, insulate these communities from the negative effects of commerce, and limit the unsettling effects of rapid wealth accumulation by creating a hereditary aristocracy entrusted with vast grants of land, a power granted the Proprietors in their 1663 charter for Carolina.

would insulate settlers from neg effects of commerce

Ashley and his fellow Lords Proprietors proposed to shield rural life in the new colony against the disorders of commerce by controlling settlement and directing transatlantic trade. As England's landlords enclosed communal land in pursuit of profits, common lands were to be resurrected around each of the towns in which planters were required to build their houses. Here they would pasture cows, "sow Corne or make Gardens," and re-create a landscape of "conveniency, Beauty and security." The sale of plantation commodities produced in the countryside would be channeled into designated "port towns," limited to a single site for each navigable river, where planters would be "bound to lade and unlade" their produce. Members of the appointed Council were to oversee "all foraigne and domestick trade" and control "faires, markets," and "all other things" concerning "publick comerse."[63] In Charlestown a grid of "regular Streets" was to prepare the colony's "great Port Town" for "increases in Riches and People" and buildings that were sure to "grow more beautyfull" as the value of Carolina's exports increased. Although a policy of religious toleration promised to quiet the conflicts that troubled Puritan communities to the north, the "lesser Townshipps" of the Lowcountry were to model themselves on New England's towns. Chesapeake settlers' dispersion across the land was an example that, if followed in Carolina, would bring the "Plantation to Ruin." The "experience of both Virginia and Maryland" proved that without enlightened direction, "men will expose themselves to the Inconvenience and Barbarisme of scattered Dwellings." Such "Rashnesse and Folly" sparked destabilizing conflicts with neighboring Indians over territory and made settlers who established "stragling and distant Habitations" more savage than civil. The "Planting of People in Townes," concluded Ashley, was the "Chiefe thing that hath given New England soe much the advantage over Virginia and advanced that Plantation in so short a time to the height it is now."[64]

Fostering a "neareness of the Neighborhood" in Carolina promised to nurture civic culture, as well as civility. In each community public meetinghouses were to become a focal point of political life. Large-scale landowners ennobled with the titles of "landgrave" and "cassique," and established as a hereditary aristocracy, would lead concentrated populations of free settlers. An entrenched ruling class, Ashley hoped, would forestall the emergence of a "numerous democracy" in Carolina. But the Fundamental Constitutions left three-fifths of all the land "amongst [th]e people" so that in "setting out and planting [the] lands the balance of governm[en]t may be preserved."[65] The scope of aristocratic privilege in this neomanorial polity was to be limited for the benefit of Carolina's settler-citizen majority. Proprietary land policies prevented Carolina's wealthiest settlers from engrossing the colony's best riverside lands. Even the indentured servants purchased to toil in the Proprietors' experimental garden, whose counterparts in the Caribbean had been "terrified" by their ill treatment and "sold as slaves," were promised possession of a house and a share of the land on which it stood when their terms of servitude ended. The Proprietors' settlement plan indeed "rooted social rank and privilege in property holding," but aggrandizing an elite was never intended to strip ordinary landowners of their political rights. Gathering planters together in coherent communities brought them under the rule of law and into relations of social interdependence, but also gave them a voice in a "quiet equall and lasting Government wherein every mans Right Property and Welfare may be . . . fenc'd in and secured." Whether or not settlers saw the advantages of upholding this elaborate social project, the Proprietors were prepared, at first, to force them to congregate in towns and live, trade, and work under the scrutiny of social superiors. The "land is ours," the Proprietors declared, "and we shall not part with it but on our own terms."[66]

Before the Proprietors' social project unraveled, Ashley had only to review the example set by the Chesapeake's self-interested settlers to anticipate resistance to his plan. His economic project for Carolina, by contrast, seemed to align the interests of planters and founders, both of whom stood to gain fortunes through the cultivation of commodities. The Proprietors encouraged the efforts of educated agricultural improvers to generate a dazzling list of "Hereditary Inriching staples, staples the Richest in Specie[,] most plentifull and exuberant in produce," for the colony's planters to grow.[67] Each seed, vine, or sapling the Proprietors gathered for experiments with "usefull plants or commodities fit for [the] Climate out of any part of the World" laid in a desirable course for economic development. James Colleton, the brother of Proprietor Peter Colleton and later governor of the colony, "brought an Olive Stick" from the Azores that once "put into the Ground, grew and prospered exceedingly." Bringing the production of "Wine Oyle and Silke" to "great perfection and profit" and introducing "Almonds and Date stones" to this Mediterranean crop mix looked forward to a refined landscape of villas, vineyards, and groves emerging in Carolina.[68] The enviable haciendas of New Spain, whose Indians and slaves processed cochineal insects into a brilliant scarlet dye and made the best indigo, cocoa, and tobacco in the world, provided another model for Carolina plantations. By emulating Spanish American commodities, Carolina might focus on "Dying Drugs," "Wood that is finely grained or s[c]ented," and "various other profitable

Plants, Druggs, and *Roots*" distinguished by their potency and high quality. Looking further afield at eastern exotics, Ashley searched for pepper-tree seed to send to Carolina, and Peter Colleton obtained a sample of "Carolina China Root" that he sent to his cousin, an English druggist, to assay its medicinal strength.[69]

Despite this global search for staples "not yet produced in the other plantations," the Proprietors and their agricultural experts encouraged planters to imitate the secondary productions and stillborn experiments of the Chesapeake and Caribbean colonies. Because Carolina's environment seemed to offer a degree of "healthfulness and pleasantness" that "noe plantation settled by the English in America" matched, planters in the Lowcountry could specialize in a grade of tobacco "as good as e[v]er was smoakt." Despite declining prices for the Chesapeake staple, a high-quality version perfected in Carolina's ideal climate might "surpass the fame of Virginia" and find a niche in a glutted market.[70] The Proprietors instructed ship captains who plied a circum-Caribbean circuit in search of provisions for the new colony to linger in "all of [the] places you goe" and to "learne as much as you can any of [the] husbandry [or] Manufactures of [the] place." In Virginia they might poach knowledge and materials to transfer a nascent silk industry to Carolina. The first colonists expected ginger, indigo, and cotton, minor West Indian commodities cultivated in sugar's shadow but "fit for the market of England," to become leading exports by the mid-1670s.[71]

At one of the Proprietors' experimental plantations, trials of cotton, ginger, olives, indigo, sugarcane, and grape vines would reveal which "sort of soile agrees best" with the "severall things plant[e]d in them." Along with shipments of food, tools, clothes, and seeds, they obtained "books of husbandry" and sought the best recent literature on the "culture of vines and olives and silk."[72] John Stewart oversaw another experimental plantation, called by the Cusabo name Makkean, in the early 1690s. With the arrogance of a threadbare but cosmopolitan new arrival to the rude colonial periphery, he reveled in his role as the planters' tutor. Stewart's devotion to the study of "projection" and "Philosophie" brought him learned insights into the "Rationales of a staple," a brand of specialized knowledge that allowed him to declare that he was Carolina's "first projector." Because of Carolina's "ixuberantly Kind" nature, he reasoned, planters could immediately cultivate "European grain of all Kinds beside ancient Maize." Stewart took the idea of Carolina as a natural garden to extremes of hyperbole, asserting that the finest British parks could not compare to the worst Carolina "desarts." Viewed through the filter of projectors' exotic commodity visions, Carolina appeared as a tractable space to which the world's lucrative produce could be transplanted. From Asia, the Mediterranean, and elsewhere in the Americas, Indian rice and indigo, Caribbean cotton, Persian wine, Chinese silk, Portuguese oranges, Spanish capers, and Greek currants called out for emulation. Stewart claimed to have promoted thirty-six separate commodities "originally and virtually in this country" and staked out a special aura of authority as a well-traveled and well-read expert. By taking up Stewart's experiments, planters would transform South Carolina from a hard-scrabble Atlantic outpost into a "fruitfull Canaan, the wonder and admiration of America."[73]

Counting "rich men" as their allies in adopting new commodities, the Proprietors praised those few "Gentlemen Planters" who took up the charge of crop experimentation and directed their hands to plant vineyards, mulberry trees, fruit groves, and tobacco patches. These were the kind of "ingenious" planters the Proprietors had envisioned inhabiting Carolina.[74] In exchange for generous land grants, a system of "good, and wholsom[e] laws," and a few years of "leisure" to make "sure of a good stock of provisions," the Proprietors expected all planters to follow the lead of the colony's "principal *Projectors*" and produce transatlantic commodities. Always "Look[ing] Abroad" to the market possibilities of new crops, the "Careful Industry" of the "prying planter" would repay the Proprietors' investments and realize the environmental promise of Carolina that they had done so much to promote. As planting began, the colony's reputation depended not only on the work of "tongues, and pennes," to sing its praises, but also on the "axes" of planters whose slaves and servants were to clear the lowcountry wilderness and cultivate valuable export crops in its soil.[75]

Ashley, his fellow Proprietors, and the projectors affiliated with them claimed a unique brand of knowledge about the best ways to animate Carolina's economy without destabilizing its emerging society. The early modern rise of technical experts in charge of English projects in navigation, mining, and harbor construction signaled a change in the very notion of expertise. These novel enterprises elevated to positions of power men who claimed that their scholarly inquiries into "how and why things worked" trumped the limited knowledge of mere practitioners, who only knew "how to do things." As advocates of economic and social reform who believed that they brought a "rare, valuable, and complicated body of useful knowledge" to the challenges of settling America, the Proprietors inherited this authority of the expert in the service of the English state.[76] As self-proclaimed philosophers of colonization, they used it to justify their far-reaching vision for Carolina's development.

The limits of the founders' expertise came to light when the experimental crops they so relentlessly promoted failed to thrive. The colony's ideal climatic position on the globe did not prepare projectors for a "great blast" of frost that "kill[e]d all things," including sugarcane and cotton, at the Proprietors' experimental plantation. A "great drought" followed, leveling plots of ginger and indigo. The only productions that survived this early encounter with environmental volatility were maize, beans, cattle, and hogs, the maligned staples of the planters' emerging economy.[77]

Settling a Planters' Landscape

Aspiring planters rejected the view of Carolina as a vast plantation in which they were subjects. Instead, they defined the plantation as an independently owned tract in which possession conveyed the power to command people and resources within its boundaries. Securing the necessities of life from the land, engaging in commercial agriculture, reinvesting profits, and passing on accumulated wealth to children put forward an understanding of the plantation as a vehicle for family improvement. Although never codified in explicit terms, as was the Fundamental Constitutions, the settlers' conception of the plantation as a privately bounded domain for enterprise entered into common usage, supplanting the Proprietors' corporatist vision in language as it did in practice. With the rise to power of the planter-dominated Commons House of Assembly and the effective end of Proprietary rule in 1719, planters triumphed in politics as they shaped the actual geography of settlement.

Planters did not reject the projecting vision for Carolina's development outright, but as they managed independent plantations, they ignored its goals and left open-ended the ultimate social and economic product of their individual enterprises. The locus of their efforts was not the "Plantation" writ large as a collective, colony-wide project, but the "plantation" writ small as a version of the independent English farmstead. Drawn like settlers everywhere in colonial British America by the opportunity to own land, early Carolina planters saw real property as the surest path to securing a "competency," that "degree of comfortable independence" that guaranteed self-sufficiency and held out the promise of profitable market agriculture.[78] The task of acquiring family wealth lacked the time constraints that urged the Proprietors to impose a constitutional framework for development that they hoped would set in motion a profitable trade in exotic commodities from Carolina's inception. Building family fortunes was an incremental process of reinvesting income in an expanding "stock" of productive and heritable property—land, livestock, and slaves—that carried the task of enlarging plantation capital across generations.

Plantation building privileged a conservative balance of risk and reward that steered labor toward ready markets and proven goods of trade rather than reaching for the most exotic, profitable, and reputable commodities as a standard for the colony's economic success. When planters resisted regulations that took away their choice of land and what to grow on it, they refused to pay the costs of establishing the Proprietors' vision out of their own capital stock or diminish the autonomy that owning land conferred in early modern English society. In their disenchantment with the progress of Carolina, the Proprietors marked planter intransigence down to plodding ignorance and a destructive regard for private gain over the security and prosperity of the province as a whole. As planters dispersed in pursuit of "good land," their actions left behind Proprietary plans for concentrated settlement. As they extracted goods from the low-country environment for sale, they bypassed the schemes of agricultural experts hired to tutor them in advanced farming methods. At every turn in the settlement process, planters challenged the Proprietors' explicit plans for settlement and economic development.

In 1680, after a decade of immigration, something on the order of 1,000 white settlers lived in South Carolina. By the end of the seventeenth century as many as 6,000 had arrived in the colony.[79] Although planters' specific points of European origin remain elusive, the bulk of early white transatlantic migrants came from England, accompanied by smaller streams of Scottish, Irish, and French Huguenot settlers. English immigrants came to Carolina from populations already in motion. Many of "2. or 3. hundred people out of London" that the Proprietors anticipated journeying to the new colony in 1670 would have been recent migrants to the growing metropolis, participants in successive internal migrations within England that concluded with a decision to embark for America.[80]

Although sailors, artisans, and other nonagricultural workers entered the ranks of Carolina's first planters, the substantial group of indentured servants, many from modest rural backgrounds, predominated. Most young men from the country labored as servants in husbandry in late adolescence. These temporary workers acquired diverse agricultural skills as they contracted for their services with a succession of farmers and migrated across England's highly differentiated farming regions. Younger sons from the lower ranks of the gentry came to Carolina with their freedom, and perhaps a little capital, but were often at least one generation removed from managing family land.[81] Members of this mobile immigrant population imported no single set of agricultural experiences to Carolina, but rather a stockpile of strategies, customs, and expectations drawn from those parts of the countryside that had once served as more permanent ancestral homes, in which they had lingered en route to resettlement in towns and cities, and through which they passed before coming to America.[82] Although only the best educated among them embraced the literature of agricultural improvement that inspired the Proprietary vision for Carolina's development, England's fascination with projects of improvement had percolated through all social ranks to reorient even the most humble farmsteads toward the market.[83] Exposed to diverse farming regions at a time when commercialization was remaking the countryside as a whole, English immigrants imported a view of the farmstead that was a flexible composite rather than a static ideal. Rather than a force for the replication of any particular farming tradition, theirs was an agricultural inheritance attuned to planting's opportunities for commerce and innovation.

Among white migrants to Carolina from other American colonies, those from Barbados loomed largest, accounting for perhaps 300 to 400 of the colony's roughly 1,000 settlers by the early 1680s.[84] Barbadians brought with them a specific template for the creation of a plantation society. From the vantage of the smaller sugar islands, "which swarme with the Inhabitants," the continental expanse of Carolina's geography seemed to remedy the deficiencies of planting in vulnerable Caribbean archipelagos. By 1670 indentured servants and slaves had long cleared the best arable land on Barbados for cane and harvested its remaining woodlands to fuel sugar-boiling houses. A chronic lack of fresh water forced planters to capture rainwater in cisterns to supply the basic needs of its concentrated human and animal populations. Ecological strains vied with exposure to hostile attacks by sea and restive black supermajorities as ongoing sources of English anxiety in the islands.[85] Against this backdrop of resource scarcity and strategic weakness, accounts of Carolina's natural abundance spoke with special intensity to the concerns and desires of Caribbean colonists. Fearing destructive hurricanes and early deaths in the intemperate tropics, Antigua settlers seemed "ready to desert" the island, "it being a meare grave." In 1672 Jamaica's governor wrote to his counterpart in the struggling settlement of New Providence Island in the Bahamas that he wished "they were all well settled at Carolina" because English colonies "can never in those islands be convenient, safe or rich."[86] Convinced that Carolina could "produce all manner [of] plants," as well as "any Comodities [that] the Charibbe Islands doe," planters from Barbados ordered slaves and servants to plant sweet potatoes, yams, and other familiar West Indian food crops along with the island's proven market crops: sugarcane, ginger, cotton, tobacco, and indigo. Barbadians worked to remake Carolina in the image of Barbados, taking the opportunity in the meantime to supply the island with the wood, meat, and materials its ravenous but resource-poor economy demanded. They looked forward to a time when the new colony would find its staple commodity and thus replicate Barbados's slave and plantation economy more completely. Led by wealthy elites, Barbados settler groups negotiated with the Proprietors over the terms of early land policies and formed a coherent and experienced class of planters around which opposition to the Proprietors' framework for development coalesced.[87]

resisted props plans

Taken with the elegance of his scheme, Ashley failed to recognize that the weak coercive powers of an early modern colonial government could do little to force planters to realize a blueprint for settlement against their wishes, no matter how artfully constructed to achieve benevolent ends. Nothing offended planters more than giving up their choice of the best land. Carolina's first surveyor general, to ensure that "the people will not inhabit [at] a distance" from one another, attempted to assign land to new immigrants "as it lyes" with "the bad and good" in every portion. Promised vast arable fields, planters found that the land they received lay in "Irregular figures," with scarce outcroppings of "good Oake Land" within larger expanses of "Pine Swamp and Marsh" wastes. Lowcountry land was "Interwoven" everywhere by "great Creeks, and Marshes." Narrow fissures of hardwood soil traced crooked paths between higher and drier pine forests and lower and damper swamps, paralleling the meandering courses of waterways in this low-lying terrain. Although Ashley wanted to steer Carolina colonists away from the example of Virginia planters, who established their plantations "scatteringly and straglingly as a choice veyne of rich ground in[v]ited them," they nevertheless followed the Chesapeake pattern. With "good land lying soe widely dispersed" and nowhere "contiguous," settlers fanned out along rivers and creeks instead of congregating in village enclaves.[88]

Seeking to incorporate the largest portions of arable land within their grants, planters set a course for lowcountry settlement that eroded the Proprietors' vision during Carolina's very first year. After parceling out lands to a party of forty-two immigrants from Barbados in the spring of 1671, Councilor Stephen Bull reported to Ashley that "wee are Sett Downe as close together as Conveniency will admit." Catering to "Every one of their p[ar]ticul[a]r desires" for land, however, meant that the Barbadians were free to survey tracts that stretched across two miles along the Ashley River.[89] For a decade before the establishment of Charlestown in 1670, prospective Barbados settlers stressed their desire to select land, among other issues, as they negotiated with the Proprietors for especially favorable settlement terms. Although the Assembly never ratified the Proprietors' Fundamental Constitutions, early settlers treated the formal "Concessions" to the Barbadians as a statement of their rights to the land.[90] With Caribbean colonists leading the way, planters staked out "Settlements scattering up & downe" Ashley River and refused lands allotted in sandy pine forests closest to Charlestown. By the early 1680s Carolina plantations, "being seated on the Rivers," formed diffuse communities in which the residents of the same waterway came together by means of "Canoo or Boat" instead of congregating at a township meetinghouse or grazing animals side by side on common lands. In the early eighteenth century Anglican cleric Samuel Thomas complained that his parishioners lived "at so wide a distance from each other" along the Cooper River that he was forced to travel more than fifteen miles and officiate at three separate services to preach to them all.[91]

The Proprietors' "Agrarian Laws" of 1672 sought to implement Ashley's vision of a new-world aristocracy. This titled nobility was to preside over a well-ordered rural society from commanding 12,000-acre "baronies" and "seignories." More modest settlers, who received the largest number of land grants in portions of fewer than 300 acres, shaped the early plantation landscape more quietly and decisively. Faced with planter resistance to early land policies during the seventeenth century, the Proprietors lowered the quitrent obligations on lands granted through headrights, provided for the outright purchase of land without rent obligations, and affirmed the titles of squatters who simply took the land they wanted, where they wanted it. When independent planters evaded land laws, subsequent legislation reduced the burdens and constraints they found onerous and affirmed the extralegal course that settlement had already taken.[92] Carolina soon bore the marks of a planters' landscape. Against the Proprietors' directives to concentrate in communities, planters dispersed across the Lowcountry. As they colonized new lands at a distance from their neighbors, they removed themselves from the scrutiny of elites and staked claims as propertied men who ruled independent domains. Their mobility across the land leveled the hierarchies Ashley hoped would flourish in his idealized villages, undermining a vertical model of social authority and entrenching one that stretched laterally to empower all white, male landowners. As colonists scattered across the Lowcountry, building plantations on plots of riverside land that reached deeper into the interior every year, they put into practice a vision for development that they never articulated in visionary terms. Although they took advantage of the law's generous provisions for headright grants that bequeathed hundreds of acres to each free, male immigrant, planters settled these tracts by the compass of their own ambitions, taking up land in ways that evaded the order of the Proprietors' land system and nullified its social objectives.

To John Stewart's frustration, "the people" remained indifferent to his agricultural projects, revealing their humble class origins as members of a "thick skul'd" rabble. Planters understood so little "of nature art or ingenuity" that they preferred growing Indian corn to tending the mulberry trees required for a colonial silk industry. All of his "Endeavors of discourse relating to my Remarks in foraigne Countrys and what they might doe and advance," he complained, were "but charming the deaf adder."[93] Planters appeared to Stewart, and to metropolitan commentators on South Carolina agriculture who were to follow him over the next century, as ignorant boors who ignored elite agricultural knowledge. The Proprietors joined him in a chorus of disapproval over the crude state of Carolina's seventeenth-century plantation economy.

In the spring of 1671 Ashley feared that Carolina planters, ever "covetous of present booty," would abandon agriculture for mining if news of gold reached Charlestown. Yet during the next two decades a different form of "rapin[e] and plunder" on the land undermined his design for a colony of "Planting and Trade." Instead of cultivating wheat and tending vegetable gardens, planters followed the model of Indian maize-and-bean agriculture by choice rather than necessity, emulating Native American methods long after early food shortages had passed. Instead of keeping livestock on village lands, planters fenced in their cornfields and let their cattle and hogs roam wild in unclaimed savannas and marshes that surrounded every plantation, making a crude commons of the Lowcountry's open wastelands.[94] For profit, they shipped surplus meat, tallow, and lumber to the English West Indies, ignoring commodities that might enhance Carolina's reputation in European markets as they generated returns for its planters and founders. When he surveyed the progress of the planters' landscape, Ashley sneered that it was the Proprietors' design to "have Planters there and not Graziers." The term reproached settlers for taking Carolina on a regressive course of development. By engrossing arable land for pasture in early modern England, "greedie grasiers" stood in the way of planting new crops and made a mockery of the faith that had been invested in landlords as agents of economic change.[95] Ranging cattle across the Lowcountry to consume its abundant forage committed the same sin of backwardness in the face of progress. To Ashley and other critics, early cattle-and-corn farming was a brand of agriculture without culture. As planters hacked fields from forests and grazed animals in wild wastes, they seemed to detach planting from the guiding force of English improvement, debase traditions of husbandry, and deprive Carolina of an economic future in line with its environmental promise. Half-wild cattle, torched fields littered with stumps, and bowls of hominy mush were signs of cultural regression to Carolina's founders.

Beneath the crude appearances of Carolina plantations, planters took part in a vigorous process of multicultural exchange that integrated African, Indian, and Latin American practices within a British agricultural framework. The creation of a rice industry in the late 1690s was the most important example of this process of agricultural synthesis, but in the first decade of settlement, Carolina's unique cattle culture bore the same marks of transatlantic adaptation. Planters pursued "Provisions and numerous Stocks of Cattle," objects of production that they "esteemed the Basis and Props of all new Plantations." As grossly distorted as Carolina's version of mixed English farming might appear to agricultural improvers, subsistence-oriented grain production, combined with livestock raising for the market, formed the backbone of the new colony's economy as it had structured the English rural economy for the better part of two centuries. Growing corn and raising cattle secured subsistence and generated income without extraordinary risks or heavy investments in labor. As imported European grain crops failed, and wresting arable land from the encroachments of nature proved an unremitting struggle, "Cattell increase[d] extraordinarily" in the Lowcountry with "litle or no trou[ble]."[96] Planters let livestock forage without confinement along the Ashley, Cooper, and Wando rivers. To keep animals from turning feral, they enticed hogs home to feed on scraps; cows returned to suckle their calves and were sometimes penned for the night. Viewed against the ideal farming system advocated by improvers, marsh grazing and makeshift enclosures seemed hallmarks of agricultural decline. Yet farmers working in the marginalized regions of western Britain (southwestern England, Wales, Scotland, and Ireland) had long raised cattle in the same ways. Later critics of colonial husbandry railed against degenerate animal bloodlines, the inadequacies of wasteland pastures, and the crude forms such practices imprinted on the agricultural landscape. These adaptations nevertheless bore strong traces of their British origins, especially those in use by fenland farmers who shared coastal Carolina's wet, low-lying topography.[97]

European planters incorporated unfamiliar practices into the familiar framework of British husbandry. Lowcountry Indians, who helped make corn and beans Carolina's dietary staples, also burned the grasslands to concentrate deer herds, giving the landscape an appearance that its first English visitors admired as a natural park. By demonstrating the utility of fire, Native Americans handed the settlers who followed a tool for increasing the grazing burdens of natural pastures. Planters in Barbados, the Leewards, and Jamaica found the islands they occupied stocked with Spanish cattle. They followed their predecessors' example, tending cattle on horseback, calling grasslands "savannas," and burning them to generate new growth during droughts. West Indian migrants imported these techniques to Carolina along with African slaves tasked to manage inland cowpens, some of which raised thousands of animals by the early eighteenth century.[98] For planters determined to acquire wealth rapidly in early Carolina, adapting to the environment meant reaching beyond a pool of British practices and enhancing husbandry with foreign techniques. Packed meats destined for the West Indies remained significant exports through the first decade of the eighteenth century, and livestock figured as a significant component of total personal wealth for most settlers. For former indentured servants and newcomers without much capital, raising cattle provided a financial stepping-stone to slave and land purchases. Livestock income funded extractive, labor-intensive ventures in lumber and tar production and, by the turn of the eighteenth century, helped finance moves into rice cultivation.[99] For those who plowed cattle profits into more diversified estates during the first decades of settlement, cheap pasturage in open wastelands allowed for unprecedented opportunities to accumulate wealth in more or less familiar ways.[100]

When he arrived in 1682, Thomas Newe carried a small stock of trade goods across the Atlantic to set himself up as a Carolina planter. As the son of an Oxford college butler, Newe's education prepared him better than most settlers of modest means to embrace the Proprietors' economic projects. The year in which he arrived was a "time of tryall" for an experimental wine industry "which if it hits no doubt but the place will flourish exceedingly." Excited by a short-lived rage for medicinal herbs as potential exports, he asked his father for "the best herbalist for Physical Plants in as small a Volume as you can get" and to "enquire at some Apothecarys what Sassafrass (which grows here in great plenty) is worth a pound and how and at what time of the year to cure it." Newe discovered that his future as a planter involved far more mundane agricultural pursuits than those pictured in promotional tracts. Most new planters were "poor and whol[l]y ignorant of husbandry." Their "whole Business was to clear a little ground to get Bread for their Familyes, few of them having wherewithall to purchase a Cow." After a few years of work "each family hath got a stock of Hogs and Cows, which when once a little more encreased, they may send of[f] to the Islands." With Barbados as a primary market, the colony produced "Pork, Corn and Cedar" for export and sold provisions to incoming shipping. Newe would be forced to pay the premiums charged by wealthier planters with "great stocks of Cattle" who supplied "new comers" like him with a breeding pair that, with effort and luck, would reproduce into a herd. A fatal bout with malaria probably killed Newe shortly after he disembarked at Charlestown. Had he survived this "seasoning" to join the ranks of Carolina's planters, his dreams of making wine and sassafras in the Lowcountry would have given way to the demands of purchasing servants and slaves, growing corn, and raising cattle.[101]

As planters defied the Proprietors' project in the 1670s, their counterparts in the Chesapeake struggled to justify their more violent challenge to properly constituted authority—known since as Bacon's Rebellion—as something less abhorrent than a revolt. Nathaniel Bacon charged that Virginia's ruling elite's claims to superior "learning and vertue" rang particularly hollow, given how recklessly they used political authority to line their pockets. Although Ashley never accused Carolina's planters of treason, he saw their disregard for his social and economic vision in class terms as the unsettling triumph of a fractious multitude that, by the force of its numbers, carved out a landscape of disorder, defacing his carefully wrought design for colonial improvement. Until "more men of Estates" arrived to aid the Proprietors in "putting our Excellent Modell in some measure in practice," a virtual "state of Warr" existed in Carolina, with humble colonists exercising an unnatural influence over government, settlement, and production.[102] As they fanned out across the Lowcountry and neglected exotic commodities for cattle and corn, planters challenged the founders' authority by disregarding their expertise.

As they synthesized agricultural traditions from throughout the Atlantic world to plant the Lowcountry, settlers became planters. Planters withheld deference to experts whose projects for ordering the landscape failed to predict nature's capacities for agriculture and miscalculated the aspirations of its settlers. Theirs was not the opposition, as the Proprietors charged, of an unlettered mob bent on upheaval and motivated only by craven self-interest. The planters' expertise derived from practice rather than theory. Merging British, American Indian, and Caribbean farming methods, planters secured subsistence and entered into exchange in the Atlantic economy. Along with slaves, indentured servants, and capital raised from sugar planting, the "well experienced planters" from Barbados imported standards for plantership that other settlers acknowledged by turning to them for guidance. Because they knew "how to setle such a Country," ship captain–turned-settler Henry Brayne argued to the Proprietors, such "men of reason that was planters" should serve on the Council. As leading figures in the political faction called the Goose Creek Men, Barbadians did ascend to political power, challenging Proprietary policies and authority into the eighteenth century.[103]

Claims about Carolina's abundance exposed a tension at the heart of early plantation society. Carolina plantations, no matter how different in appearance from English farms, followed a basic principle of arable-pasture land use. Such farmsteads, reconstructed out of the materials at hand in subtropical America, however, were to produce goods that no English farmer could. Reconciling the familiar potential of lowcountry land with its exotic promise demanded a new kind of knowledge about agriculture. The planters' landscape, even as it supplanted the environmental visions of Carolina's founders and indigenous inhabitants, was a product of culture and agricultural synthesis.

Four groups sought to shape Carolina's seventeenth-century landscape. Native Americans parlayed their knowledge of the land and their presence on it into a short-term tactical advantage, steering settlers to establish a colonial outpost in the midst of Cusabo country. As officials gained independent access to the Indian interior and colonists took up lowcountry land beyond the Ashley and Cooper rivers, this short-term advantage disappeared, leaving the Cusabos in a position of long-term geographic and strategic vulnerability. Within a few years planters had learned to grow what they called Indian corn for themselves, and their dependence on Indian agricultural knowledge subsided. As outsiders to the English colonizing process, coastal Indians failed to sustain the influence that came with their long occupation of the Lowcountry, a position of strength that native groups deeper in the interior, such as the Catawbas and the Cherokees, were able to put to use diplomatically to survive the colonial period.

As racial outsiders relegated to the status of dependent subjects, enslaved Africans influenced the character of this emerging plantation society without official power. As environmental agents who stood between planters and land, however, slaves assumed a customary scope of influence over the cultivation of crops. This practical control over planting shaped the domestic economies that sustained black families. As rice became more important as an article of trade than as an article of consumption, Africans set precedents for slave labor that ordered plantation work long after planters claimed slaves' agricultural experience with wetland agriculture as their own.

The colony's Proprietors exercised their legal title to Carolina as if the scope of their official authority conveyed the power to implement their schemes for settlement, society, and production. Their dilated visions of exotic commodities, new-world aristocrats, and village communities failed to appreciate how little settlers wished to be subjects. As the primary agents of colonization, planters united explicit authority as owners of land and masters of dependents with the practical authority that came with living on the land and directing plantation settlement and production. They succeeded where others failed by integrating the environmental visions of their rivals into a plantation system under their command.

The contending visions of growth that pitted projecting founders against improving planters, however, shared much common ground. Long after they deposed the Proprietors, planter legislators imposed upon themselves the constraints they never tolerated during the colony's beginnings. After South Carolina and allied Indian forces expelled Yamassee insurgents to end the war of 1715, the Assembly reserved their lands to attract white immigrants. Legislators envisioned these yeomen farmers, too poor to buy slaves, populating a strategic buffer zone on the southern frontier. In the early 1730s the provincial government reserved townships along the inland edge of the settled Lowcountry for poor white Protestants to claim. South Carolina's Assembly enforced prohibitive duties on slave imports, in part to finance these townships, but primarily to slow the growth of the black population.[104] Government schemes to restrain this plantation society scrutinized its weaknesses and continued to ask planters to tally the costs of settling the land by the light of their individual economic interests.

Both founders and planters looked forward in time to picture South Carolina plantations remaking the coastal Lowcountry through commodity production for European markets. Both took the English farm as a starting point from which to create a new form of agriculture. Founders and settlers alike conceived of Carolina as a landscape "languishing from a lack of an informing vision" under Native American possession, which made it seem especially "receptive of white design." Projectors introduced planters to the environmental and market possibilities of three crops—rice, indigo, and cotton—that would determine South Carolina's economic future. By the first decade of the eighteenth century, as rice production remade lowcountry plantations, they continued to parade visions of silk, wine, almonds, and other exotics before planters' imaginations.[105] Ashley's well-ordered village communities never materialized, but Charlestown's growth as a central place for exchange, government, and culture realized part of his vision for a rural society infused with the civilizing forces of urbanity. The members of this charter generation were not born in Carolina, but their experiences on early plantations laid the foundations for an economic culture that, in its initial openness to cross-cultural influence and willingness to shed normative models, was creole in character.

— 2 —

Rice Culture Origins

From above the Lowcountry's freshwater swamps, European colonists watched African slaves plant an edible species of grass that distinguished itself from wild forage in late summer. As its heavy panicle of rice matured, the plants appeared to bow to the ground under the burden of the grain.[1] As rice moved from provision grounds and experimental plots to the commercial centers of plantations, and as plantations themselves changed from enclaves of arable land to encompass larger swampland tracts, planters and slaves fashioned a model for expansive colonization that had eluded the colony's founding generation. In many ways, people transplanted from Europe and Africa found this portion of coastal North America to be a wasteland. To English eyes, the cleared wetlands in which rice flourished seemed at first unproductive wastes compared with the higher and drier land settlers migrated across the Atlantic to claim. To grow rice for sale abroad, planters learned to cast off the categories of conventional husbandry and prize such lands as the Lowcountry's most valuable endowment for plantation agriculture.

As a place in which masters and slaves struggled to reconstitute familiar ways of living, South Carolina was a wasteland in a different sense. When wheat rotted in lowcountry fields, settlers reconstructed a new domestic economy from materials drawn from other societies, growing a multicultural array of crops that the land could bear in preference to those that affirmed their identities as English people. Slaves faced a world in which their bondage narrowed the time and space they could take to cobble together acceptable African meals. Abundant supplies of maize, called "Indian corn" throughout colonial British America, sustained black and white bodies alike, but it also symbolized a shared estrangement from

53

the American subtropics that both groups tried to overcome by growing new crops to take its place in their diets. The origins of South Carolina's distinctive eighteenth-century plantation economy lay in the adaptation of rice agriculture to the lowcountry environment. Rice's standing as a food for both slaves and masters paved the way for its transformation into a commodity. Just as the first settlers created a new-world version of the British farm using Native American methods, a later generation of colonists appropriated the example of African American wasteland farming to focus their plantations on the production of a new market crop.

As rice rose to the status of a staple commodity after 1720, it changed South Carolina's external relationship to the Atlantic economy, opening lines of credit, generating private fortunes, and drawing hundreds and then thousands of new slaves to the colony every year to grow more rice for export. This watershed moment also transformed the internal dynamics of the plantations. By intensifying work and multiplying the number of enslaved dependents, rice's demands put disruptive pressures on plantations as households, reconnecting individuals to one another along new lines of authority, dependency, and expectation that produced the region's distinctive task labor system. Slaves took part in these transformations, influencing this new world of production and consumption as they reacted to its onerous new demands. African experience with rice was not, however, the critical element that ushered in this eighteenth-century plantation regime. Planters entered into a multicultural dialogue on how best to bring the land into cultivation, appropriating Indian and African agricultural strategies to shape and reshape the plantation landscape. They applied the innovative approaches of "improved" British agriculture to make this foreign crop their own. Increasing racial rigidity and the brutal subjugation of people on the land went hand in hand with cultural and agricultural flexibility in South Carolina's early plantation society.

That members of Europe's most ethnocentric imperial culture should also prove to be so open to non-European methods poses a paradox. Unraveling it hinges on a new reading of rice's origins that stresses the first function of agriculture, providing food for those who cultivated land. Contemporaries and historians alike have looked to rice's beginnings to discover how this distinctive plantation culture came into being. This search has put forward three figures that, by adapting agriculture to the

Lowcountry, might make a claim to be remembered as the founders of South Carolina's staple economy. Eighteenth-century colonists favored a protagonist built after their own image, a heroic planter who erected a refined landscape on the cultivated acres of once-forbidding swamps. Modern historians first credited the Lords Proprietors as farsighted economic planners who brought both the first rice seed to Carolina and experts who knew how to raise it. Others have contended on behalf of South Carolina's slaves, crediting them with importing an effective African rice system to the Lowcountry. Successfully planting the wastelands, however, depended on finding ways to synthesize and put into practice the different sorts of knowledge that settlers, officials, and slaves possessed. The early years of settlement opened a window for cross-cultural exchange across lines of race that soon closed.

Agricultural Agency and Historical Memory

Pondering the moment at which rice seeds first germinated in lowcountry soil involves stringing together a series of technical events by which European and African immigrants implanted an old-world cultigen in the new. Explaining how the critical materials of this plantation economy were first assembled remains this society's most compelling origin story. At stake in these accounts is a model for economic development that rests on human ingenuity and the attribution of credit—to white colonists or black slaves—for first introducing a crop that made such innovative use of the Lowcountry's swamps. Rice's story serves as a genesis narrative of economic and social creation on Britain's colonial periphery.

European colonists mythologized their staple's beginnings as the story of their own triumph over nature. Contemporary accounts written between 1731 and 1809 pinpointed the moment of introduction at different times and credited several different elites as rice's progenitors. Virtually all agreed, however, that a "fortunate accident" brought rice to Carolina. Various ships bearing the first seed hailed from exotic points of origin— North Africa, Indonesia, India, Egypt, and Madagascar—outside the normal range of the colony's commerce.[2] In one version, happenstance led to a meeting between a British East India Company official and a Charlestown merchant at a London coffeehouse. This encounter brought "a money bag full of East India rice" to South Carolina. The Madagascar ship (said to have arrived in 1685, 1696, or 1713) "happened, in distress, to put into the port of Charles Town." The captain of a "Barbary" vessel "by Chance brought with him a Bushel or two of RICE to feed his Poultry."[3] Perhaps "it was by a woman that Rice was transplanted to Carolina." Perhaps a "ship, on its return from India, ran aground on this coast . . . laden with rice; which, being tossed on shore by the waves, grew up again."[4] Storytellers marveled at the "small begin[n]ings" from which "have sprung the quantities of that grain which now cover our fields." They focused on whichever bag, peck, or bushel of rice their story claimed as the source "from which small stock it . . . increased" to cover thousands of acres of cleared swamp fields.

"From this small beginning did the staple commodity of Carolina take its rise, which soon became the chief support of the colony, and its great source of opulence," wrote Alexander Hewit in his 1779 *An Historical Account of the Rise and Progress of the Colonies of South Carolina and Georgia.*[5] Once initial trials with the grain proved successful, these accounts praised the planters who transformed nature and entrenched a thriving industry armed with only a small supply of seed. Only after white settlers exploited the potential of freshwater swamps did rice cease to be an empty innovation. After struggling with the inefficiencies of growing rice like English grain, "experience . . . taught the husbandman to clear and cultivate the swampy grounds." When planters discovered such wastelands to be "perfectly adapted" to the crop, their efforts working on the land made it "the great staple of the country."[6] Planters told the story of how they commandeered the land for commercial agriculture. Theirs was an early modern epic of colonization pitting virtuous colonists against unpredictable fortune.

The first apocryphal account of Madagascar seed finding its way into the hands of a colonial official was published in 1731, four decades after the seminal event it described took place.[7] Origin-story authors projected the practices of their own times into the past to spin coherent narratives out of misremembered facts. Thomas Lamboll recalled that when he was a child walking to school near plantation fields in 1704, he saw "some planters, who were essaying to make rice grow."[8] This memory took shape during an era in which elites throughout the Lowcountry devoted plantation land to trials with silk, oranges, hemp, potash, and, most successfully, indigo. In his 1809 account David Ramsay shifts the locus of experimentation from the countryside to the city, claiming that Governor Thomas Smith first planted rice in a "low and moist" spot of his East

Bay Street garden. Ramsay assumed that the late colonial rage for amateur botany that inspired urban elites to plant new crops next to their town-houses held sway a century earlier.[9] Was it Governor Nathaniel Johnson in 1688, Indian trader Henry Woodward around 1690, Thomas Smith in 1693, or East India Company treasurer Charles Du Bose in 1696 who deserved to be recognized as rice's critical disseminator? Putting even the slightest pressure on colonial origin stories to reconcile them reveals their distorted view of the past.[10]

Unlike their counterparts elsewhere in colonial British America who venerated their founders, lowcountry colonists did not see themselves as lesser men and women whom worldly acquisition had made into pale versions of more heroic forebears. "So great was the economic boom" in mid-eighteenth-century South Carolina, Jack P. Greene has argued, that it seems to have "eroded most of the traditional fears of prosperity and to have produced a remarkably complete adjustment to the conditions of abundance." Planters paid tribute instead to second-generation settlers who laid the foundation for their plantation society's prosperity. This generation's willingness to leave the "high land" and cultivate rice in "fresh water swamps" was a critical environmental adaptation. It set them apart from the first, somewhat-hapless settlers who had revealed themselves as "men of little knowledge and substance" and "utter strangers to the arts of agriculture" for renouncing the wastelands.[11] This move to the swamps, argued Charles Pinckney in 1744, was all that stood between the Lowcountry's thriving plantation society and a savage, undeveloped landscape that might have been.

> Our Fathers avoided the running out those rich and deep Swamps, so proper and necessary for the Cultivation of RICE; and terminated their Platts with the Bounds of the high Lands; giving up all beyond as dangerous, impassable and of no Use . . . had they not . . . *ventured* upon the *new* laborious and dangerous Experiment of entering into thick and deep Swamps, and there cultivating RICE, how many fine Estates would to this Day have remained ungotten; and how many valuable Tracts of Land would now have remain'd in the very Heart of our Settlements wast[e] and uncultivated, and Harbours only for Beasts and Tygers and other Beasts of Prey?

The accomplishment of transforming rice from an inert import—a handful of seeds—into the "staple and principal Commodity of this Province" resolved the threat of failure that hovered over newcomers in a hostile environment.[12] The contrast between rice's chance beginnings and its vast influence made the efforts of the first successful planters seem all the more remarkable.

Although their self-regard was distinctive, the planters did not construct their origin story out of wholly new materials. The literary model to which it aspired was the georgic, a neoclassical verse form that celebrated the "heroism of staple agriculture" and relished the details of soils, seasons, and production.[13] Georgics insisted that the dominant discourse of political economy, which evaluated colonies in terms of their contributions to imperial commerce, had misplaced what was important about new-world agriculture. These agricultural epics envisioned the work of "pioneer planters" turning a wild frontier into a "landscape of cultivated estates." Where mercantilist tracts saw staples as articles of transatlantic exchange, georgics celebrated their production and the "creative extension of human design over profuse nature" that made it possible. South Carolina planters admired the sight of "flourishing fields" that they took as signs of their own "diligent husbandry."[14] They focused on the last decade of the seventeenth century, more than twenty years after the establishment of the colony, as a moment of transformation in which unlucky settlers became the kind of enterprising planters with whom they could identify.

Historians have demystified such fabulist tales of transformation in a brave new world. Rice's first modern scholars have insisted above all that the commodity was "not the result of an 'accident,' " but rather a planned innovation of the colony's founders.[15] Two recent economic studies of the plantation economy dispense altogether with the questionable facts of the planters' legend. Compared with structural dynamics that changed South Carolina's relationship to the Atlantic economy, finding the right type of seed and conquering the swamps appear as mere epiphenomena on the surface of the industry's market-driven acceleration.[16] These interpretations retain European colonists as the story's protagonists, but they downplay the significance of the planter imposing "his will on the chaos of a coastal Carolina swamp," as well as the "lucky accident" that made such an accomplishment seem extraordinary.[17] Far from being changed by their encounters with a new crop grown on unfamiliar land, colonists, in the view of these historians, found in rice a means of realizing expectations for commodity production that they brought with them from Europe.

Casting Africans as the originators of rice agriculture has made the transformative power of black agency a staple of the revisionist historiography of slavery. Peter H. Wood's *Black Majority* identifies parallels between cultivation, irrigation, and processing techniques in West Africa and the Lowcountry, thus crediting black rather than white pioneers for setting a course for the plantation economy.[18] Building on this association to argue that African skills remained critical to South Carolina's eighteenth-century expansion, Daniel C. Littlefield stresses the logic behind planters' preferences for slaves from rice-growing regions. By showing how slaves might have brought "more than just brawn to the development of plantation society," Littlefield suggests that the influence of their ingenuity extended well beyond the moment of rice's introduction.[19]

Honing Wood and Littlefield's associations between old- and new-world techniques into harder analogues, Judith A. Carney points to underlying similarities between tidal rice agriculture in South Carolina and mangrove rice systems in West Africa. Reasoning that slaves must have parted with knowledge this advanced only in exchange for something of value, Carney claims that slaves traded rice skills to planters to secure the benefits of independent production within the Lowcountry's task labor system. No documentary evidence supports this contention that "knowledge of growing rice by submersion provided slaves leverage to negotiate" for the task's limit on daily plantation work. Because white contributions to the historical record have enforced the "denial of African accomplishment," however, *Black Rice* seeks to set the record straight with its "counternarrative . . . to the dominant one that attributes rice history in the Americas to European agency."[20]

Each of these interpretations of origins credits rice growing to a single cultural group. Colonists who celebrated rice as a white achievement wrote Africans out of the story of South Carolina's development despite their vast numbers and the familiarity of some with farming in subtropical lowland environments. Telling tales in an atmosphere of heightened racial repression, planters saw field slaves more as "hands" deployed to enact their masters' agricultural designs than as minds capable of so critical an innovation. When Virginians experimented with rice in 1648, by contrast, they made no secret of their appeal to black expertise. Their "Negroes affirme[d]" that "the ground and Climate [were] very proper" for the crop, "which in their Country is most of their food."[21] It took a French commentator on British colonial development to broach the suggestion that rice "may have been carried" to the colony "with slaves." Yet South Carolina planters left behind no hint that Africans had anything to do with early rice growing beyond physical labor. So complete was this suppression of rice's possible black origins that in 1770 Governor William Bull credited the "experience of the Po and Ganges" with technical precedents for late colonial advances in rice irrigation.[22] Most who have followed in his wake have continued to privilege European agency to the exclusion of those without formal power to direct the economy.

The revisionist counternarrative has exchanged planter heroism for ignorance when it came to rice. English colonists "knew nothing at all" about rice, according to Wood. Because they possessed "no prior rice-farming knowledge" and in particular lacked any "expertise in wet rice farming," Carney concludes, the "origin of rice cultivation in Carolina is indeed African."[23] Making a case for slaves as the necessary agents behind rice culture assumes precise, one-to-one correspondences between source and destination regions in the technical evolution of South Carolina plantation agriculture. Africans knew and grew rice, and Europeans did not. Awarding slaves the laurels they have been denied by a "long-standing research bias against Africa and its peoples" thus steers us away from seeing transatlantic transmission as the intercultural exchange of precedents, technologies, and materials.[24] Puncturing the planter elite's self-admiration, revisionist historians have, with a few qualifications, argued that South Carolina's rice culture was an exclusive African creation.[25]

Asking the question, who first made rice grow in South Carolina? understands the first instance of rice planting as the beginning of a process of economic growth rather than as a cultural activity within contemporary material contexts. To examine dynamics of cultivation and culture on their own terms in the period 1670–1700, we might begin by asking, instead, why rice? For both planters and slaves, it was an improbable choice. It is counterintuitive rather than self-evident that slaves would devote that precious margin of their labor that they controlled to tending a plant so sensitive to drought because some had grown and eaten it in West Africa. Hardier root crops such as yams and sweet potatoes deliver the same number of calories at a fraction of the man- and woman-hours required to cultivate rice. Furthermore, approximately six out of every seven slaves transported to South Carolina before 1740 came from regions that produced little or no rice. For most Africans in the early Carolina Lowcountry, rice was as unfamiliar a grain as it appeared to northern Europeans.[26]

European settlers, although aware that rice might be grown for export, had at first limited interest in doing so. The commodity was a minor article of European exchange that supplied largely untried markets before it was shipped from Charlestown in large quantities. That rice could be sold for profit is a necessary but not sufficient explanation for why planters singled it out for production. A minor prospective commodity among many others that promotional writers encouraged, this modest grain lacked luster next to the other signature commodities of plantation America. Virginia's tobacco was a powerful psychotropic drug associated with exotic Native America; Barbados's sugar satisfied deep-rooted desires for sweetness, nobility, and purity.[27] Ginger, silk, wine, indigo, and cotton each seemed more promising staple candidates in the 1670s; decades later both indigo and cotton would prove to be lucrative exports.[28] A few projectors promoted new commodities, but their designs were frustrated by rank-and-file settlers interested in clearing land, growing maize, and raising cattle. For most colonists in early Carolina, the quest for a staple was a secondary pursuit rather than an all-encompassing search powerful enough to place any viable commodity, no matter how obscure, at the center of plantation work.

In cultural terms, planters had much to lose and, it first seemed, little to gain by focusing land and labor toward commercial rice production. By moving agriculture into the swamps, they lost the opportunity to create a plantation landscape that resembled the English countryside. British critics later railed against wetland rice as a brand of agriculture that subverted standards for improved husbandry, sacrificing order for disorder, independence for suffering, and tillable soil for murky swamps.[29] Organic metaphors for growth seem apt to describe a course of development that depended on the cultivation of *Oryza sativa*, the species sent to European markets in increasing quantities after 1699, but its emergence as a staple was by no means natural or inevitable. South Carolina's economy might well have followed the pattern set in North Carolina, where eighteenth-century exports of tar, meat, corn, and lumber built a more modest transatlantic trade out of a set of early subsistence and extractive enterprises that both colonies shared. As rice's *deus ex machina* appearance in the planters' narrative suggests, the crop was an unexpected arrival and a strange agricultural bequest.[30] How planters became cultural omnivores, valuing and appropriating Native American and African American approaches to agriculture on early plantations and, at the same time, laying the foundations of one of the Western Hemisphere's most exploitative societies, demands an explanation that reaches beyond appeals to the profit motive.

Although the revised story of "black" rice overturns the planters' story of white agricultural achievement, it cannot sustain its tone of celebration. Only by framing the slaves' transplantation of African rice to Carolina narrowly in time, to the moment of its introduction and early adoption as a plantation crop, does this innovation appear as a meaningful expression of black agency. When projected beyond the Stono Rebellion of 1739 and into the brutal work regimens of the large-scale rice plantations of the second half of the eighteenth century, the view of rice as an African "accomplishment" or "contribution" should evoke irony rather than appreciation. As white planters mastered the techniques of rice cultivation, irrigation, and processing, black "skills rapidly lost distinctiveness."[31] As the commodity's success brought thousands of new slaves to work in the rice swamps, any influence that special knowledge may have given slaves over the terms of labor disappeared. Illuminating a moment of black ingenuity shows slaves to have exercised capacities for innovation under duress, but they were unable to control the influences their agricultural decisions would have into the future. If slaves intended to use their rice skills to "reshape the terms of their domination," then introducing South Carolina planters to their staple crop worked against this goal by entrenching African slavery, multiplying the number of its victims, and making plantation work and life far more repressive than it had been.[32]

The descendants of Brazilian maroons, as Carney has recounted, describe rice culture originating in the moments after a single captive disembarked from a slave ship. Before a forced sale separated this African mother from her children, she tucked grains of rice into their hair. When the planter who purchased one of them discovered the grains, he demanded to know what they were. "[T]his is food from Africa," the child replied. The planter seized this first Brazilian rice seed and forced slaves to grow it as a commodity for sale.[33] Perhaps slaves in colonial South Carolina told a similar story, whose central element is almost certainly a fiction. Ships that brought slaves to Bahia and Charlestown alike took on rice as provisions in West Africa. As he took on captives in Gambia, for example, Captain Robert Heatley provisioned slave trading voyages to Jamaica, Dominica, and South Carolina with "Guinea Corn, Rice, and

Cuss-Cuss."[34] Fortunate accidents and extraordinary subterfuge were thus not required to circulate rice seed in either South Carolina or Brazil. But just as the planters' origin myth documents the crop's sudden appearance and a new engagement with the land that made its cultivation possible, the maroon tale contains an important narrative truth that applies to the early Lowcountry as well. Slaves used rice as food, valued it as a crop that linked individuals to one another in new-world families, and saw it wrenched out of this context of domestic production and consumption by an act of white appropriation.

In seventeenth-century South Carolina, growing crops for food took precedence over generating exports for Europe. From 1670 to 1699, a period in which the transatlantic focus of planting had yet to be determined, the rules of mastery and slavery were up for negotiation within a general framework of coercion. The boundaries between black and white households were fluid rather than fixed as all faced the challenges of how to produce and consume food on new settlements. Rice's meanings changed over the course of these three decades for those who came to grow, eat, and export it. Practically all that we can know with certainty about the early rice economy flows from three documented instances of rice growing: in 1674, four years after the colony's founding, an isolated shipment of rice was produced and exported; in 1689 and 1690 colonists planted the crop experimentally with the intention of producing it as a commodity; and in 1699, hundreds of slaves working on scores of plantations produced the first significant crop for export. Within each of these moments, one can find a threshold crossed by settlers and slaves in their perceptions of rice as something to eat and something to sell. Rice's versatility as a food to both Africans and Europeans distinguished it from a number of other plants that might have been grown for consumption and for profit. For slaves, rice was a grain in an independent domestic economy based on precedents set in the Caribbean but adapted to the environmental conditions on the mainland. For planters, it became an ingredient in their bread, a foreign crop suited to advanced agricultural methods, and, finally, a plantation staple with which they imposed new burdens on slave workers. Where these very different desires for the crop intersected, Carolina rice culture grew and spread. Rather than offering an authoritative origin story, this inquiry into the changing function of rice as food and commodity explains how slaves and settlers experienced and imagined American agriculture. As rice became a commodity in early South Carolina, racial repression went hand in hand with agricultural exchange.

Transatlantic Foodways

If runaway servant Charles Miller, brought before Spanish interrogators in St. Augustine in 1674, had not told them that "some rice which is grown on the soil" was sent to Barbados, there would be no record of rice growing in South Carolina during its first two decades. Miller's three companions mentioned only barrel staves and tobacco as the colony's articles of trade.[35] With only a few hundred inhabitants living in English Carolina, this rice was perhaps a onetime surplus from a single plantation. Whatever its source, Miller's observation reveals how open early plantations were to non-English crops as masters, servants, and slaves, both Indian and African, worked to secure a reliable subsistence. This singular instance shows that any crop, no matter how obscure, might be sold in Charlestown's nascent marketplace. That producing food was the most important object of early plantations is made clear by another documentary milestone. We do not know the name of the first enslaved African mentioned in South Carolina in 1670, the year of the colony's founding. Barbados ship captain Henry Brayne simply listed what he called "one lusty negro man" among the "stock" of people, animals, and supplies he imported to establish a plantation. What we do know about the first Afro-Carolinian of record is that he drank milk twice a day, helped slaughter a pig against his master's wishes, and was one of several workers who were eating through a supply of imported provisions as they cleared land for planting. Seventeenth-century South Carolina was a multiethnic society in which all were preoccupied with food. In simply getting enough to eat, Brayne asserted, "we have made a beginning."[36] The Proprietors provisioned migrating colonists with the "seeds and roots" of food crops gathered throughout the Atlantic world. As the first settlers attempted to "trye English graine and to sow . . . English wheat," officials urged them to make do with "Irish potatoes" that might be "boyled, roasted and baked" as a last resort in times of dearth. By 1671 colonists had planted and consumed "Indian Corne," "English pease," and "Guiney Corne," among other crops. Stocked with provisions from England, Barbados, Virginia, Bermuda, and New England, South Carolina was from its inception a place in which foods from Native America, Africa, and Europe were cultivated and consumed together.[37]

Because the colony was supplied with diverse foods from diverse sources, there was no "starving time" in early Carolina like that which nearly put an end to English Virginia more than fifty years earlier. But Africans and Europeans resisted the maize that sustained them. In Barbados, from which most South Carolina slaves were transported before 1700, Africans rejected rations of a cold maize gruel, named "loblolly" for its resemblance to the oatmeal eaten by English sailors. The "Negroes, when they come to be fed with this," reported Richard Ligon, "are much discontented, and cry out, *O! O! no more Lob-lob.*" Their aversion to maize served in this way violated their standards for what made food good to eat. Perhaps slaves found this "thinne boyled," "slovenly" dish so unpleasant because its loose consistency prevented them from taking a portion in hand and dipping it into a relish after the West African fashion.[38] Its "heavy and lumpish" texture contrasted with a preference for uniformity, and its ambient temperature made a sorry meal for people used to eating heated grain dishes. The monotony of receiving it, day after day, as an unsalted ration contributed to their distaste for loblolly. Throughout the West Indies, when planters provided a single, dominant provision, slaves complained that unrelenting supplies of Indian corn, Guinea corn (sorghum), or yams constituted "miserable fare."[39] When toasted on the cob and eaten as a vegetable, corn was a welcome addition, but as a starchy staple at the center of the diet, slaves found maize both unpalatable and, perhaps because of its low protein content, insufficiently nourishing. The nutritional advantages of starchy staples, which feature high calorie content compared with volume, are enhanced by the low cost per calorie that modern agronomists have found universally for cereals next to every other food source. Starches are also remarkably flexible foods, capable of figuring as a key ingredient and substituting for one another in "bread, pasta, pastries, cakes, biscuits, noodles, porridges, grits, gruels, tortillas, and chipattis."[40] It is for these reasons that premodern, and many modern, cuisines across the globe have focused on a single complex carbohydrate as a core food, to which oils, vegetables, meats, and spices have served as a fringe complement. Once established, such signature crops took on values that transcended their material advantages. Staple foods nourished people and represented them, just as staple commodities sustained and stood for an economy.[41]

In seventeenth-century Barbados, early Carolina's primary culture hearth, slaves took part in a food culture that drew ingredients from "a vast variety of vegetable production, maize, Guinea corn, and many edible roots." White settlers prized ripe bananas, but slaves gathered plantains green, before they became sweet, and boiled the flesh, "making it into balls, and so they eat it."[42] Although loblolly was still part of the slave diet after 1700, it no longer predominated. The most common food crop by the early eighteenth century was sorghum, with maize, plantains, cassava, sweet potatoes, and bonavist (a tropical kidney bean) figuring as supplementary starches.[43] Slaves in Barbados complemented such rations with imported fish and cast-off meats they received from planters. To make a better relish for their bread, they grew vegetables on small garden plots (such as an asparagus-like root "of which some of the Negroes brought the Seeds, and planted") and gathered palmetto-tree fruits and red sea crabs.[44]

Throughout the Africanized Caribbean, colonists and slaves assembled a global array of crops, providing ingredients that could be mixed together and substituted for one another in new-world versions of old-world dishes. In Jamaica, where slaves controlled what they planted and ate to a far greater degree than did their counterparts in Barbados, they pounded red-pea flour and maize into a protein-rich paste called *tumtum,* perhaps an onomatopoetic term from Akan that mimics the sound of a pestle striking a mortar. Naturalist Hans Sloane recognized the varieties of Jamaican "Pease, Beans, and Pulse" as different from their European cousins. Colonists ate them green, but as a standard part of the slaves' provision they were transformed by boiling into a malleable ingredient.[45] Even before enslavement forced some Africans to rebuild domestic economies in America, crops introduced by Europeans allowed those who remained behind to experiment with new foods by choice. In the early fifteenth century Portuguese mariners brought maize to the Gold Coast, where Africans named it "overseas millet." Women working at European slaving factories used it to prepare *kenkey,* a fermented dough wrapped in plantain husks that diffused into the surrounding countryside. Slaves throughout the Caribbean re-created *kenkey,* mixing plantains and yams with its "traditional" maize base. Those detached from their societies by the slave trade did not re-create static ways of planting, cooking, and eating. These and other "fusion foodways" reveal that Africans in the Atlantic world improvised within the broad confines of a starch-centered diet, integrating new foods into old recipes. Those caught in the slave trade continued this adaptive approach to cuisine, taking charge of the foods that came to hand to reconstitute reasonable meals in plantation America.[46]

Although rice was never as dominant as maize nor as widespread as sweet potatoes, Africans grew it throughout the greater Caribbean as one such versatile, starchy food. Its culture crossed imperial boundaries from the sixteenth through the nineteenth centuries. Less than twenty years after Columbus named Hispaniola, slaves were growing rice along with African yams and pigeon peas. Ranked the third most important grain in late seventeenth-century Jamaica behind Guinea corn and Indian corn, rice was "planted by some *Negroes* in their own Plantations, and thrives well."[47] Slaves grew rice in Martinique, Surinam and Brazil and on the Pearl Islands off the coast of Panama.[48] They did not, however, grow it in Barbados, which lacked surface water required to nourish the crop and a surfeit of wastelands that planters elsewhere gave slaves to grow their own provisions. Making food, eating food, and expressing preferences about it were arenas in which the enslaved controlled the character of their material lives. In their domestic economy, enslaved people could live multidimensionally. A small act such as turning up one's nose at a bowl of loblolly was one of many basic cultural performances that controlling food under slavery made possible.[49] Slaves sent to South Carolina from Barbados or Angola (places in which rice was not commonly grown or eaten) and those from Jamaica and Senegambia (places in which it was) came prepared to reconstruct shattered connections to culture from the ground up, so to speak, by cultivating starchy food crops and combining them in new ways to create a truly transatlantic way of eating.

Although there is no record that slaves grew rice for food in seventeenth-century South Carolina, they instituted a version of this Afro-Caribbean food culture, within which rice was a minor but persistent crop, from the colony's inception. Throughout the colonial period slaves made use of the marginal and wild spaces between cleared plantation fields, gathering and cultivating plants, raising and capturing animals, and venturing into woods and swamps that planters owned but that slaves had mastered.[50] In 1700 an enslaved man sold naturalist John Lawson "some small quantity of Tobacco and Rice," perhaps the product of his own provisions plot. Eighteenth-century slaves grew minor African crops such as peanuts, okra, and sesame and more substantial starchy staples such as Guinea corn and "Spiked Indian Corn," an African variety of maize. After touring the Lowcountry in the mid-1720s, naturalist Mark Catesby reported that these grain crops were "rarely seen but in plantations of Negroes, who brought it from *Guinea,* their native country, and are therefore fond of having it." Planters used Guinea corn for chicken feed, but slaves cooked ground sorghum into a porridge, making "bread of it."[51] Plantations produced two varieties of the Asian rice species *Oryza sativa* for export, but another kind, perhaps the African *Oryza glaberrima* or another *sativa* variety cultivated for their own consumption, persisted into the nineteenth century in slaves' independent provisions grounds. Planters worked to eradicate this "Guinea Rice" (a grain "principally cultivated by negro[e]s") because its distinctive red color appeared to invade otherwise white fields of rice grown for export.[52] The ongoing production of these independent food crops suggests that Africans in early South Carolina undertook a broad and successful search for usable cereals to take the place of, and to be served alongside, Indian corn. In the 1670s a few hundred slaves, most of whom had been forced to migrate to Carolina from Barbados, worked on small settlements along the banks of the Ashley River.[53] It would have taken only a few to produce the isolated parcel of rice that Miller reported in 1674; it would have taken the deaths of only a few African American farmers or enterprising European planters, or their decisions to cultivate another cereal crop, to put a stop to this stillborn rice culture.

By the time of this single shipment to Barbados prior to 1674, rice had a minor but well-established place in British cuisine that did not depend on what slaves grew for food. In 1672 the Proprietors shipped "one barrel of rice" to Charlestown along with larger quantities of provisions, gunpowder, and arms. Letters that came with these supplies aboard the *William & Ralph* made no mention that the rice was to be planted, or that it came unprocessed so that it could have in fact germinated if sown as seed. At this early stage of establishing a "publique Plantation" for commodity trials, all that was to be done was to "clear the ground, and plant provisions."[54] Hungry colonists probably devoured this rice, but it is unlikely that they dressed it with rose water and cinnamon as a dessert, boiled it with pigeons, or prepared it with beef to create an exotic "Turkish Dish of Meat," as recommended in *The Accomplish'd Lady's Delight in Preserving, Physick, Beautifying, and Cookery.*[55] Discriminating English consumers found supplies of imported Italian rice plentiful enough during the seventeenth century to enjoy these and other "good and wholesome dishes, some thicke, some thinne, some baked, [and] some boyld." When mixed with any ground meal and baked into biscuits on shipboard galleys, this bread was "too pleasant and too strong" for daily fare, but could be used weekly as a "physicall nourisher, or for the comfort of sicke and diseased men."[56] Those who found this single barrel of rice in 1672 among larger quantities of flour and beans anticipated an evening's reprieve from the Indian corn that made up their everyday diets.[57]

It would be difficult to overstate the importance of wheat bread to English colonists in America. As Roy Porter has noted, bread was "indispensable for the needs of life [and] health" in early modern Europe. It "stood for the Body within Christian symbolism. Making, breaking, and distributing bread carried profound connotations of friendship, communion, giving, sharing, [and] justice." When the first colonists reached Carolina, wheat was the grain of choice in England and was on its way to becoming the "universal bread corn of the whole people, of all classes and occupations."[58] Bread made of temperate wheat kept the vital humors of temperate English bodies in balance. Encouraged by promotional writers to expect bountiful harvests of "all sorts of *English* Grane," settlers immediately set about growing wheat to make bread.[59] Being able to transplant this keystone of domestic material culture indicated that English identities could be sustained in the new world. In 1672 colonial official Joseph Dalton proclaimed that the country was "excellent for English grain, and will afford us the convenient husbandry of wheat." He was overly optimistic about creating a domestic economy centered around wheat bread and featuring mutton, beer, and cheese, all foods that colonists produced with difficulty when they could make them at all in Carolina's subtropical climate. Mold and rust attacked wheat in the field; what grains survived were encased in an unusually thick hull and, when ground, yielded dirty-colored flour.[60]

It was a dispiriting realization for English men and women to learn that they would be forced to eat bread made from "that savage graine maze." Medical theory ranked maize as a heating food, liable to upset English constitutions, induce fevers, and derange the digestion. The notion of assimilation, which treated food as the matter out of which the body's flesh was restored, offered colonists the menacing prospect that with every bite of Indian corn, they were hastening a physical and moral transformation into Indians.[61] Officials blamed a deadly outbreak of dysentery among new settlers on the shock caused by eating Native American provisions. Long a marker of gentility, white bread set the refined eater apart from the rabble and their coarse brown and black breads. "I care not if I tell you our diet," wrote Mary Stafford to relatives in England in 1711. In place of proper bread she was forced to make meals of "Indian Corn . . . boiled stiff and eaten with milk. It "is called homony," she reported with disgust.[62] Even those without Stafford's tastes found in their daily bowls of maize mush a betrayal of the colony's environmental and social promise. After hearing "glowing tales" of Carolina, John Hash signed away his liberty "in order to improve his fortune" as one of its first servants. Instead of easy abundance, he and his fellow runaways to Spanish Florida found only "want and suffering . . . especially as regards food." Philip Onill, whipped for throwing the "provisions allowed him and his fellow servants to the Doggs" in 1672, made it clear that his mistress had failed in her responsibility to provide food fit for European stomachs.[63] Across English plantation America settlers who first tasted maize labeled it "coarse and meane fare" and "savage trash." Although Carolina colonists learned to eat such nonwhite bread every day, they never called maize by the generic term "corn"—it was always Indian corn, Turkey Wheat, or Virginia Wheat. The very language settlers used to describe maize labeled it as foreign and inferior.[64]

Some held out hope that the immigration of women to this disproportionately male settler society would dethrone maize as the colonists' dietary staple. With more "huswives" skilled in the arts of making bread, cheese, and beer, environmental obstacles to re-creating an English domestic economy might be overcome.[65] Along with the failure to raise wheat, early struggles to establish dairies, plant gardens, and raise wool-bearing sheep boded ill for this society's future as an English place capable of sustaining itself. In the meantime, settlers mourned the absence of "Malt Beer," concocted fruit liquors, and drank water in its raw state against their best judgment. The first imported vegetable seeds "did not thrive," and those "English fruit and garden herbs" that later did shared space in plantation plots with strange produce never seen in England.[66]

Of all the minor crops grown in seventeenth-century South Carolina, rice stood out as an ingredient that could whiten colonists' bread. One of the first rice plantations along the Ashley River produced and sold the grain for export, but also in small parcels to neighborhood planters for consumption.[67] John Norris's 1712 pamphlet *Profitable Advice for Rich and Poor* took the form of a fictitious dialogue between an English farmer interested in emigrating to Carolina and an experienced planter willing to advise him. "If Wheat . . . is not plentiful," asked the farmer, "how are you supply'd with Bread?" The planter replied, "The Country Planters that hath not *English* Grain mak[e] Bread for their Families with *Indian* Corn and Rice, of which is made very good Bread, not much Inferior to your fine Wheaten Bread, especially Rice Bread, whilst new, eats as pleasant, and is as White to compare with the Finest Wheaten Bread."[68] John Mitchell wrote that the region was so barren that colonists "can only get the necessaries of life . . . by means of Rice, and are daily obliged to run the risque of their lives in clearing the destructive swamps in order to get Rice to supply the place of Wheat." Because he claimed that this substitution "was the occasion of planting Rice in *Carolina*" as part of a broader anticolonial critique, it is difficult to tell whether his remarks summarized a now-lost rice origin story once in broader circulation or merely reflected an animosity toward American planters.[69] Unlike poor English consumers, who combined whatever grains they could find to make bread in times of scarcity, colonists found themselves plentifully supplied with Indian corn. But the cultural dearth of doing without wheat inspired English settlers in plantation America to refine maize with cassava or rice flour to make a "mixt sort of bread."[70]

Colonization changed the ways in which Africans and Europeans turned crops into food. As they adjusted their domestic economies to the environmental conditions of tropical and subtropical America, settlers and slaves engaged in a process of transatlantic adaptation. Placing rice within this context as a minor article of material culture that both groups used to make bread makes no progress toward identifying either as the commodity's originators. Instead, it reveals that the small parcel of rice exported from South Carolina prior to 1674 had meanings as food for the slaves who grew it and for the planters who sold it. In the old world rice had specific roles that determined its proper function. The minority of lowcountry slaves captured from rice-growing regions in West Africa knew the crop as the staple of their diet and the central object of community labor. For colonists from northwestern Europe, imported rice was an obtainable luxury served on rare occasions. By conscripting rice into service as a complement and alternative to maize, new uses eroded established ones. Slaves, most of whom "had never seen a rice plant,"[71]

grew it alongside other strange and well-known cereals in wasteland provisions patches; planters learned to value it as a commonplace flour rather
than as a restorative pottage or a spiced dessert. Rice's utility as food, not
its familiarity, gave it an initially small role in the much larger cultural
transformations brought about by colonization. As "individuals tran-
siently and opportunistically reassign[ed] things to functions other than
their proper ones," they renegotiated roles for objects—whether imported, found, or appropriated—that could be used to sustain life and
support households in plantation America.[72]

Knowledge and Practice

Two decades after the Lords Proprietors put their faith in the economic
leadership of landed elites, a rich period of agricultural experimentation
began bearing fruit. With the support of Governor James Colleton, projector John Stewart conducted crop trials on his patron's Wadboo Barony
for seven years before capturing the attention of those outside his circle
of wealthy officials.[73] In 1690 a rage for cotton planting extended from
Stewart's experimental fields. Sixteen ninety-one was to be a year for silk.
Already, future governor Nathaniel Johnson had planted 24,000 mulberry
trees on his nearby Silk Hope Plantation and dispatched boats to collect
"wild and plantation leav[e]s" along the river to feed his silkworms.
Granted a 500-acre tract as a reward for promoting these "profitable
commodyt[ie]s" and "cares't everwher[e] for [his] success and discovery
in silk," the Scottish agricultural expert turned next to rice.[74]

After his thirteen-page discourse on "managing silk, cotton, [and] rice"
failed to wean the generality of risk-averse planters from "any kind of
produce but that of maze," Stewart took another tack. Because "sensible
demonstration" was "the only mathematicks that the Crude understands,"
he redirected his efforts from the "learned" to those "Judicious and well
meaning planters" who could be swayed by the sight of growing crops.[75]
He mocked those settled along a Cooper River tributary as the Goose
Creek "philosophers" for their clumsy attempts to grow rice as an English
farmer would grain. Although their method of planting it in rows had
been "the generall way of the country last year," the rice came up "so
full of weeds" that few who tried it cared to repeat the experiment.
Stewart vowed to undo the damage this abortive trial did to rice's prospects as a commodity. He tailored cultivation techniques to the Low-

country's environment, selecting twenty-two plots of "differing ground" that ranged from hickory highlands to "Marsh Swamp." At the end of this experimental season, he advocated clearing dry swamps, fitting fields with drains to carry off excess water, and broadcasting a thick layer of seed on the soil. He gloated when his "rectified" mode of rice husbandry yielded, on two separate multiacre plots, "glorious and hopefull" crops.[76]

As he sought to claim the honor of perfecting Carolina rice culture, John Stewart's account revealed that he was not the only one pursuing the new commodity. Before his Wadboo experiments, others had devoted land and labor to rice, some of which had already been shipped to Jamaica, where it was "better esteem'd" than the European variety.[77] What brought rice to planters' attention at this moment is a matter of speculation. If Africans had already grown rice for food, then planters had only to look down from their upland houses to see it growing in lowland provisions grounds. Planters may have already begun eating maize bread whitened with rice flour, perhaps prepared by enslaved African or Indian women employed as cooks. Although slaves may have preceded the Scottish projector in showing that it was possible to raise rice in swamps, Stewart gave the imprimatur of agricultural science to this enterprise. The irrigation methods later used to grow rice on a massive scale circulated in the literature of improvement that Stewart avidly studied. The sight of his rice, "growing a yard high, and like the thickest barly f[ie]ld . . . green as grass," anglicized wasteland farming for settlers who had little previous interest in planting untried crops on undesirable lands.[78]

Whether the model came from Africa, East Asia, Italy, or South Asia (Stewart called it "India's Rice"), planters could draw on a range of English precedents to make swamp rice production a European endeavor. In England rice had piqued the interest of Samuel Hartlib, who asked in 1650, if it "groweth in the Fenny places of Milan . . . why may it not grow in our Fens?"[79] On the eve of Carolina's settlement, improvement-minded promoters foresaw rice fitting the profile of a "new crop" that promised to strengthen England's economy. As an import that drew hard currency from the kingdom, rice might be produced in the warm-weather colonies that expanded the ecological reach of the empire, improving its balance of trade with the Mediterranean. Robinson Crusoe, the quintessential improver abroad, grew rice on "Desolation Island," his fictitious Caribbean home. As a product that could be grown on reclaimed wastelands, rice (which whitened paper and stiffened collars in addition to making puddings) could serve, like rapeseed and linseed, as a raw material for industry.[80] Part of a "vast, distant, experimental annex" of Europe's "fastest-developing economy," Carolina added hundreds of thousands of potentially productive acres to help fuel England's growth and strengthen its commerce with the world.[81] That so much of the Lowcountry seemed to be soggy wasteland made the tactics of improvers all the more relevant. They saw in wetlands repositories of fertile soil that could be made productive by controlling the water that pooled in swamps and ran across meadows. From the late sixteenth century travelers to China and India and, closer to home, Italy described rice as a grain that required rich, well-watered soil. Improvers judged Britain too cold to produce so promising a commodity, but imagined that it would flourish in warmer, "moorish" sites in the Chesapeake Tidewater, the Delaware River valley, and, finally, the Carolina Lowcountry.[82]

Eighteenth-century planters directed slaves to embank the borders of cleared swamp fields. Running water collected behind upper dams, creating reservoirs; at the lower dams, to which water flowed, drains drew off the surplus. These were the same methods that allowed English farmers to create and enrich pastures.[83] From the mid-sixteenth century fenland farmers drained and embanked wetlands to extend grazing ranges, and those exposed to the sea and along the banks of large rivers channeled water and reclaimed land for crops and livestock.[84] When improvers descended on the fens in the seventeenth century, they initiated contentious, large-scale projects, "drayning Fen, Reducing Bog, and Regaining Sea-lands" to make them yield bumper crops of grain and materials for the textiles industry.[85]

Water mills, common sights in early modern England, involved damming, reserving, and conducting water, as did irrigating rice swamps. Settlers and slaves along the Ashley River gained experience with this technology as they worked for wages maintaining dams at the colony's first large-scale sawmill, built in 1701. Planters later drew water from the networks that irrigated their rice to power other mills, putting the stamp of English methods on the plantation landscape.[86] Tide mills in Britain, some of medieval vintage, made use of coastal lands near the sea, capturing the daily overflow of water in reservoirs to work their machinery.[87] By the 1760s advanced models worked "both with the flux and reflux of the tide" and were equipped with a type of floodgate that regulated water flow and "shuts again of its own accord to prevent the tide from over-

flowing the country."[88] No tidal rice planter needed to travel to the metropolis to see such marvels at work; his own plantation made use of the
same techniques.

Europeans in South Carolina possessed sources of agricultural knowledge suited to rice that did not depend on slaves. Methods for reclaiming
wetlands for agriculture were broadly shared among northwestern European farmers by the eleventh century.[89] Colonists unfamiliar with these
practices found directions for watering land in published agricultural
tracts. Resident improvers such as John Stewart put long-standing visions
for rice as a prospective commodity into practice on lowcountry land.
British colonists had no previous experience producing tobacco in Virginia or sugar in Barbados, but this did not stand in the way of building
plantation economies around the Atlantic world's two most lucrative staples.[90] The improvers' creed was antitraditional. It called for growing new

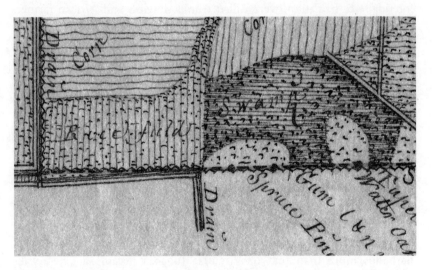

Figure 2.1. Inland swamp rice field. Cleared freshwater swamps were the
principal sites for rice production during the colonial period. Slaves readied a
field for cultivation by building an earthen dam across a swamp formation.
The dam arrested the flow across a landscape gradient that would have
otherwise caused water to drain toward lower-elevation creeks or rivers. As
water backed up behind it, a reservoir formed that could irrigate growing rice
in times of drought. Records of the Court of Common Pleas, Writs of
Partition, box 1777–1792, folder 10A (detail). Courtesy of the South Carolina
Department of Archives and History.

crops on new lands with whatever obscure or foreign methods proved effective. This sanction to innovate suited the improvisational character of American farming throughout colonial British America. Settlers engaged in "persistent experimentation as they learned by doing" and created a "new system of agriculture" that was synthetic rather than purely British, Amerindian, or African in character.[91] It was clear to metropolitan critics that South Carolina's wasteland agriculture, in which the hoe-wielding slave replaced the horse-drawn plow, set the new-world plantation apart from the old-world farm. Slaves used to growing rice in West Africa also found distortions along with similarities in American swamps. The reservoirs that dominated the lowcountry landscape for much of the colonial period were novelties to farmers who had relied on rain and tides to water crops. African and English precedents converged in generic solutions to common problems. The buried, wooden channels that regulated the flow of water between rivers and fields, a technology essential for tidal rice irrigation, were called trunks. English and African farmers alike had long hollowed out logs to channel water, but only Europeans had previously made use of the hanging floodgates that came into general use in South Carolina.[92] Plans "for draining fens" and constructing "sewers & bankes against inundation" were in place from the colony's first year, and the first settlers used ditches to draw water off their fields "according to the English manner."[93]

Planters did not need African knowledge to initiate commercial rice planting in South Carolina. Integrating the crop within this dynamic model for British husbandry was the key innovation that made it South Carolina's "staple Commodity, as Sugar is to Barbadoes and Jamaica, or Tobacco to Virginia and Maryland."[94] They did so, however, with an established labor force of experienced African American farmers. In this respect, South Carolina's path to its staple commodity resembled that of Barbados more than that of Virginia. Tobacco became a Chesapeake staple produced largely by European indentured servants. The region's rising slave imports in the late seventeenth century incorporated African workers into an agricultural system in place for more than half a century. In Barbados, by contrast, twice as many slaves as servants labored on diversified plantations just before midcentury, years before sugar became the dominant export. Only after a period of experimentation did West Indian planters realize the advantages of imposing "gang labor with its lock-step discipline and liberal use of the whip to force slaves to work as hard as possible," a labor innovation that made sugar the island's signature commodity.[95]

South Carolina's early economy featured a similar time lag between the creation of an Africanized labor force and the intensification of commodity production. South Carolina was a slave society from its inception in 1670 and a black-majority province by 1710, but rice became its unquestioned staple only after the surging exports of the mid-1720s. During a period of trial and error with rice, roughly 1690–1720, the colony experienced a boom in exports led by naval stores (tar, pitch, turpentine, and ship lumber) and provisions. During this prelude to the rice economy, South Carolina planters, like their Caribbean counterparts before them, worked slaves harder to make them produce more goods for sale abroad. Before colonists focused intensively on rice production, the process of gearing plantations to serve European markets was likewise already under way. They learned different lessons about how to organize labor and land, however.

The material demands of rice as a staple commodity encouraged planters to select freshwater swamps as sites for cultivation and divide work into individualized tasks. These diverging practices set rice plantations apart from the model of the Barbados sugar estate. Although African rice farmers were not the indispensable agents behind the implantation of rice culture in South Carolina, planters never grew rice without slaves. Practically all enslaved men and women grew their own food and worked at a versatile range of farming jobs on these early, diversified settlements. The general skills they adapted and acquired to perform their daily labor were probably more important in assuring rice's establishment as a viable commodity than was the specific knowledge possessed by a few experienced rice growers.

Europeans and Africans brought different sorts of agricultural knowledge to South Carolina and had different capacities to put this knowledge into practice around 1690. A few slaves knew how to grow rice, but they lacked the power to direct plantation resources toward its cultivation beyond their own provisions grounds. Planters commanded land and labor, but they had never planted rice before. They were drawn to the promise of rice, however, and cobbled together the means to make it grow. They knew it as one of several new commodities promoted by the Proprietary government, were familiar with irrigation practices that could turn swamps into fields, and had access to a resident corps of improvers and improvement-minded elites who showed them how to adapt British techniques to the culture of this foreign crop. To disregard Stewart's experiments because he had never "planted a crop that was not even grown in the country of his birth," Scotland, underestimates the impact of applying the methods of "improved" British agriculture in America. Despite his "small actuall experience in the world," he claimed a "universall Knowledge by reading and converse in all Kind of Human learning" that he put into practice.[96] As John Stewart considered how much seed to sow, weighed the merits of planting even rows or by broadcast, and plowed under a first growth to strengthen the soil, he displayed the modus operandi of a committed improver.

In Stewart's view, African influences on the development of Carolina's economy were limited to mere "toyl of the body."[97] But enslaved workers filled in the details within the outlines of the agricultural systems that he imposed. Wadboo Barony slaves sowed the seeds and tended the plants that flourished so well under Stewart's direction. The talents that made his "dry swamps" yield good crops might have been too subtle for the improver to recognize, especially one who never lost an opportunity to boast of his own comprehensive knowledge of farming practices from around the world. In their search for alternatives to Indian corn, slaves cultivated their own food crops on hilly, sandy, rocky, and watery lands throughout plantation America.[98] When Stewart charged planters to clear well-drained swamps for rice, their own slaves reinforced this contrarian advice by demonstrating how well the grain could grow in these so-called wastes. South Carolina slaves sowed rice in a distinctively African way, pressing a hole into the soil with the heel and then covering the seed with dirt brushed across it with the foot.[99] There are many ways to plant a seed, and this one was not indispensable. Few British servants, however, could have demonstrated such an assured feel for planting cleared wetlands. Whether born in Upper Guinea, Barbados, or Carolina, slaves who grew their own food learned to read the landscape with a "visual acuity" that could well have proved useful in identifying viable sites for production, once planters learned to see swamps as central, rather than marginal, to plantation production.[100]

Indirect recognition of African capabilities came decades after the rice trials of 1690. From 1760 slave factors occasionally announced the sale of captives from the "Rice Coast."[101] To planters who almost came to blows at Charlestown markets in search of scarce slaves, regional origins meant less than age, gender, health, stature, and, above all, price in determining a willingness to buy. Merchants nevertheless hoped that planters might pay a premium for slaves they sometimes advertised as "accustomed to the planting of rice."[102] In marketing African captives in this way, slave dealers urged planters to see those imported from the "Rice Coast" as workers prepared to enter immediately into field labor. Those "from the Windward Coast where they cultivate rice," reasoned one prospective planter in 1764, "may be soon trained to plantation business." New African slaves served typically as field hands, entering labor hierarchies at their lowest rungs. After midcentury planters placed little stock in the knowledge of such "weak, raw, New Negroes" that they imported in rising numbers, even though many more came from rice-growing regions than had around the turn of the century. Instead, they valued the demonstrated competence of those "strong seasoned handy Slaves" who were born in South Carolina or had risen through the ranks to become skilled workers.[103] Planters who lived in Charlestown for much of the year relied especially on their drivers, experienced men who supervised day-to-day field labor and, in the absence of overseers and planters, effectively managed plantations themselves. One driver attended his master in town to receive specific directions about which swamps to clear, how to extend irrigation to new fields, and how to set daily labor tasks. He returned to the plantation to impose these orders on field workers.[104] Almost a century after Stewart's experiments, but near the very spot where they took place, Henry Laurens spoke with some of his slaves at Mepkin Plantation, making "Enquiries of the Negroes ... respecting the Value" of a nearby tract he wished to purchase. To settle a family land dispute, another planter relied on experienced slaves to identify "the best pie[ce]s of High land on the Whole Tract" and remember how it had been planted in the past. These planters valued the judgments of slaves who had cultivated the land for years and who spoke English they could understand well.[105]

Planters saw South Carolina's landscape with new eyes in the eighteenth century. A surveyor sent to the Georgia frontier in 1767 to select land for a new rice plantation was instructed to return to Charlestown with an "account of its several qualities." He was to detail "how much Savanna & cleared Plantable Land in all, what quantity of unclear'd Tupelo or other Swamp, if any part of it is subject to be overflowed by Saltish Water, what capacity for dams & reserves, & what quantity of Oak & Hickory & Pine Land & of what use such high Land may be to the Plantation."[106]

Planters with such knowledge of water and terrain no longer needed the guidance of agricultural experts or the example of enslaved cultivators to value land or direct rice cultivation on it.

The influx of larger numbers of African rice farmers into lowcountry slavery in the later eighteenth century was not the only pool of potentially valuable agricultural knowledge that planters neglected to acknowledge. When British forces deported Acadia's French inhabitants in 1755, South Carolina reluctantly accepted its allotment of more than 1,000 uprooted people. The provincial Assembly dispersed most of these deportees into the countryside and urged local parishes to indenture them to defray the costs of their maintenance. Not only were they "well acquainted with agriculture," but many also had extensive experience constructing dykes and embankments. At a time when planters were developing river tide-lands for rice, they were presented with an opportunity to purchase the labor of expert wetland farmers who knew how to desalinate fields and irrigate crops on tidal floodplains. Acadians who migrated to Louisiana soon used these skills to grow "rice in small ponds" and along riverbanks for food. There is no record that British colonists did anything but shun the Acadians as a dangerous internal enemy and condemn them as a "bigoted" people, incapable of assimilation into South Carolina's plantation society. Those who survived this second displacement made their way back to Charlestown, where some managed to escape from the province and others became impoverished wards of St. Philip Parish. Only 210 remained alive in the colony by 1760.[107]

The first rice planters opened their economic culture to new and foreign methods for turning lowcountry land to account. Their successors kept their own council, priding themselves on being agricultural experts in their own right. They occasionally gathered information about advanced European technologies to enhance rice productivity, but they did not seek out the expertise of people they subjugated. Once they learned how to remake land and control water, planters were far from ignorant pupils who depended on slaves as knowledgeable "tutors" to grow rice.[108] By the second decade of the eighteenth century, colonists had mastered the techniques of rice irrigation and cultivation and integrated these skills into a British agricultural framework. This act of synthesis whitewashed the thought of African or African American influences from colonists' collective memory.

Work and Households

In the three decades before 1700, Carolina planters had secured a lack-luster position in the Atlantic economy. The first settlers sold cattle on the hoof and packed meat in barrels bound for the West Indies. Their small contingents of servants and slaves sawed planks and made shingles by the thousands for Caribbean planters who had cleared their own forests for vast sugar estates. A few aggressive settlers monopolized the trade in Indian deerskins, the colony's only significant export to Europe. Carolina's promoters had promised settlers a secure place for commercial agriculture, assured by the fertility of the Lowcountry's lands and the temperance of its climate. Rather than generating exotic produce, seventeenth-century planters carved out farmsteads and cattle ranges within a landscape that seemed alternately rank and barren, a resource that constrained their fortunes even as they accumulated capital through farm building.

After a visit to the Lowcountry in the late 1690s, customs collector Edward Randolph reported that South Carolina had crossed an economic threshold from a vulnerable American outpost into a true plantation colony. With rice as a reliable commodity, it was now capable of contributing to England's commerce and increasing the "revenue of the Crown." A little more than a barrel went to Jamaica in 1695. By the 1699–1700 shipping season rice was a full-fledged transatlantic export, with "above 300 Tuns shipped this year to England," 30 tons more "to the Islands," and more produced than there were "Ships to Transport" it.[109] The "trade of cotton-wool, indigo, ginger, etc. not answering their expectations," planters left aside those once-desired productions, each of which had seemed poised to play the role of staple commodity. Instead, the "inhabitants are now upon making of pitch, tar and turpentine, and planting of rice." After a decade of difficulties, Randolph suggested that recent breakthroughs by which they "found out the true way of raising and husking Rice" had paved the way for this promising turn toward transatlantic commerce.

South Carolina's Assembly encouraged the invention of a rice-processing machine in 1691 and again in 1698, revealing that the problem of "husking" rice (removing the grain's outer hull) and "polishing" it (scouring out its inner cuticle of germ and bran) persisted. There was an effective, widely known way to prepare rice for market. It required neither a government patent nor an engineered design, only a log hollowed into a mortar, a large pestle carved out of pine, and hours of rigorous manual labor. As every African woman who had grown up pounding rice by hand knew, the work demanded tremendous exertion, as well as a practiced touch to clean the grains without breaking or "burning" them. Mortar-and-pestle rice processing was an African technology. So was separating the chaff from the grain by tossing hulled rice in the air in coiled grass baskets. Had slaves not introduced these methods by 1699, colonists might have stepped up their search for workable animal- and water-powered mills, machines that came into general use in the 1750s. Every grain exported in 1699, however, was milled in the African fashion. Hundreds of field hands, comprising a significant proportion of the total black population, pounded this rice by hand, a few pecks at a time, to produce the 330 tons (739,200 pounds) Randolph reported. As exports rose sharply during the first three decades of the new century, planters forced thousands more into the labor of clearing land, cultivating it, and pounding the rice they grew.[110]

More effective irrigation systems deployed over the course of the eighteenth century increased the quantity of rice each slave could grow in a season. Such productivity gains turned manual processing into a brutal productive bottleneck.[111] Hand mills eased the labor of hulling by the late 1720s, but the "very laborious and tedious" work of using mortar and pestle to remove the "inner film which clouds the brightness of the grain" continued. This "excessive hard Labour," planters believed, "killed a large Number of Negroes" each year.[112] Exhausted by "beating much Rice by hand," slaves evaded the heaps of grain that awaited the mortar after every harvest by "lying up," or pretending to be sick. After James Gray "work'd his Negroes late in his Barn at Night" and then the "next Morning before Day, hurried them out again," he found the building "burnt down to the Ground" along with all the rice within it. Pushed to the limits of their endurance, slaves took advantage of the anonymity of fire to bring this grueling labor to an immediate end.[113]

Those African Americans who had lived in the colony before planters found their staple witnessed their frontier society become a plantation society. Instead of living with their masters as members of a small "interracial family unit" that included Indian slaves and European servants, most blacks in rice-growing districts after 1720 found themselves within larger communities, their numbers swelled by recently imported Africans. In St. George Parish, whose surviving tax return for 1726 provides the colony's earliest demographic profile, over two-thirds lived on plantations with more than twenty white and black inhabitants. Thirty-eight percent of the parish's black population lived on seven plantations, each with fifty or more slaves, the largest with ninety-four. Instead of working alongside their masters in fields and forests and undertaking a versatile range of tasks on their own, most labored in the swamps.[114] Gone was the rough equality of material conditions shared by settlers and slaves in the seventeenth century. More than any specific technical advance in its production, the first transatlantic shipment that Randolph reported in 1699 rested on the social innovation of recasting the rules for labor.

Planters wrenched slaves into this new world of work with violence. Backed by the coercive power of the state and sanctioned by a version of the Barbados slave code, every master enjoyed the liberty to brutalize enslaved dependents within his household. In an era before planters learned to weigh their words about the punishments they inflicted, a recent immigrant stated plainly in 1711 that those who could "get a few slaves and can beat them well to make them work hard" stood to prosper in the colony.[115] That planters possessed the willingness, as well as the freedom, to impose this repressive racial order explains how slaves were forced to make so much rice. Sheer force does not, however, account for the universal labor system that took shape on plantations by the mid-eighteenth century. In contrast to the gang labor common throughout the rest of plantation America, lowcountry slaves worked by the individual task. Slaves completed a daily labor assignment, such as hoeing weeds out of a quarter-acre portion of rice field, at a pace set by the worker. A driver, overseer, or planter beat those who failed to complete their tasks. Those who finished their tasks before the day was through reclaimed a few daylight hours to use as they wished. Many grew crops, tended livestock, and made crafts for sale after their work in the fields was done, entering into the market economy as small-scale producers. Rice was suited to the task system. Unlike tobacco and sugar, cultivating it did not demand direct supervision to control quality and coordinate interdependent tasks. By letting slaves work on their own and holding them to account at the end of the day, planters spared themselves the trouble and the danger of lingering too long near malarial swamps. The system offered incentives for slaves to complete field work that mitigated the constant, destabilizing use of the whip. Once the task system was put in place, considerations of disease, motivation, and management entrenched it as a distinguishing feature of South Carolina slavery that no other slave society in the Americas followed as a standard way of organizing work.[116]

Why and how the task system came to be the universal mode by which "negroes [were] put to labor" in the Lowcountry remained as obscure to planters as their staple crop's origins.[117] They knew only that it was a custom so well established by past practice that any attempt to marshal slaves into gangs would provoke resistance.[118] Judith A. Carney has suggested that slaves received the benefits of the task system in return for teaching planters how to cultivate rice. This quid pro quo exchange would have been unlikely for three reasons. First, this knowledge was neither exclusive nor proprietary. Once slaves demonstrated rice techniques, whether remembered from West Africa or developed to grow their own provisions, they lost the ability to restrain their dissemination or use them as "leverage to negotiate and alter some of the terms of their bondage."[119] Planters could appropriate what they saw Africans do and integrate their methods within applicable European farming strategies without the need to offer compensation. Second, specific African knowledge was limited rather than general within a seventeenth-century population dominated by slaves from non-rice-growing regions, born in the colony, or imported from the Caribbean. Later planters rewarded slaves with special skills individually, giving artisans food, alcohol, clothing, cash, and the ability to work and travel without supervision. It is possible that a small contingent of experienced rice farmers who worked with planters to select land and direct cultivation became the Lowcountry's first drivers. That all slaves should gain the task system in exchange for agricultural skills that the vast majority did not possess seems implausible. Third, there was no explicit and collective bargaining process over the terms of labor in colonial South Carolina. Slaves could not agree with one another as a group to withhold rice knowledge any more than they could represent to planters that they intended to do so unless their demands were met. Negotiations over labor took place in one-on-one encounters within individual plantations and across the inequalities of a legal and social system in which slaves had no standing as people and masters made frequent use of their monopoly on coercive authority.

Why, then, did planters, some of whom had profited from working slaves to death in Barbados, tolerate the task system's limits on rice labor?[120] Unlike the Chesapeake and Caribbean colonies, South Carolina "became a slave society before it developed a plantation regime."[121] West Indian slaves were among the colony's first inhabitants. To answer the subsistence challenges of living on new seventeenth-century settlements, slaves took (and were granted) time and space to provide for themselves. They enjoyed thereafter a "share of Liberty to keep themselves, their Houses, and their Plantations sweet, and clean." This sphere of autonomy surrounding their domestic economy had taken on the status of a "sovereign Rul[e]" by the early 1680s.[122] For thirty years they labored on new settlements that were called plantations but functioned like small farms, more focused on securing subsistence than making commodities. Seventeenth-century colonists strove above all to "clear a little ground to get Bread for their Familyes," and for another two decades or so after the first transatlantic rice shipment of 1699, their successors devoted labor and land in roughly equal proportions to growing food and making goods for sale. Except for tar and lumber, everything early plantations produced served "as well for the kitchen as the market."[123] As slaves spent more time growing rice, the division between producing food and making commodities became more sharply defined. As these onetime farms abandoned a "safety-first" strategy of securing provisions and devoting surpluses to the market, the intensifying demands of plantation labor pushed the slaves' search for food to the margins of the agricultural calendar, into weekends and after dark. Independent production, a distinctive "freedom" within slavery protected by custom, became under these conditions a form of enforced privation.

Planters exploited this custom to save themselves the costs of feeding and clothing their dependents. They forced slaves ("from whose wounds they extract their estates," a sympathetic minister observed) into the swamps for more days every year and longer hours every day.[124] Always short on cash and long on debt, planters linked their futures to the new staple as a way to speed the pace of capital accumulation. Improving land and breeding livestock were farm-building activities that increased the value of lowcountry estates by gradual degrees before 1720. The dramatic rise in the average worth of inventoried estates in the decades that followed depended on selling rice and reinvesting the proceeds in new African slaves. As their peers died around them in early Carolina's "funereal lowlands," survivors saw how narrow was their window of opportunity for building family fortunes. Keenly motivated to cut costs and increase revenue in the here and now, planters left slaves to their own devices to secure life's necessities.[125] Before work by the task took shape as a universal system sometime after 1720, planters "free[d] themselves from the trouble of feeding and clothing their slaves" by no set rule other than to cut the time slaves were allowed to feed and clothe themselves to the barest minimum. Striving settlers imposed a regimen of "imoderate labour" so severe that some slaves ran away for "want of Victualls and rest," risking the tortures masters inflicted on disobedient slaves (among them branding, castration, and ear cropping) rather than be worked to death on the plantations.[126] Many planters allowed them "one day in the week to clear ground, and plant for themselves as much as will clothe and subsist them and their families." "In order to do this, some Masters give their slaves Saturday, some half that day, and others Sunday only," a fragment of the week in which to grow enough to eat, as well as a surplus to sell in exchange for a few "old rags" that served for clothes. "Autonomy" on such terms, even as it allowed for the retention of African foodways and enabled slaves to become active buyers and sellers, must have seemed more a curse than a blessing.[127] Slaves suffered as planters mobilized land and labor away from subsistence and toward the market, yet the principle of compensating slaves for work that took them away from growing their own food and for any surpluses they chose to sell was left in place. Slaves listed in Newington Plantation's account book in the period 1699–1707 were paid for their rice, cotton, turnips, potatoes, and other goods. When dispatched from field to forest to make tar, they received cash payments and food and rum rations as long as they labored at the kiln.[128]

Horrified that slaves were "Sufferd, some forced—to work upon Sundays, having no other means to subsist," Anglican missionaries urged their parishioners to reserve the "Lord's Day" for slaves' religious instruction. Only when "Slaves shall be fed and provided for by the Masters," one argued, would the "whole time of the Slaves . . . be their Masters." A few "truely Religious Masters" followed this advice out of concern for their slaves', and perhaps their own, souls.[129] The rest began providing rations for the more worldly reason of imposing order on plantations in the throes of destabilizing change. A rash of poisonings, runaways, barn burnings, and suspected conspiracies followed the rice shipment of 1699. Such disorders, culminating in the 1739 uprising at Stono River, were triggered by the rising burdens of field work and the violence used to compel slaves to perform it. We might also see in this surge of resistance a reaction to the strains placed on slave households by the shift toward commodity production. As many an enslaved man struggled to secure "food and raiment and the support of his family" on the weekend, he watched rice's escalating demands enforce a new standard of poverty on its material well-being, threatening "all that is dear to him in this world."[130]

Rations stabilized plantation households after a period of flux in which the question of how slaves would eat was open to variation from plantation to plantation and contention between masters and slaves. In 1721 a missionary monitoring this change for its effects on Sabbath labor observed that slaves "formerly . . . had Considerable quantity of provision of their own produce, whereas now for some years past they have had nothing but what has been given them by their owners." To his disappointment, most slaves freed from the desperate weekend pursuit of food failed to seek Christian instruction and instead redoubled their Sunday labors on their own plots.[131] Rationed sweet potatoes provided a "great Support to the Negroes" by the mid-1720s. Every master now planted a "Patch, or inclosed field, in proportion to the number of his slaves." Setting tasks in provisions fields and distributing harvests of maize and sweet potatoes eased the pressure that rice labor put on producing food. Tasked labor emerged at roughly the same time (c. 1720–1740) as rations as a standard plantation practice. The new labor system added weekday afternoons to the time allotted slaves to produce food crops, provided they could complete their daily tasks. In place of the uncertainty that came with rice's widening demands on slaves' time, tasking inscribed on the land, with a contractual clarity, the quantity of plantation work for which each field hand was responsible. Overseers and drivers measured off field tasks with a pole or chain, marking the boundaries of 105-foot-square plots that made the basic quarter-acre unit of work visible to all.[132] These new rules for rations and labor reduced the anxiety that slaves faced as they attempted to get enough to eat by increasing both the supply of food and the time available to grow it. It placed the South Carolina Lowcountry between the "allowance" colonies of Virginia and Barbados, where slaves subsisted almost entirely on rations, and the protopeasant society of Jamaica, where slaves grew and sold much of what everyone on the island, black and white, ate.[133]

The rice regime disentangled blacks from once-unified, multiethnic households and resettled them away from white residences, near the fields or around the pounding barns.[134] Clustered together in cramped huts across the plantation countryside, slaves "labour[ed] together and converse[d] almost wholly among themselves" as if they comprised a "Nation within a Nation."[135] The African-influenced forms of ceramics, dwellings, and yards in early slave quarters reveal that slaves organized domestic spaces and activities around their own preferences.[136] Slaves working by the task established "little plantations" on "as much land as they can handle." Those who were "skillful and industrious . . . plant something for themselves after the day's work," buying "trifles," as well as "necessary things," with the proceeds.[137] By the 1770s slaves worked in "their own private fields, consisting of 5 or 6 acres of ground, allowed them by their masters, for planting rice, corn, potatoes, tobacco, &c. for their own use and profit." The original, functional rationale for independent food production—that it was necessary for survival—no longer applied. "They do not plant in their fields for subsistence, but for amusement, pleasure, and profit, their masters giving them clothes, and sufficient provisions from their granaries."[138] But after producing their own food for more than half a century, the custom of independent provisioning endured as the material foundation for a distinctive and autonomous African American culture.[139]

As food producers and marketers, slaves "tasted freedom," anticipating lives beyond slavery that their command over productive property foreshadowed.[140] By exploiting the regard for custom that was woven into planters' conceptions of legitimate authority, they also found ways to shape their dependency within it. Once established, independent slave work became one of many "Custom[s] of the Country" that British settlers respected as legitimate ways of doing things that were "Calculated According to the Local Circumstances of the Place" rather than imposed by law.[141] Despite differences in household governance in Europe and Africa, societies throughout the Atlantic world honored the "legal and political *space* for custom."[142] Dependent laborers in both western Europe and West and Central Africa could make claims for the means to subsist on those who commanded them, either by receiving food or the time to procure it themselves. Tenants, slaves, and others forced to labor for social superiors who demanded rent or tax often did so by performing a set quantity of work to fulfill such obligations.[143] Custom, that "powerful protector of the weak against the strong," enforced limits on repression that even the most severe "tyranny is forced in some degree to respect," reasoned John Stuart Mill. Even the South Carolina master, with the rule of law utterly at his disposal, declined to "strain that law to the utmost, and every relaxation of it has a tendency to become a custom, and every custom to become a right."[144]

Especially when masters and slaves encountered one another for the first time across the uncleared wastelands of a just-settled plantation, the rules by which they would interact were open to innovation. Whatever expectations they brought to Carolina about dependency, authority, and how workers should get enough to eat lacked the force of custom in the new world. Tasks combined with rations stanched the erosion of time devoted to food production on new rice plantations. This solution reflected the needs, desires, and influence of both planters and slaves, and in this sense it was a negotiated settlement after more than two decades of contentious expansion following the exports of 1699. The new balance between the domestic and commercial sides of plantation work did not, however, emerge through a process of mutual agreement that the term "negotiation" implies. As in Jamaica, where slaves claimed broad rights to time and land to cultivate crops, rice planters and field slaves inherited the task system but no longer remembered the original reasoning and intentions behind the custom.[145] Jamaica's extensive slave-controlled farms gave their cultivators control over food and at the same time saved planters the "expense of feeding" them. This "happy coalition of interests between the master and the slave" privileged practices that answered distinct objectives across slavery's racial divide. South Carolina masters were not required to recognize African ingenuity, sympathize with their slaves' fears, or capitulate to demands that the boldest among them risked to see the merits of the task system. For their part, slaves were not required to see their stakes in their "little plantations" as a form of accommodation to slavery that bound them to obedience or enforced the gratitude of dependents toward generous patriarchs. Agreeing to a common order for work and food rewarded both. The independent slave provisions ground was a site at which divergent, even antagonistic, goals intersected.[146]

The story of rice's rise cannot be separated from the cross-cultural search for food on Britain's subtropical colonial frontier. As a stray shipment to the Caribbean in 1674, an improver's commodity project in 1690, and an initial transatlantic export in 1699, rice straddled the domestic and commercial sides of early plantations. These three windows into the cultural and material contexts out of which South Carolina's staple commodity emerged give little support for attributing rice exclusively to either the pioneering heroes of the planters' myth or the ingenious enslaved farmers favored by revisionist historians. Wherever rice grew, members of both groups staked out interests in its production and consumption that brought together desires to eat and sell it, methods to cultivate and process it, and experience doing so in lowcountry swamps—all critical factors to the crop's future as a staple commodity. Understanding rice as a collaborative project of European planters and African slaves risks celebrating it as a multicultural accomplishment, as if each should be awarded a share of credit in an inclusive story of American development. This conclusion conceals the experiences of privation, brutality, and wrenching cultural and economic change that any account of origins should place at the center of analysis. An old-world crop implanted in the new, rice took on new functions for the settlers, black and white, who implanted its culture. Its earliest cultivators saw it as a starchy substitute, an exotic delicacy, an experimental export, and a means of survival, among other things. By the mid-eighteenth century one meaning—as a commodity that dominated plantation work and fueled the Lowcountry's expansion—loomed above all others.

After 1699, when ships departing Charlestown began carrying thousands of barrels of rice every year for sale abroad, South Carolina's early food culture changed for both Africans and Europeans. Spurred to use rice for food in Carolina because of a shared aversion to maize, eighteenth-century masters and slaves learned to accept Indian corn into their diets. In the 1720s it was eaten "not only by the Negro slaves, but by the generality of the white people." Of all the ways to prepare corn, colonists and slaves learned to relish hominy, sometimes thickened and fortified with West Indian bonavist beans to make it a heartier starch. The *sativa* rice that slaves grew for themselves after completing their daily tasks was too valuable as an article of trade to consign to the cooking pot. When eighteenth-century slaves ate rice, it commonly took the form of broken grains, the unsalable by-product of the processing they performed after every harvest.[147]

By the close of the colonial period whites enjoyed desserts such as rice and sweet-potato puddings and fruit topped with roasted peanuts, dishes that brought West Indian and African ingredients into Anglo-American cuisine. Instead of taking bread with their morning coffee or tea, Charlestown elites ate thin rice cakes that tasted vaguely of almonds.[148] "All the poor, and many of the Rich, eat Rice for Bread, and give it even a preference," despite the fact that backcountry farmers produced enough grain to supply every table in town with wheaten loaves.[149] A century after rice growing began in Carolina, planters had embraced rice and other distinctive foods as their own for so long that they seemed exotic only to visitors. During a 1772 stay among the lowcountry elite, Philadelphia merchant William Dillwyn "dined on Turtle," "drank punch," and smoked tobacco mixed with sumac in the Native American fashion after eating this remarkable meal.[150]

Growing rice demanded that English immigrants alter their initial expectations for land, labor, and agriculture. The crop forced planters to revise one of their core cultural inheritances, a sense of the land's value, as its cultivation elevated wetlands from disrepute to esteem. A crop produced on wastelands, rice offered planters and slaves alike a way to eat well. Tracing the progress of rice from provisions patches to plantation fields, from the domestic to the commercial economy, helps us see early Carolina as a place of intercultural adaptation. That English planters came to grow "black" rice to make white bread is a painful irony. Those who later proved to be closed to the merits of non-European cultures opened their sensibilities to value and then appropriate a foreign crop. Rice became visible to settlers because it flourished at a place of cultural intersection, where it meant important but very different things to white and black producers and consumers. South Carolina's plantation society was built in accretive steps without overarching design, following a course beset by contingency rather than inscribed by destiny. The origin of rice culture was not a single event, but rather a process. Multiple introductions of techniques, seeds, and, above all, interest in the crop culminated in making rice grow in seventeenth-century South Carolina. In fits and starts this transplanted culture diffused from a few sites of experiment and innovation to become a powerful model for orienting the plantation economy more intensively toward the transatlantic economy. Only in retrospect was rice a staple-in-waiting that required agricultural heroes, black or white, to realize its commercial potential. As Africans and Europeans pursued material comfort in the most basic and intimate ways through food, they set in place customs for labor, land use, and material exchange that shaped this society's later development. Satisfying small desires during the colony's formative years set precedents that reverberated with unanticipated force as African and European cultural aspirations converged on rice in early South Carolina.

— 3 —

Transforming the Plantation Landscape

A vision of the plantation as a self-contained world detached from connections beyond its borders has become an emblem of the American South. This myth of autarky floated above the realities of a plantation landscape better characterized by flux than stasis. Toward the close of the eighteenth century prominent planters tied their identities to their best-developed country seats. Linking themselves to the land in this way put forward messages of occupation across the generations from which a measure of social legitimacy as masters of slaves derived. To distinguish themselves from one another, each of three cousins named Elias Ball took the name of his home plantation (Wambaw, Commingtee, and Limerick) as a kind of second surname. These showplace estates celebrated the family's rootedness, but were in fact fairly recent acquisitions, put together in a series of eighteenth-century transactions by the several Elias Balls, their fathers, and their grandfathers.[1]

Turbulent land histories lay just beneath the surface of these claims to lineage, stature, and achievement. In response to South Carolina's volatile environments, colonists changed how they bought and sold land as they configured and reconfigured plantations. They ascended a steep learning curve of environmental adaptation that came with relatively recent occupation of the colony. This process of engagement with nature, slaves, and long-distance exchange revealed itself in a series of dramatic changes in how they understood the land's value as a resource for commercial agriculture. The complex patchwork of property lines that parceled out the coastal plain into individual landholdings shifted over time as planters who first avoided wetlands as wastes learned to prize them as the very heart of a well-improved rice plantation. Within these boundaries planters

92

marshaled their slaves to reengineer the landscape for a form of rice agriculture that could withstand dangerous environmental extremes. In huge landholdings that marked off hundreds and even thousands of acres for development, colonists worked to cobble together "complete" plantations that took more comprehensive advantage of the region's varied types of land and began stringing these plantations together into multiple-plantation enterprises that spanned the extent of the settled Lowcountry. The plantation landscape was formed through a process of colonization that put people in motion across the land.

[handwritten margin note: built multiple-plantation enterprises]

Memorials of Landscape Change

Although they misremembered the story of rice's origins, planters knew the histories of their lands. Those who wanted to secure their ownership of real property were required by law to place themselves in connection to its past. The Quit Rent Act of 1731 was designed to rationalize a land system thrown into disarray by the contentious, drawn-out transfer of Carolina from the Proprietors to the Crown during the 1720s. It asked colonists to link the land they claimed to an initial grant by which it had first passed from the state to an individual. This single, legitimating moment in the past served as a progenitor of every valid title with the credibility to sweep aside competing claims. Seeking to establish a legal chain of connection to the land across decades ravaged by lost records and through the many transactions by which it had changed hands over the years, planters gathered what moldering paperwork they could. Few could walk into the auditor general's office in Charlestown clutching every one of the documents that authenticated their ownership. Using these papers as mnemonic devices, planters told the stories of how the lands they occupied had entered legitimately into their possession. These legal accounts of the land's history, called memorials, replaced the chaos of South Carolina's land system with a uniform new series of documents.[2]

The memorials provision of the Quit Rent Act was an attempt by royal officials to establish authority over the colony as a whole. It also gave planters an opportunity to shore up claims to their discrete pieces of it. During the 1730s landowners were compelled to remember this landscape as a volatile stage for enterprise in which they played only the most recent leading roles. In reconstructing the often-complicated narratives of their lands' ownership history, they generated a unique record of landscape change as a plantation society took root in the colonial Lowcountry. The memorials registered 1,415 tracts encompassing 617,770 acres.[3] As they filed their memorials, 488 individuals recalled the disruptive process of colonization that stood behind their own occupation of the land. Their records noted fires that destroyed caches of legal papers along with the dwellings that housed them. Whether planters understood these disasters to be acts of God or acts of subversion by overworked slaves was left unclear. Stories of lands taken up in anticipation of future production, long since lost to financial insolvency, reminded their current owners of how perilous planting could be.

Titleholders "perished in the Indian War of 1715" along with their documents. Landmarks shifted over time, leaving once-meaningful geographic names as archaic notations on deeds and plats, as these rough official sketches that recorded a property's boundary lines were called. A later eighteenth-century colonist navigating by terms such as Cubbus Swamp, John Wommily Creek, and the "path to Peters Cowpens" would soon be lost in the Lowcountry.[4] The memorials also created an archive of a displaced landscape that had been shared in the seventeenth century by settlers and Indians. One tract was once intersected by three paths that had linked Native American towns, long since deserted, to English Charlestown. Others located a lost Anglo-Indian frontier. Seventeenth-century property lines once adjoined an "Indian Settlement Marsh" and the "Lands of the Cussoe Indians," a coastal Cusabo people attacked by the English in 1671. What the colonists called Foster's Creek was once "called by Indians Asseeboos Creek." The place "known formerly by the Indian name of Pathehon Plantation" when it was granted in 1694 was known by some other name, if it was named at all, when William Brandford filed his memorial for 150 acres along the Ashley River in 1732.[5] As English settlers displaced Indian inhabitants, they imposed an English geography of occupation. The experience of establishing a chain of title into the distant past evoked memories of conflict and contingency on a contested middle ground.

The memorials reveal the process by which the second and third rice-planting generations assembled landed estates. These records expose the founding vision of an ordered social landscape in tatters by the booming 1730s. The Proprietors had attempted to control settlement by linking the size of a headright grant to the number of dependents (free, slave, and indentured) capable of cultivating it. Few planters found their desires for land confined by the social objectives of South Carolina's first rulers or tied in large measure to what their parents left them in their wills. Colonists who filed memorials in the 1730s purchased more land than they inherited, putting up their own cash and drawing on increasingly available lines of credit as the most common way to acquire real property.[6] The Proprietors awarded large-scale patents (five or six 48,000-acre "seigniories" and a dozen 12,000-acre "baronies" were actually surveyed) to establish a hereditary aristocracy in Carolina. Instead of founding enduring estates, recently minted caciques and landgraves sold their property to London firms and carved off portions for sale, restrained only by the desire to let their vast, undeveloped holdings gain in value until new waves of settlers were ready to buy them up piecemeal.[7] The Colleton family's Wadboo Barony, the site of John Stewart's rice experiments, was the only such patent registered intact in the memorials, as well as the only one retained through the colonial period by a single family.[8] The tracts of land planters claimed reflected their own resources and aspirations more than they depended on the bequests of the previous generation.

As much as the experience of filing a memorial brought the past into view, it also revealed the plantation landscape as a work-in-progress geared toward the future. Lowcountry colonists took part in an active land market that circulated real property. Tracts of land changed hands frequently during South Carolina's first half century. A small minority of tracts, just over one-tenth, were subject to a single transaction: the grant that conveyed them to an initial owner. About three out of every four tracts had changed hands at least once or twice more, and a sizable minority were subject to complex alterations that involved four or more exchanges.[9] There were some colonists who settled on their grants, built plantations, and willed land to children who would have been in a position to clear more land, buy more slaves, and grow crops on a paternal estate. Just under one-third of all recorded tracts fit this stereotypical profile of the southern planter class's attachment to the land. The same proportion, however, had been sold within ten years from the date of an initial land grant. For every bequest that sought to keep land within a circle of consanguinity, there were half again as many conveyances by which real estate was alienated to neighbors and strangers.[10] Within this dynamic land market, land was South Carolina's most important commodity after rice.

Just as planters' relationship with land changed over time, it also became more articulated across space. The shift to rice after 1699 left its mark on the memorials, changing the ways in which planters brought together tracts to establish plantations. The memorials reveal colonists on the move, staking out varied claims to real property as rice growing and the demand for new land accelerated apace. Although a sizable minority registered a single tract, landholdings with more than one tract predominated. More than a third owned at least three tracts of land. The 71 individuals who registered more than 2,000 acres made up just 14.5 percent of the total group of 488, but those in this land-rich minority each filed memorials for eight tracts of land, on average, and together claimed 59.2 percent of all acres registered. Three decades into the rice economy, there was still a place for smaller producers who owned and worked a single plantation. This imbalance between a land-rich gentry class and a majority of smallholders captures South Carolina in the 1730s in the process of becoming a plantation society that was beginning to form a characteristic social pyramid topped by a small, disproportionately wealthy elite.

The shifting ownership of land is one index of flux in this emerging plantation landscape; the changing spatial forms etched by property lines across the terrain are another. Tracts of land first granted years earlier were then fractured into smaller portions for sale, annexed to adjacent holdings, and fused together to form expanded plantations. Forty-five percent of all registered tracts were altered in one or more of these ways from the initial grants from which they derived.[11] The desire to acquire wetlands for rice production was a driving force behind this reconfiguration of the landscape. Surviving seventeenth-century survey plats show that the first settlers, seeking arable upland tracts, avoided including wetlands in their land grants. Excavated settlement sites confirm that they valued elevated terrain—a match for English arable land—along deepwater river routes to Charlestown. Early surveyors made allowances for "Swamp & Marsh" when they laid out these tracts in the seventeenth century, including such terrain within a grant's boundary lines when it could not be easily avoided, but not counting such acreage toward the maximum allowed by a settler's warrant to claim land.[12]

After the first rice shipments to England turned an agricultural experiment into a transatlantic commodity, planters scrambled to acquire "marsh" excluded from their original grants.[13] Large landowners represented in the memorials shed small tracts of 100 or fewer acres for sale in parcels too small to support a plantation, but well situated to provide neighbors with access to swamps that their own grants had excluded. After receiving a gift of "back land" from his father, John Anger purchased a 55¼-acre tract that extended his holdings to the wetlands on the banks of the Ashley River.[14] When the land office reopened under royal authority in 1731, planters inundated the Council with petitions for these "water lots" excluded from seventeenth-century surveys.[15] Richard Allien made one of many such bids to join a "considerable quantity of low lands lying waste and uncultivated" to his "upland" tract near the Santee River in 1735. To add to their rice fields, planters cannibalized land originally laid out in town lots, undermining the last vestige of the Proprietors' plan to implant an idealized version of the English countryside in America.[16] South Carolina's first historians burnished the legend of the planter pioneer as they celebrated this early eighteenth-century acquisition of swamps for rice growing. Because the first settlers were "utter strangers to the value and fertility of the low lands," argued Alexander Hewit in 1779, the "swamps were therefore carefully avoided, and large tracts of the higher lands, which were esteemed more precious, were surveyed, and marked out for estates." The move "to the swamps was highly advantageous," concurred David Ramsay in 1809, because it "gave use and value to lands which before were of no account, and by many deemed nuisances."[17]

During the first three decades of the eighteenth century, the emergence of rice as the colony's staple commodity was marked by a surge in transatlantic exports. Some 6,000 settlers, black and white, witnessed the birth of the rice economy around 1700, when annual rice exports averaged less than 270,000 pounds. In the years that followed, African slaves imported to clear and cultivate new rice swamps outpaced the increase in European migration. Approximately 10,000 white colonists and 20,000 black slaves sustained South Carolina's economic growth around 1730, when exports averaged nearly 17 million pounds per year.[18] Masters and slaves had put in place a strategy for making the land pay that propelled plantation settlement into new territory. Colonists participated independently in this active market for real property more than they found themselves bound by constraints of kinship and schemes for social interdependence when they brought land into cultivation. In a literal as well as a figurative sense eighteenth-century planters did not inherit this landscape, they remade it. A century before the myth of the static South romanticized the plantation as an ancestral estate, the memorials reveal that planters' relationship to "the land" was marked by tumultuous change.[19]

Volatile Environments

In the mid-1740s, with the rice trade languishing because of a disruptive transatlantic war and the prospects of a nascent indigo industry uncertain, planters watched oranges ripen on the branch. Long an emblem of desire in Britain's warm-weather colonies, these fruits, sweet tasting and delicate, realized the environmental promise of South Carolina. Planters ornamented their grounds with trees that yielded fruits "of all sorts extremely fine and in profusion." Along with live turtles destined for the soup tureen and parcels of fine pudding rice, Charlestown merchants shipped oranges by the crate to their British correspondents. Such tokens of esteem put the province's exotic bounty on display before discriminating metropolitan palates.[20] In the 1730s and 1740s some had enlarged these plantings into commercial groves capable of producing tens of thousands of fruits each season. With the first of some 300,000 oranges harvested in 1746 en route to America's cold-weather colonies, growers eyed the London market with expectation.[21]

When planters awoke on 7 February 1747 to an unusually cold morning, their dreams of a lucrative citrus trade were shattered by a blast of frost so harsh that it had "destroyed almost all the Orange-Trees in the Country" in a single night. Coaxed by a mild winter, the trees' "Juices were so far risen" that they were "ready to blossom." This unexpected "Frost burst all their Vessels, for not only the Bark of all of [the trees], but even the Bodies of many of them were split, and all on the Side next to the Sun." When another destructive freeze descended twenty years later, there was no industry left to kill, only the spirits of colonists who had grown accustomed to eating oranges, pomegranates, and other "Delicates." Without fragrances, flowers, and tastes to anticipate, they were left "much in the dumps," suddenly aware again that tender, fruit-bearing trees were a "precarious growth in this Climate."[22]

Because Carolina was relentlessly promoted as lying in the "same latitude with some of the most fertile countries on the globe," its first settlers believed that they were entering a charmed space for agriculture. More experienced eighteenth-century colonists seldom took up the undiluted optimism of this environmental cant. Instead of a temperate terrestrial paradise, they saw their surroundings governed by dangerous extremes. South Carolina turned out to be colder than "many countries in our latitude," but it also experienced the "summer heat" of "tropical countries."[23] The colony's inhabitants ran a seasonal gauntlet of "Egyptian plagues" that included "violent heat," "dreadful drought," "much thunder and lightening, and muskatoes and sand flies in abundance."[24] "[O]ne minute serene, the next cloudy and tempestuous," the weather confounded prediction. "[C]hangeable and erratic" winds, bearing startling cold or warmth, hailed from "different Points of the Compass, without any regularity." Punctuated by "surprising Extreams," South Carolina's "Strange & irregular Seasons" made its agriculture uncertain.[25]

Hurricanes became a symbol of this superabundant natural world, a place of "wild luxuriance" that brought forth remarkable bounty along with the ever-present threat of natural disasters. Tropical storms and full-blown hurricanes descended on the Lowcountry and, as they advanced across its "low and flat lands[,] have spread their desolation far and wide."[26] In the punishing hurricane year of 1752 Henry Ravenel watched the skies darken into what looked like "Smoak" from Hanover, his Santee River plantation. These threatening clouds blotted out the sun, making the "Earth so dark that I could scarce desern my Wife from the front Porch to the back." Winds ripped the roofs off his "Negroe Houses" and "Blow'd down our Fowl House." A deluge of rain flattened stalks of growing corn to the ground and "put Water over the Ears of the Rice." The hurricane washed away bridges, ran ships seeking safe river anchorage aground, and did "unconceivable Damage & . . . vast havack among the Trees." Travelers could not but recall the historic fury of the storm as they made their way along roads that "for Years afterwards, were incumbered with Trees blown and broken down."[27] Philadelphia naturalist John Bartram, visiting Charlestown in 1765, witnessed panic among his hosts when strong, sustained northeast winds began to blow. At first he chalked such fear up to the "feminin[e] weakness" of elite women, "supposing thes[e] grievous calamities came but once in an age." Only when mature, sober men assured him that such winds were the telltale sign of an impending hurricane, the frequent bane of Carolina, did he share in their "anctious concerns" and, perhaps, rushed to join the women seeking secure shelters.[28]

Even when storms did not devastate the countryside, the everyday volatility of South Carolina's climate made planting unpredictable. At each stage of development too little or too much water posed a threat to the growth of the rice plant. In the initial vegetative phase during which the shoot emerges and lays down a root system, dry conditions made for the "most extraordinary good Weather for planting." The planters' saying "that a dry Spring produces a large Crop" hinged on this ecological requirement. All too often, however, slaves returned to muddy fields to replant seed that failed to sprout and take root after especially wet weather. This delay forced plants to mature later in the season, when cooler autumn temperatures made for poorer-quality rice and less of it.[29]

Although the rice plant is adaptable to a range of environmental conditions, it is particularly intolerant of drought. Rice's reproductive phase was marked by the emergence in late summer of the rice panicle, the grain-bearing head of the plant, an event that planters called "earing." Plants cut off from sustaining showers of rain during the "critical Season of Earing" could wither and die before producing a single grain. Planters without "great resources of Water damm'd in" to preserve their crops during the drought of 1762 "lost them beyond recovery." August was thus "always the ticklish Month for Rice." Whenever the rains stopped for a week or more, fields carved out of muddy swamps dried up until it seemed as if they would "burn like dry fu[se]."[30]

After reaching its full height and extending its panicle, the rice plant entered a final ripening phase in which the grains developed, a process that planters sometimes called "filling." "[T]empestuous" harvest weather could wipe out rice that had survived a dry summer. Before a crop had weathered the storms of autumn, the second of its two "most dangerous Stages" after earing, few were willing to predict its size.[31] Because South Carolina's "Seasons [were] so precarious," no one took stock of "Country produce till it [was] in the barn." A "Hurricane or some such disaster to the Harvest" could undo the work of even the most "uncommon succession of seasonable Weather," cutting in half a crop that slaves had tended for months in a matter of hours.[32]

Planters' sense of the weather, like all attempts to describe fluctuation beyond the norm for any climate, focused on a "subjective collection of atmospheric phenomena, among which the temperature and precipitation stand out," because these factors, more than any others, affect the growth of cultivated plants. A mutual dependence on the seasons, and the unrelenting uncertainty this involved, was a common point of experience that American planters shared with English farmers. As grain growers, both watched spring sowings and fall harvests as times of particular vulnerability to nature's extremes. Charlestown merchants found planters, with their never-ending complaints about the weather, "much of the disposition of the English Farmers (addicted to groul without a real cause)."[33] These similarities of environmental experience aside, colonists planted in a continental climate featuring "extremes of heating and chilling," while their old-world counterparts farmed in more temperate, maritime conditions. Whatever damage storms and droughts might inflict on the diversified English countryside, they did so region by region and crop by crop; catastrophic losses to any one of South Carolina's three dominant eighteenth-century crops (rice, maize, and indigo) had the potential to plunge the province as a whole into crisis.

Dominated by a long "Hott season" in which droughts alternated with fierce storms, the Lowcountry's agricultural year concluded with an unpredictable "Hurricane time" that might leave town and countryside in chaos.[34] Colonists lacked a store of well-worn weather proverbs that foretold the coming of good and bad seasons. The look of the lunar surface or the clarity of the air on a saint's day, for all their faults as predictors of weather to come, placed anxious English farmers at the front of a generational procession of fellow tillers of the soil. By invoking old saws and sayings, they stood with those who had endured the uncertainties of the climate before and survived to pass on environmental knowledge.[35] Planters faced their "violent" world alone, without the comfort of illusions that seemed to hearken back to time immemorial. Although they regarded what the "oldest man can remember" about the weather, this search for benchmarks with which to pin down a sense of what was normal reached back only across the span of a single lifetime, no more than "40 Odd years" into the past. The sweep of weather cycles that took place even earlier, before the "Settlement of South Carolina," remained opaque, especially after the dispersion of coastal Indians who had once shared their own weather lore during the brief time that Native Americans and the colony's first generation of settlers lived side by side in the Lowcountry.[36]

Merchants paid keen attention to the impact of the weather on planting. Few letters to British trading partners concluded without at least a hint about the projected size of rice and indigo crops. Together, their more than 300 extant crop observations comprise an agricultural chron-

icle that spans most of the eighteenth century.[37] Because they were concerned with predicting the level of supply in any event, commodity traders
reported record yields and harvest shortfalls alike. Although they had as
much reason to describe good as well as bad seasons, they had far fewer
opportunities to do so. Their comments on the weather's impact on agriculture picture the lowcountry environment as an unrelenting and menacing challenge to planters. In fifty-three seasons for which crop descriptions have survived, merchants told of only fifteen that were ideal for rice.
During these few extraordinary years the weather's fluctuations seemed
designed to complement the needs of growing rice plants. Beginning with
dry springs just right for sowing seed, these kind seasons then nourished
young plants by soaking the fields with steady, gentle rains. Pessimists
feared that such good fortune would be undone by the destruction of a
violent storm, only to find that the "Hurricane Season steals off in smiles"
to preserve bumper crops.[38]

In twenty-five other years, however, South Carolina's volatile climate
asserted itself. Saturated springs, arid summers, and bouts of extreme
weather made it seem "as if heaven and earth Were combin'd against us."
As droughts and floods swallowed up dreams of bountiful rice harvests,
planters salvaged what they could from their fields and prepared to plant
again to pay off mounting debts. The environmental record of indigo,
which joined rice as a second staple commodity in the mid-1740s, was
even more checkered: only four seasons passed muster as unqualified
successes, while twenty-one others were marked by disasters small and
large for this source of blue dye for Britain's textile industry. Hard frosts
dealt the same death blow to indigo as to oranges. Long droughts left the
"Weed . . . so stunted that it was scarcely worthwhile to cut it." Indigo
plants could "mend" miraculously with timely showers, but the leaves for
which the crop was cultivated absorbed damage with every harsh encounter.[39] Rice, grown for its seeds, proved to be "of a more hardy nature." The temperamental chemistry by which compounds in indigo
leaves were extracted into usable dye was particularly sensitive to cold
spells. South Carolina indigo was saddled with a reputation for poor
quality that resulted, in part, from growing a tropical plant in the subtropics. The "planters almost to a man make it as good as they can, but
there is something at times either in the air or water that is not discover'd," they came to believe, "which confounds those of the best experience."[40] The different vulnerabilities of these two crops provided little

in the way of protection through diversification. Compared with the seven recorded years in which a bad season for one staple crop was balanced by a good season for the other, in seventeen others the violent weather of South Carolina hurt both of the plantation economy's mainstays.

Commanding Water

Confronted with this volatile natural world, planters transformed rice growing to withstand environmental extremes. Destructive floods and withering droughts posed creative disruptions to agricultural practice.[41] Punished by crop losses, planters shaped land and channeled water to protect growing rice from the elements. Some late colonial contemporaries imagined the first planters as upland growers who produced "providence" rice, so called for its dependence on whatever rainfall the skies happened to provide. In this view early planters bypassed the "swampy grounds" that later proved so well suited to its culture and instead "exhausted their strength in raising it on higher lands" as an English farmer would grain, an approach that "poorly rewarded them for their toil."[42] The few descriptions of agriculture for the period 1690–1725 offer scant details of production methods, but they do suggest that rice was a wetland crop from the very beginning. John Stewart demonstrated rice's viability by planting it in intermittently "dry swamps," one sort of underused wasteland that he and other early modern improvers treasured first for its promise of renewable fertility. The precedent he set along the banks of the Cooper River in 1690 seems to have drawn early rice planters into engagement with land defined by its relationship to flowing water. They sought out "low moist lands" for their "rich and moist soil," selecting sites for planting that, by virtue of their topography, were probably dry enough to plant but were inundated irregularly by overflowing rivers and heavy rains. By the mid-1720s, if not earlier, the typical planter was able to control water with more certainty, putting "two feet of water" on the fields and keeping it there for "at least two months in the year."[43]

The first English scouts who reconnoitered the region for the Proprietors sought out tracts of high and dry land shaded by the canopies of large hardwood trees. Experienced planters overturned this preference and came to the conviction that the Lowcountry's "*high* lands are the poorest and the *low* the Richest in the world" because these swamps were either "naturally covered with water the greatest part of the year" or

enriched by heavy rains or overflowing rivers that pooled in their re-
cesses.[44] Colonists learned to lower their gaze from the uplands, taking
in the fluid dynamics of swamp terrain, places where a line of control
would have to be imposed between land and water in order to produce
rice. They watched where tidal surges pushed water over the riverbanks
with every flow and drew them away again at every ebb; they monitored
the impact of "freshes," or freshwater floods, fed by mountain-borne
rivers from the interior; they saw how quickly heavy rains engorged
swamps, pushing their waters across the Lowcountry's flat expanses to fill
every dried-out pocket and depression. When planters marked out
swamps for rice fields, they identified places where the land could be
girded by embankments, cordoned off by dams, and ringed by ditches
and drains. As planters deployed slaves to remake the swamps for rice,
they arrested the flow of water across the land's surface, disrupting the
landscape gradient along which it was accustomed to flow. In doing so,
they harnessed the power of flowing water and put their fortunes in its
unpredictable path.

When the *South-Carolina Gazette* printed the first of more than 3,300
advertisements describing land for sale in 1732, issues of the colony's first
newspaper opened a documentary window onto a process of agricultural
adaptation in full swing. These advertisements, an unofficial census of
planting practice, clarify two points about the landscape changes that
came with rice's rise: first, that the dual threat of drought and flooding
was the driving force behind technical innovation in planting; and second,
that the single most important feature of plantation land was the "command of water" it made possible.[45]

Some lands advertised in the 1730s offer a sense of what earlier rice
plantations might have looked like. These plantations made comparatively
simple alterations to the land that took advantage of the existing contours
of its topography. Charles Starns's rice field lay at the foot of a gully
framed by two high bluffs. A short dam between them was all it took to
keep water from flowing across 100 acres of cleared inland swamp. Once
slaves constructed this barrier between the swamp above and the field
below, a reservoir of water accumulated with which the field could be
"overflow'd" in a dry season.[46] Aided by such natural land features, the
most basic freshwater swamp irrigation system was a packed-earth dam,
two or three feet high, that traversed the swamp formation and issued a
"fine stream from its waste in the driest time." As they enticed buyers

eager to bring new rice land into cultivation with their descriptions of land for sale, planters noted when their swamps' position next to higher-elevation terrain made their lands "convenient for damming." After slaves cleared Alcimus Gaillard's Winyah River swamp of its cypress, they could easily build a 180-yard dam at its upper border, creating a field that produced 200 barrels of clean rice after every harvest. Lands ordered for agriculture by a "very moderate Charge of Labour, in raising Dams and Water stops, which would preserve great Quantities of Water, sufficient to supply the same in the dryest Summer," played to the pocketbooks of planters who sought the greatest return on the least investment of labor.[47]

Swamp formations placed by nature to suit rice culture, however, were few and far between. After planters took up these small and scattered wetlands that were comparatively easy to improve, those who planted on a grander scale altered the land more intensively to achieve a command of water. Water stagnated in many of the Lowcountry's larger arable swamps, virtual "dead levels" on the land. To irrigate these fields, planters ordered slaves to dam up more distant wetlands and excavate "large artificially dug ponds" to capture their runoff. Slaves dug a network of connecting channels from these reservoirs to "throw Water" onto growing rice. On these flat expanses, labor-intensive methods for "letting off Water" were as important as those that put it on. Ditches carved into the edges of fields carried off "overplus Water" to lower-elevation drains. To create the conditions under which just-sown rice could vegetate, drainage systems ensured that these "low Grounds may be drained, planted, and kept dry."[48] They secured plantations from the "highest Freshes" and rendered them "safe in planting against any sudden rains." Settling lands at lower elevations surrounded them with abundant sources for irrigation, putting them in the path of higher water draining toward the sea and within the floodplains of overflowing rivers. Positioned to expose their fields to water descending from above and surging from below, swamp plantations were vulnerable to floods that struck quickly and with devastating effect. To counter the "Danger of the Freshes," known to "Rise thirty nay forty foot in one Night," demanded the construction of the "artful trench, to make the floods retire," and "pow'rful banks" capable of repelling the tides.[49] Ditching and draining such swamps changed their hydrology, putting water in controlled motion across the surface of the land.[50]

These more intensive landscaping efforts allowed "for the flowing of the Rice Land with Water, which may be let off again at pleasure." Compartmentalizing field sections enhanced water control even further, allowing for their discrete irrigation. One hundred acres of John Lining's Santee River plantation were "ditched in, and divided by cross dams, into small squares of about 10 acres into any of which, water may be let in, when necessary from a large reserve of back-water."[51] Lands located on the low banks of rivers that surged and retreated to the rhythm of the tides were entirely reshaped by slaves to control the flow of water between river and field. When the lay of their lands took in both freshwater and tidal swamps, some planters joined these two sources together to irrigate their fields. Whether washed by rising rivers or steeped in freshwater pools, planters valued these swamp tracts for their command of water. Every rice plantation was a unique adjustment to the local conditions under which land met water in the Lowcountry.[52]

Setting aside the horse-drawn plow for the hoe-wielding slave and turning from dry uplands to soggy wastes to grow their staple crop, planters set themselves apart from most European grain farmers, but the methods they used to cultivate rice in wetlands adapted technologies long employed in English husbandry. Swamp irrigation systems bore a strong resemblance to those used to "float the water meadows." The simplest of these man-made pastures diverted stream flow "over a hillside . . . and back into a stream lower down," much in the same way that rice planters exploited topography to bring swamp waters on their fields across a landscape gradient. More developed English water meadows employed "a complicated arrangement of hatches and ditches" to channel river water over land in a "slowmoving sheet," just as planters tapped swamps and exposed their rice fields to controlled river flooding. English farmers floated the water meadows to nurture a supply of feed grasses in defiance of dry or cold conditions, thus "smoothing out the fluctuations of the seasons."[53] The same defensive incentive—shielding agriculture from the impact of the weather—stood behind both systems.

From the crudest inland swamp dam to the most thoroughly regulated tidal system, control of water protected rice fields from volatile weather. Good rice-growing conditions prevailed in these man-made microenvironments, even as extremes of wet and dry weather swirled across the Lowcountry. Improved swamps were "drained and cultivated with such banks as to keep out torrents of water in planting season," and their reservoirs supplied "artificial rain" in the "very driest of times." Such control allowed planters to impose a seasonal rhythm—dry springs, steady moisture through the summers, and dry harvests—under which rice plants flourished. Paul Mazyck's plantation was so tightly embanked that a brief downpour laid the "whole [240 acres] under Water" and so well drained that "after the greatest Freshes ever known the water goes off in 24 Hours or two Days at most."[54] After the long, dry summer of 1760, an absentee planter was warned, rice that grew beyond the reach of irrigation perished, but "as far as your water Covers you[']ll have good Rice." Natural disasters taught persuasive lessons about the benefits of agricultural improvement. In another drought-stricken season one of the Elias Balls watched his own rice fail because his plantation lacked a "suf[f]icient command of water." Those who could "flow the[ir] fields immediately after planting," he observed with jealousy, made good crops. A map of his lands drawn seven years after he suffered this setback reveals a dam built through Turkey Hill Swamp forming a vast reservoir that

Figure 3.1. Tidal swamp rice field. Increasingly during the second half of the eighteenth century, planters invested in cultivating river floodplains at the "pitch of the tide." These locations exploited the rising and falling water levels of coastal rivers caused by the pulse of the ocean tides. After slaves created a geometric grid of embanked, leveled fields, rice crops could be irrigated at will by admitting and releasing water through channels, called "trunks," embedded in the banks. Records of the Court of Common Pleas, Judgment Roll 1788, no. 223A (detail). Courtesy of the South Carolina Department of Archives and History.

provided more water to the fields below.[55] The lure of tidal river flood plains was first and foremost the guaranteed supply of water they offered, making rice crops in antebellum South Carolina "the most certain in the world." Planters without "Tide Lands or back water" and those "who have not great resources of Water damm'd in" suffered serious losses.[56]

The tyranny of harsh seasons made the persistent case that slave labor should be invested in reservoir, bank, ditch, and dam construction. Planters emphasized precisely such hedges against environmental volatility when they advertised plantations for sale, promoting their lands as "extremely well water'd in the dryest of times" and "of Consequence not subject to the Droughts." A "swamp with an entire command of water through or around it" allowed planters to keep the fields "dry or drowned at pleasure." Once the "Tedious and expensive" work of building "Banks and drains" was done, one planter reckoned, "we can make good crops in spite of G—ds teeth."[57]

With "great banks and deep ditches" planters secured rice from the elements. Should the planter "not have the water at his command," commented naturalist Bernard Romans, "the noxious growth in dry weather, or a profusion of water in wet weather, would equally destroy the crop."[58] This drive to command water was part of a larger quest by colonists to gain control over the many volatile forces that made planting a precarious enterprise. The well-irrigated rice field was a keystone technology that made planters more effective agents across the board, arming them with the means to respond to crisis. Achieving a command of water gave planters a way to reduce slave labor to a more predictable routine and thereby diffuse the resistance that slaves mounted when faced with unexpected or unusually severe work. Two harsh labor tasks—hoeing weeds in overgrown fields and hand processing the harvested crops—were flashpoints in master-slave relations. Planters drew a hard line of distinction between grass species they called weeds from those they cultivated as articles of commerce, but swamp fields promoted the growth of these genetic cousins equally. Slaves forced to weed rice by hand and hoe endured work that masters acknowledged was especially "toilsome." Weeds that infested the fields mimicked the appearance of the rice plant, developing a high degree of phenotypic plasticity to survive alongside it. Barnyardgrass (*Echinochloa crus-galli*) took root in swamps as slaves cleared them for agriculture. Manual weeding introduced a powerful act of selection that made this opportunistic species almost impossible to distinguish from rice after only a few growing seasons. Slaves spoke with their feet when grass-choked fields made their daily tasks unreasonably hard. After one overseer beat three slaves who could not complete their impossible tasks, they fled to Charlestown to bring this grievance to their master. Plantation agent Josiah Smith Jr. ordered "lenient treatment" and offered the "encouragement of a Beef & some Rum" to persuade slaves under his management not to run away when the "Grass was very bad."[59]

On the "old plantations" grass invaded the fields after only two years of cultivation and "covered the earth like a fur," sometimes sprouting up "again on the same day on which it was removed." On "river swamp plantations, from the command of water," however, irrigation displaced the hoe as the planter's primary weapon against weeds. After slaves hoed through new rice plants once, a flow of water suppressed the grass, "while the growth of rice is much accelerated." The best-regulated tidal fields were "so exceedingly Rich that many of them which have been planted above Sixty years without rest or Manure of any kind produce as good Crops as at the first settling and are deemd inexhaustible." After preserving a crop against droughts and floods, the "great object" of rice agriculture was "to keep the land clean from weeds." Doing so effectively removed a bone of contention that, if left unresolved, might prompt slaves to challenge their masters' authority. When land was laid out in embanked "squares, or small fields," each task was "proportioned to the strength of the negroes who work them, in such manner that they can be planted, or hoed through, in the course of a week."[60] Fields so ordered preempted confrontations over what constituted a fair day's work in the rice fields. Control over irrigation narrowed a space for conflict, taking much of the guesswork out of setting tasks and making it more difficult for an overseer or driver to single out a slave for reprisal by burdening him or her with punishing tasks.

As more effective irrigation increased the amount of rice each slave could produce, it intensified the labor required to prepare it for sale. Slaves had long taken to the swamps and resorted to arson to evade the annual ordeal of pounding rice by hand. Water-powered mills improved the capacity of rice processing and set a course of technical innovation that resulted in its extensive mechanization by the end of the century.[61] The first advertised plantation that featured a site for a water-powered "pounding mill" appeared in the *South-Carolina Gazette* in 1752. Those that followed used the same technologies for irrigating rice—dammed wetland reservoirs and overflowing tidal rivers—to turn waterwheels that moved as many as "twelve pestles by water," automating West African–style mortar-and-pestle pounding.[62] Several integrated "water pounding machines" directly into irrigation systems built for agriculture. Reservoirs did double duty on these plantations, providing "water for the whole spot of rice land" and working a "pounding mill in the winter" that could "beat out any Quantity of Rice." The first advertised "water machines" that worked by the ebb and flow of the tides adjoined the fields of a Pee Dee River plantation in 1756.[63] The eighty-five colonial-era advertisements in the *Gazette* that mentioned them reveal that water-driven mills were a widespread, if not yet commonplace, technology in the late colonial period.

The "planter who has water at command" to power a mill pounded rice "cheaper than . . . by horses or by the manual labour of his slaves." These machines processed larger quantities more quickly than the animal-powered "Pecking-Machines for cleaning Rice" that were used to supplement slaves' hand labor.[64] The best animal mills performed the same work as "16 Negroes from Sun to Sun can do," producing about 2,100 pounds of clean rice every day. Planters claimed that their least effective water machines matched this rate and their most productive models doubled it. These high-capacity mills cleaned rice at a rate of approximately 4,240 pounds per day, taking on the tasks of thirty-two slaves working by hand.[65] Early planters and those without the capital to invest in such specialized machinery forced slaves to process the entire crop manually, sometimes working them into the night in the pounding barn after a day's work harvesting the grain. The few slaves needed to tend the water mills, by contrast, worked "between sun-rise and sun-set" and sometimes finished their work "by Dinner Time." As planters pushed slaves to prepare the crop for market, every barrel of rice packed at the machine house was one that a slave did not have to fill by beating rice in the mortar, a few pecks at a time. By the early 1770s many "wealthier" planters, one of whom adopted the technology expressly to "ease his People," switched to water power.[66] Technical improvements put in practice in the 1790s made water mills the standard means of processing rice for export. "[C]ommanding water, both for making rice and pounding machines," smoothed out the labor demands of rice production.[67] As water submerged weeds and set the pestles in motion, these uses for the well-irrigated plantation softened sharp spikes in the intensity of labor. Particularly in colonial South Carolina's slave society, which maintained social order through the unwritten rules of the task labor system, impositions of work that went beyond customary expectations always had the potential to destabilize master-slave relations on the plantations. What slaves gained in terms of the transparency of field tasks and a reprieve from the brutality of hand pounding, however, they lost to another kind of "laborious" work. The price planters forced them to pay to achieve the "certain promise of the cultur'd field" was year-round labor building and maintaining the massive earthworks that channeled water for rice irrigation.[68]

Planters' increasing command of water also gave them the material resources needed to produce indigo as a second staple commodity. South Carolina's advancing rice monoculture ran up against a serious economic crisis during the 1740s. British hostilities with Spain and France unleashed privateers into the Atlantic Ocean and Caribbean Sea that preyed on shipping. When the risk of a ship's capture as a prize of war was factored into freight and insurance charges in Charlestown, rice earnings could barely "defray the expence of cleaning" the grain. With returns from their first staple in sharp decline for want of an economical means of exporting it, planters heeded the warnings of agricultural improvers who used the depression to "bring the Planter off from his Darling Rice" and fulfill a long-standing goal of diversifying the export economy.[69]

Those who planted indigo to weather this market crisis learned that although the crop did not match rice's voracious need for irrigation, its processing consumed vast quantities of water. Once the plants were harvested, slaves steeped and agitated them in large vats to extract the dye. The vital importance of water supplies was hammered home after the drought of 1755, when many "lost fine Fields of Indigo for want of Water to work it." Armed with experience manipulating water for rice, planters put slaves to work damming up streams and swamps, sometimes supplying the "rice land and indigo vats" from the same reservoir.[70] To pursue South Carolina's second staple, they maintained "reserve[s] of water sufficient to work several sets of indico vats in the dryest season."[71] When the approach of the Seven Years' War threatened once again to "turn things upside down," one merchant reflected in 1755, "we have the satisfaction to think a War now cannot affect this Country a Quarter part so much as the last did. Every one now can make Indigo when their necessitys drive them to it & in the former they had nothing to depend upon but Rice."[72] Although making good indigo was never easy in the Carolina subtropics, planters' practiced control of water ensured that the crops they saved from bad weather could be turned into marketable dye.

Achieving a command of water made possible another kind of diversification. In a pinch, swamp fields built for rice could be made to grow any of South Carolina's crops. The versatility of "Tide Swamp Land" enhanced its value. When "properly banked in, and your trunks and dams in perfect good order," it yielded indigo, as well as rice.[73] Although most indigo was grown on drier ground, those who planted the vast tidal floodplains of the northern and southern coastal frontiers found higher terrain in short supply. John Channing's plantation produced bumper crops of rice but lacked uplands on which to grow provisions. After investing the proceeds of the 1769 harvest in twelve new slaves, he ordered twelve new lowland acres banked in for a "small field of Potatoes" to feed them. His other slaves subsisted on corn grown in a cleared swamp that he claimed could "produce beyond any high ground was it once dammed in & put in order." When a bad season decimated the colony's provisions crops, planters avoided paying high food prices by sowing their swamps with corn. By the turn of the nineteenth century, some refashioned these fields to grow cotton.[74] Once cleared, leveled, embanked, and drained, each of the wetland types planters could discern across their soggy landscape could be "well adapted to the culture of rice, indico and corn." Subjected to controlled irrigation, "River Swamp," "high champion swamp, "choice tupelo swamp," and "fresh water marsh or tide land" alike could be made "suitable for any thing."[75]

In 1670, the colony's first year, John Locke summarized Carolina's natural promise in a terse but tantalizing memorandum under the heading "*Country*": "Healthy, delightful, bears anything." The lure that drew the first settlers was, in part, the idea that the world's most prized commercial crops could thrive in lowcountry land. Although transplanted far from their exotic points of origin to grow in the colony's soil, "were the seeds brought into it," these lucrative productions, early colonists believed, would be nurtured to perfection.[76] In the flexibility of their swamplands planters realized, in a modest and practical way, this dilated seventeenth-century vision of the Lowcountry as an infinitely malleable space for agricultural enterprise.

Making indigo helped planters better weather the fluctuations of a global commodities market easily upset by the shocks of imperial warfare.

Its addition to their productive repertoire "persuaded Carolinians that their creativity played a major role in delivering the colony from depression, that they could deal with adversity, and that they were competent to shape the future."[77] This bid to smooth out the volatile terms of transatlantic trade was part of a larger quest to limit vulnerability and exert greater influence on disruptive forces arrayed against them. As planters disrupted and simplified ecosystems and enforced a brutal work regime on slaves, the rigid modes of control epitomized by the gridlike pattern tidal plantations left on the landscape could themselves be prone to unanticipated disorders. Seen as one element of a larger "design for mastery," lowcountry plantations sometimes shared the fate of other attempts by American slave owners to impose their will on land and people they owned but could never control absolutely.[78] The strongest banks could not withstand a hurricane, and many plantations never reserved enough water to compensate for the longest droughts. Even slaves who found their tasks lightened were never thereby rendered utterly obedient. Measured against the standard of unchallenged agency, South Carolina planters and their plantations fell well short of the mark of "mastery." But these agricultural transformations gave planters meaningful leverage against violent weather, restive slaves, and unpredictable markets, supplying the material foundations of a more reliable "command."

Plantations in Motion

Although every tract's boundaries were rendered in deceptively solid lines on official survey plats, from ground level these borders were an abstraction of dominion. In practice, the threshold between nature and culture amounted to a shifting frontier, both within individual landholdings and across the colony as a whole as it expanded to claim new territory for plantation agriculture. Every plantation was a site of colonization writ small in which slaves wrested new fields from swamps and forests to feed a growing slave population and produce more rice and indigo for the transatlantic market. A typical plantation encompassed 500 acres.[79] Although most actual boundary lines traced a far more irregular figure across the landscape, we can visualize the scale of such a space by imagining it as a perfect square whose perimeter stretched for about 3.5 miles and whose interior was large enough to contain 378 American football fields (including their end zones). At the same time as planters were developing such massive tracts, some Massachusetts colonists were strug-gling to maintain farms of just 30 acres, the bare minimum thought necessary to sustain a family. The status of the English yeoman, a social template for colonial conceptions of landed independence, rested on a holding of just 50 acres.[80]

Eighteenth-century surveyors sighted lines around the sinuous shapes of swamp formations when they marked off colonists' warrants to take up land. Dividing the land in this way centered new plantations around valuable wetlands, but also included a broad range of other land types.[81] The situation of these tracts on landscape gradients that sloped to meet rivers, streams, and low-lying swamps stocked plantations with a mix of soils. Ecologists have categorized such diverse terrains in terms of their exposure to water, dividing bottomland forest wetlands into five distinc-tive ecological zones, each with its own agricultural potential.[82] Above the wetland portions of plantation tracts perched a drier world whose slightly higher elevation kept it free from water under all but the most cata-strophic conditions. These uplands were dominated by large swaths of sandy pine forests and interspersed with hardwood outcroppings. Al-though planters after 1700 acquired land for its swamps, these potential rice fields amounted to, on average, only 40 percent of the total acreage.[83] The largest parts of their holdings sampled a broader ecological and top-ographic diversity.

Although colonists sorted these lands into a finely graded range of soil categories, a basic distinction between "high and low" lands defined their plantations' purchase on the landscape. Acres marked out for use within their large holdings sliced across uplands and lowlands to incorporate both into working settlements. Tracts that were "well diversified with swamp and high lands" supported plantations with one foot in the export economy and another in the domestic economy, providing land on which to grow rice and land needed to grow food crops, erect buildings, harvest lumber, and chop firewood. Those plantations composed almost entirely of valuable tidal swamps still required "sufficient high land to settle on" to function as places of human habitation.[84] On patches of cleared forest above the wetlands, slaves built makeshift villages—identified as "settle-ments" on plantation maps—that included dwellings, provisions grounds, barns, and workshops. From this island of opened, developed space at the settlement, the working plantation expanded outward in fits and starts to take in lands for rice, corn, cattle, and indigo that were often scattered across the tract. As British forces converged on Charlestown in 1780, an officer noted with surprise that the woods had been "only clear'd about the Houses" of the plantations his regiment passed. Even in this long-settled, densely populated district near the Edisto River, this uneven pattern of developing land created a space that resembled a rough frontier rather than a thoroughly cultivated landscape.[85]

Instead of being an integrated place of work and life, the lowcountry plantation was spread out across space. Its patchwork of fields under cultivation, denuded forests, uncultivated swamps and woods, and played-out plots—converted into makeshift pastures or abandoned for nature to reclaim—provided the land resources that slaves needed to build an independent material culture. The impermanent "huts" in which slaves lived were sometimes located within the core of the settlement, often next to the pounding barns where they processed rice after every harvest. As plantations stretched out across the land, slave quarters tended to migrate away from this seat of white scrutiny. Settled near the fields in which they worked, slaves might be left to their own devices for much of the time provided they completed their assigned tasks.[86] Africans ventured routinely beyond the edges of the settled plantation to hunt animals, gather plants, and sow their own crops. This accessible wilderness began within the broad acres of their masters' lands and extended into a surrounding countryside that other colonists might have registered via grant, deed, and memorial, but that slaves used as if it were an open resource to exploit. This margin of material autonomy, a distinguishing feature of South Carolina's slave society, was made possible by a plantation form that spread out across the land to make use of the Lowcountry's heterogeneous mix of riverside terrains.[87]

Within these large and diverse tracts a pioneering phase of settlement continued well beyond the colony's formative years. Throughout the eighteenth century colonists and slaves recapitulated the frontier experiences of carving out new fields from a perceived wilderness. The snapshots of development provided by plantation advertisements indicate that slaves had cleared only a small portion of the land, about one-fifth of total tract acreage on average in the period 1732–1775.[88] Over time, the working plantation's footprint on the landscape changed form within the larger tract. One sign of this movement was the hasty erection of impermanent split-rail fences to mark a boundary between cultivated and uncultivated land. To protect growing crops from wandering livestock, permitted by law to roam, slaves split trees into rails as part of their annual routine of land-clearing tasks and then interlocked them in a zigzag pattern that required neither nails nor postholes. Seventeenth-century colonists attempted to transplant the hedgerow to Carolina, "intrenching Ground with Quicksets, according to the English manner." Their eighteenth-century successors, who saw their plantations less as permanent places of improvement than as temporary sites of production, made do with these cheap but inelegant "worm" fences.[89] Planters relinquished grassy plots "for pasture, and clear[ed] new ground of its woods." In a "country abounding in trees," it made little sense to tend hedges. Instead, when they were not left to rot or burned for fuel, slaves took apart fences around fields that were "exhausted" and "forsaken" and reassembled them around new lands just cleared for cultivation.[90]

Along with the drive to bring fresh soil under the hoe, planters colonized their lands more intensively as they added slaves to their labor forces. So voracious was their demand that it seemed as if "*Negroes* may be said to be the Bait proper for catching a *Carolina* Planter, as certain as Beef to catch a Shark." After importing slaves by the hundreds every year during the first two decades of the eighteenth century, planters began buying by the thousands to propel the expanding rice economy after 1720. They forced approximately 110,900 Africans into slavery between 1700 and 1790, most of whom were destined to work in the rice fields. If only half of these survived to work as field hands, their labor would have made possible the planting of upwards of 200,000 acres in rice alone.[91] South Carolina plantations were already large communities by the 1720s, when most lowcountry blacks lived on units with twenty or more slaves. After midcentury their populations grew larger still, with about one-third living on plantations with fifty or more slaves in the 1750s, a proportion that rose to about one-half during the 1770s. When rice and indigo prices rose in one year, planters rushed to take advantage of what they hoped were sustained market upswings by reinvesting their earnings in new slaves to plant more land in the next.[92] A group of "New Negroes" purchased for Ralph Izard in 1765 were immediately set to work clearing 30 new acres for rice, enough land to make 150 barrels and pay back part of their purchase price. John Lining first settled his 1,000-acre Buck Head Swamp plantation in 1758, initiating production with 100 acres of indigo. In less than two years his slaves had added 50 new acres for indigo and cleared 100 acres of "exceeding good swamp for rice."[93] Surging slave imports drove the plantation economy into new territories and intensified the development of land within existing plantations.

After developing every usable acre of one part of their tracts, planters sent contingents of slaves into the undeveloped reaches of their lands to clear a new section of swamp and settlement land. Naturalist William Bartram, traveling across an isolated beach on horseback, feared for his life when he saw a "party of Negroes" approaching "armed with clubs, axes and hoes." These potential weapons turned out to be the field slaves' stock in trade. As the members of this land-clearing expedition separated to allow him to pass, their "chief informed me whom they belonged to, and said they were going to man a new quarter at the West end of the bay."[94] Slaves dispatched to found new settlements could traverse a wilderness without stepping across their masters' property lines. At first they lived in rough camps or undertook long daily treks to clear new swamps "on which no buildings are as yet erected." On the colony's northern coast, a 879-acre tract famous for producing the "largest crop that was made in the province" featured a high-volume water pounding machine but not a single structure to house the slaves who supplied it with rice. Tracts laid out to take in elongated swamp formations could span several miles, making a single landholding into a space large enough for sustained internal colonization.[95] The first pioneering crews were often followed by a fuller complement of plantation personnel: field hands and their families, drivers, overseers, and slave artisans who built more permanent upland settlements near the swamp.

As colonists settled ever-larger numbers of slaves on the land, plantations cleaved into multiple units of residence and production as if by mitosis. Some tracts of 1,000 or more acres advertised for sale featured two or more "compleat settled and well improved plantations," several white residences and barns, and, in one instance, five distinct settlements outfitted with "good dwelling-houses and out-buildings."[96] This process of internal expansion was a brand of capital accumulation through "farm building" on a grand scale. Early settlers throughout colonial British America, although their material comforts might have been few and crude, generated substantial wealth simply by clearing land and preparing it for agriculture.[97] Some South Carolina planters did divert planting wealth toward luxurious consumption, building elegant mansions and manicured pleasure grounds for which this colonial elite is best remembered, but many others sacrificed material refinements in favor of

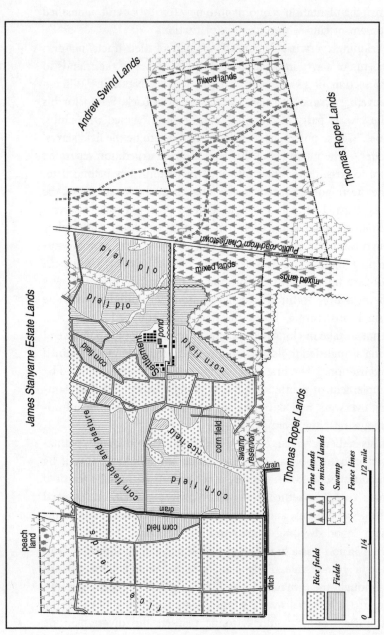

Figure 3.2. A lowcountry rice plantation, c. 1789. Rice plantations were typically vast, diversified holdings made up of a patchwork of land types. This 814-acre plantation intersected two branches of Stono Swamp. Slaves had embanked both of its narrow, wetland tracts to grow rice. Patches of higher land supported provisions fields, livestock pastures, a small peach orchard, and a residential "settlement" that included a slave quarter. Beyond the public roadway that linked this plantation to Charlestown, much of the land was in pine or mixed woods, useful for fuel and building materials, but less desirable for commercial agriculture. Figure by Philip A. Schwartzberg. Source: Records of the Court

building for the future. Although they owned thousands of acres and perhaps hundreds of slaves by the 1750s, the branch of the Allston family that occupied Oakes Plantation along the Waccamaw River made do with a dirt-floored, posthole dwelling for years after the tract was settled.[98]

There was nothing modest, however, about the ways in which colonial planters acquired vast, speculative landholdings. Taking up and developing large tracts created opportunities to realize wealth outside the transatlantic marketplace for their commodities. In 1725 an Anglican minister cast a critical eye on his planter-parishioners for their tendency to "engross more lands than it is possible [to improve] a tenth part of and yet to be greedy after more."[99] There was some method to this apparent land madness. As planters "acquir[ed] every year greater strength of hands, by the large importation of negroes," these purchases gave masters the right to claim new headright grants for land. Long before colonists built plantations at the unsettled frontiers of the province, surveying expeditions descended to claim "all the valuable lands on navigable rivers and creeks" in "exorbitant tracts." Planters with "foresight and judgement" early on "began to look out and secure the richest spots for themselves," confident that over time the plantation economy's centrifugal expansion would enhance the value of even the most isolated wilderness tracts. Many reaped impressive rewards after selling long-held lands for prices that reached tens of thousands of pounds.[100]

The rising price of land confirms that advances in irrigation and cultivation techniques made rice planting more productive as it made it more secure. The value of land increased even as the price of their staple commodity fluctuated significantly in the short term. Colonists believed that their lands could generate higher future earnings despite unpredictable season-to-season market returns, or else they would not have paid premiums to buy new land. Higher yields helped Carolina planters establish their grain in European markets of consumption despite stiff competition from other grain suppliers in the 1720s. Producing more rice, more reliably helped many weather the rice depression of the 1740s. As rice's price trend swung upward after 1750, planters were poised with the technologies and methods needed to realize their land's advancing worth.[101]

New planters who had just purchased or inherited slaves, but lacked enough land to work them, made eager buyers for tracts "in proper order for planting immediately," saving themselves the "great trouble and inconvenience incident to the settling of a new plantation." The moment the deed was transferred, a slave owner could arrange to take possession of houses, livestock, and fields "well fenced in, under good dams," and the "ground fitt for putting in the seeds." Land put in such "exceeding good order" was "ready for putting a good Gang of Negroes immediately to work upon it." If one could pay the purchase price, he might buy a plantation slaves and all, with a crop of rice and corn growing in the field, and become a full-fledged planter in an instant.[102]

Colonists claimed far more land than they could possibly develop with their own slaves. Of the 3,330 tracts advertised in the *South-Carolina Gazette* in the period 1732–1775, 40 percent betrayed some signs of development, from a few cleared acres to fully functioning, well-improved plantations. The bulk of these advertised lands were undeveloped tracts, and they were, on the whole, much larger than those that had been settled. These advertisements introduced 2,220,184 acres onto the land market, 63 percent of which belonged to unsettled tracts. The most prolific land sellers in the newspaper, brothers Charles and Jermyn Wright, were speculators first and planters second. Over the span of a quarter century, they put up for sale 51 tracts of land totaling 40,724 acres. From the 1730s, when sellers advertised about the same number of developed and undeveloped tracts, South Carolina colonists speculated more aggressively in new lands, offering them for sale in subsequent decades in larger number and greater sizes than tracts on which working plantations had been settled.

Those with deep pockets developed plantations in promising new areas rapidly, buying up land and transplanting slaves to live and work on onetime frontiers. After he retired to England as an absentee planter, George Austin owned one of the few large-scale plantations on Pee Dee River until 1772, when two wealthy colonists suddenly joined him by settling three new "respectable Plantations" on this tidal river. Rawlins Lowndes bought his land outright for £20,000. Benjamin Huger swapped an undeveloped tract for his two Pee Dee plantations, uprooting his slaves from Horse Shoe Savannah in the central part of the province and moving them north.[103] Once they learned the advantages of owning rice lands watered by the tides, planters with means were constantly "on the look out" for a "good River Swamp Plantation." Finding one in the right place at the right price triggered the forced migration of slaves from long-settled plantations closer to town to new lands at either end of the province's southern or northern coastal frontiers and into the new colony of Georgia.[104]

Those without fortunes to begin with could find sellers willing to extend generous terms. Sixty-one percent of tracts advertised through the *Gazette* that detailed financial terms were to be sold at a year's credit, a standard that allowed new planters a full season in which to recoup the costs of buying land by selling commodities that slaves produced on it. Some planting land could be had without full payment for two, three, or, in one extraordinary case, eighteen years. Selling plantation land on long credit attracted aspiring planters of limited means as buyers. Generous terms promised sellers a predictable annual bond payment and offered a stream of income to estates managed for the benefit of minors. Only about a quarter demanded "ready money" or payment within a year, a condition that tended to reflect an estate that had been seized for debt or one in distressed financial straits. These were sold at a deeply discounted price.[105] Whether because of failing health, advancing age, looming debts, or opportunities that beckoned abroad, some sold off their lands and slaves, "intending to give over the planting business." As they departed, they found others eager to acquire their slaves and seeking "a Plantation or two more" on which to put them.[106]

To acquire wetlands for rice agriculture, the memorials reveal, early colonists broke apart grants, joined them together, and changed the pattern by which individual domains were carved from the lowcountry landscape. A similar transformation continued after 1730 as planters worked to form "complete" plantations. To make "one good Plantation" out of widely dispersed wetlands, uplands, and watercourses, planters acquired new grants bordering their own and bargained with their neighbors for pieces of their adjoining properties.[107] Those without neighborly impulses put such vital tracts up for sale to the highest bidder, offering up one tract "which would be very convenient for the place where Roger Pinckney, Esq. is now settling" and another that "lies back of the rich rice plantations upon Savannah-river," land needed by "those places as a settlement for raising provisions."[108] Colonists added tracts on which they could dam up reservoirs for expanding rice fields. When they had shorn a long-settled plantation of its trees, they purchased additional pineland tracts, some a few miles away, to secure timber and firewood.[109]

A "valuable and compleat Plantation" possessed a basic natural-resource independence, lacking nothing in the way of land and water required to engage in large-scale commodity production. Its borders enclosed sources of irrigation that none could divert, as well as a stockpile of virgin wetlands for internal expansion. Only after "50 Acres of fine Swamp" had been "Cleared & planted" and added to Mepshew Plantation's existing fields would the settlement, with its 120 acres of rice capacity, merit the description of a "Compleat" plantation.[110] Diversified to take in stands of trees, indigo lands, and provisions plots and close enough to river landings to bring commodities easily to market, such plantations had "every conveniency and advantage of water, situation, soil, and timber, that can render a plantation either pleasant or profitable." What made Samuel Stevens's 1,000-acre tract "as compleat a plantation as any in the province" was its vast swamps for rice, facilities for cutting and transporting timber, and a well-developed settlement featuring a two-story cypress house with a piazza.[111] The ideal eighteenth-century plantation aggregated the Lowcountry's heterogeneous lands to support long-term production and habitation, even if planters were quick to realize their value by selling them rather than occupying them forever.

A complete plantation was, almost by definition, one that focused on the production of rice or indigo for export and grew maize and sweet potatoes for slaves' food rations. When planters suggested commodities that could be produced on the lands they had for sale, they listed rice in seven of every ten advertisements. They promoted indigo in about half of all advertisements published after its introduction as a market crop in the early 1740s. Indigo's time demands complemented the rice calendar. The dye crop was planted along with rice in the spring; slaves harvested it once during July and obtained a second "cutting" from the same plants in August. Indigo harvesting and dye processing occupied slack times in the rice schedule. Governor James Glen described rice plantations and their complementary productions in 1749, drawing special attention to "how conveniently and profitably, as to the Charge of Labour, both Indigo and Rice may be managed by the same Persons; for the Labour attending Indigo being over in the Summer Months, those who were employed in it may afterwards manufacture Rice, in the ensuing Part of the Year, when it becomes most laborious; and after doing all this, they will have some Time to spare for sawing Lumber, and making Hogsheads and other Staves, to supply the Sugar-Colonies."[112]

So many lands were promoted as fit to grow "rice, corn, and indico" that this phrase became something of a mantra, included in some form in the text of one out of every four published descriptions, and was simply assumed as an essential capability for most other viable plantation lands. Changes in these lists of suggested productions point to the rise of a common plantation complex devoted to these three crops, once replicated across the greater British Lowcountry, from North Carolina's Lower Cape Fear to the St. Mary's River in East Florida. From the 1730s, when published advertisements first appeared, the early plantation economy's general focus on livestock and naval stores—activities that were extractive in character—was already on the wane. By the close of the colonial period large-scale cattle raising had become the specialized focus of a few vast "cowpens." After tar, pitch, and turpentine peaked and fell as widespread plantation commodities in the 1720s, those who rendered these naval stores from pine forests concentrated in just a few areas, particularly Black Mingo Creek on South Carolina's northern coast.[113]

In place of these activities and alongside the central place of rice, planters shifted slaves in large numbers to producing indigo dye during the 1750s. Not only did indigo, first mentioned in a 1745 advertisement, offer planters an alternative to rice in times of disrupted or depressed markets, but the crop's tolerance for different soil types suited the heterogeneity of the region's riverside terrains. In rich soils and poor, on cleared uplands and lowlands, growing indigo allowed for the more intensive use of plantation land. "When you abuse their pine barrens," named for their notorious infertility, "a Carolina planter will answer you by saying, that they do for their richest crop, indigo."[114] Indigo's rapid adoption as a plantation commodity gave planters as lucrative a use for their uplands as rice was for the lowlands.

Cutting down trees to clear new fields for planting had made firewood, shingles, and milled lumber some of the colony's earliest exports. This extractive trade in high-bulk, low-value wood products actually grew in importance even as the plantation economy focused on rice and indigo as its most valuable exports. In the mid-1760s lumber had "become a very profitable, quick saleable, and ready-money Article." Charlestown's growing population demanded fuel and building materials. Having cleared their own forests for sugarcane fields, Caribbean planters looked to the Lowcountry's expansive forests for their wood. With thousands of new slaves clearing tens of thousands of new acres every year, South Carolina plantations kept up with this rising demand for the humblest of commodities by keeping, and then expanding, a foothold in the "wood

business." By the close of the colonial period about a third of all plantations for sale were said to have good timber land, "conveniently situated" close to waterways so that it was profitable to transport pine boards
for building, staves for rice barrels, cypress shingles, red-oak bark for
Charlestown's tanneries, and firewood for its hearths.[115] As planters mobilized rising numbers of slaves across the Lowcountry, they made new
and more intensive use of its diverse lands, generating wealth through
commodity production, farm building, and speculation. South Carolina
plantations marked off the landscape for colonization and commerce
during the eighteenth century.

Describing planters' perceptions of the environment in terms of "volatility" and their interactions with it as a brand of "agency" would have
rung false in early modern ears, particularly because these concepts seem
to describe disorder and order as absolute states. As they commanded
water and shaped land, bought and sold real property, and bought more
enslaved workers who brought more acres into production, colonists
changed their position in relation to the natural world. Challenged by
their exposure to nature's extremes, they sought a stance of virtue with
which to contend with unpredictable fortune. Acquiring experience on
the land gave rise to the kind of expertise needed to transform it. The
first settlers were confounded by the scarcity of land thought best for
English husbandry and dispersed along the banks of rivers to claim it.
Those who followed made increasingly intensive use of swamps and pine
forests, uplands and lowlands, integrating the Lowcountry's diverse lands
and altering them to build plantations. This change in how plantations
made use of land, from their limited selection of uplands and pastures
to an exploitation of practically every type of riverside terrain, reveals the
extent to which colonists had adapted agriculture to the Lowcountry's
unique environment.

This changing material foundation for South Carolina's plantation
economy underwrote broader social and cultural transformations. The
idea of the planter as patriarch, the resident head of an extended household who ruled directly over enslaved dependents, lingered past its prime.
Even as this patriarchal model began to lack salience to describe the new
realities of the multiple-plantation enterprise and the rising numbers of
seasonal absentees who made their home in Charlestown, planters re-

tained it as an ideal. In practice, if not in theory, the increasing physical distance between slaves and masters disrupted the idea of the plantation as a world in and of itself. Using the methods of merchants and the sensibilities of colonizers, planters directed production and consumption on far-flung settlements, more often than not from Charlestown, an urban place deeply connected to the Atlantic world.

Seated in comfortable dominion over "my flocks and my herds, my bonds-men, and bond-women," Virginian William Byrd II saw himself living in plantation America like "one of the patriarchs." This vision of the colonial Chesapeake as a "silent country" in which masters and slaves were locked in place on the land bore little relation to the dramatic changes that South Carolina colonists initiated to develop their own plantation landscape.[116] Despite the eagerness with which elite colonists dwelled on the idea of the plantation as an entrenched estate, planters, by and large, were notable not for their attachments to land but for their willingness to buy and sell it, their tendency to move slaves to other, more promising spots for agriculture, and their accumulation of developed and undeveloped tracts across the vast extent of the region. Robert Wells preserved a shred of family dignity by noting that he "must make a reserve of his family's burying place" before selling it off. Others revealed such loose connections to their properties that they purchased them sight unseen after looking over a surveyor's map in town or prepared to sell lands that they owned, but had never seen, based on secondhand "intelligence."[117] Across a country described as "one continued plain and forest," they settled plantations "upon the sides of the rivers and watercourses."[118] By 1770, wrote the royal surveyor for the Southern District, this process was all but complete; "all lands upon and along the sea coast upon and between navigable streams and rivers are occupied, and at this time become private property."[119] Claiming the Lowcountry's lands in this way initiated a dynamic process of adaptation that continued long after surveyors laid down the line and compass.

— 4 —

City, Hinterland, and Frontier

For weeks after merchant William Dillwyn arrived in Charlestown in 1772, he scarcely ventured out of sight of the harbor. He devoted his days to a stock of imported dry goods and attending the city's small Quaker meeting. When he could spare a few moments of leisure, he admired the sights, including St. Michael's Church with its "pretty steeple." Already opposed to slavery in principle, Dillwyn would soon become a more "energetic friend of the Negro" as an active member of an inner circle that campaigned against the slave trade from London and Philadelphia.[1] His diary of this visit, however, betrayed no sign that he endured his stay in one of colonial British America's most repressive slave societies as an alienating ordeal. Far from experiencing any special revelation about the evils of human bondage, he reported feeling at ease at one associate's house because "his Negroes looked happy in their Situation." Neither was Dillwyn immune to the charms of the plantation countryside when he toured a Goose Creek neighborhood shortly before his departure. He appreciated the majesty of the "stately *Live oaks*" that lined the path to one "genteel" settlement. He marveled at a nearby "Seat" with its "Gardens Fish Ponds & Walks," a landscape of rural pleasures that stretched across twenty acres. Slaves cultivated small fields of the colony's staple commodity "here and there," Dillwyn observed, damming up small bottomlands to "raise a little Rice on." Had there been "fewer Negroes in Sight," he reflected, "we might have imagined ourselves in some Parts of Jersey."[2]

During the century that separated South Carolina's establishment as an English colony and its independence as an American state, colonists transformed the Lowcountry by adapting their plantations to its natural en-

126

vironment. They modified a British agricultural inheritance to settle the colony as a self-sustaining society in the seventeenth century. As they learned to plant swamps with rice after 1700, this shift to the wastelands changed the way planters valued land, accelerated their acquisition of it, and increased commodity production for the Atlantic economy. To pursue commercial agriculture despite turbulent weather, volatile markets, and restive slaves, colonists commanded water to develop their lands more intensively and on a grander scale. These changes on the land took place and had their most profound impacts within the boundaries of plantation tracts. The landscape that emerged from these changes after 1750, however, was more than the product of the same plantation form reproduced over space. A wider geographic view of landscape formation reveals the emergence of a sharp divide within the late colonial Lowcountry. What Dillwyn took to be a representative portion of the colony as a whole was in fact a diversifying core area of settlement characterized by small tracts, increasing material refinement, and production for the urban marketplace. What he did not see was the region's expanding frontier, a place of huge plantations, impoverished material culture, and an intense focus on growing rice for export.

This differentiated landscape grew out of a tension at the heart of South Carolina's territorial expansion. As plantation settlements expanded outward across space, they were also linked more effectively to Charlestown, the colony's only important city, port, and commercial center. To extend the geographic reach of the plantation economy beyond the handful of waterways that emptied into Charlestown harbor, colonists invested in building roads and clearing rivers during the first half of the eighteenth century. This flurry of improvements integrated an area for plantation settlement that clustered around the provincial capital. After 1730 the most adventurous speculators hunted for lands far beyond this plantation pale. They surveyed larger tracts of productive, tidal swampland along the colony's northern and southern coasts. To reach the isolated, sparsely settled rivers of this emerging plantation frontier, planters and merchants launched schooners into the ocean that delivered slaves, tools, cloth, and food and returned to town filled with barrels of rice.

Boundaries between core and frontier were never marked on any map, but the differences between the two zones structured basic working conceptions of the Lowcountry's economic geography. Centered on Charlestown as the hub to which all plantations connected, the core made the

planters resided in the city

frontier possible. Planters took up residence in increasing numbers in and around the city, making urban townhouses and hinterland retreats head-quarters from which they managed far-flung settlements. What the fron-tier lacked, the core provided. Overseers tasked slaves working on pro-ductive new tidelands first and foremost with rice work. Planters sent provisions grown in the core so that slaves could keep digging, em-banking, and hoeing on the frontier. The frontier's lucrative specialization in rice likewise made possible the core's increasing refinement and diver-sification. When they added frontier lands to multiple-plantation enter-

Map 4.1. Zones of settlement in the Lowcountry. Map by Philip A. Schwartzberg.

prises, planters no longer expected their core holdings to generate the bulk of their rice earnings. Relieved of this focus on commodity production, planters redeveloped their core plantations to make the most of their proximity to Charlestown consumers. As they populated a crude and brutal frontier with new slaves, colonists redesigned core plantations to make them comfortable for white bodies, more beautiful to British eyes, and as pleasant as they were profitable.

Shaping the landscape into these contrasting, yet interdependent, places was a culminating adaptation to the Lowcountry that changed the practice and meaning of plantership. As colonists extended the geographic reach of their enterprises into new zones of settlement, planting became an activity initiated from the city and enacted in the countryside. Although planters transported commodities to town routinely from even their most remote lands, some distances were not as easily bridged. The expanses that separated planters from plantations and masters from slaves changed the ways in which colonists exercised authority over slaves, overseers, and land. As patriarchal masters became distant managers, the plantation landscape diverged into a world of productive slave labor camps and well-cultivated market farms.

managers more than masters?

Zones of Expansion

Settlers linked together this fractured landscape, with its distinctive core and frontier zones, in spite of geography, not because of it. Only at the close of the colonial period did the Lowcountry, "low and unhealthy as it is," appear as a single place, designed for unimpeded "commerce and navigation." Its coastal plain, the largest in eastern North America, extends for some 500 miles along the Atlantic seaboard and reaches up to 50 miles into the interior. When rushing rivers descend from the mountains, they "lose their velocity when they reach the plains, through which they glide smoothly along, in a serpentine course, to the ocean." The ebb and flow of ocean tides across much of this flat expanse pushed watercraft into the plantation countryside and drew them back to the coast every day. Because the region was "every where interspersed with navigable rivers and creeks," the cost of bringing rice to market, "which otherwise would have been intolerable, was thereby rendered easy." Rice shipped from deep in the lowcountry interior bore transportation expenses comparable with those of plantations from which the masts of oceangoing ships could be seen.[3] Such a traversable, interconnected landscape seemed designed by nature for commercial agriculture.

Few working planters imagined the Lowcountry as a unified space for enterprise. Instead, they saw their region from within, as a differentiated patchwork of settlement stitched together over time and across space. Theirs was the view of the colonizer who saw the landscape from the comparative security and refinement of Charlestown. At the center of this region was a densely developed core plantation zone that took in the province's port city and its first-settled rivers. Surrounding the core like two cupped hands, the Edisto and Santee rivers anchored a secondary zone of settlement into which planters moved next in their search for new rice lands. Flanking this enlarged, central plantation district were two huge frontier zones, one along the southern coast and one along the northern coast, each of which was about the size of the core and secondary zones put together.

This core zone encompassed the watersheds of four rivers—the Stono, Ashley, Cooper, and Wando—that flowed into Charlestown harbor from four different directions and extended no more than forty miles inland. Few places in the Lowcountry were more constrained by the short reach of its rivers. Only the Stono connected the core beyond the range of these four waterways. Instead of discovering arteries of colonization that penetrated deep into the interior, the first settlers to reach their headwaters found themselves bogged down in impassable swamps. From the beginning, South Carolina was a society dispersed along the lengths of its waterways. Eighty-seven percent of tracts registered in the memorials, which track settlement patterns for the period 1673–1724, located land along one of the Lowcountry's rivers or on a tributary creek or swamp formation. With practically "all Plantations being seated on the Rivers," it took less than two decades for settlers to claim most of the lands along the Ashley and the Cooper, the two longest rivers of the core.[4] Charlestown, "pleasantly Seated, at the conflux of [these] two pretty rivers, from which all the Country product is brought down, and in return all imported goods are sent up the Country," grew from the colony's initial beachhead into the nucleus of an expanding plantation society. Immigrants who came over too late to acquire valuable river frontage were tempted to take up less desirable inland tracts by reports that one could "hardly plant your self 7 mile[s] from a navigable river." To claim their portions of the region's scarce uplands, the first planters settled far apart from one another, "scattering up and downe" the riversides.[5]

This dispersion undermined the development of market towns and villages that gave order to English rural life. Instead, planters, servants, and slaves lived in atomized sites, connected by "Creeks, which have a Communication from one great River to another," and oriented toward Charlestown by virtue of their common occupation of a single drainage basin. Although these small-scale rivers limited settlement within the core during the colony's first decades, this topography integrated early plantations into a ready-made transportation network. Spread out along deep-water routes, residents of the core went "to and fro by Canoo or Boat" and so rarely by foot or horseback that people went about unshod, as did their mounts.[6] Flat-bottomed boats, called "pettiagers," plied streams that "glid[e] on, gently," until they "mee[t] our larger Rivers," where "almost every Planter has the Pleasure of Sailing or Rowing with their Slaves, Carrying or Re-Carrying their Goods to or from their Market Town." Seaworthy schooners, carried inland on the flow of "one tide," could furl their sails as they navigated to plantation landings. This ease of water communication gave rise to a modern sensibility, one that typically depends on the reliability of automated travel, of space measured in "Hours distance from Town" rather than by miles.[7]

Just beyond the "narrow compass" of this core settlement zone, settlers in numbers from the late 1690s began claiming land along two great rivers, the Edisto and the Santee, that lay just beyond the core. During the first decade of the eighteenth century colonists were in the process of "seating" these "two New Rivers [,] . . . one in the South, the other in the North." Prospective planters converged on this secondary zone, recently the site of Anglo-Indian violence, for the chance to acquire "the choice of the best Land" that those who first settled the core had all but engrossed for themselves.[8] Lands granted on the Edisto and Santee extended the frontier of settlement to approximately forty miles from Charlestown in every direction.

Like most of the major rivers beyond the core, the Santee and Edisto flow from the interior directly to the coast, bypassing rather than intersecting with the nexus of waterways that defined the core. This fact of geography forced planters who settled in the secondary zone to put their slaves to work building passages to town that nature had failed to provide. Because both rivers were navigable for only the smallest vessels, this landscape had to be altered by human hands to connect secondary plantations to Charlestown, where rice, pitch, and other bulky commodities could be loaded onto oceangoing ships.[9] Planters colonized the southern, Edisto

River side of the secondary zone first, particularly around a coastal branch called the Pon Pon. Much of the land around the river consisted of "fine cypress swamps" regarded as "the best for rice." Despite the lure of so many productive acres, only a small portion of this "very valuable" terrain had been cleared for plantation fields by 1730.[10] The maze of "low islands, . . . innumerable creeks and narrow muddy channels" through which commodities were forced to pass to reach the port limited more thorough development. Only after slave gangs carved strategic "cuts," connecting channels that cleared a direct route to Charlestown, did the Edisto River grow into a viable extension of the core.[11]

Santee River lands altogether lacked the natural advantage of a navigable water route to town. Deploying the "great Industry" of conscripted

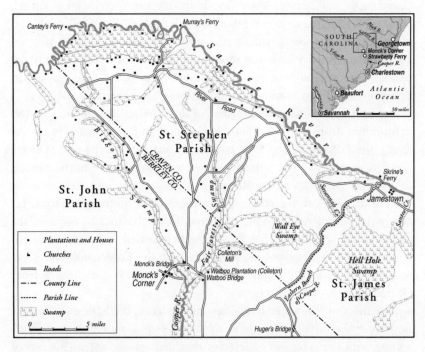

Map 4.2. Plantation settlement along the Cooper and Santee rivers, c. 1785. Colonists and slaves extended the reach of the rice economy into a secondary zone of settlement along the Santee River from the 1690s with a network of roadways that converged on the trading town of Monck's Corner. Map by Philip A. Schwartzberg. Source: Henry Mouzon Jr., *A Map of the Parish of St. Stephen, in Craven County* (London, 1773).

slaves, parish road commissions built a fan-shaped network of roadways between the Santee and the core zone. These wagon roads funneled the commodities produced by plantations scattered along the banks of the river to one of the core's most traveled waterways, the western branch of the Cooper River. Slave teamsters left their riverside plantations with loads of rice and, later, indigo to reach Monck's Corner, a small village of storehouses where schooners anchored to take on these commodities and ship them to town. By midcentury the sandy, well-maintained roads of the Lowcountry had "been made level, dry, and comfortable for driving, riding, and walking." A flurry of internal improvements between 1720 and 1740 established thoroughfares "for the benefit of carriages and coming to market" that linked the dispersed plantations of the secondary zone to Charlestown.[12] Only after the Lowcountry's pine forests were "conveniently traversed with publick roads" and its rivers "made passable with well-constructed wooden bridges" did the plantation landscape expand beyond the natural limitations of the core zone's topography.[13]

Before 1750 a sparsely settled frontier zone lay roughly 40–100 miles from Charlestown, on the Lowcountry's northern and southern coasts. No river route or roadway connected the province's vast extremities to its core. Land-hunting parties blazed overland paths through savannas and forests to prospect for new plantation sites. Planters took passage on schooners that voyaged into the open ocean to reach the "remote" plantations they established there.[14] Settlement along rivers of the southern coast was limited before 1750 because this area was located in a violently contested imperial borderland. A Spanish raid in 1686 dispersed the contingent of Scottish colonists that founded Stuartstown on Port Royal Island. Yamassee Indian attacks in 1715 "destroyed most of the out settlements of [the] province" between the Savannah and Edisto rivers, as well as some plantations within the recently established secondary zone.[15] In 1719, four years after colonists and allied Indians rallied to disperse the Yamassees, opening their territory (known as the "Indian Land") for white occupation, "all the land" south of Port Royal was still "deserted and intirely uninhabited." Only after the war had been over for nearly two decades did Henry Woodward, whose grandfather had abandoned an Ashepoo River plantation during the war, return to reclaim his inheritance. Settlers along the southern coast, as late as 1743, fled to the more secure core when rumors of a French or Spanish attack reached them on the eve of transatlantic conflicts.[16]

Despite the dangers of living at a distance from the colony's better-defended core, the opportunity to acquire fertile rice lands along the "banks of those larger rivers, that have their sources in the mountains," drew colonists to the frontier zone. Members of a surveying expedition to the northern coast's Waccamaw River in 1733 camped out in an apparent wilderness. They found a "great deal of good land," but also signs that others had been there before to claim it. These promising rice swamps were "all entirely taken up for above forty miles."[17] In 1736, at the colony's southern end, "all the Lands on the Carolina Side" of the Savannah River "were already run out" for some sixty miles inland. Planters contended with one another to possess large, flat tracts inundated by tidal rivers. Water that flowed over these plains left a "richness behind" that produced the "best Crops of Rice." Although the Savannah "had so long lain neglected whilst 'twas a remote Frontier of Carolina," the drive to own these productive swamplands had become so intense after 1730 that rival scouts literally raced one another to stake their claims.[18] The abundance of low-lying lands that made the frontier attractive for rice agriculture also made overland traffic through them unreliable. The roads were "often submerged and ruined by the overflow of rivers." Once settled in earnest after midcentury, plantations in the northern and southern wings of the coastal frontier featured river landings where the largest vessels could "lie close to the shore and load."[19] In place of the small craft that shuttled goods between town and countryside in the core, 100-ton ships and boats that could carry 100 barrels or more appeared at frontier plantations, many isolated in "remote Corner[s] of the Province," to take rice back to Charlestown and leave behind imported supplies.[20]

Of all tracts first granted before 1700 in the memorials, about seven out of every ten were claimed within the core. A few seventeenth-century grantees invested in the promise of the secondary zone. The acreage registered from these secondary zone grants amounted to just a quarter of what was claimed in the core. The early development of the frontier was even more tentative, amounting to a comparative handful of tracts granted in the period 1673–1699. Following close behind the Cooper and the Stono, the two dominant rivers of settlement in the core, were more than 20,000 acres derived from seventeenth-century grants along two other core rivers, the Wando and the Ashley, and the "populous" Goose Creek, a Cooper River tributary.[21] Tracts in the secondary and frontier zones, by contrast, centered almost exclusively on one or two rivers. So concentrated were early land grants along the rivers and creeks draining into Charlestown harbor that the colony was, for all intents and purposes, synonymous with its core zone. This clustering of landholding within a small area of settlement reveals early plantation society's meager purchase on an immense landscape that remained largely unoccupied by Europeans before 1700.

After 1700 the beginning of the transatlantic rice trade intensified plantation development in the core and secondary zones and propelled it into the coastal frontiers. The core remained the Lowcountry's most active zone of settlement in the first decades of the eighteenth century, as it had been in the last decades of the seventeenth. Total acres granted in the core and later claimed in the memorials increased by 134 percent from 1700 to 1724 compared with the earlier period. Despite this torrid pace of land acquisition, the core's share of the whole declined. Fourfold increases in acres granted in the secondary zone kept pace with the drive to possess new rice lands as these became scarce in the core. Threefold increases in the frontier zone reflected the rapid development of new, distant rivers. On the southern coast colonists surveyed the sea islands and became the first to stake claims along the Chehaw, Coosawhatchie, and Savannah rivers. In Winyah, as the northern coastal frontier was called, early eighteenth-century grantees took up lands along each of four rivers that merged to form Winyah Bay. Measured by the total acres recorded in the memorials, the size of English Carolina doubled during the first twenty-five years of the new century. Over the entire period 1673–1724, just over half of all acres granted fell within the dominant core, joined by another one-fourth granted along the increasingly integrated rivers of the secondary zone. About a quarter of all acres were claimed on a single core-zone river, the Cooper, the same proportion claimed throughout the entire frontier. Twenty-five years after the first large shipments of rice sailed for England, South Carolina's economy featured an intensively developed central planting district flanked by two large spaces into which planters and slaves were just beginning to advance.

Dividing colonial South Carolina into core, secondary, and frontier zones holds up an analytical frame to chart the plantation economy's expansion across territory. The language planters used to describe their landscape makes clear that this division was also a contemporary artifact of their geographic consciousness. They spoke of the most intensively developed core as the "Heart of the Settlements."[22] Seeing the Lowcountry from the perspective of ongoing, outward colonization put Charlestown at the center point of a widening semicircle of settlement. One radius of expansion traced an arc at "100 miles of Charlestown" that took in the whole of the Carolina Lowcountry, including the promise and vulnerabilities of its two large coastal frontiers. Another arc at "50 miles of Charles-Town" took in the well-integrated neighborhoods of the core and the "Midway" plantations of its secondary extension.[23] This 50-mile mark distinguished the interconnected hub that lay within this unofficial boundary line from the recently settled sites that fell beyond it. The "Out-settlements" to the "Northward" and the "Southward" became known as much for the tremendous yields of their rice fields as for their remoteness from settled society. As they extended the reach of their plantation economy by taking up lands and moving slaves across this line, planters saw the Lowcountry divided into distinctive zones for enterprise. Measured in terms of "Distance from Charlestown," this imagined division between core and frontier marked off a space for civility and refinement from one of crude productivity.[24] This particular sensibility of space undermines the image of the plantation as an isolated domain, detached from the larger society. Instead, when they imagined this expanding landscape, in commercial as well as cultural terms, colonists rendered every part of it in terms of connection to Charlestown, the colony's economic, political, and cultural center.

Core versus Frontier

That Charlestown should serve as this plantation colony's vital urban center, much less grow to become British North America's fourth-largest city, poses a troubling exception to the idea of the South as a fundamentally rural place. Like a streetscape of facades on a Hollywood soundstage, some have pictured Charlestown as a false city, one capable of dazzling the eye with the opulence of its elite material culture but little more than an empty shell when it came to paving the way for dynamic economic growth. Entrenched at the tip of a peninsula that projected into a busy ocean harbor, Charlestown has seemed a dependent outpost of transatlantic culture and commerce. It lacked the power to restructure production and exchange in the coastal interior, nurturing no significant "supporting hinterland towns" that could lead the plantation economy down a path of self-sustaining specialization and diversification.[25] Georgetown and Beaufort, two seaside towns located on either end of the frontier zone, amounted to little more than "inconsiderable villages" and served chiefly as places for schooners to take on rice for transshipment to Charlestown.[26] As the colony's first site of settlement, its seat of government, and the port through which people and goods passed between the colony and the Atlantic world, Charlestown reinforced its status over time as the only town that could claim the title of city. Rice's leading commercial characteristic—that it was bulky compared with its value and therefore expensive to ship—sealed Charlestown's dominance as the colony's central place of trade. Disembarking in 1767, a British visitor believed that he had arrived in the "Metropolis of South Carolina." Historians of Charlestown's anomalous growth have begged to differ. A fluke built on the accidents of geography and circumstance, British plantation America's largest city appears to have been an unlikely creation that stood apart as an "island of urbanization in a rural sea."[27]

To its prosperous white residents and their well-heeled guests, Charlestown emerged in the second half of the eighteenth century as the "liveliest, the pleasantest, and the politest place, as it is one of the richest too, in all America." Yet it did not become a force for the urban-led development of the Lowcountry as a whole. From a long-term perspective, the countryside's plantation focus blunted the potential impact of its city, diminishing the economy's capacity to shift resources from plantation agriculture to industry and leaving it vulnerable to volatile shifts in global commodities markets of the kind that proved its ruin by the early twentieth century. In the shorter span of time in which colonial planters settled the Lowcountry, however, the integration of town and country was the critical ingredient in stimulating economic growth. It was also the basis for South Carolina's distinctive pattern of social development, featuring a high degree of political unity among propertied whites. Early colonists, often divided by religion and residing in separate ethnic enclaves, competed with one another for power under the Proprietary government. By the mid-eighteenth century a largely native-born elite converged on Charlestown as a central place of trade, culture, politics, and residence. Wealthy planters and merchants joined together to rule the colony from town as a "rural-urban squirearchy" that dominated the ranks of the Commons House of Assembly, cemented ties through intermarriage, and shared a common stake in the fortunes of the plantation economy.[28]

Although colonial Charlestown did not prepare South Carolina for a dynamic industrial future, its role as a consumer market helped diversify the productive range of core-zone plantations. As settlement spread into the frontier zone after 1730, the plantations on direct water routes to town became smaller, more developed, and less focused on rice and indigo production. In 1776 only Philadelphia, Boston, and New York surpassed Charlestown's 12,800 residents, a large population by early modern standards.[29] Planters tasked slaves in the core to produce goods suited for the urban market. Tracts along routes to town sprouted warehouses, stores, taverns, and inns. Artisans escaped the city's ruinous rents by settling small, sandy tracts "only suitable for a tradesman." They became part-time planters and fully vested citizens as they practiced their crafts and put their slaves to work on modest workshop-plantations.[30] Easy transportation to town encouraged the manufacture of basic early modern materials such as lime and leather and a profitable trade in specialty lumber shaped for ship masts, wagon wheels, barrel staves, and hoop poles. Such was the demand for firewood on the peninsula, largely stripped of its forests by 1700, that a planter with a good stand of trees close to a river landing could "pay the purchase money three times over" just by selling fuel for urban hearths. A brick-making industry grew along the banks of the Wando River to supply the city with fire-resistant building materials.[31] One sign of this specialization in urban-focused production was the shrinking scale of landholdings nearest town. Plantations within five miles averaged only 266 acres, about half the median size of advertised plantations throughout the province. Only past the ten-mile mark—which we can see as a border between Charlestown's urban hinterland and its plantation countryside—did tracts exceed 500 acres and approach the typical scale required for rice production.

"What with the Nearness to the Market," these hinterland plantations became a "Kitchen-Garden for the Town." Sarah Woodward's James Island plantation, located "within sight of Charles Town," was surrounded by an orchard that produced figs and peaches, as well as an orange grove of forty bearing trees. She fattened "neat Cattle, Sheep, Hogs, Turkies, Geese, Ducks, and other Poultry" for sale in her pastures and pens. Richard Brailsford advertised more than 6,000 acres in small tracts along the Cooper River. These were unremarkable rice lands, but because they were located just nine miles from town, their value multiplied along with their uses. One could buy them to pursue "sawing, brickmaking, lime-burning, cutting firewood, marketing, or keeping stock upon for butchering, supplying the ship carpenters with spars and whiteoak, and the blockmakers and wheelwrights with ash." Rice, indigo, and maize still prevailed as dominant core-zone crops, but the diversification into manufacturing, commercial services, and "market-truck" that did occur in colonial South Carolina concentrated in the core zone on plantations prized for their "Vicinity to the Metropolis."[32]

Rice emerged as a plantation commodity within the core zone during the 1690s. For the next fifty years colonists settled more acres with more slaves there than anywhere else. In cleared freshwater swamps along the banks of the Cooper, Wando, Ashley, and Stono rivers, planters and slaves adapted rice growing to the Lowcountry, fashioning a plantation form that would serve as a template for expansive colonization. By 1750, however, it was clear that the core was past its prime as a bellwether for South Carolina's development. Peter Manigault spoke to its faltering reputation when he made light of a destructive summer storm that hit the colony in 1768. Those like him who planted in the "Less fruitful Plains of Goose Creek," he pointed out with irony, were "never uneasy about our Crops, because We have none to lose."[33] William Dillwyn confirmed that "Little Rice is now raised in this Neighbourhood." The very Wappo Creek tract on which Eliza Lucas conducted indigo trials during the early 1740s, launching the dye crop as the colony's second staple commodity, was later recommended as a place best suited for chopping wood, burning lime, and grazing cattle. Those still inclined to plant indigo and corn could do so, but there were only a few "patches fit for rice."[34]

The future of planting lay far from Charlestown in the "extremely fertile" rice lands of the frontier zone. Tidal rice agriculture began as a frontier innovation in the mid-1730s. Seven out of every ten tidal tracts put up for sale in the *South-Carolina Gazette* in the four decades that followed were located in the frontier. Irrigated by overflowing rivers that ebbed with the ocean tides, these lands produced "amazing Crops." Planters who reported their record harvests became "famous" for such feats of productivity, accomplishments made possible by massive investments in slave work to reshape the floodplains for agriculture.[35] These expert producers came close to achieving a perfect command of water on the tidal frontier and used it to irrigate rice, drown weeds, and replenish field fertility. This command generated extraordinary yields of six barrels per acre. Those who planted inland swamps in the core, by contrast, celebrated harvests that were half as productive.[36]

The frontier was a place that seemed "entirely adapted for Rice." In the core less of the land within each tract was suited for rice growing, about one-third of total acreage, compared with just under one-half in the frontier. On larger frontier tracts the size of these arable rice swamps was much larger as well, averaging 372 acres, compared with 204 in the core. Planters believed that the number of working hands that could be "employed with advantage" on a typical frontier plantation was about forty, compared with only twenty-five in the core. So few hands, warned Henry Laurens, could "plant very little more than will provide for themselves and afford the Family a little Rice & Corn." Twenty hands were enough to settle a "Snug and improvable little Estate," but twice as many slaves working twice as many acres would be required to begin amassing a fortune. So "middling" in quality were some of the wetlands in the core that sellers suggested turning them into "pasture land" or "rich Meadow" instead of planting them with rice. Frontier planters bragged that their lands were "inferior to none in the province for rice." More modesty was required in the core, where landowners qualified praise for their lands, describing them as being as "Profitable as any of their size" or as "good as the land in general is so near the Town." "A little plantation is a sorry undertaking," one planter of 200 acres noted with resignation.[37]

While slaves in the core planted rice in scattered spots, planters accentuated the scale of frontier swamps by presenting their dimensions in miles. Because such a small portion of these large potential rice fields had been cleared for cultivation, planters saw the frontier as a space for unlimited expansion. The region had so much of the "best of land"—some 40,000 acres on the Carolina side of the Savannah River alone in the 1760s—that one could imagine hundreds of slaves toiling "for ever" before exhausting its potential.[38] Compared with the concentrated patchwork of smaller, more developed lands in the core, the frontier zone was a place of large and largely unsettled landholdings. So intense was speculation in the promise of the frontier that undeveloped tracts outnumbered settled plantations by more than two to one in advertisements that listed them for sale. Next to the well-cultivated fields of the core, expanses of frontier river swamp formations were thick with standing cypress and tupelo trees, an indication of their fertility and a sign that they were "fit for a large rice plantation." In the core there were few new lands to settle and many that bore signs of long-term occupation, including "Old Fields" first cleared by lowcountry Indians and depleted rice plots rotated out of cultivation and then reintroduced "as new land." For those who sought high returns on expensive slave laborers, such tracts held little attraction. They were no match for "never planted" frontier lands, "FRESH and NEW and therefore the BETTER." When Peter Manigault bought up lands at Wassamsaw, one of the last unclaimed areas within the core in 1770, other planters ridiculed him for "playing the Fool."[39] Those inclined to follow the trend toward the frontier uprooted their slaves, sold their core lands, and founded new plantations in Georgia and Winyah and along the great tidal rivers of the southern Carolina coast. The slave populations of some core estates dwindled over time with these out-migrations as planters colonized new settlements far from Charlestown. Trading a "delightful prospect" of the Ashley River for a chance at larger rice profits, Peter Stone "remove[d] to the Southward" in 1768; Stephen Drayton abandoned the "pleasant healthy Situation" of another Ashley River plantation before heading to the "Northward" in 1771.[40] The core was the site of the colony's rice-planting past, but the frontier defined its productive future.

Labor Camps and Genteel Retreats

Nothing celebrated the plantation as a place of refinement more than a pretentious name. Seeing plantations as transplanted aristocratic estates has been a leading fiction in the myth of the Old South, one steeped in "archaic romanticism" since the mid-nineteenth century. Every notable estate, in retrospect, has seemed to require an ennobling name. A few colonists, to be sure, helped sow the kernel of truth on which it was based. Sir Alexander Nisbett insisted that his Cooper River plantation be called Dean Hall instead of its less elegant common name, Coot-Baw. Although William Donning had been content to call his settlement on the notoriously soggy lands at the head of the Ashley River Ponds Plantation, his wife, Frances Donning, strove without apparent success to rename it Weston Hall.[41] Such names took one of several paths to invest rough colonial places with a sign of gentility. They celebrated family prominence (Middleton Place, Drayton Hall), evoked English places (Hyde Park, Hillsborough), or preserved an exotic Amerindian past (Mepkin, Wambaw) that lamented, in a burst of "imperialist nostalgia," the peoples colonists had themselves displaced. Every site Samuel Gaillard Stoney memorialized in *Plantations of the Carolina Low Country* (1938) bore one of these kinds of status-elevating names.[42] One might expect that colonial newspaper advertisements would present an extensive catalogue of high-toned plantation names as sellers sought to add luster to their properties on the cool medium of the printed page. In fact, fewer than one in ten mentioned a name of any kind. Many of these names merely pointed to local geography (Cherhaw Bluff) or turned surnames into eponyms (Goddard's Plantation). Some, such as Bugby's Hole and the Ratt-Trap, even veered toward the vulgar. If we look only at those names that planters affixed to their plantations to enhance their cultural value, the actual landscape occupied by the new-world aristocratic estate shrinks smaller still. Only 61 plantations out of 1,343, less than 5 percent of all those advertised in the *South-Carolina Gazette*, bore such a status-elevating name. Most of these were confined to the core zone of settlement, and a mere handful were scattered across the length and breadth of the colony's expansive frontier zone.[43]

Beyond the clustering of named plantations, other signs point to a fundamental cultural and material divergence between core and frontier. By the turn of the eighteenth century a few planters had invested in dwellings designed to impress. With their brick walls, symmetrical forms, and multiple hearths, these were plainer versions of midsize English houses, but compared with the prevailing standard of "clumsy and miserable huts"—most of them dirt-floored, "earthfast" structures secured by wooden posts sunk in the ground—they stood out. By midcentury many more planters in the core built houses that could provide comfort, display wealth, and ensconce their white inhabitants in a bubble of modest luxury. Crowned by steep-gabled "Dutch" roofs, encircled by piazzas, and "painted, glaz'd and plaiseter'd" within, some of these structures were grand enough to merit the title of "Mansion-House." Rural white dwellings grew larger during this time, and many followed a "double-pile" plan with four rooms above and below.[44] This increase in the number of rooms allowed for greater specialization of the activities that took place within them. Interior space was a resource that encouraged eating in furnished dining rooms and hosting company in designated parlors. Within these walls planters ornamented rooms with "raised cornishes" and filled them with "genteel Household-Furniture," including glass cabinets "made after the newest fashion" to display books, china, and other prestige-bearing imports. Sunlight streamed through multiple "sash'd" windows (one planter boasted of his "30 Lights"), illuminating the clean lines and shining surfaces of these interiors. Detached kitchens, washhouses, and privies kept the inevitable smoke, heat, and stench of human life at a distance from privileged white senses. The multiple partitions between rooms functioned as "social buffers" that distinguished the material lives of whites within from those of blacks outside.[45]

A refined white residence was the central structure in an array of outbuildings that, together, gave a feel of permanent occupation. Beginning with a "genteel Dwelling-House," a truly "well-settled Plantation" required a small village's worth of buildings that centralized the plantation's dual functions as a place of production and consumption. White needs came first here, served by greenhouses and gardens, dairies and smokehouses, and chicken coops and stables. Corn cribs stored slaves' rations, and rice barns brought commodity processing into this circle of residence and oversight. Some kept these structures "neatly boarded and painted," built barns and storage sheds out of brick, and made these functional buildings "all of the best stuff . . . erected without any prospect of ever selling them."[46] Such care and expense remade one small portion of a rough plantation tract into a civil space for white residence. Most plantation structures were framed, roofed, floored, and paneled with pine and cypress that slaves harvested on-site as they cleared land for planting. When an old wooden dwelling house fell into disrepair, masters tasked slaves with cannibalizing its timber "for the building of a new." Using durable brick instead of perishable wood displayed wealth—bricks had to be bought and moved—as well as serving as a sign of entrenchment.[47] As an alternative to scarce stone out of which English manor houses were often constructed, brick met a higher standard for "neatness" and regularity compared with wood. Charlestown's plan imposed a grid of "Straight, broad and Airy" streets on the cityscape. In a countryside that could appear to whites as an unruly, Africanized wilderness, colonists invested in materials, finishing, and craftsmanship that set the best plantation compounds apart as places of intentional order. As the internal colonization of plantation land slowed within the core, planters with means commemorated their occupation of it with memorials of brick, glass, and carved wood.[48]

Planters pursued refinement most intensively within the core zone of settlement. The use of brick for building and the construction of dwellings large enough to devote rooms to consumption were materials with which colonists pursued refined lives in the countryside. The piazza, that sig-

nature architectural feature of the "Carolina taste," connected white residences to the surrounding landscape with refreshing breezes and gratifying views.[49] Gardens and orchards provided a buffer zone between the
built environment of the settlement and the rougher world of fields,
swamps, and forests that surrounded every plantation. Although the frontier held every advantage for rice production, core plantations dominated
each of these indicators of refinement. The core's share of all plantations
for sale was about twice that of the frontier's, a proportion reflected in
the number of white dwellings of any kind mentioned in newspaper advertisements.[50] Yet this densely settled zone was considerably more than
twice as refined by these measures. In relative terms, planters were far
more likely to invest their domestic spaces with the trappings of gentility
in the core than in the frontier. In absolute terms, colonists and slaves
experienced these settlement zones as contrasting material worlds, one
"improved" and "settled" and the other crude and in flux.

George Ogilvie came to South Carolina in 1774 to manage his uncle's
multiple-plantation enterprise. To inspect Charles Ogilvie's three properties "almost at the Oposite Corners of the Province," he imagined a
"Vagabond's life" as a plantation manager. So bad were the roads linking
"one Country Place to another" beyond the core and secondary zones
that he would be forced to undertake epic, 500-mile journeys that always
passed "thro the Metropolis of the Province" to reach Belmont in the
Backcountry or the settlement at Indian Land (Yamassee territory until
1716) on the southern frontier. He took up residence on a new island
tract in the Santee River delta, a landscape of broken tidal flats, and
immediately felt the weight of his isolation. This neglected border area,
straddling secondary and frontier zones, was as undeveloped as most
riverside lands in the core had been a century earlier. The future author
of the georgic *Carolina; Or, The Planter* took shelter in satire when physical comforts of any kind were hard to come by. "Myrtle Grove a terrestrial Paradize!" he declaimed in an irony-laced letter to his sister. On his
first night on the property he found himself "at least four miles distant
from any white Person—like the Tyrant of some Asiatick Isle the only
free Man in an Island of Slaves." The arrival of an overseer, his wife and
children, and other white visitors eased his racial isolation but sharpened
his sense of living rough in an encroaching wilderness. Now "Seven
Whites besides two or three Negroes" shared "what we call a House," a
shoddy structure made from a "few Rough boards naild together so nicely
as to admit the wind and the light through every seam."[51]

This impermanent dwelling stood on a solitary pine-barren knoll, practically an island within an island. Standing only "five feet above the level of the water," it was thus fully exposed to the "aguish vapours and in-fever'd air" thought responsible for deadly outbreaks of malaria infection. From this modest perch Ogilvie beheld a vast "open field" of level tide-lands, as ideal a setting for rice agriculture as it was ill suited for human life. Scattered here and there across the island's 3,000-acre expanse, a "few sandy Hillocks," amounting together to less than 5 habitable acres, remained above the rising waters that "covered the whole Island . . . and all the neighboring Islands once every twelve hours." In winter whites huddled in a shared bed, and a few blacks clustered around a kitchen fire as water seeped into the kitchen, glazing over with a thick coating of ice. Ogilvie used such images of nature breaching the thin defenses of a ramshackle house to illustrate the "Craziness of my Mansion." These waters receded to reveal a maze of "thick woods so matted with Briars and Shrubs . . . that there was no passing thro them without a Hatchet." On "Charming walks" across the property, "every step was up to the knees in Mud whilst swarms of Muskitoes [drew] Blood at every Pore." By surrounding himself in "Pavilions of Gauz," Ogilvie defended the few square feet of his bed every night as a refuge from these "devils in Minature." If it were not for this thinnest of barriers, the six interminable months in which the insects swarmed would have made "this Country Hell upon Earth."[52]

At Myrtle Grove "there was no ancestral farm that had flourished long and profitably." The experience of living on the frontier, "in the solitude of those forests that surrounded [his] infant plantations," informed Ogilvie's poetic portrait of Carolina planters as "*de novo* creators." Forced to turn this wilderness into a rice plantation, fifty slaves logged harsh tasks every day, hacking away undergrowth and excavating mountains of waterlogged soil. They retreated to houses he neglected to describe. Although the rudimentary measures that protected his own body from the elements—a few feet of distance from standing water, a working hearth, mosquito netting, and clapboard walls—were a constant source of complaint, one can imagine that most of the island's slaves desired these meager comforts as part of a desperate quest for survival. By the time Ogilvie arrived, they had cleared and embanked 100 acres, doubling the land's value before planting a single seed. Looking beyond his own suffering to tally the human costs of developing this "Sickly" place, he reported with relief that only one woman had died. Myrtle Grove's workers would soon be reinforced by a group of "New Negroes" imported to enlarge Ogilvie's command of land and water for rice. These recently enslaved Africans, first "seasoned" for good measure at his uncle's "old Plantations," would endure another disruptive migration before arriving on South Carolina's plantation frontier.[53]

Colonists who thought that they knew the province well could be shocked when they came face-to-face with conditions on this rude frontier. Instead of the "agreeable place" they expected, a party of weary travelers arrived at Black Mingo Creek in 1773 to find only a "very mean dirt timbered house" surrounded by "nothing but a wilderness." Some planned, in time, to construct "better Buildings" than the rough-hewn log or board structures that sheltered whites on newly settled tracts. Others, never intending to live on these distant holdings, provided only a dwelling that, while "neither wind nore watertite," was thought good enough to "serve an Overseer." With little time and what materials they could scavenge (excepting "a few nails"), slaves built their own "Negro Houses," mixing West African and European design elements to fashion "open temporary cabins." Planters expected these "huts" to molder into disrepair within a few years.[54] On tracts of land bought with an eye for how much rice they might yield, planters like Charles Ogilvie forced overseers and slaves to squeeze dwellings and low-yielding provisions grounds onto "pieces of high sandy land dispersed in the swamp." The space for settlement on one 300-acre Savannah River site was as cramped and exposed as that on Myrtle Grove. Its 4-acre "Knowle of high Land, just fit for the necessary Buildings," was surrounded by 296 acres of swamp, flooded and drained every day by a strong-flowing tide.[55] One could hope for a "sufficiency of good corn-ground" on a tidal plantation, where the "high Land, at best, is but bad," enough perhaps to provide a bare subsistence for the slaves who cultivated rice there. In this landscape of swamps, water necessary for advanced rice cultivation encircled places of habitation, "surrounding the Buildings," impoverishing material life, and limiting self-sufficiency in food and wood.[56]

As ambitious planters transported their slaves to the frontier in pursuit of rice profits, Charlestown's elite refurbished the long-settled plantations of the core into country seats. Determined to transform her father's Starve Gut Plantation into a proper "rural retreat," Alicia Hopton relied on Carolina friends abroad to send her maps and sketches, including one of Twickenham, Alexander Pope's famed "Sweet Retreat" outside London, to use as models.[57] When wealthy merchants grew "weary of attending the store, and risking [their] stock on the stormy seas," they idealized their new plantations as places of independence and solitude. Despite a professed "retirement" to the countryside, they kept a hand in commerce and a primary Charlestown residence. Benjamin Guerard promised the "Gentleman" discerning enough to buy his Ashley River plantation a "delightful RETREAT . . . well situated for Pleasantness and Agreeable Prospects." With a "Carriage and Four or Six Horses," he might also "come to his Business in Town in the Morning, and return to his Family in the Evening." Those city dwellers who yearned for rural gentility but lacked the means to buy such seats might yet afford one of the "little places of retirement," sold in parcels of "ten acres and upwards" just seven miles from town.[58]

This imported, late colonial aesthetic prized the "picturesque comfort" of the cottage over the imposing artifice of the Georgian mansion. Owning a "villa" in the core offered the gentleman planter and his family above all a "commodious" environment. When "contagious Distempers rage[d] in the Metropolis," the ability to retreat from town to country could be justified as something more than a fancy for rustic charm.[59] In a house seated on a "fine airy Hill," "open to the refreshing south-west and westerly breezes" that came in from the sea, a white family could escape the stultifying heat of the city in midsummer. Piazzas that opened dwellings to circulating air promoted "healthful ventilation and climatic comfort," along with other "conveniences" (including "Shade rooms" and brick cellars "fit for dwelling in summer") that could "moderate the rigour of a hot climate." Guided by standards for physical comfort that were fast defining urbanity in the Atlantic world, those whose parents had lived with less remade old plantations into places suited to this elite's recently acquired sensitivities.[60]

The success of rice agriculture was matched by a failure to replicate the English countryside in the Lowcountry. Slaves planted swampy wastes, left the stumps of trees to clutter the fields, and subsisted on crops of Indian corn when wheat failed to thrive. As the colony became a more settled place, early promoters insisted, it would become more English as well.[61] Although the debased material life of new frontier settlements exposed this progressive premise as so much wishful thinking, signs of anglicization multiplied on core plantations. One Ashley River property was "proper for a Gentleman's Villa," but it was not clear if its owner thought of it as a plantation, possessing as it did "every Building necessary on a FARM." With seventy acres "Cleared, and free from Stumps and Roots," it could be plowed and sown with wheat or hay grass but not planted in rice. The owner of Epsom Wells Plantation improved the land to make it yield "all sorts of English Grain." Others followed, cultivating wheat, rye, and oats once thought impossible to grow well in the humid Low-country.[62] The practice of letting livestock forage in wild savannas had long stigmatized planters as slovenly agriculturists. In the core, planters practiced better methods of animal husbandry, enclosing pastures, making hay, and planting special feed grasses. Well-cared-for cattle, pro-vided with ample fodder, were not allowed to stray past the fence line into the wilds beyond. In 1711 new immigrant Mary Stafford, com-plaining bitterly of the scarcity of mutton and beer, among other indig-nities, yearned to "return home to England where there is no want of any thing." Had she arrived in the core a half century later, she would have found more familiar comforts and fewer alienating differences. Low-country beer was still a rarity, but sheep, horses, and cattle, some "of the English breed," were common sights. Few "old settled plantations" were without a team of oxen.[63] Although tended by enslaved "dairy wenches" rather than English "huswives," the "good tame milch cows" of the core, often penned in old rice fields to "glean after Harvest," produced "good Butter and Cheese."[64]

Flowering next to exotic peach and pomegranate trees, groves of cherry, apple, and plum made some orchards "resemble old England." Intensively cultivated rural and urban gardens remade small parts of the landscape into preserves of English sensibility. Instead of the functional, but ugly, worm fences that kept roving cattle out of the corn, these "pretty little garden[s]" were marked off from their surroundings by neat pales.[65] Often under the supervision of elite white women, black gardeners hauled manure, raised beds, and pruned trees, employing the most advanced English techniques for enriching and cultivating the soil. Whites strolled down walkways of shady orchards and inhaled the fragrances of gardens for "pleasure and kitchen" that gratified the senses a second time when their fruits and vegetables came to be eaten. Focused on English vegeta-bles, the first provincial gardening manuals detailed routines for Irish potatoes, but no sweet potatoes. Beyond a few appropriated ingredients (okra, squash, and watermelon), this intensifying "spirit of horticulture" that took hold "in the vicinity of Charlestown" left the produce of the slave plot and Indian field by the wayside. The manuals instructed gardeners how to grow asparagus, radishes, and carrots, as well as a variety of "aromatic herbs" traditionally used to flavor English foods, including hedges of rosemary, thought to cleanse the air and "guard domestic spaces against polluting odors."[66]

Just as eighteenth-century English landowners transformed their least productive farmlands into "Parks and Pleasure Grounds," their Carolina counterparts followed suit, building bowling greens, keeping hives of bees, and grafting "English Fruit-Trees" onto native stocks.[67] Slaves had always ventured into the wilderness beyond plantation settlements in search of food and game. Their masters, by contrast, enjoyed their plantations as places for the genteel pleasures of "Fishing, Fowling, and Hunting." In winter their fields became game preserves; in summer they cast lines into artificial ponds stocked with "Perch, Roach, Pike, Eels and Cat-fish." Some built "well connived Aviaries" to house pigeons and doves. One planter so treasured his "tame fat Fawn" as an exotic pet that he was willing to pay for damage it caused grazing at will in the neighborhood.[68] Planters ornamented plantation settlements with gardens and orchards in large numbers before midcentury, but the rage for larger, formal sites began shortly before American independence. A few such gardens have been located in the secondary and frontier zones, but surviving material evidence suggests that they clustered disproportionately within the core. Despite planters' efforts to remake the core into a recognizably English rural place, most of the plantation countryside "neither afford[ed] flowers to regale the senses, nor the vegetables necessary to the comfort of [their] families." With "so great profits from the cultivation of rice," colonists "neglected the culture of gardens" on their most productive plantations. The staples of the English stewpot (cabbages, potatoes, and onions) continued to be imported from more temperate colonies to the north.[69]

Planters in the Chesapeake imposed "great houses" on the landscape, symbols of rank meant to be gazed at from far below by social inferiors. Lowcountry planters were more interested in sightlines that traveled in the opposite direction, from houses that offered views of the surrounding landscape to white eyes. From its "rising eminence" on the banks of the Pon Pon River, Benjamin Fuller's house opened an "agreeable Prospect on every side." Charlestown's mansions and churches and its bustling harbor were visible from the high bluffs that overlooked the city. Those farther inland took pleasure in seeing the houses and grounds of their neighbors. From its "pleasant healthy Situation" high above the Ashley River, one plantation had the "Command of Fourteen or Fifteen Gentlemen's Seats on each Side of the River." Another looked out on the "agreeable Prospect of the Honourable *John Drayton*, Esqr's Palace and Gardens."[70] These sights confirmed membership in a community defined by a shared commitment to material improvement. Above all, landowners prized "delightful" and "beautiful" prospects "up and down the River." As the key visual element in landscape paintings, an emerging genre in this era, water could be turbulent or still, a cue that told the viewer which of nature's two sides was on display. Planters liked to admire their rivers at peace. Watching their waterways flow toward the harbor reminded them that although they retreated to their plantations, they were never locked there in rural isolation. These rivers kept them in constant connection with Charlestown.[71]

Planters displayed images of the English countryside on the walls of their country homes. One of the Elias Balls, just "compleating the decorations" of a new house, commissioned "two handsome Landscapes of Kensington & Hyde Park" adorned with views of "Woods, Fields, & Buildings & some little addition of Herds, Huntsmen, &ca." Barnard Elliott ransacked London's print shops to find English farming landscapes that could "ornament" the "Hunting Hall at Benfield," his friend's country seat on the Ashley River.[72] On the frontier, where the view from ground level could be dispiritingly crude, the distance between this rural English ideal and the realities of large-scale rice agriculture were difficult to reconcile. Far from Charlestown, prospects bore even more of the weight of the notion that plantation settlement improved the landscape, making it more civil and more English. James Deveaux's 906-acre plantation contained "rice land enough to employ 70 working hands." The picture it presented of a new plantation neighborhood was not only that of crude productivity. From his piazza one could take in a "prospective view of Sheldon," the "seat" of the lieutenant governor, as well as the new brick church, "esteemed the compleatest piece of building in any country parish in this province." Anchored by these two landmarks of refinement in the still-rough environs of Prince William Parish, the rest of the plantation landscape appeared in a new light. The three rice plantations visible on the other side of Tomotley Savanna appeared less like rough labor camps and more like "so many small villages." With "their rice fields before them," they "exhibit[ed] so delightful a scene, that the sight is ravished and the mind charmed therewith." If one squinted, it was possible to see an image of the English countryside even on the rice frontier. Viewed from above and afar, the swamps, long a symbol of South Carolina's crude landscape, could make a "pretty prospect."[73] This vantage was less a panorama of command than a chance to refine the aesthetics of the plantation landscape from a distance.

In 1739 near the banks of the Stono River, one of four waterways that defined the core zone, slaves attacked and killed as many as twenty-five colonists. Two years after the uprising Henry Hyrne advertised a plantation on the river featuring a "Chaise House" and a "very good Orchard." On any given night by the 1770s "seldom fewer than 40 or 50 fugitive slaves" might be concealed "within 10 miles of Charles-Town," the capital's diversified hinterland. Hundreds traveled between town and countryside to exchange goods for sale and scores gathered on the city's outskirts to take part in a "Country-Dance, Rout, or Cabal of *Negroes*." Colonists remade parts of the core zone into a recognizably English rural place. The bucolic landscape they imposed, however, was a veneer that can conceal the material world created by its black majority. Swept dirt yards, provisions fields, and palmetto-thatched dwellings marked out "as 'twere a Nation within a Nation." In "all the Country Settlements," slaves lived in "contiguous Houses" and "labour[ed] together and converse[d] almost wholly among themselves."[74] Increasing white material refinement took place alongside the articulation of black life in the densely populated core zone. African Americans in the Lowcountry cultivated a degree of cultural autonomy throughout the eighteenth century, but these spaces for independent activity did not remain unscathed. As core and frontier developed into contrasting plantation zones, this divergence changed the slaves' world by reshaping their labor.

Changing Tasks

Mobility was this society's most powerful expression of practical power. It demonstrated the freedom to move from places of disease, ugliness, and suffering to those of health, comfort, and conviviality. The ability to traverse settlement zones was a key to survival and a pathway to achievement. The rich whites who ruled South Carolina moved between town and country with magisterial ease. When British naval forces converged on Charlestown harbor in 1780, spectators watched the exchange of cannon fire between Fort Moultrie and the invading ships. As soon as this defense of the city ceased, a Hessian officer watched as "everyone disappeared from the ramparts," followed by a "quantity of small vessels sailing up the Cooper River into the country."[75] This extraordinary exodus was part of an ordinary pattern of white flight from dangerous environments. When faced with smallpox in the city or malaria in the country, whites moved out of the path of disease outbreaks, shifting the epidemiological burden of plantation production onto slaves and overseers forced to remain behind.

Expansive colonization changed the work of planting. As planters acquired lands across the Lowcountry, their roles shifted from direct mastery to distanced management. After his visit to Charlestown during the winter of 1764–1765, Lord Adam Gordon reported that the planters he met there had "made a trip to the Mother-Country," had enrolled their children in British schools, and seemed prepared by temperament and wealth to leave their American province for a "home life" as absentees. What kept them in Carolina were the demands of managing their plantations, which required the "immediate overlooking of the Proprietor." At the same time, he observed that "every family of Note have a Town residence, to which they repair on publick occasions, and generally for the three Sickly months in the fall," a busy phase of the agricultural calendar that coincided with the rice harvest.[76] As his elite hosts provided the details that filled the pages of Gordon's journal, perhaps across the polished dining tables of their well-appointed townhouses, he might also have wondered what was taking place on the plantations as they spoke with such authority about South Carolina's distinctive society and economy.

Even the most attentive planters, those who spent more time in the malarial countryside than in Charlestown's refined environs, could not be in more than one place at the same time. As colonists acquired lands scattered across the Lowcountry and settled slaves to work them, this extensive mode of planting marked a sea change in the development of plantations as units of production and as places of social order. Increasing white wealth underwrote the acquisition of multiple plantations. With few alternative investments that could match the promise and security of planting, Lachlan McIntosh segued from trading into land and slave ownership in the early 1760s in order to "realize some part of [his] loose money." Ralph Izard wondered what to do with £5,000 sterling he had "in the Bank." His agent recommended settling a new indigo plantation and adding "ten Negroes apiece to the other Plantations. Thus the money will do very well." Izard's 1777 tax return recorded that he owned 8,070 acres and 508 slaves and still had thousands of pounds for which he could find no better use than to lend out at interest. From a modest brick house on his "home" plantation on the Ashley River, called Burton, or from his elegantly furnished Meeting Street townhouse, he directed six other plantations. Another planter found himself without "rice land sufficient to employ all the Negroes" and "embarrassed how to dispose of about 20 to 25 workers." With rising numbers of slaves came the increasingly commonplace practice of managing more than one plantation to put them all to work.[77]

As the ownership of multiple tracts of land in the memorials suggests, it was "very common for Men to keep several plantations at once in their own Hands" from the late seventeenth century. What had changed by the later decades of the eighteenth century was the scale of these multiple-plantation enterprises and the distance of their component parts from one another. About one-third of all individuals who advertised lands for sale in the *South-Carolina Gazette* had more than one tract to sell; about one-tenth had more than one developed plantation to sell.[78] Because sellers probably advertised only a part of a larger estate through the newspaper, these proportions offer only the most conservative estimate of how pervasive multiple-plantation ownership actually was. At the more modest end of the spectrum, seventy-two planters put up for sale at least two of their plantations; at the most extreme, Francis Yonge offered the most of any seller, fifteen separate plantations over a span of forty years. Favorable inheritances, wealth-concentrating marriages, and strong commodity earnings for much of the 1760s and 1770s enlarged late colonial estates into multiple units of production. Although Joseph Allston had "begun the world with only five negroes," he had amassed an estate of "five plantations with an hundred slaves on each" before his fortieth birthday. At the time of his death in 1780, John Drayton, a visitor marveled, was "very rich, had 10 plantations & about 1000 Negros."[79]

Another effect of multiple-plantation ownership was the creation of a new class of plantation managers. Planters relied on overseers and enslaved drivers to run the day-to-day business of planting. Hiring other planters to "undertake the direction and inspection of the overseers" had once served as a temporary expedient, bridging the gap when planters died with only minor heirs or made an extended trip to Europe. By the 1760s the post of plantation manager became a permanent supervisory position.[80] With plantations scattered across the Lowcountry, planters appointed local or itinerant planters on the prudent grounds that "no Overseer at a distance from his employer should at any time be without an Overlooker." A manager visited the plantations, inspected the land and slaves, interrogated overseers, and exercised decision-making authority, backed by his own elite status, on the planter's behalf.[81] Merchant-planter Peter Manigault criticized the increasing reliance on "Gentleman Managers," reasoning that "every man can see better to his Business himself than any other person can for him." He refused to hire William Moultrie to manage one of Ralph Izard's indigo plantations because "he manages his own Affairs so wretchedly that, he ought rather to have somebody to overlook him." Although Manigault railed against the use of "these Super Intendants," his commitment to a tradition of direct planter management was out of step with the demands of newly enlarged enterprises.[82]

As planters acquired slaves, they added "House to House" and laid "Field to Field" across the extent of the settled Lowcountry.[83] Rather than presiding over work and life at their plantations, they orchestrated the transfer of slaves between individual holdings, established new settlements, and managed integrated enterprises from afar. The role of water as the sine qua non of rice production made it possible for planters to design a plantation's irrigation system without being there to implement it. They made strategic choices about building fields, reservoirs, dams, and ditches from the comfort of their urban residences. After inheriting slaves and land in 1766, Richard Hutson returned home from Philadelphia College with a divinity degree and the intention to "turn Planter." He imagined that his new calling would mean spending a "great part of my time in [the] Country." After the better part of a year living in his "little house" on his rural estate, Hutson returned to town. He had gained enough experience in the "planting business" to issue confident written orders to his overseer about the importance of clearing the plantation's drains after the rice harvest. Although his James Island plantation was an easy boat ride across the Ashley River, he saw no reason to leave Charlestown to direct the project himself.[84]

Daniel Ravenel's plantation encompassed a complex swamp formation with four separate branches. Deciding how to "unite and concentrate these into one, and bear off the water when in excess, as well as distribute it into the fields," was the critical task of the season. Since Ravenel "resided in Charleston during the summer months when the work had to be chiefly carried on," he summoned his driver to town to take his orders. Removing the carpet from the floor of the hall, he chalked out a map of the plantation's "swamp, the creeks, [and] watercourses" for the "driver's study and understanding."[85] After charging overseers and drivers with building new fields and extending irrigation channels to water them, planters held their subordinates to account during periodic visits to see how well work on the ground fit their vision for the plantation's productivity, order, and expansion. Gideon Dupont Sr. proudly led visitors to his property on horseback to behold its newest project of improvement in progress: 130 slaves digging a quarter-mile-long ditch designed to divert the flow of a nearby river into a "large piece of low ground above two hundred acres to water it for rice." "[I]f you do not make good crops" on good tidal land, one experienced planter advised another, "you or your overseer deserve censure and not your Negroes." High yields reflected how well any planter had shaped land and water to suit the unique conditions of his tract.[86]

For a multiple-plantation owner who lived in town, it paid to have a "Half-Way Place to his Southward Plantations." On periodic tours of inspection he could stop overnight and load provisions en route to the frontier.[87] Such nonresident planters saw their plantations less as places to rule and more as systems of production to keep in motion. They thought of individual plantations as component parts of a larger enterprise and worked to integrate them from Charlestown by organizing an internal commerce in provisions, cloth, and commodities. We know something of this view of planting from the images colonists commissioned to represent their plantations. These maps took a bird's-eye perspective on the land, which was abstracted into a network of fields and irrigation works that could be managed in absentia. Like English estate maps, these images were both working documents with which to plan development and a graphic representation of the overarching command to which elite planters aspired.[88] This view from above presented the plantation as a field for enterprise on which slaves could be mobilized by proxy to expand, maintain, and cultivate. Planters measured the reach of their irrigation systems by the number of acres they could "flow."[89] John Martin estimated the annual income he expected from an inherited rice plantation based on a labor force of about fifty working hands. These slaves would cultivate approximately 170 acres. Because every acre yielded three barrels, every barrel weighed about 650 pounds, and rice would sell at 43 shillings per hundredweight, by his calculations the plantation was capable of producing the small fortune of £1,000 sterling every year. Martin, a recent English immigrant, made explicit an equation that other planters knew by rote. Directing the work of so many slaves on so many acres from a distance, they estimated the profit per year for each slave worker, "clear of all expenses," before a single seed had been planted.[90]

For most slave workers, intensifying labor demands in the rice and indigo fields framed a very different view of the plantation from within rather than from above. As planters moved across the landscape and orchestrated flows of goods and people from town, overseers drove field hands to work longer and harder, spending more hours every day and more weeks every year engaged in commodity production. The work required to irrigate rice stretched out the seasons that slaves spent completing tasks.[91] With water enough to drown the weeds, slaves spent less time working in the fields attacking "grass" with hoes. Creating and maintaining well-irrigated tidal squares, however, required a new regimen of tasks between the fall harvest and spring planting. Slaves now worked through the winter, once a lull in the agricultural calendar, extending and repairing the irrigation infrastructure that made it possible to water rice by the tides. During the spring and summer months they spent more time leveling ground, clearing drains, repairing banks, and cleaning ditches than they did sowing rice seed or hoeing through the growing crop.[92] These improvements lightened the burdens of field labor but dramatically increased the work of building the irrigation systems themselves.

As planters initiated monumental efforts to reshape the land for rice agriculture, they insisted on not making "a Barrel less" of rice.[93] A planter who owned thousands of acres and hundreds of slaves across the northern frontier, Joseph Allston had "the best dams in So. Carolina." His well-ordered rice plantations were made possible by notoriously heavy ditching tasks of 600 cubic feet per day. At this rate, each worker excavated, with hoes, spades, and hands, enough soil to dig his or her grave four times over every day. Former slaves hated cold winter "mud work" so much that they refused to do it at all during Reconstruction.[94] Lowcountry slaves, like other preindustrial agricultural workers, had become accustomed to alternating between intensive labor, especially during crop harvests, and periods of lighter work. Planters, like other calculative capitalists of the era, sought to increase returns per laborer by investing in technologies to increase productivity and fill gaps in the productive calendar with more work.[95]

Slaves and masters embraced the task labor system, put in place during the origins of South Carolina's rice culture in the early eighteenth century, because it eased the disruptive pressures that intensive commodity production placed on slave households. Under its rules, slaves who completed a daily work allotment before dark could take what remained of the day for themselves. A mutual adherence to past practice sustained the system, which flourished in the space where the antagonistic desires of masters (for a noncoercive means of compelling labor) and slaves (for time to use as they wished) intersected. Although this arrangement had hardened into a customary right by the end of the colonial period, a second wave of agricultural change after midcentury eroded its effectiveness as a means of limiting the plantation's demands on slaves' time. The advent of large tidal rice plantations and indigo as a second major export commodity weakened the task system as a barrier against the more comprehensive exploitation of enslaved workers.

The simple principle behind tasking made it so adaptable to different kinds of labor that it survived slavery itself in the Lowcountry. Despite changes in production, masters continued to apportion work by the individual, daily quota. By midcentury each phase of corn and rice cultivation, from sowing seeds to harvesting grain, had been assigned a task value, usually between one-quarter and one-half an acre of work per slave per day. Rice processing was measured by the peck or mortar, and with the expansion of irrigation systems slaves dug ditches and drains by the cubic foot or the "quarter." So thoroughly did planters extend tasking to new types of labor that their synonym for a working slave was a "taskable hand."[96] Despite the persistence of the task system, the demands of field work intensified as planters put in place more elaborate irrigation systems to achieve a greater command of land and water. Overseers tasked slaves to exhaustion and beyond, keeping them "so closely to hard labor" that the Assembly attempted to prohibit working days longer than fifteen hours in 1740. Hannah was one such overtaxed worker. She came so "late out of the Field from her Work" one typical evening in 1749 that she "laid down upon her Bed with all her Cloaths on, and fell asleep." Slaves worked so "hard to Compleat their Task" of processing rice by hand that planters believed that some literally worked themselves to death, sometimes through the night "by the light of pine torches."[97] Older and weaker workers, if they were not able to draw on the assistance of "able young Negroes," were often unable to complete their tasks, much less produce rice or corn on their own accounts.[98] Although it was sometimes "impossible" for slaves to complete the work they had been assigned, masters and overseers nevertheless inflicted "30, 40 or 50 lashes" routinely on those unable to bear the burden of their daily tasks.[99] Only the strongest, healthiest workers could expect to complete their tasks in time to set themselves up as independent producers. On tidal rice plantations with heavy daily work burdens, they relied on their masters' largesse for a few days off every season to plant and harvest their own crops.[100]

As much as tasked labor preserved the principle of the slave's own time in the face of agricultural change, it did not stand in the way of a net expansion of labor demands over the course of the year, nor did it prevent changes in the character of labor that were bad for slaves. Its very survival as a barrier against unmitigated planter control over work has seemed to mark a "victory for the slaves" by demonstrating that slaves retained their agency and expressed their humanity under the most repressive conditions.[101] The idea that the task system, once introduced, opened a breach in the operation of plantation slavery ignores the plight of field workers in the second half of the eighteenth century. This thin-edge-of-the-wedge reasoning imagines that the system created a sphere of slave autonomy that only grew larger over time, that planters were powerless to challenge its encroachment, and that it acted as a solvent on the stability of this plantation society, gradually undermining slavery by exposing its internal contradictions.[102]

The task system's persistence in the Lowcountry reflected slaves' tactical agency, but it did not protect them against strategic shifts in labor that worked against their interests. Even as the system continued to reserve a place for slaves at the metaphorical negotiating table, its role as a bulwark against the appropriation of labor time eroded. When planters altered the mode of rice production, they moved the benchmarks for what was considered "Proper and Necessary" labor. Claims of urgent necessity justified exceptions to the rule of tasked labor, trumping claims of long-standing custom without igniting widespread slave resistance. When flooding rivers damaged the irrigation works on one plantation, the overseer forced slaves into the fields throughout the winter of 1772. The "Negroes indeed complain'd to me," wrote the plantation's agent, "that they had been hard work'd; but for this there was a kind of necessity, . . . to have the Banks

secur'd was to save the Crop from being hurted by overflowing Tides."
When Richard Hutson's plantation drains needed repair, he wrote from
town to order the overseer to "be with [the slaves] as much as possible
and see that they lose no time." Instead of working at their own pace,
his slaves now rushed to complete the job under direct white supervision,
working much as gang laborers throughout plantation America did.
Without fail, water eroded earthen embankments, and debris clogged the
drains. For those who reinvested their rice profits in new slave workers,
there were always new fields to carve out of the swamps and new canals
and banks to extend to water them. Putting a rice plantation in "good
order" opened a claim on slaves for "essential" work that took precedence
over all else, including the task system's daily limit on labor. Planters used
agricultural change to justify heavier work loads as necessary and therefore reasonable demands.[103]

After its introduction in the mid-1740s, indigo production claimed the
time of thousands of enslaved workers. As a new crop for lowcountry
slaves, indigo lacked a work history and thus fell outside the customary
labor arrangements that masters and slaves had negotiated decades before
to ease the introduction of rice into the plantation economy. Some slaves
probably cultivated indigo plants by the task, but these assignments never
gained the universal status of rice's "quarter acre." One improving planter
urged that slaves "should be always kept in Gangs or parcels & not scattered over a field in Tasks," but slaves, with customary right on their side,
successfully defended the task system in the rice fields. For indigo, however, planters imposed gang labor throughout the productive process. "It
is customary," wrote one indigo planter, "for every gang or set of hands to
work, from the beginning, the land belonging to the respective set of vats
for which they are designated, and to perform all the requisite duties in
their several departments, without interfering with each other's gangs."[104]
Intensive work from the first July cutting to the first frost of the season fell
across that part of the agricultural calendar that slaves used to produce
their own crops. Depending on the size of the indigo works, five to ten
hands rotated between the fields and a set of processing vats during the
harvest, moving through a synchronized set of duties as the plant was
transformed into dye. They reaped the plants, pumped water for the vats,
beat the infused liquid, and, finally, pressed and cured the indigo "mud"
into cakes of dye for export. Specialized indigo plantations might run five
sets of vats or more, engaging scores of workers in these routines.[105]

Indigo in Carolina, like sugar in the West Indies, imposed a processing phase that, because it was both time and quality sensitive, encouraged direct supervision and the coordination of interdependent tasks. From the moment that slaves began harvesting the plants, indigo production demanded the sunrise-to-sunset commitment of slave labor. During the "making season" indigo planters took away the slaves' Sundays to keep production on schedule. As Peter Sinkler supervised the processing of his first indigo cutting, he returned so late every night and woke so early every morning that he "never for three weeks saw the face of his wife or daughters." One can imagine little respite for the slaves who worked under him.[106] Unseen chemical transformations, by which compounds in the plants' leaves were turned into coloring agents, determined dye quality and volume and thus the market value of the year's crop. Indigo makers took extraordinary care with each step in the process, imposing inflexible standards on workers, who had to cut the stalks at the exact moment of maturity, carry leaves cautiously from field to vat, and beat without pause the fermented fluid in which the plants had steeped. Planters held hired and enslaved indigo makers accountable for the final product, encouraging them to impose a rigid work discipline. A novel staple with exacting processing requirements, indigo insinuated gang labor into the task system's stronghold.

Figure 4.1. An indigo plantation during the "making season." Detail of Henry Mouzon Jr., *A Map of the Parish of St. Stephen, in Craven County* (London, 1773). Courtesy of the South Carolina Historical Society.

Agricultural change hurt most field hands, forcing them into more intensive labor on the land. At the same time, it privileged those who filled new positions in more elaborate labor hierarchies.[107] Workers on tidal rice plantations could aspire to become "trunk minders" who maintained and operated irrigation gates or operators of water-powered processing mills. Indigo makers joined slave drivers as part of a small class of enslaved managers. Those entrusted with finishing the dye put down their hoes for the iron tools that shaped indigo cakes. Slaves throughout the Lowcountry worked as carpenters, coopers, and sawyers—the three most common skilled slave jobs.[108] In the densely settled core these and other craftsmen could work as itinerant "jobbers," plying their trades in the city and from plantation to plantation, returning to their masters to hand over a portion of their wages. With farm production for the urban marketplace came new jobs that took slaves out of the rice fields. Before black cooks placed dishes of English vegetables, orchard fruits, and barbequed fowl on the dining tables of the urban elite, slave boatmen carried produce and livestock to the Lower Market, where enslaved marketers, many of them women famous for their shrewd dealing, monopolized the sale of "poultry, fruit, and eggs . . . brought thither from the country for sale."[109]

At the end of the colonial period, as many as one in four slaves worked in specialized jobs that offered the most promising path toward acquisition, mobility, and autonomy.[110] Slaves entrusted with these jobs were loath to return to field work. Planters exploited this point by demoting them to "perform a task every day," punishing them for shoddy work or unruly behavior with a degrading descent in rank. Peter Gourdin provided posthumous protection for Billy in his will, insisting that he "not be put to any field work, but be kept a jobbing on the plantation and in the proper seasons to tend the Indigo works about the Vatts as in my lifetime." Quackow, who supervised rice labor on a Pee Dee River plantation, was not as lucky: for his "dishonesty," the plantation's agent was to "degrade him from his present office of Driver, into that of a common Field hand."[111] For slaves forced to labor as taskable hands, agricultural innovation in rice and indigo production amounted to an assault on customary work limits preserved by the task system. As conditions in commodity production worsened for most slaves, diversification within the core increased the need for skilled slaves who could work on their own between town and country.

Precise profiles of plantation demographics are hard to come by, but the frontier's focus on field work seems to have skewed the composition of slave communities there toward disproportionately African, young adult, and male populations. Compared with the Chesapeake Tidewater, as well as the nineteenth-century Lowcountry, few colonial South Carolina plantations featured balanced distributions by age and gender, a reflection of disrupted populations unable to reproduce naturally over several generations. Examples from the frontier in particular show spikes in the 20–40 age range, an absence of children, and imbalanced sex ratios.[112] Thirty-four "plantation negroes" lived on one Georgia plantation, twenty-seven of whom were male. On a Combahee River settlement there were a few children, but only four slaves out of fifty "whose Ages exceed Thirty-five Years."[113] Colonists who sought to sell core plantations along with their slaves pointed routinely to the high proportion of the labor force that was "country born" and to the presence of "handy boys and girls" and listed a broad range of specialized occupations for "fine sensible slaves," "very useful in many Things." Such details seldom appeared in advertisements for frontier plantations, where the labor force was likely to include only a few skilled woodworkers.

Masters clearly considered the frontier to be a disordered place for slave life. They exiled their most dangerous slave "rogues" to Winyah, the colony's northern frontier zone, selling them away from communities in the core.[114] Enslaved workers who toiled on large, productive rice fields lived in comparative isolation on the sparsely settled plantations of the frontier. Recent forced migrations disrupted their communities, a form of social instability that continued with new African arrivals purchased from the slave trade. While masters forced slaves to move to the frontier, slaves in the core moved of their own accord, exploiting new economic opportunities on diversified core plantations geared to the Charlestown market.

For a rising proportion of wealthy planters, life on distant plantations was detached from their own experiences. They were places visited rarely but thought about frequently, whose slaves figured more as entries in ledger books or tax returns than as real people bound into personal relations of mastery and subjugation. The rounds of planters' own movements increasingly fell within a circuit that took them between Charlestown and the most habitable of their rural plantations. Fleeing the seasonal outbreaks of malaria near the swamps, planters and their families relinquished the countryside to slaves and overseers. By 1775 almost one in three whites took up primary residence in town.[115] Charlestown was built to project an impressive image to the Atlantic world. Passengers on incoming ships beheld a panorama that took in the "sumptuous Exchange & Custom House." Even a Loyalist in the process of fleeing her rebellious home city had to admit that British-held New York made "no figure from the water: nothing to equal the order and regularity" of "beautiful Bay Street of Charlestown! Every house for a mile, three stories high!"[116] Those who resided within the city and retreated to the tidy plantations that sprang up in its shadow insulated themselves from the violence and crude conditions of distant labor camps. Strands of the myth of the southern plantation incubated in this distorted view of landscape and economy, gaining a purchase in South Carolina's port city and urban hinterland, but masking the realities of plantation slavery in the wider countryside.

[margin note: most elite masters lived in Charleston]

Sources that describe the Lowcountry, especially those that do so with an eye for the credible details of lived experience, have helped bring the core zone into sharp focus and place it squarely in the foreground of historical perceptions of South Carolina's plantation society. Those articulate visitors who disembarked in Charlestown eager to record their impressions seldom explored the coastal interior beyond the showplace plantations of their hosts. Merchants drafted their correspondence from town- and countinghouses, binding copies in durable letter books. The urge to ponder, characterize, and digress, pen in hand, was a luxury of those who could afford to do so from the comfort of South Carolina's most refined places. Next to lavish accounts of their home plantations, planters often published spare descriptions of their more valuable, but also more remote, lands. They complained at how infrequently they received news of life and work on their distant plantations. Those few letters that have survived, full of the halting prose of unlettered overseers (expected only to "write and cipher sufficient to measure boards"), help explain why we know so little about the colony's frontier zone.[117] The distortions of this uneven documentary record, slanted to make views of the core seem a comprehensive picture of the Lowcountry as a whole, have concealed a fundamental contrast between core and frontier plantations.

At the close of the War for Independence, planters took pains to describe themselves as humane masters. The social environment of the core did much to affirm their sense that just as the landscape seemed to be more settled and more English, so slavery seemed to have ameliorated over time. Because masters "do not always reside at their plantations" and in fact had "several settlements a considerable distance from the place where they usually live," they insulated themselves from the violence of slave labor. Acknowledging the claims of "humanity," some disowned policies of treating slaves "in a harsh manner." They could be persuaded that physical suffering should be relieved by building "Comfortable Negro Houses" with brick foundations, brick chimneys, and glass windows. In the absence of planters as masters, however, the "charge of negroes is given to overseers" who often worked for a share of the crop and thus had a strong financial incentive to resort to "hard Driving" and the whip.[118] In 1778 Catherine Piercy decided to sell her slaves at auction, but asked her brother to handle these transactions, "for it requires more courage th[a]n I am mistress of to stand against their intreaties." Once she learned of the high prices paid for them, however, she calculated that her "Interest" had effectively doubled in value after the sale.[119] Planters took refuge in their distance from the everyday violence that marked the struggles for authority on plantations, but they were aware of the "discipline of a rice Plantation" that took place far from town, even when they did not give the order for "another flogging" directly.[120]

Reconstructing the distance that separated planters from plantations helps explain how they reconciled desires for gentility and a path of economic expansion that created so many rice-producing slave labor camps. The rising refinement of material life within the core insulated planters from the harsh realities of the frontier, laying a foundation in the sights and sounds of their everyday experiences for the belief that the countryside was approaching British standards for what such a landscape should be. It was this disjuncture that J. Hector St. John de Crèvecoeur sharpened into an attack on South Carolina slave owners as early American despots: "While all is joy, festivity, and happiness in Charles Town, would you imagine that scenes of misery overspread in the country? Their ears by habit are become deaf, their hearts are hardened; they neither see, hear nor feel for the woes of their poor slaves, from whose painful labours all their wealth proceeds. Here the horrors of slavery, the hardship of incessant toils, are unseen; and no one thinks with compassion of those showers of sweat and of tears which from the bodies of Africans daily drop and moisten the ground they till. The cracks of the whip urging

these miserable beings to excessive labour are far too distant from the
gay capital to be heard."[121]

This contrast between white urban pleasures and black rural suffering
indicts planters for their luxury, as well as their brutality. It also explains
how they were able to shield themselves from an ever-present awareness
of their moral accountability. In the second half of the eighteenth century
colonists built two worlds across the distances of South Carolina's settlement zones, one in which to live and the other from which to profit. By
mobilizing dependents to plant the frontier, they isolated themselves
within landscapes of refinement built to gratify their senses. When
planters left the countryside for Charlestown, they attempted to leave
behind their identities as taskmasters, even changing out of their
"Country Garb" and substituting a "Sword and Perriwig" for "Frock and
Trousers."[122] Cultivating refined identities out of plantation profits depended not on exercising authority from fixed seats of command but on
moving goods and people across a divided landscape.

The word "plantation," historian Peter H. Wood has argued, has become so saturated with nostalgia for the Old South that its use cannot
but conceal the realities of racial repression in early America. He urges
us to speak more often of slave labor camps, a term that punctures comfortable illusions and forces attention toward the violence that turned
commercial agriculture into a profitable agent of new-world colonization.[123] The plantation myth that many still find compelling was not entirely a product of modern denial of the present-day legacy of slavery's
past. Plantations that gave rise to this myth did exist in colonial South
Carolina, but they occupied one small part of a larger landscape. Conceived as places of order, they exerted a magnetic attraction on colonists'
sensibilities as they staked claims to gentility. They functioned as cultural
shelters that allowed planters to see the promise of cultural improvement
realized in the dramatic territorial expansion of their society in the eighteenth century.

— 5 —

Marketplace of Identity

As late colonial planters erected mansions on the ruins of the decayed, impermanent structures of their predecessors and their slaves laid out gardens in place of stump-strewn cornfields, South Carolina's elites made a bid for recognition as an American gentry class. An intensive engagement in developing land and working slaves in the Lowcountry secured the wealth that made possible such refinement, but they looked abroad to validate their status. No matter how great their fortunes, colonists found that cultural success could not be purchased from overseas. In contrast to an idealized Britain, they found their own society wanting. When they put pen to paper to reflect on how living in a distant colonial province undermined their quest for civility, they came, more often than not, to the same pessimistic conclusion. The distinguishing features of their plantation society—commercial agriculture and African slavery— seemed checks on its progress. Only through a cathartic break from Britain that came with the War for Independence could once-dependent colonists, freed from their own "profound craving for metropolitan acceptance and approval," measure their characters and accomplishments without "constant reference back to . . . the standards of the metropolitan center."[1]

Colonists' adaptations to the lowcountry environment, however, built a material foundation for a more viable provincial identity than this model of colonial cultural dependence permits. Homegrown experience, not imported models for emulation, yielded the critical innovations that made planting possible, profitable, and secure. This agricultural legacy engendered an elite, white, and male culture that evaluated its members by how well they met standards for planting expertise. These standards

166

centered on how to value and improve land, but to do so well required more than technical proficiency with growing crops in the American subtropics. The ideal of plantership elevated a set of inner virtues that defined the planter's character. This sensibility favored flexibility in the face of volatile change and a preference for practical, rather than abstract, knowledge as a guide to practice. Despite the temptations to build a life of refined consumption that could be elevated from the commonplace concerns of agriculture and commerce, the best planters remained deeply engaged in the work of planting. They drew no hard line between the polite and prosaic worlds they inhabited.

South Carolina planters were, like their counterparts throughout colonial British America, preoccupied intellectually with the problem of provincialism. By remaking agriculture with advanced technologies, for example, they sought to put to rest the gnawing belief that their colony was doomed to remain a backwater in a modernizing world.[2] Although colonists looked to Britain as a cultural sun around which South Carolina orbited, they were also engaged in work that bound them together in a community, set up its own rules for behavior, and generated normative values from inside their society. As it gave planters the means with which to fashion a corporate identity, the work of planting was as much cultural as it was economic, social, and environmental.[3] This economic culture centered on distinctive planting expertise developed in tension with an intensifying quest to emulate the home country. In the decades before American independence, the distances that separated the colonial periphery from the metropolitan core served to keep these differences from precipitating a cultural breach, much as a sharp divergence in conceptions of how the empire was governed remained unresolved without becoming destabilizing before the Revolutionary era.[4] As colonists sold their commodities in the Atlantic economy and took part in transatlantic discussions about the development of the colonial Southeast, however, contrasting judgments of who planters were and what they were worth could not be concealed.

Through the routine exchange of commodities and in the course of planning new colonial ventures on the southern frontier, South Carolina colonists found their society, as well as their characters, held up for critical evaluation from London. Over ledgers in Bay Street countinghouses and beneath the masts of oceangoing ships on the Cooper River's wharves, they saw how Europeans valued their place within Britain's American empire. They basked in the recognition that came with high prices and glowing reports of commodity quality, and they harbored resentments against corrupt forces when the markets turned against them. As the slave trade populated the countryside with African workers, slavery's rise in the Lowcountry drew a chorus of disapproval from Britain. Such criticism influenced programs of settlement in the Backcountry, Georgia, and East Florida that attempted to distinguish these new colonial regions from South Carolina, which, despite its robust economic growth, posed strategic as well as cultural problems. As its black majority grew, South Carolina seemed to become more African than European, more savage than civil, and more of a liability than an asset to empire.

This exchange of critiques and defenses fixated on how to know and evaluate human character. Explaining how people changed in terms of morality, temperament, and capacity was part of a broader early modern search for the foundations of identity. In a world distended by long-distance exchange and transoceanic colonization, what things and people were worth was made especially uncertain as individuals gauged their interests within extended commercial networks, occupied positions in the new multiracial hierarchies of colonial societies, and sent back new crops for sale from the new world.[5] To locate character was to move beneath the superficial and try to grasp "qualities that seemed rooted in the things themselves."[6] Character was a fundamental property that anchored the self in this changing world where appearances could be deceiving. Describing character pinned down the true value of the socially ambiguous person and the fluctuating commodity alike and fixed the essence of both so that they might be inserted into a stable matrix of understanding. Because they were one of its objects, colonists were intensely concerned with how this process of characterization worked and with the positive and negative judgments it rendered. For planters fighting for cultural legitimacy on Britain's colonial periphery, determining character was no idle philosophical exercise.[7] At stake was a positive sense of the relationship between place and self in South Carolina amid charges that colonists had become as savage and as volatile as the African slaves and subtropical environment on which their society and economy depended.

Expertise and Provincial Identity

Agricultural writer William Marshall saw three distinct types of farmers cultivating Britain's countryside toward the end of the eighteenth century.

The Aboriginal was, at worst, an "illiberal sloven." His "fields are foul,—his crops wretched,—his live-stock pitiable;—his whole life is a scene of cunning, toil, poverty and wretchedness." The mirror image of the Aboriginal was the Aerialist, a "volatile, speculative, and credulous" figure who knew nothing of farming but what he read in books. "He has read the TOURS,[8] and seen the PATENT-PLOW!" Because the Aerialist disregarded practical knowledge, however, his "ridiculous" academic schemes came to nothing. Between these extremes stood the Scientist. Although he respected traditional agriculture, the Scientist took nothing for granted "which proceeds not directly from ANALYSIS, EXPERIMENT, and OBSERVATION." With his eyes focused on achieving "UNIVERSAL PLENTY" for his countrymen, his hands were frequently soiled with useful work, none of which he found demeaning. The Scientist farmer walked between the "FIELD OF QUIET" and the "FOREST OF NATURE" and "sits down satisfied."[9] The provincial Aboriginal, the arrogant Aerialist, and the determined Scientist each possessed a different moral character from which followed his particular approach to farming. South Carolina planters claimed the sensibilities of the Scientist for their own, but those who criticized the plantation landscape as an alien departure from the English countryside ranked them as an American kind of Aboriginal. In the eyes of metropolitan critics, the planter revealed Aboriginal tendencies toward meanness, cruelty, and a disregard for the future. A plantation's crude appearance—teeming with half-wild cattle, corn plots littered with tree stumps, and fields sooner abandoned than renewed—revealed its proprietor's rude heart.

In addition to plantations' disordered appearance, planters departed from standards that even the most debased farmer at home honored. In place of wheat there was African rice and Indian corn; instead of a horse-drawn plow, scores of Negroes armed with hoes; instead of well-drained arable land, swamps rank with disease. Although colonists were busy cultivating the core zone of settlement in English ways, their critics singled out the large rice labor camps of the frontier to represent their society. Britain would be better off without the "Rice Grounds or Swamps of *Carolina*," argued John Mitchell, for they "destroy more people than they are worth." Because "human nature is not fit to undergo *the slavery of Planters*," even the robust bodies of Africans failed in such an "unhealthful" and violent place. The horrors of rice work stirred another critic to picture slaves' suffering in excruciating detail. Standing "mid-leg deep in water, which floats an ouzy mud," they were "exposed all the while to a burning sun, which makes the very air they breat[h]e hotter than the human blood; these poor wretches are then in a furnace of stinking putrid effluvia: a more horrible employment can hardly be imagined, not far short of digging in Potosi." This comparison put South Carolina rice swamps on a par with the infamous silver mines of Peru, notorious to British readers as the new world's most oppressive place.[10] This potent scene of slaves at work in the swamps stressed the exoticism, danger, and cruelty European audiences already associated with both Africans and the intemperate subtropics and wove them together into a singularly negative space for the development of a transplanted English society. As the warp and weft of a dystopian image, the colony's natural and social environments fastened the curse of a new "black legend," once reserved for Spanish atrocities in America, onto South Carolina's rice planters.[11]

Critics of plantation America painted a deeply unflattering portrait of settlers whose very personalities, they charged, had been made volatile by the violence, heat, and immorality endemic to life in subtropical and tropical slave societies.[12] Born and bred to "tyrannize from their infancy," reflected one visitor, "they carry with them a disposition to treat all mankind in the same manner they have been used to treat their Negroes." Planters who saw themselves as particularly "able" masters believed that they could bear the "Short Comings of Negros" without resorting to the whip on every occasion. In the eyes of British observers who spared sympathy for the slaves, however, the commonplace use of "rough means" immersed colonists in a world of coarsening violence.[13]

The idea that presiding over a slave society unbalanced English temperaments was part of the broader eighteenth-century discourse of degeneration that focused attention on the volatile natural world colonists inhabited. Just as transplanted flora and fauna seemed to decline in quality in South Carolina, the colony attracted its first settlers from the "lowest classes of mankind." As rice emerged as a profitable staple, the planters who produced it were still, in the opinion of one Anglican cleric, the "Vilest race of Men upon the Earth." They had "neither honour, nor honesty nor Religion enough to entitle them to any tolerable Character." The remarkable enrichment of the planter elite after midcentury did little to ennoble its members, their critics contended. Colonists concealed their debts with excessive consumption and sank into a state of indolence made possible by slave labor and the work of poor white overseers. The promise of the Lowcountry, that newcomers of modest means might dramatically raise their social and economic status within a single lifetime, also suggested a "meanness of origins" that deprived the society of a respectable ruling class.[14]

To be sure, planters were stung to find themselves represented in print as cruel and careless, American cousins to English Aboriginal farmers. Yet they did not take such critiques to heart on their merits. Leaving played-out fields for fresh ground rather than fortifying them with manure appeared as a kind of "sloveness in husbandry," admitted John Drayton, "which, to an experienced farmer, would bespeak ignorance, and inattention." "This, however, is not the case," he insisted, for the "crops generally produce good returns."[15] Those who wanted plantations to resemble farms could be seen as harboring a rigid regard for what was superficial about agriculture without taking stock of planting strategies that had developed over decades of experience on the land.[16] With labor dear and land cheap, America's resource endowment was the inverse of Britain's. It was therefore unreasonable to expect to find the hallmark signs of improved English husbandry in South Carolina's most productive plantation districts. Why tend meadows when cattle could graze in unclaimed canes? Why enrich old fields when new planting land could be had almost for the taking?[17] Planters laid claim to the virtues of the Scientist farmer, in their view, not by mimicking English forms, but by constructing a brand of new-world agriculture suited to the Lowcountry's environment.

With an Aerialist's devotion to "speculative knowledge derived from Tull[18] & other favorite Husbandmen," merchant Lachlan McIntosh attempted to begin a new plantation on the model of an improved English farm. As his more experienced patron remarked, such agricultural theorists had "contributed not a little to starve you." Only by proceeding "from *your own* knowledge" of conventional planting methods, he counseled, would McIntosh "gro[w] Rich."[19] As planter-poet George Ogilvie described the "experienced Planter's" art, it rested on a detailed knowledge of the land and a determination to reshape it. The planter identified good sites for rice production by surveying "Nature's wild landscape" with a "searching eye" for the right kind of swamps. He then transformed the land he found, draining the "deep morass," embanking cleared swamps with "strong mounds," and channeling the waters of rivers and swamps to make a formerly "steril desert yield / The plenteous harvest of the richer field."[20] Planters saw wetland rice culture as the product of their own engagement with the natural world rather than as an agricultural inheritance from Britain.

After years of experience, some planters became known as especially "good Judges" of land, but all claimed some ability to value it through visual inspection. Tracts put up for sale bore reputations that circulated among planters, who compared one another's estates, talked about who owned the best and worst lands, and were invited to view growing crops before buying new properties. A printed description of a 970-acre tract on Johns Island was unnecessary because it was "generally esteemed one of the most valuable and improveable plantations in the province."[21] It became something of a custom for a host to lead guests on long strolls around the perimeter of his rice fields. Planters walked the swamps on their own, mastering the details of the terrain at their disposal and monitoring the work they had ordered done.[22] A planter demonstrated competence in his calling by having an intimate knowledge of his land's value and utility. When William Gibbons Jr. and Joseph Ottolenghe could not come to terms on a proposed Georgia land swap in 1764, talk of lawsuits began. Each belittled the quality of the tract he was to receive in the deal, a tactic that called into question the judgment of the other, who, in turn, vouched for the virtues of the land he had contributed to the bargain. This dispute hinged on whether an island tract was marshy and worn out or merely "a little hurt Round the edges with the Salts" and how much of an upland tract was considered "bad pine." As neighbors became adversaries and each enlisted witnesses to support their different assessments of land qualities, their private dispute turned into a public battle over who possessed more certain planting expertise.[23]

Planters admired those who, in addition to being good judges of land, devoted scrupulous attention to its improvement. Good planters exercised direct, managerial authority over their plantations. The men and women of the Manigault family performed "hard labor" themselves when they arrived in the colony in the 1680s, "working the ground like a slave." By the mid-eighteenth century Africans, enslaved in fact, performed this work, and hired overseers took on the day-to-day management responsibilities of the many plantations owned by Manigault descendants. The "great care, attention and activity" required "to attend properly to a Carolina estate" entailed planning a season's work, determining when slaves would be shifted from task to task, and overseeing the flow of supplies to the plantations and commodities from the plantations to market.[24] The estates of British absentees were never as profitable as those run by the planters who owned them. These "able Planters" were "ever employ'd in contriving every thing that can make for their Advantage" and saved "every Expense that can possibly be avoided." By "hard-driving," pushing slave workers to the limits of endurance and beyond, such planters risked violent resistance in order to "save a Crop from destruction."[25] Even those

Figure 5.1. George Roupell, *Peter Manigault and His Friends*, c. 1750s. The scion of a family of Huguenot émigrés, Peter Manigault (1731–1773) lived a life that joined together commerce, land ownership, and authority. After training as a lawyer at London's Inner Temple, Manigault returned to South Carolina to work as a merchant, planter, and plantation agent and rise to the political leadership of the Commons House of Assembly. His diversified fortune, one of the largest in colonial British America, included a Charlestown townhouse and a Goose Creek plantation residence, either of which might have been the setting for this image. Seated at the left of the drawing with a bottle in his hand, Manigault presided over a gathering of men who traded toasts and jokes while being served by an enslaved boy. Ink drawing on paper. Courtesy of Winterthur, Museum Purchase.

who lived in town, leaving everyday toil in the swamps to slaves and overseers, descended on the countryside at critical junctures during the season to enforce order and ensure production. The Commons House of Assembly adjourned to allow its members to oversee sowing and harvesting rice on their plantations. Despite their reputation for high living in Charlestown, planters returned to the sea islands off the southern coast, where they became "wholly attentive to the Cultivation of Indigo."[26]

Unlike their counterparts elsewhere in colonial British America, Charlestown elites admitted the mundane world of production and exchange into polite society.[27] Planters and merchants seemed to love nothing more than talking business across the dining table, contending amiably with one another for the distinction of having bought the best land, produced the most rice, or received the highest price for a cask of indigo. Bostonian Josiah Quincy expected the "more elder substantial gentlemen" who attended the Friday-Night Club to engage in polite banter in the belletristic style. Instead, he was surprised to find that talk turned consistently toward "negroes, and the price of indigo and rice." At another club colonists gathered to compare crop yields after the harvest. Whoever produced the most rice per acre was credited as being the most "attentive Planter" of the season. Ranking the planter who "shall bring the largest crop to market" far above "who shall put his estate in the most beautiful order," they competed for this honor with an intense spirit of "emulation."[28] On Charlestown wharves curious onlookers were perpetually "peeping into Indigo & giving their sentiments & making comparisons between one parcel & another." South Carolina society had its share of drinkers, gamblers, and "idlers," those ne'er-do-well sons of the wealthy who loom large in representations of the antebellum South. But a commitment to business became a normative standard around which elites oriented their values in the colonial era. "Nobody, be he ever so distinguished," wrote one observer around midcentury, "is ashamed of work in economic things."[29]

Just as those who wore unfashionable clothes in Charlestown could suffer "much humiliation and mockery," derision punished those who failed to live up to basic planting standards. Planters who "from inattention" left their rice fields "neither completely wet or dry" were ridiculed for the "*sobby state*" of their lands. When reproaching a fellow planter for being a "bad manager, they do not observe such a person's plantation is not clean, or is weedy," but rather used a well-worn turn of phrase.

[handwritten margin note: talked business in polite society]

Saying that "such a man is in the grass" mocked him for an inability to manage slaves, a tendency to push a modest labor force beyond its means, or simple carelessness. By meeting basic standards for cultivation, quality, and productivity, those who owned land and slaves could aspire to be included within the circle of reputable planters.[30] By recognizing that these criteria defined the expert planter, individuals demonstrated their membership in the group and, together, gave the lie to metropolitan notions that planters were Aboriginal hacks rather than experienced Scientists when it came to agriculture.

Developing a discerning eye for land and learning the "method of Planting and managing Rice, Corn, & Indigo" and the "usual Management of Negroes" were the benchmarks by which planters judged one another.[31] These skills might be obtained fairly rapidly. Newcomers who were "not expert Carolina Planters" could, "under the tuition & assistance of a capable overseer," master them in a few years. More than any technical or managerial skill, qualities of character, acquired over a lifetime, made for a good planter. Novices who demonstrated "understanding & industry," and who were "honest & sensible," "quick of apprehension," and "dilligent & Carefull" gained the support of experienced patrons. Some European immigrants, driven to South Carolina by their "Indigence" at home, lacked the "Spirit" to become planters. They were mere farmers, content with a bare subsistence. As their children grew to maturity in the Lowcountry, however, this creole generation promised to make "good Settlers" after acquiring ambitions and habits of industry that their parents lacked. Truly able planters looked at their world as a vast space for enterprise and improvement. Over the course of the eighteenth century, planters overturned assumptions about what constituted good land, used irrigation to transform rice production, diversified and specialized their productions to take advantage of market opportunities, and managed larger numbers of free and enslaved dependents. Good planters realized that expertise distinguished them, not by providing an all-purpose store of knowledge, but by inculcating habits of innovation and responsiveness to the Lowcountry's volatile environments.[32]

Planters saw themselves as participants in a broader Anglo-American movement of agricultural improvement. Reaping larger crops and greater profits came with practicing efficient farming methods, but amassing wealth was never the ultimate goal of a campaign to turn wastes into flourishing fields and poverty into plenty.[33] Over the course of little more

[handwritten marginalia: qualities of character made a good planter]

[handwritten marginalia: industry innovation]

than a century, colonists had transformed what they took for a savage wasteland into "one of the most opulent, and most increasing Colonies in America."[34] Planters' command over land and slaves had turned a cultural "desert" into one of British America's "cultivated, cleared, populous, and improved spaces" whose rapid growth, as Jack P. Greene has observed, was "without parallel in the known history of the West."[35] Even critics who held up the sufferings of slaves as a negative emblem of plantation society could not entirely deflate planters' sense of accomplishment on this score. Planters argued that African slavery and swamp farming were calculated adaptations to the unique constraints of their environment rather than degenerate departures from improved methods. Without them, South Carolina "would revert to a state of nature," and its "extensive rice fields which are covered with grain would present nothing but deep swamps, and dreary forests[,] inhabited by panthers, bears, wolves, and other wild beasts."[36] Because planting laid the economic foundation from which white colonists could aspire to British standards of civility, their achievement validated in their own eyes the means by which it had been achieved, however unconventional or repressive. Through this work on the land, planters came to set the terms for who they were and how much their experience was worth.

Commerce and Character

Charlestown's marketplace was the stage on which planters took their place within the Atlantic world. As an active site for exchange, the colony's dominant port city was like no other in plantation America. Chesapeake and West Indian producers tended to consign their staples for shipment to Europe, maintaining ownership of commodities until British merchants brokered a sale and sent back news of the crop's proceeds. The tidewater gentry seemed disengaged from the details of Atlantic commerce, for how any hogshead of Oronoco leaf fared in European trade was a distant event they paid others to manage. In contrast to the consignment system, which diffused transactions over time and far from home, planters sold almost all their rice and most of their indigo in town for an immediate return.[37] Direct, American sales made every shipping season a drama performed by actors who saw their fortunes determined before their eyes. Planters held out for the highest price. They stood toe-to-toe with local export merchants just as determined to offer the least they could for the planters' crop. This annual contest over the value and quality of commodities was a performance more engaging than anything enacted by visiting players on the stage of the Queen Street Theatre.[38] The goods planters brought to market represented a year's work of slaves on the land and the entire product of their capital stock for which they sought a return. Along with their money and time, they invested their characters in casks of indigo and barrels of rice.

While planters elsewhere waited for their accounts from Britain, those in the Lowcountry angled for advantage in the local marketplace. Crop seasons flowed into shipping seasons in South Carolina, filling the calendar with year-round activity. Planters' economic lives shifted between production and exchange, activities that were as indispensable to one another as they were different from one another. Each marked off a sphere for enterprise with its own scale of magnitude. Planting focused attention on a world measured in concrete increments: acres and tasks, bales of Negro cloth and families of slaves, grosses of iron hoes and head of livestock. During the months of marketing, planters adjusted their gaze to figure out how sweeping changes across the Atlantic world altered international demand for their commodities. The annual transition from planting to trade not only enlarged the sphere in which planters acted, but made it more uncertain and far less under their control. Masters commanded others on the plantations, but in the Atlantic economy they were marginal participants, subject to unseen market forces and the influences of powerful metropolitan merchants and officials.

Charlestown was a physical rather than a metaphorical marketplace. Goods changed hands here in personal, face-to-face encounters. The town encompassed just over 300 acres by the close of the colonial period, the size of a modest plantation tract. Trade took place in storehouses, countinghouses, and wharves clustered together in an even smaller portion of the city on the eastern, Cooper River side of the peninsula.[39] Approximately 230 mercantile firms traded here in the late eighteenth century. The interests of some 2,000 planters were represented by about 40 "country" or "rice factors" hired to sell plantation produce in town.[40] Exchange was a highly visible process in this small-scale marketplace. Merchants listened to planters discuss the weather and toured plantation neighborhoods to gain an early sense of the size of the crop. As rice collected at "Sundry Country Landings" and was then stored in town, the scale of rice and indigo production for the season became even clearer.[41] Knowing local demand was even more straightforwardly visual: ships in the harbor and their approximate freight capacities were available for all to see and were reported in the *South-Carolina Gazette* for good measure. The local market's transparency, in which known personalities gathered to buy and sell physical goods in the open, gave eighteenth-century Charlestown a superficial resemblance to a medieval European market town, sometimes romanticized by early modern thinkers as an idyll of fair dealing and stable value. Social critics tallied the moral costs of trade in commercializing Britain by pointing out that the literal marketplace had given way to an abstract market in which "invisibility, concealment, and *mis*representation" reigned.[42] The immediacy of trade here, however, did not immunize Charlestown from distortion and deception as if it were an enclave of premodern exchange rather than an outpost of the Atlantic economy, deeply tied to long-distance networks of credit and commerce. Instead, its intimate environs intensified the moral drama of trade, subjecting every gain and loss to accusations of unfair advantage and calling into question the characters of buyers and sellers.

Price quotations litter the accounts and correspondence that survive to document exchange in this contentious marketplace. How many shillings were given for rice by the hundredweight and indigo by the pound, always carefully tallied to record a transaction, was never a numerical abstraction to those who bought and sold commodities. These figures represented windfall profits and painful losses; they reflected good and bad turns of fortune; they testified to the success of a well-executed marketing strategy and put a hard value on grievances against people, seen and unseen, suspected of manipulating the market for their own advantage. During the eighteenth century prices given for rice and indigo increased in real terms. Viewed from far above the details of the ledger sheet, the Atlantic economy rewarded planting, driving this society's economic development and making white South Carolinians one of the Anglo-American world's wealthiest groups.[43] Planters and merchants experienced the market within this positive long-term price trend. On the shorter scale of time in which they acted, the value of rice and indigo rose and fell dramatically. In absolute terms, indexed rice and indigo price series for the eighteenth century show sharp departures from the index year, frequently amounting to more than 25 percent in the average annual value of the commodity.[44] Merchants and planters saw this short-term market volatility in action as they watched the price of rice cut in half or double during a single shipping season. From their perspectives within the process of commodity exchange, rice seemed "very uncertain...in its Value." "[U]nexpected turns" rocked the market without warning. So "very fluctuating" was the value of rice that it "Varies very much in price every Week" and "often sold at different Prices in one Day."[45]

Trading within these volatile swings, planters and merchants staked their economic lives to commodity prices. For planters, selling a crop was a moment of reckoning when the value of the labor, debt, and capital they had risked over the past year was determined. Even in the "worst of Markets" the planter needed "more from his Plantation than will defray his ordinary Expences" to stay one step ahead of his creditors and prepare for the next season. In better times planters invested their profits in "Slaves preferably to any thing else," reaping the benefits of good markets while they lasted. The "only point with them" when they decided how much to lay out in new laborers was "what price the Value of their Produce will enable them to give." Planters held out for the highest price even when this meant extending credit to merchants who could not make immediate payments, a reversal of the typical creditor-debtor relationship. A twenty-shilling turn in the price of rice moved planters toward two different futures, one in which the provost marshal sold off seized land and slaves at public auction and another in which new slaves cultivated new acres to make more to sell the following year.[46]

Price was also the hinge on which traders' fortunes turned. Charlestown's export merchants bought rice and indigo with their own money, sometimes selling it on their own accounts, but more often shipping it to British merchants who later reimbursed them their costs plus a commission. A small circle of wealthy merchants earned lucrative commissions selling African slaves, the colony's most valuable import. In the one branch of trade that most independent merchants financed directly, the sale of imported manufactured goods, competition glutted the local market by the second half of the eighteenth century.[47] With part of their capital laid out every year to buy commodities and the rest languishing in stocks of dry goods sold at long credit, merchants, in the opinion of one observer, became "mere prey to the Planter."[48] When planters gained higher prices than the market at home could bear, merchants waited for payment from the importers who sold the season's rice at a loss. Without this cash in hand as the new crop came in, "Younger Traders" with weak balance sheets failed. Only the best-financed merchants could dig themselves out of the hole by buying another crop and hoping for lower prices and better returns. In 1754 John Guerard complained that high rice prices made the merchants' prospects "Dull & Gloomey." He concluded that the "Planting Business is now become the most advantageous & if times do not mend I believe I must Resolve to become a Planter for Good and all or Else go behind hand." Guerard left behind his calling and "turnd Planter" six years later. Many others, perhaps the majority with the means to buy land and slaves to "retire" to the countryside, followed his example. With such antagonistic interests, it was no wonder that the "planters and the merchants look[ed] at one another with an evil eye."[49] During every shipping season members of this generally unified elite strained to reconcile their particular economic interests with claims that each served the common good of the province they ruled together.

As they battled over price, planters and merchants did not know what rice or indigo was really worth to consumers abroad. The time it took to cross the Atlantic, typically ten weeks to Britain and six to Carolina, opened the work of valuing commodities to wide-ranging conjecture.[50] Local merchants remained "watchfull & vigilant," eager "to learn what is going forward & to improve upon the earlyest intelligence." Well-informed traders kept good information private, urging associates to "keep [it] to your Self" to avoid moving the local market before they had a chance to act.[51] Because ship captains opened "their Bag or Box of Letters Im[m]ediately on the Wharf . . . or in the Street & Sometimes at a Private house or Tavern, where any Person may Take them," this information edge could be easily lost. Some merchants received letters with their seals broken after some "curious" party had "satisfied their itch by perusing the contents."[52] Accounts of European markets, arriving in port when ships did, were "plenty at one time and scarce at another." Despite their pleas to British correspondents for the most recent updates, export merchants made do with news that was often so "out of Date" that it was "not worth reading."[53] Few knew how to begin to set a price when they were "quite without news."[54] Even the freshest intelligence described market conditions out-of-date by at least one month, the time it took the swiftest packet boat to reach Charlestown from London.

Commercial gossip took over where reliable news failed. Planters and merchants ordered fragments of market information into scenarios of rising and falling commodity prices that they continually revised in light of new indicators. News of a "late Great Rise in [the] price of Rice in

London" gave planters the clout to demand high prices; "dismal advices
... in all the European Markets" gave merchants the ability to force them
down.[55] In an atmosphere of rumor-driven buying and selling, competing
stories of demand circulated in Charlestown as each side tried to turn
the local market for rice and indigo to its advantage. Claims for price
were linked to the size of the Italian rice crop, the damage wrought by a
hurricane in the West Indies, and the state of grain harvests throughout
Europe.[56] Despite a "vast Crop" and "scarce one Ship" in port waiting to
take on rice, prices rose late in the Seven Years' War when hints arrived
that Britain and France were on the "very brink of a sudden peace." When
the ship *Success* arrived bearing accounts of the Treaty of Paris in January
1763, the planters' position improved again in a matter of hours.[57] Armed
with intermittent bursts of outdated commercial news, buyers and sellers
constructed global narratives of war and peace, dearth and plenty, and
calamity and prosperity to make a case for the prices they wanted.
Planters and merchants, locked in competition in their small corner of
the Atlantic world, behaved as if they acted on an expansive international
stage.

Although they controlled nothing about commodity demand beyond
its interpretation, planters used their command over supply to influence
the local market. From the first week in November through the end of
May, agriculture gave way to commerce. As soon as casks and barrels
were processed and packed, slave boatmen and teamsters hauled them to
town for sale.[58] While rice and indigo were still growing in the fields,
local export merchants estimated the size of the rice and indigo crops for
British import merchants who used these reports to determine the tonnage required to carry off South Carolina's commodities. Environmental
volatility humbled rice-crop observers who concluded that "there's no
determining of the product of that precarious article before it is in the
Barn." Only when barrels began stacking up in Charlestown warehouses,
long after ships had departed for America to take them on, was the true
size of the crop known. Planters capitalized on this uncertainty by
spreading false information. They gloated over expected large harvests
when they knew full well that bad seasons had damaged their crops. When
the planters' disinformation circulated in Britain, import merchants there
caught wind of this enthusiasm and dispatched large fleets to take on
small crops, a situation sure to drive up the local price. Charlestown
merchants chided their British counterparts who were "deceiv'd" into

"bad adventures by the sound of large Crops" in midsummer. They railed against the "many unwary & some artful people" who had spread "grand Accounts of the approaching Crop."[59] Less conniving planters were still "too discreet to complain openly" of droughts and other natural disasters "untill the Ships are fairly harbour'd in the Winter." Only after this die was cast did they reveal that "the Crop is short and that the prices must be in proportion."[60] Planters could do little, season to season, to control the impact of the weather on the rice and indigo supply. Shifts in European demand were beyond their prediction. By manipulating perceptions of the "Plenty or Scarcity of a Crop," however, they strove to turn their financial aspirations into self-fulfilling prophecies.[61]

Once ships anchored in Charlestown harbor, the battle over price was joined, and time was of the essence. No matter how uncertain and complex were the signs that indicated European demand, waiting ships "could not Lye & must be dispatch'd one way or other." For every additional day in port, the accumulating expenses of a transatlantic voyage ate away at the chance to return to a "saving market."[62] Although hundreds of ships called on Charlestown every season, so sensitive were local commodity prices to the number of waiting vessels that a few new captains seeking cargoes gave "Encouragement to the Planter to insist upon a high Price for his produce." Merchants attempted to "keep down the price of Rice" by delaying the arrival of incoming vessels.[63] The first barrel of rice that changed hands was the opening act in this drama of exchange. The planters' asking price at these times could be "exhorbitant & must distress the waiting Ships." Whatever was offered in this initial transaction set a precedent for the season; "breaking" or "fixing" the price established a benchmark for negotiations that followed. The "disagreeable necessity of fixing a price" set the machinery of local commerce in motion, and planters exploited their control over the supply of commodities to force purchasers to set a high opening price that reflected their own self-interested reading of the market.[64]

Planters withheld crops from the market when prices declined. This "method of the Planters keeping Back their Rice til they are Sattisfied with the Price" was performed with theatrical gestures. Planters "stop[ed] their Boats" from coming to town. Rice factors "lock[ed] up their Stores." Weeks could pass "at great expence" to desperate shippers before this tactic forced the price to "advance 5 or 10" percent.[65] As ships came and left toward the end of the shipping season, the two sides usually "split the difference by & by." But these standoffs left both parties feeling aggrieved, convinced that trade was a zero-sum game between American planters and British-backed merchants in which one's success came at the other's failure. As planters regulated the flow of commodities into the Charlestown market with tactical intent, merchants, in their frustration, condemned their motives as mercenary. It was the "nature of our Planters," wrote John Guerard, to "get as much as they can not regarding whether the Adventurers Gain or Los[e] by it."[66] In their staunch demands for high prices, they seemed "avaricious," as well as "Obstinate," unwilling to bend in the face of changing market forces and "always amusing themselves that Rice will rather rise than fall, & that there will be the same Demand for it in Europe this Crop as was last." Against the dictates of common sense, planters kept "*Rice* at home, 'till the Merchant is forced to give the Price they please to demand."[67] Manipulating the supply of plantation commodities and raising local prices beyond what the market could bear seemed selfish and reckless. These schemes might reward the individual for the moment, but collectively, by scaring off British merchants, they threatened to place the commercial health of the region, and the fortunes of planter and merchant alike, in jeopardy.

With price as the crucial variable that governed aspiration, planters exerted what leverage they could over the local sale of commodities with a clear conscience. Why should they shoulder so many of the costs of Britain's precarious colonial commerce? At the risk of their own lives and fortunes they had colonized the Lowcountry, a feat that generated strategic and mercantilist benefits for the kingdom. The punishing financial consequences of crops destroyed by hurricanes, frosts, and floods fell to their lot alone. John Drayton expected something on the order of 300 barrels of rice from 120 acres in 1768. After his newly planted crop was first washed away by floods, replanted, and then withered by drought, his slaves only managed to make 30 barrels. This would have "come to nothing" had he sold it right away, but Drayton made his "Small parcel of rice turn out to near half a crop" by withholding it from the market and selling it as the price peaked later in the shipping season. By standing out "stiffly for a price," Drayton and his fellow planters stretched the returns of short harvests to cover their costs and debts and survived to plant again.[68] Fortune was to blame for bad seasons, but planters also held the human agency of metropolitan officials at fault when their interests were subordinated in the making of imperial policy.

When it came to assessing the quality of their rice, colonists saw the Atlantic economy as a benevolent place that validated their expertise and their characters. As their primary staple gained and maintained a reputation as the "best rice that is brought to England from any part of the world," they found their skills as planters endorsed every shipping season. The cultivated Lowcountry in which they had brought rice culture "to the highest perfection, and as such known in all the European and American markets," seemed itself affirmed by this high international regard.[69] When the first Carolina indigo cakes arrived in London in the mid-1740s, however, they crumbled on inspection into "Pieces about the Bigness of Horse Beans, with grey, mouldy, or dull Edges." The low esteem in which European buyers held lowcountry indigo never improved. In 1791 Claude Louis Berthollet, author of the first empirically rigorous study of dyeing chemistry, categorized indigo into three classes: the best "indigo flore," good "copper indigo," and "much less pure kinds, as that from Carolina." Throughout the colonial period and beyond, South Carolina's second staple commodity seemed to "Labour under so bad a Character" that it became a byword for inferiority.[70]

Colonists struggled to remove the stigma of their commodity's quality by improving it, but few produced good indigo consistently, perhaps because the Lowcountry's volatile climate made the process "extreamly troublesome and intricate." Although the most proficient Carolina makers met the London market's standards for symmetrical shape and luminous color on occasion, their dye never sold as well as what planters in Guatemala or St. Domingue managed to ship every year. When a parcel of seized French indigo came to Charlestown to be sold as a prize, it commanded high prices despite appearing to be "a good deal inferior" to the local product. Such revelations piqued colonists' suspicions that indigo's reputation, good or bad, reflected the machinations of metropolitan merchants more than any stable use-value for coloring cloth. Some planters bridged the distance between regional reputation and reality by masking their dye's origins. They sent their indigo to Jamaica, cleared it there as French, and found it greeted in London with acclaim.[71] Such strategies traded the market liability of a bad reputation for the price premiums paid for a good one, but further revealed the artifice behind Carolina indigo's bad image.

When Henry Laurens traveled to London to present his own batch to "some of the Wise Men call'd Brokers and Dyers" in 1772, they "admired it much for East Florida indigo." They were "sorry we could not make such Indigo in Carolina," even though this sample was the product of his own Cooper River plantation. Convinced that he and his fellow planters had been unfairly maligned and perhaps cheated by such "Prejudices," Laurens abandoned the British market for the French after independence. Rumors that South Carolina planters adulterated their indigo with dirt to increase its weight added the accusation of fraud to the standard charge of carelessness that attached to their indigo's bad reputation. Its poor quality and low prices characterized their plantation society as a crude place, defined more by degeneracy than discernment. "[T]is realy a piece of Cruelty," insisted Laurens, that London's biases against Carolina indigo worked to "damp the Sale of a Comodity from our Own plantations of so much utillity to the Nation." That the colonies of Britain's imperial rivals, Spain and France, should benefit from this humiliating disparity made the apparent unfairness of this reputation even more galling to patriotic Britons in America.[72]

Rice paid substantial duties to the Crown as an enumerated commodity. The mercantilist requirement that it be shipped to Britain and then reexported to its primary markets of consumption on the Continent made it more expensive to transport and harder to profit by.[73] On top of this long-standing burden, King George's War plunged the rice economy into a sustained depression during the 1740s. As prices declined, the proceeds of entire crops "would barely pay the Outgoings of a plantation." Even some of the colony's "most careful Planters" were "reduced to the greatest Distress" during this crisis. Many others fled with their mortgaged slaves, leaving dishonored bonds behind them. At this critical juncture Parliament threatened to end all rice exports to Britain's adversaries in the conflict, France and Spain. Planters imagined this additional constraint on their faltering export economy as a final, destabilizing straw that might plunge the colony into chaos. They envisioned a nightmare scenario of cascading bankruptcies and slave insurrections as their economy collapsed.[74] In part because of the vehemence of their protests, this bill to restrict the colony's trade did not pass. Planters' sense of dependency, however, lingered. In their own eyes they were not the greedy predators of the merchants' accusations, but rather vulnerable prey, subject to destructive forces and malicious influences beyond their prediction or control.

As they threw their weight around in Charlestown trade, merchants recognized planters as a united group, even as they condemned their aggregate power as a mercenary combination. When it acted in concert, the planter class seemed to betray single-minded qualities of discretion and discernment.[75] Planters eyed the short-term price shifts in their local market as a singular opportunity to bring the Atlantic economy into a forum in which they could exert influence. Against the merchants' control over shipping and private access to market information, they countered by regulating the pace and perception of supply. Their most powerful weapon in this regard, forming cartels to withhold crops from the market, brought the dynamics of long-distance trade over which they had little control into a sphere in which their actions and expertise could shape their participation within the Atlantic economy. The image of the autonomous lowcountry patriarch who was "independent of all persons" except the slaves he commanded, "separated from his surrounding neighbors by the recognized boundary of his broad acres," and "practicing there his own peculiar system" of agriculture described an antebellum figure far removed from its colonial precursor. Rather than retreating from the wider world, planters deepened their commitments to the market every year. Seasons of large crops and high prices allowed them to clear their debts, buy more slaves, and "strain upon a next Crop to increase their Stocks both for themselves & their Children."[76] Rather than allowing them to retreat to the countryside to rule their plantations, the distinctive terms of trade in Charlestown brought planters into engagement with one another as a coherent provincial class.

Slavery and the Future of Plantation Society

Planters thought through the consequences of plantation slavery for their society's developmental future as they engaged in debates over new colonization in the region. Plans initiated from London to settle the southeastern frontier treated South Carolina's plantation society as a problem to be remedied rather than as a model to be emulated. Schemes to populate the Backcountry, Georgia, and East Florida against the image of the lowcountry plantation complex were greeted by planters at first as a necessary means of achieving territorial expansion with security. With each proposed alternative to their plantation society, however, came a critique of their character. The charge that slavery weakened security was also an accusation of private selfishness against the public interest. New settlers

[handwritten margin note: indicted SC society]

in Georgia's social utopia and Florida's natural paradise, by contrast, would become more rather than less virtuous. When the idea of confining large-scale slavery and plantation agriculture to the South Carolina coast was put into place, it began to grate against planters' self-image, offering an indictment of their society and imposing a suffocating limitation on its growth.

As they settled rice plantations across the Lowcountry, colonists surrounded themselves with slaves. Serving "all the Settlements in *North-America*" as a "Frontier," white South Carolinians faced the geopolitics of Indian, French, and Spanish designs on the continent with their internal security undermined by a rising black population.[77] To some critics, developing the coastal plain in this way also undercut colonists' claims that they were turning a savage Indian land into a civil European one. By outward appearances colonization had Africanized rather than anglicized the Lowcountry. After experiencing its vast black majorities in 1737, Swiss immigrant Samuel Dyssli declared, "Carolina looks more like a negro country than like a country settled by white people." Another newcomer could almost believe that his white host had "conducted me to Africa, or Lucifer's Court," rather than guiding him to Charlestown.[78] The first attempt to reverse this demography of vulnerability took place only a few years after blacks surpassed whites in the province. After the Yamassees were pushed out of their territory on the southern coast in 1716, the South Carolina Assembly at first reserved this depopulated "Indian Land" for non-slave-owning yeoman farmers to settle. Governor Robert Johnson, the first to take charge of the colony after the formal end of Proprietary rule in 1729, initiated a more ambitious scheme. His Township Plan, implemented in the early 1730s, encircled the plantation zones with nine enclaves of land reserved for European immigrants to claim in modest, fifty-acre headright grants.[79] By 1735, however, the Assembly opened several townships to settlement by South Carolina residents, and individual planters used legal and illicit means to consolidate township lands into new plantation settlements.[80] However compelling the logic of reform, few planters wished to pay its costs by limiting their access to cheap new planting land.

If the Township Plan applied a bandage to the strategic problem of slavery in South Carolina, then Georgia was to be a miraculous antidote. Its Trustees put forward a vision for development intended to reverse the consequences of unbridled economic freedom that plagued its long-established neighbor to the north. Slavery, along with alcohol, was banned outright. Georgia was to be a haven for white families who would labor on small farms and congregate in villages. Land laws hamstrung specu- lators and sought to keep settlers focused on improving their properties instead of dashing to new frontiers to claim the best new tracts. Against South Carolina's legacy of Indian conflict, political turbulence, and re- pressive bondage, the Georgia Plan laid out a social design for the pro- motion of virtue, stability, and security, benefits to be enjoyed by the impoverished settlers, drawn from among the wayward poor, who would redeem themselves there. For the empire as a whole, Georgia promised to shore up an exposed southern frontier and strengthen claims to moral superiority over Spain in the quest to justify imperial rule in North America.[81] Recognizing the strategic utility of the planned colony, white South Carolinians at first praised its prospects. In addition to financial support from their government, parishes in the colony took up charitable collections to aid the first Georgia settlers after their arrival in 1732.[82]

By the early 1740s, however, South Carolina planters had soured on Georgia. An account of the 1743 death of William Sterling served as a cautionary tale for those who might be lured to venture there. After "Nine Months Confinement in a Palmeta Hut," Sterling and his fellow colonists were reduced to begging food from soldiers at a nearby fort before "Ne- cessity and the Approach of Rain obliged all the Settlers to abandon their Improvements."[83] Further criticisms were directed at the Bethesda Or- phanage, a benevolent experiment founded in 1740 by George Whitefield, the charismatic preacher whose travels through the colonies fanned the flames of a religious awakening. After contemplating Bethesda's struggles to educate its wards in silk making and self-discipline, one South Carolina satirist mocked Whitefield's "gilded Scheme" as a "silken Dream." Located on "barren and unprofitable" land, Bethesda made a tempting target for those who sought to tar the Georgia Plan and Methodism with the same brush of overreaching idealism.[84]

As Georgia foundered, the "planters of Carolina" soon treated "their poor neighbours" with the "utmost contempt," holding them to the stan- dards for good plantership with which they praised and mocked one another. Lacking slaves and stymied by the pursuit of one failed com- modity experiment after another, the colonists who sought to achieve Georgia's progressive vision had become mired in a profound commercial "Backwardness." Unwilling to adapt their agriculture to the region's nat- ural environment, the "poor and ignorant planters" of early Georgia attempted to grow wheat and rye, crops that failed and "left them, after all their toil, in a starved and miserable condition." Contemporary historian Alexander Hewit looked back at the failure of Georgia from the 1770s and concluded that the "imagination of man could scarcely have framed a system of rules worse adapted to the circumstances and situation of the poor settlers, and of more pernicious consequences to the prosperity of the province."[85] After two decades of struggle, the Georgia Plan was dismantled. Once the Trustees' laws were repealed and slavery was allowed in the early 1750s, South Carolina's plantation society expanded southward. Georgia had begun in opposition to rice and indigo, slavery and luxury, and swamp fields spread across a black-majority plantation landscape. As planters moved their slaves south across the Savannah River to settle its tidal floodplains, they transplanted these hallmark features of South Carolina's economy and society and took credit for ensuring Georgia's survival as a British colony in doing so.

"When I got into *Georgia*," recounted J. B., a Charlestown "Gentleman" writing in the *South-Carolina Gazette* in 1754, "I was disappointed every where. . . . It may be a good country in time but, in my opinion, it can never, never come up to *Carolina*." He claimed that he heard Georgians discuss an "unusual phœnomenon" said to have afflicted South Carolina during his visit. Out of the swamps of the Cooper River there reportedly arose a "terrible monster, having *twelve* heads of different sizes." This creature "made a terrible bellowing noise" as it threatened nearby plantations and advanced on Charlestown like an early modern Godzilla. Each of its heads "was cornuted, some with fifty, some twenty, and some fewer horns; and that one head in particular appear'd to have its horns tipt with gold." When the traveler returned home, he discovered that no one had heard these "roarings of destruction." Despite the certainty of the "grave sober men" who had predicted South Carolina's demise, "these philosophers either were mistaken, or the monster gone to sleep." This monster was, of course, slavery, or, more precisely, a caricature of the way in which idealistic Georgians had imagined slavery as a social pathology that would prove South Carolina's ruin. Cobbled together from the Book of Revelation's beast from the sea and the unconquerable Hydra of Greek myth that grew two heads for every one cut off, it represented the problem of slavery as an impending disaster, driven by greed ("horns tipt with gold") and capable of paralyzing white colonists with fear with every rumbling of a "Negro insurrection."[86]

South Carolina planters ridiculed Georgians' excessive paranoia about this menace, but they did not dismiss the potential for disorder as an empty threat. Perhaps the monster was a "fiction," J. B. concluded; perhaps it was merely sleeping.[87] They monitored the rise of subversive "rogues" among their slaves with contained anxiety. By regulating the kinds of people brought into the colony through the transatlantic slave trade, they convinced themselves, they could reproduce a population of practical, sensible, creolized slaves who seemed to pose less of a threat to social order than did "savage" Africans.[88] Georgia's collapse as a slaveless farming society helped bolster the idea that their brand of plantation slavery imposed more virtues than vices on the landscape. Despite the weaknesses that came with extensive African slavery, human bondage also appeared as an indispensable motive force for bringing the southern frontier into agricultural order. Remove slavery from the calculus of colonization, and the result would be underdevelopment of the land, which if left in the hands of Indians would fall prey to rival imperial powers with designs on North American expansion. South Carolina society came under imperial scrutiny in the 1730s as two major initiatives, the Township and Georgia plans, were put in place to limit slavery's expansion in the Lowcountry. Critiques of their plantation society put slave owners on the defensive as officials schemed to make the region into a more secure outpost of empire. As planters recolonized Georgia to resemble South Carolina after 1750, the doomsday scenarios in which slavery figured as British plantation America's fatal flaw had lost their urgency as a guiding principle of imperial reform. That antislavery's star fell along with the Georgia Plan can be seen in the pleasure with which South Carolina elites depicted its architects and supporters as alarmist zealots, badly out of touch with the realities of what was necessary to impose order on a disorderly landscape.

After Britain secured an unprecedented hegemony in eastern North America and the Caribbean following the Seven Years' War, land speculation and settlement in East Florida intensified this debate over the future of plantation America. With the seaboard safe for the moment from French and Spanish intervention, planters critiqued the new colony's program for development as a dangerous fantasy. Visions of Florida as a landscape of tropical villas worked by European servants, they insisted, would come crashing down, leaving behind a wilderness of uncultivated swamps and pine barrens along the Lowcountry's southernmost frontier. The region's third major eighteenth-century settlement scheme once again put planters on the defensive. The feverish tone of William Stork's 1766 *Account of East-Florida* "has sett us all Florida mad," reported Lord Adam Gordon, a prominent absentee investor. Wild claims for the colony's natural abundance did seem like a kind of insanity to experienced planters. With an unshakable faith that Florida's climate and soils guaranteed its economic success, the new colony's promoters promised the same exotic commodities (olives, cotton, and sugar among them) that had once enchanted seventeenth-century Carolina projectors. Florida would not ban slavery as did Georgia, but its planners deemphasized it in favor of indentured white labor, urging the migration of Huguenot winemakers, Bermudan shipbuilders, Greek farmers, Scottish peasants, persecuted German and Swiss Protestants, and even reformed London prostitutes.[89]

The settlement of Florida reanimated British conceptions of the Southeast as an exotic space in which any crop that could be desired might be produced in abundance and to perfection. Speculator and promoter Denys Rolle wrote in 1766 that "Everything in nature seems to correspond towards the cultivation of the productions of the whole world, in some part or other of this happy province, the most precious jewel of his majesty's American dominions."[90] The very name of the colony evoked legendary fertility, a lush capacity for improvement that would be realized when British industriousness replaced Spanish "sloth & laziness." For naturalists "tired with the same seeds over & over again," Florida offered an astounding new space with which to satisfy metropolitan curiosity. Its insects "increase in size and beauty," and its flowers surpassed those of Carolina and Georgia "in beauty of fruit & sweet scent." Alexander Garden welcomed Florida as a remarkable natural frontier that promised novel exotica compared with the mundane, increasingly well-settled South Carolina Lowcountry. "Think that I am here," he wrote to fellow naturalist John Bartram, "confined to the sandy streets of Charlestown, where the ox, where the ass, and where men as stupid as either, fill up the vacant space, while you range the green fields of Florida, where the bountiful hand of Nature has spread every beautiful and fair plant and flower, that can give food to animals, or pleasure to the spectator."[91] Grand and untried settlement ventures, however implausible, seemed to match the mythic promise of such a place.

Settlers who believed that they would gain easy plantation profits in East Florida seemed to recent British immigrant Frederick George Mulcaster to be suffering from an infectious mental disorder. "There is a certain something in the Air of St. Augustine or some curs'd Power . . . which actually turns the Brain . . . some it seized violently the moment they set their foot on Shore, others do not catch it till some days after their arrival, even I with all my resolution could not with stand it." After dreaming that he owned a plantation producing "Indigo Rice Cotton &c, in great abundance," that magically transformed into "Corn wine & oyl" on arrival in England, he agreed to buy a Florida plantation. Mulcaster noted the irony of first criticizing Florida as a lunatic asylum and then suddenly becoming "the most desperate Petient in it," one of the "incurables" to whom every outrageous encomium that took stock of East Florida's natural abundance was understood as evidence of certain agricultural success.[92]

Carolina planters faulted eager new landowners for their lack of economic realism. Without any experience in "Planting & affairs of Husbandry," they expected vast crops and instant returns. So flawed was their knowledge of the land they sought to plant that they were armed with maps that "might as well serve for any part of Germany as for East-Florida." Those "infected" by enthusiasm for Florida settled isolated tracts where they lacked "Neighbours, Navigation, & Markets" required to translate the land's potential into profits. A new Florida planter might reasonably begin by harvesting swamp cypress, selling indigo seed, or renting land to immigrants who "might get Bread & even in the course of Years earn some Negroes." Those who imagined that the land's abundance would allow them to bypass the arduous process of land clearing, road building, and raising provisions "must expect the fate of those who have died before in Swamps." Particularly galling was the arrogance with which Florida's novice planters ridiculed South Carolina lands as infertile and spoke of rice as a "common or unclean" commodity.[93]

As planters heaped criticism on the Florida scheme, they applied "cracker" as a term of derision that later gained currency as an epithet demeaning poor, white Southerners. The term featured prominently in the correspondence between Henry Laurens, who sought to dampen enthusiasm for Florida, and James Grant, who presided over the colony's settlement as its governor and held out particular hopes for producing sugar there. Laurens urged his friend to prepare himself for the first hard frost of the season: "down goes all your Sugar Canes & hopes of Canes! My Dear Governor don't encourage people of worth to throw away their Money in that Country . . . it never will be more than a Cracker Country."

Laurens refused to accept Grant's retort that his own new settlement on Georgia's Altamaha River was a "Cracker Plantation." "[I]f it is," Laurens replied, "I wish all East Florida was Cracker too." Only "under the delusion of [his] present affections" could Grant call Laurens a "Cracker." The rapid development of Georgia's tidal rice lands by the "many old & knowing heads" who had forsaken Florida for this alternative frontier proved the difference.[94]

This debate between a South Carolina planter and the East Florida governor, each advocating a different version of plantation society, points to deeper concerns for social disorder beneath the surface of a good-natured exchange of insults. Florida was not all it was "cracked up" to be, a modern idiom that retains the meanings that surrounded "cracker" in this context. The early modern term exposed the ignorance of "vain and empty fellows" and typically targeted a "man of small capital and great appearance" for ridicule. In the early modern Scottish vernacular, a cracker was a braggart, a figure described by Samuel Johnson as "a noisy, boasting fellow." By midcentury tidewater and lowcountry observers used the term to disparage the Scotch-Irish settlers who inhabited the disordered Backcountry. When used in America, "cracker" meant a specific kind of rogue who was not only a deceitful vagrant, but also an unwelcome newcomer to colonial society. The word's Scottish origins made for a stinging, ethnically specific, rebuke to backcountry settlers' claims to political influence, class standing, and cultural position.[95] As propertied vigilantes known as Regulators battled with a "people called Cracker" for control of the Backcountry during the 1760s, general charges that poor settlers were a people of "abandon'd Morals, and profligate Principles—Rude—Ignorant—Void of Manners, Education, or Good Breeding" became vested in a specific group of hunters and squatters to which "Cracker" was affixed as a proper noun.[96] Implicated in violence on the Indian frontier and brutal raids during the Revolutionary War and extremely resistant to political control or standards of civility, "Carolina Crackers" embodied the threat of American degeneracy by which ordered society might slide into barbarism.[97]

The southern migration of landless whites reached Spanish Florida by 1755. These "rootless people called Crackers" were a "species of white renegade" that resisted all civil authority. The most debased of the group were "nomadic like Arabs," gained renown for their "depraved cunning," and constructed "Indian-style huts in the first unpopulated space fit to grow corn that they stumble upon." But "the best caste of *crackers*" adopted more stable, if still-crude, ways of life, building cabins and planting crops. The slave-owning Crackers of the St. Mary's district included 200 white settlers who "cloth[ed] their families . . . through the aid of homemade rustic looms."[98] In the last years of British rule, East Florida had become a haven for those who sought to escape the demands of government authority and appeared indifferent to the spirit of emulation that drew colonists elsewhere closer to the metropolis through their consumption of material goods.

That the "men of the first rank" who received East Florida grants were compared to Crackers and their nascent settlements ridiculed as "cracker plantations" bleached such derision of its class connotations.[99] The leading roles played by Scottish planters and investors in the new colony, however, may have retained the ethnic insult built into the term. Few who maligned East Florida with such language could have believed that British elites would end up spinning the cotton for their own garments, squatting on the Indian frontier, or shunning the marketplace. What this critique did imply, however, was that elite entrepreneurs, in their heedless pursuit of unrealizable settlement schemes, would fail spectacularly in their undertakings. Florida would become a "*Cracker Country*" as environmental and commercial constraints on plantation development asserted themselves and the land bubble that sustained migration and investment in the colony deflated. When elites abandoned the province, and speculative fervor gave way to disillusionment, the disconcerting presence of poor whites at the fringes of East Florida society would move to its center. After the "desertion of its Planters," East Florida would fall away from civility and incubate an all-but-savage society inhabited by the "Crackers in that Country" left behind. The colony's economic collapse in the 1770s seemed to confirm this scenario of declension. Only after abandoning hopes of "dubious article[s] of culture" and by learning to make rice and indigo did some Florida plantations avoid bankruptcy. Many others "lost such large sums of money as to break up some of the plantations and give no slight languor to them all." That Florida, "that Paradise . . . from whose Bourn no Money e'er returns," survived by building South Carolina–style plantations assured planters that their own expertise was indispensable for expanding British dominion on the subtropical mainland. The new colony's failure seemed also to prove that "Negroes are the most useful Servants in these Southern Climes."[100]

So "fevered, dilated, [and] overreaching" was its design, so out of touch with the realities of planting, that it was as if the colony had never been settled by British colonists at all when the Crown returned the territory to Spain in 1783. As a young man, William Bartram toured the new colony with his father John, whose rapturous report helped spur the first Florida land craze. The Bartrams believed their own hype. William had only just settled a plantation on the St. Johns River when "insolent" slaves and a bout with malaria ended his career as a planter. Returning as a naturalist in his own right a decade later, the younger Bartram reflected on the failure of the Florida enterprise as he walked the remains of Denys Rolle's ambitious settlement, its "old habitations . . . mouldering to earth." White servants brought to work there died or escaped its "constant contagious fevers" by migrating to the "more fruitful and populous regions of Georgia and Carolina." Instead of improving Florida, mourned Bartram, the most noticeable mark that British settlers had made on the landscape was to destroy "those extensive, fruitful Orange groves" that had once testified to the land's exotic environmental potential.[101]

The intention to make silk and grow sugarcane in Georgia and East Florida dusted off commodity ventures tried and abandoned decades earlier in Carolina. Reflected in the luster of these economic visions was the dull image of commonplace rice and mediocre indigo that enriched but did not ennoble their producers. In the transatlantic marketplace of opinion, South Carolina planters angled for advantage and sought to vindicate their characters. Perhaps the most damning attack against their society and themselves as its architects could be found here, in the re-imagination of the mainland subtropics apart from plantation slavery. To disregard the Carolina plantation complex as a blueprint for territorial expansion was to judge it dysfunctional, deem it incapable of reproduction, and discard the expertise of those who sustained it. A muted attack on slavery as a moral evil was subordinated in these charges to concerns about reproducing a British domain in America that was as secure as it was extensive. Whether it emerged out of a humanitarian sensibility linked to an emerging global capitalism or was attracted to the colonial Southeast as a place in which progressive social reform might be attempted, attacking the planter as a tyrant lodged this incipient antislavery perspective in British understandings of plantation America's prospects.[102] Planters fought for their future, as colonists and masters, when they worked to undermine these settlement schemes. As Georgia and East

Florida failed, leaving plantation slavery unchallenged as the only effective mode of extending British dominion over the Southeast, they could make positive claims that their plantation culture was an indispensable asset to empire.

South Carolina colonists agreed that planting had changed them, but contested the idea that they had become exotic, taking on the features of their unruly surroundings. Although planting created a distinctive new occupation and social category in America, it was not only a British enterprise in practical terms but also one created to extend British culture and society into newly colonized places. Against the caricature of the volatile, debased slave master that circulated in transatlantic commentaries about plantation America, colonists put forward a positive counterimage of the planter that stressed his role as an experienced cultivator. George Ogilvie's heroic protagonist in *Carolina; Or, The Planter* (1776) demonstrated a skilled capacity to make wilderness productive. In the most thorough statement of the self-image to which colonists throughout plantation America aspired, West Indian sugar planter Samuel Martin sought to redeem his fellow planters from their reputations as "Creolian despots" in the eyes of the world. He expanded the idea of planting as an economic activity to the status of an all-encompassing identity that he termed "plantership."[103]

In *An Essay upon Plantership* (1750) Martin celebrated the planter as a "practical philosopher" of the soil who combined the virtues of a life of husbandry with the sensibilities of entrepreneurs. A good planter was deeply involved in the details of production, and it was his duty "to inspect every part of the plantation with his own eyes." One was not born into this calling, but brought to it a mind shaped by a "liberal education," and a willingness to systematize "what he sees every day in common practice."[104] This ideal planter was "adept in figures and in all the arts of œconomy; something of an architect, and well skilled in mechanics." He was most "particularly a very skilful husbandman" who used his own experience above any imported model to determine the "right culture of his soil," on which depended the "*quantity,* and in a great measure the *quality* also of his produce." The ultimate object of plantership was not the profits that such diligence was sure to create, but rather the "conquest, or government," of his own "human passions." This conception of plantership justified mastery as legitimate, provided that masters honored the "laws of humanity" with "due benevolence" toward slaves. Martin's planter combined an improving farmer's knowledge, a merchant's acumen, and a just ruler's governance. His vision of planting as a new-world calling promised to refine the planter's character and rehabilitate his tarnished reputation as an American tyrant.[105]

Planters took seriously the critique of their characters, their agriculture, and their slave society. Negative assessments of South Carolina's plantation society rested on a vision of progress powerfully articulated by eighteenth-century political economists that privileged commerce over agriculture as civilization's highest state.[106] Another mark of advancement that South Carolina plantation society failed to achieve was imposed by British agricultural standards. To those who saw the arable, well-tended field as a universal ideal, the sandy pinelands and freshwater swamps that slaves planted in the Lowcountry were aptly named "barrens" and "*dismals.*"[107] Falling short of these standards for economy, culture, and landscape left colonists anxious about their claims to civility, but not without resources with which to make claims of their own. Just as English farmers in the fens defended their lands, characters, and methods against elites who sought to improve them, every "professed Planter" knew that slavery in the rice swamps made productive use of the land even as it created a landscape that departed from the image of the English countryside.[108] A century's worth of "time and experience" had "taught them the useful discoveries" of how to make commercial crops grow in the Lowcountry's volatile environment.

In debates over agriculture, as well as politics, Britons at home and abroad weighed empirical experience against principles deduced from reason as the lodestones that should guide their efforts to improve the world.[109] Their critics were armed with centralized standards by which the qualities of societies and people could be measured; colonists worked to show how the unique circumstances of American planting called for adaptation. By this empirical reckoning, the departures from form that defined South Carolina were distinguishing features rather than aberrations that flew in the face of reason. The leading idea behind schemes to settle the Townships, Georgia, and East Florida was that South Carolina did not have a viable future as a slave society. As plans to implant virtue failed to take hold in the greater Lowcountry, slavery and plantation agriculture proved their utility. Some colonists campaigned to end high duties on new slave imports, imposed by the Crown to slow the growth of South Carolina's rising black population, because this restraint impeded "the better settlement of the Colony." From 1750, South Carolina planters settled slaves along Georgia's tidal rivers and into the Lowcountry interior, an expansion that promised to secure Britain's southern frontier in North America.[110] This debate over slavery's place in American expansion on the continent was far from settled at this moment. It would be revived again, in sharper terms, after American independence. But it reveals that although some critics shaped imperial policy around the idea of plantation slavery's strategic weakness for a time, slavery's demise was far from a foregone conclusion in the late eighteenth century. South Carolina colonists found their views seconded by a critical mass of European intellectuals who affirmed plantation America's ongoing potential for economic and territorial growth.[111]

When read from the inside out, from the perspective of the officials and intellectuals in the imperial core, the charge of provincialism attached a stigma of inferiority to social difference. Colonists adopted this view of themselves at times, holding their societies against metropolitan standards and finding them inadequate by comparison. But this perspective was not the only one that they used to assess character and attribute social value. South Carolina planters also read provincialism from the outside in, from the vantage of living in distinctive regional places within a composite British empire.[112] This view of culture was shared by most people who inhabited Britain's non-English component countries (Scotland, Ireland, and Wales), resided in its many overseas extensions, or saw themselves as part of a disenfranchised class or out-of-favor region within England itself.[113] That colonists defended their provincial ways against metropolitan standards did not mean that they were preparing a precocious foundation for American cultural independence, casting off an old-world matrix of values like a suit of ill-fitting clothes. Such claims of American "exceptionalism" give too little weight to the intensifying desires of colonists to see themselves and to be seen as legitimately British to 1776 and beyond.[114] Planters made a case for their characters that merged British standards and American experiences as mutually reinforcing sources of value. In a sense, they reversed the polarity of the cultural relationship between colony and home country when they justified departures from normative standards as an adjustment to new-world conditions that entailed necessary changes in society, economy, and culture. Slaves and swamps, as much as these representative emblems of their plantation society interfered with their quest for civility, were also a robust source of growth that generated wealth required for material refinement, brought disordered land into orderly cultivation, and secured British territories against the claims of European rivals. Like the exotic staples they sent back to Britain, things of merit could emerge from the fringes of empire.

— 6 —

Henry Laurens's Empire

Henry Laurens was a "man well versed in the traffic of the world." From the 1750s he parlayed a fortune trading rice and slaves into a private plantation empire. More than 300 slaves, along with a dozen or more free white dependents, lived and labored under his command on five separate settlements. As he established new rice labor camps in Georgia's coastal plain, he purchased diversified estates in the Charlestown hinterland. The "store of commercial knowledge" he acquired over two decades spent managing long-distance exchange helped integrate dispersed plantations into a single interdependent venture. From his first plantation purchase in 1756 until his death in 1792, his extraordinary wealth, the ambitious reach of his plans, and the dramatic collapse of his enterprise during the War for Independence made his plantation empire distinctive.[1] As one of many merchants who invested in planting and as one of many planters who integrated several plantations into a coordinated venture, however, Laurens serves as an exemplar for the possibilities and vulnerabilities of extensive planting. The story of how his business came together and fell apart in the second half of the eighteenth century brings into view fundamental changes in organization and authority that remade plantation slavery in the Lowcountry at the close of the colonial period.

The idea that plantation economies stood outside early modern capitalism as islands of feudal social relations reconstituted with African slavery has given way to a picture of planters as calculating, profit-conscious participants in a world market for their commodities.[2] The Laurens enterprise exemplified a mode of plantation business that was not only attuned to the opportunities of the marketplace, but was also governed operationally and politically by commercial strategies. A mer-

200

chant turned planter, Laurens invested more than £100,000 in land and slaves. By any standard his plantations generated impressive returns on this investment. Because he kept precise accounts and one of his master ledgers has survived, we can calculate his profits and gauge the plantations' internal workings in detail. A voluminous body of surviving correspondence through which Laurens directed his business from afar complements his unique account book, a document that appears to have recorded every plantation expense and sale over eight years, from 1766 to 1773, a period of unbroken prosperity for the plantation economy.[3] Beyond showing that one particularly well-run plantation venture made a great deal of money for its owner, this reconstruction of life and work under Laurens's rule shows how governance changed as planters and slaves lived at opposite ends of the settled Lowcountry.

Landscape paintings of colonial plantations lead the eye up rising slopes to revere the great houses of the planter elite.[4] The idea of the rural mansion as symbol and seat of plantation command had no analogue within the Laurens holdings. The constant movement of people and things across this expansive enterprise, recorded by more than 1,600 transactions, challenges the very idea of the plantation as a place with a center. Nowhere was Laurens's authority as a master of dependents reinforced by his ongoing physical presence. Laurens and his family visited Mepkin Plantation, easily accessible from Charlestown and the only one of the five equipped with a suitably refined residence, for a "few days of amusement" from time to time, especially when he wanted to view the sowing of the season's crops or "fix" a new overseer in his position.[5] When he mounted a rare expedition to New Hope, Broughton Island, and Wright's Savannah plantations to the south, his slaves must have viewed him, with caution, as a powerful stranger. An intimate arbiter of their lives and work, he was rarely present to put a human face on the power he wielded through written directives to his proxies. To plantation landings on the Cooper, Santee, Savannah, and Altamaha rivers he dispatched schooners that took in the rice, wood, indigo, and corn enslaved men and women spent their lives producing and delivered the cloth and food on which they depended. Laurens played the role of master most persuasively as a merchant who circulated the goods that connected plantations to one another, to Charlestown, and to the wider Atlantic world.

On maps that chart the flow of goods for sale in the early modern Atlantic economy, arrows pointing across the ocean identify South Carolina as a consumer of slaves and manufactured goods and as a producer of rice and indigo. The demands of cultivating and processing these crops imposed a material matrix that shaped slave labor, land use, transatlantic commerce, and every other facet of the Lowcountry's economic culture. Defining Atlantic places by their commodities, however, obscures the vast energies that went into making and circulating commonplace items of consumption. An active domestic economy within this enterprise complemented its role as a supplier to the export economy. For a colony whose leading staple was something to eat, as well as something to sell, there was no hard line separating the two. As a patriarch who rarely saw his slaves, Laurens maintained his authority by doing what he had learned to do well over a twenty-year career as an importer, exporter, and commissions merchant. He satisfied some of their material wants, dispatching a fleet of small schooners to bring them bushels of maize and yards of cheap woolens and selling them small indulgences—tobacco, handkerchiefs, and the like—in exchange for the rice they produced on their own time. As his most distant plantations, those located more than 100 miles from Charlestown, began generating impressive profits, the success of his mercantile approach to planting suggested that there might be no limit to the plantation economy's expansion across space. Instead of a plantation mansion, Laurens and his family inhabited a compound on the outskirts of town that featured its own Cooper River wharf. This dwelling house and countinghouse in the suburb of Ansonborough was far from each of his plantations but served as a central household to them all.

The War for Independence severed these commercial connections between master and slaves, planter and plantations. Laurens abandoned his frontier plantations as British forces invaded the Lowcountry in 1778. Instead of rebuilding his enterprise on the same distended scale after the war, he gathered his surviving slaves together and lived among them until his death in 1792. Laurens immobilized the circulation of goods and people that had been so profitable before the war, treating slaves less as consumers to be supplied and more as subjects to be ruled. This retrenchment was designed to ease the conscience of a negligent master as it eased the burdens of slave life for those who survived the war. By the early 1780s a fourth of his slaves had disappeared, some as runaways and many others as victims of disease and privation from which he had failed to protect them. Laurens's headlong expansion into planting during the 1760s had been charged with optimism for slavery's expansion into new frontiers. As master of Mepkin Plantation in the 1780s, Laurens pondered

the future of South Carolina's plantation society with more circumspec-
tion. Stasis, rather than the constant movement of people and goods,
reigned as his contracted enterprise's governing ideal.

From Merchant to Planter

When Henry Laurens purchased a one-half interest in Wambaw Plantation in 1756, his social prospects changed instantly. As the new copro-
prietor of 1,500 acres in St. James Santee Parish, he met the province's
landholding qualifications to stand for election to the Assembly, which
he did, successfully, the following year. Laurens and John Coming Ball,
his partner and brother-in-law, pooled their slaves to work in Wambaw's
corn and rice fields, shared its horses and cattle, and owned jointly the
schooner *Wambaw* that made the frequent thirty-mile voyage between
the plantation's Santee River landing and Charlestown. As he sent more
than fifty slave hands into Wambaw's vast inland swamp, Laurens retained
the role and, in the very deeds that made him a planter, the occupational
title of "merchant."[6]

Despite the image of the southern planter as an autonomous patriarch,
South Carolina settlers had long made use of planting partnerships to
share the burdens and rewards of commodity production. In Laurens's
mercantile world, private partnerships managed long-distance commercial ventures as a matter of course. Those who joined as equals in the
"communion of profit and loss" pooled diverse areas of expertise, worked
to integrate operations efficiently, and spread their financial risks.[7] Acknowledging his "poor notion of Plantation business," Laurens relied on
Ball to take "all the care" of slave management and cultivation off his
hands, leaving him to market the plantation's rice and procure its supplies. Like partners in a trading firm, they shared Wambaw's proceeds
"half to each" and bore "every expence & even every Loss" together.
Laurens once sent slaves to Wambaw without tools, not yet aware of the
planter's precept that Negroes were "useless without . . . a broad Hoe &
an Axe to each." He made up for such novice lapses by organizing the
Wambaw's voyages, chartering oceangoing vessels to "carry off our Crop"
to the most favorable European markets, and importing cloth, rum, and
tools at wholesale prices. A comfortable segue into planting for Laurens,
the Wambaw partnership also brought new savings and coordination to
Ball's multiple-plantation enterprise.[8]

In 1762, six years after joining Ball to "plant in conjunction," Laurens paid £8,000 for Mepkin, a 3,100-acre tract thirty miles by water from Charlestown, on which stood a small existing settlement. He populated his second plantation with twenty-four slaves who were put to work— men, women, and boys alike—in fencing fields and repairing the property's Negro houses.[9] Mepkin's commercial situation sparked Laurens's interest in making a diversified plantation out of this underused portion of a large seventeenth-century land grant known as Wadboo Barony, the site of John Stewart's 1690 rice experiments. Located downstream from Monck's Corner, a regional entrepôt where wagons loaded with rice and indigo converged, the plantation was also within view of Strawberry Ferry, an anchorage to which oceangoing vessels retreated from the damaging salt water of Charlestown harbor. With its deepwater landing open to the colony's busiest site for exchange outside its Atlantic port, Mepkin's produce enjoyed cheap freight rates and ready transport to market. Its transportation and marketing costs, at only 1 percent of commodity sales, were half those of Wambaw's. Even when Laurens, who renovated Mepkin's house as a family retreat, lingered "more in the Country" than "in the Counting house," he was never more than an easy half day's river voyage from town.[10]

As a young clerk serving in a London firm during the mid-1740s, Laurens learned the intricacies of the Carolina trade at a time of plummeting rice prices and devastating plantation losses. Wambaw derived over 90 percent of its income from rice sales. His second plantation, which Laurens made a showplace for the profitability of commodity diversification, offered shelter from another rice-market collapse. Mepkin was perched on a fifty-foot bluff overlooking the Cooper River, and its high elevation, rich soil, and abundant forests seemed to create a temperate oasis in the sultry Lowcountry "capable of producing Indigo, Corn, Wheat, & all the produce of the best high Lands." By 1768 he had doubled his Mepkin workforce to more than fifty hands who generated more than £4,400 in earnings from sales of firewood, indigo, corn, and lumber, but "very little Rice."[11]

Although Laurens alone owned Mepkin, John Coming Ball directed both plantations until his death in 1764. Even before Ball died, however, Laurens had offered to buy out his partner. When he moved his family into their new house on the outskirts of Charlestown, Laurens had already converted much of his trading capital into land and slaves and set himself up as a planter on his own account.[12] Still dependent on the advice of

more experienced planters in matters of agriculture and slave management, he kept his own council as he added new components to his expanding multiple-plantation enterprise. As a surging rice market raised
the price of land close to Charlestown, Laurens was among a handful of
early colonists who set their sights on developing plantations along
Georgia's isolated Altamaha River in the 1760s. Broughton Island Plantation offered "1,000 Acres of as good River Swamp as in the Universe,"
ideally situated to create a vast tidal rice plantation.[13] In the spring of
1766 Laurens transported more than fifty slaves "to attempt a settlement
on that Island." In the same year he purchased a fourth plantation,

Map 6.1. Henry Laurens's plantations, 1756–1792. Map by Philip A.
Schwartzberg.

Wright's Savannah, on the South Carolina side of the Savannah River. His first Broughton Island rice crop yielded sixty bushels, generating enough income to defray the expenses of establishing it. Acquiring a bargain at half the price of land in South Carolina, Laurens settled a fifth plantation, New Hope, on the south side of the Altamaha River in 1768 and diverted slaves from Broughton Island to begin rice production there in 1770. To Wambaw and Mepkin, two long-settled plantations within easy water communication with Charlestown, he added in rapid succession three distant tracts, each newly carved from lowcountry swamps and focused on producing rice with the most advanced irrigation methods.[14]

Before devoting more than £50,000 to these new tidal rice lands and the slaves to work them, Laurens subjected his southern plantation venture to a merchant's calculus: he weighed the land's remarkable productivity against the costs of shipping rice to market. Its river swamps were "undoubtedly good as any Land can be but that alone would not induce me to plant bulky commodities upon it if the Navigation was not equally good." Altamaha's commercial promise lay in its openness to the largest transatlantic ships, which could ride the tides along a deepwater channel to "within one hundred Yards of my Barn." Such accessibility inspired feverish visions of the new region's rapid economic development. Laurens fantasized that someday he would watch "300 sail of Vessels," as many as called on Charlestown every year, venturing up the Altamaha River to load everything from silk to lumber.[15] Although transportation costs for the Georgia plantations, at 4 percent of earnings, were high compared with Mepkin and Wambaw, his fleet of schooners made this settlement in the plantation economy's outlying frontier both "convenient" and "profitable." By the late 1760s Laurens continued to "move on in the commercial Circle" as a regional shipper who "commanded Vessels to go here or there where ever a Freight is to be made." Whenever his plantations, separated by hundreds of miles across the Lowcountry, had commodities to send to town, Laurens dispatched a schooner "without dependence on any intermediate Market." Laurens did not abandon his identity as a merchant, but rather redefined the scope of his commercial activities to become a planter. Building a profitable multiple-plantation enterprise in the 1760s meant controlling regional water traffic as much as mastering slaves or developing land.[16]

Laurens's decked schooners docked at Rattray Green, his new residence and headquarters in suburban Ansonborough. Its shallow-water wharf could not admit the 100-ton rice and slave ships that Laurens had directed as a transatlantic commission merchant. As he narrowed the scope of his trading "within a small circle on my own Account," Laurens invested in a small fleet to ply the Lowcountry's rivers and coastline between his plantations and his countinghouse.[17] The *Wambaw, Ann, Baker, Brother's Endeavor,* and *Broughton Island Packet* were the sort of "small Vessels" that planters had long "employed . . . in carrying necessary articles from Charles Town . . . returning with the produce of their Farms & Plantations." In the summer of 1767 the *Wambaw* departed on one of these voyages bound for the Georgia plantations. Loaded with corn to feed Altamaha slaves, it returned with 50,000 shingles they had made after clearing a new rice swamp of its cypress trees.[18] Such commonplace internal commerce became a subject of high political dispute when customs inspector Daniel Moore seized this schooner and two others engaged in carrying goods between Charlestown and the southern plantations. Laurens's fight to reclaim his condemned boats in Vice Admiralty Court, publicized by a heated pamphlet war, gained him continental renown as an opponent of British encroachments into customary economic freedoms.[19]

Colonists resented attempts by customs officers, "who did not understand the situation in S.C.," to subject these coasting voyages to regulatory scrutiny. The prospect that new efforts to enforce navigation laws might cut off traffic to the new Georgia settlements was also a chilling corrective to their vision of the Lowcountry's developmental future. Cultivating Georgia's coastal plain depended on unfettered transportation across provincial boundaries as much as it did on planters' newfound ability to irrigate rice fields from the overflowing tides. Laurens held up Moore and Vice Admiralty judge Egerton Leigh to public censure for the irregularities of the proceedings in a series of critical pamphlets. Privately, Laurens mused that if customs officials extracted a fee whenever one of his schooners entered the open ocean to serve outlying plantations, he might be forced to "break up my settlement upon Altamaha River" or at the very least "contract" his planting empire "within the sphere of a large Canoe."[20] Such a retrenchment, forced by the hand of metropolitan authorities, would cut off his three southern plantations from access to supplies that made their focus on rice possible.

In his 1769 rebuttal to Laurens, *The Man Unmasked,* Egerton Leigh invoked traditional suspicions of merchants as duplicitous political actors.

Leigh pictured Laurens in his element at the counter of trade devoting "poring attention" to the "intricate concerns of pounds, shillings, and pence." With vulgar familiarity, Laurens associated with every man he met on the street and "every *Skipper* in the trade." His "*vanity* and *self-intoxication*" were gratified as a respected "arbitrator . . . in little differences of accounts and reckonings." Laurens loved nothing more, according to Leigh, than "sitting at home in all the pomp of *oracular* importance, ready to advise *raw beginners* in the *mysteries of trade.*" Laurens was a "Machiavel" at heart, as incapable of pursuing his case as a disinterested fight for justice as he was of dispensing alms without making sure that others witnessed his scrupulously public acts of charity. That this "*little obscure man*" in South Carolina should rise above his social rank and limited abilities to become an aggressive "dabbler" in law and politics revealed Laurens as a "quack." He was driven not by "patriotism, but private pique, malice and revenge" against those he believed had done harm to his interests. Laurens was a creature who could only understand the world within the orbit of his own "partial, personal, and local" concerns. At the end of the day, who could take seriously charges of fraud and abuse against the king's officers from a "mere *marker* and *shipper* of Rice"?[21]

Because Laurens's schooners, their hulls rotting in the harbor, languished in legal limbo for much of the period covered by his account book, this dispute has impoverished the data from which we might reconstruct the role of coastal shipping in his enterprise's finances. The controversy surrounding these seizures, however, exposes the crucial role merchants played in coordinating the multilateral exchanges that made long-distance planting ventures possible. When he criticized those who supported Laurens in his acrimonious quest to regain his schooners as "*mercantile patriots,*" Leigh appealed to South Carolina's planters as a class of gentlemen whose landed wealth gave them special claims to political authority. If such was his intention, Leigh failed to appreciate South Carolina's evolving political culture. His choice of words gave Laurens the opportunity to claim that Leigh wrote them with "a kind of *sneer* or *derision*" to "stigmatize" his merchant opponents in this controversy as social inferiors.[22] Despite the fact that they squared off against one another over commodity prices, wealthy merchants and planters saw one another as economic, social, and political partners by the 1760s. As merchants like Henry Laurens entered plantership, these very occupational categories blurred into one another, challenging the political inheritance that cast suspicion on traders while seating virtue in the exclusive hands of a landed gentry.

Leigh ridiculed Laurens's mercantile habits as the practices of a supercilious personality, but this attack, as personally vicious as it was, captured its target's obsessive regard for the quotidian tasks of economic life. Laurens paid scrupulous attention to his accounts and transactions. He set his own conduct as a model of rectitude for others to follow and, with self-righteous confidence, chastised those who failed to live up to his standards. He took obvious pride in his mastery of commerce and could not resist the impulse to instruct those who sought the advantages of his patronage or fell, like slaves and children, under the sway of his authority. Laurens seemed to resent most the charge that he was a "dabbler" who had reached beyond the narrow sphere of his competence. This insult challenged his belief that men of integrity could reinvent themselves in the Lowcountry, that character trumped skill in the quest for position and fortune, and that he himself could translate proficiency with the minutiae of trade into the expertise required for his new life as a planter and political leader.[23]

Over the course of his two-decade career as a merchant, Laurens constructed a network of associates on which his trading ventures depended. For every critical contribution to his business made by correspondents in London, Bristol, Philadelphia, or Bridgetown (Barbados), Laurens worked to reciprocate by selling their goods, chartering ships, providing market information, and sending tokens of appreciation from Charlestown. In addition to the hundreds of letters he wrote to maintain these transatlantic "friendships" in virtually every North Atlantic port, he found himself called upon to stand security for debts, enter into new commercial partnerships, and help establish junior traders. Asking his British associates for access to his own money, denominated as credits in their books, could be a tender subject in difficult economic times. Compared with the "constant hurry of Trade," planting promised Laurens and other merchants an opportunity to shun debt, "procure contentment" on his own terms, and focus his energies within a more "narrow compass."[24]

Throughout British plantation America the idea of the plantation as an arcadian retreat provided a vision of independence that merchants saw as a release from the interdependencies demanded by commerce. Merchants envied what they saw as planters' absolute command over slaves and land. Schooled in the arts of long-distance business integration, how-ever, merchants-turned-planters learned to coordinate timely transpor-tation and maximize returns by squeezing savings from every conceivable expense.[25] These sharpened sensibilities for exchange prepared them to become plantation agents and proprietors of extensive new multiple-plantation enterprises. In practice their commercial approach to organ-izing plantations as interdependent units of production and consumption and linking them to the Charlestown marketplace belied the romantic vision of the plantation as an isolated rural idyll. Bringing commercial sophistication to planting made Henry Laurens a great deal of money. Within his lowcountry empire, he circulated goods and orchestrated exchange as if planting was another branch of trade.[26]

Integrating Core and Frontier Plantations

The social relations cobbled together on new colonial plantations must have been jarring in their artifice. Laurens dispatched slaves to occupy vacated buildings on Wambaw and Mepkin that someone else's slaves had once made their homes. Others, axes in hand, were destined for Wright's Savannah, Broughton Island, and New Hope, where they cleared spaces on the knolls of high and dry land at the edges of swamps on which to build crude shelters. Laurens's power as master over his slaves was all but absolute in law, but in practice most of his slaves knew him only through brief encounters when he purchased them in town or made a rare plan-tation visit. In his absence an array of hired employees exercised authority on his behalf. Spanish moss surely dangled from the live oaks that lined Mepkin Plantation's avenue, but those who inhabited Laurens's enterprise would have seen few of the symbols that a later generation would use to tint their multigenerational occupation of the land with the patina of legitimacy. As colonists settled new tracts during the eighteenth century, plantation life bore the awkward adjustments of new construction.

During the 1760s Laurens created two distinctive kinds of plantations, one marked by long-term occupation and the other by recent settlement. Mepkin, located within the core zone of settlement, featured commodity diversification, entrenched slave households, proximity to Charlestown, specialized farm buildings, and well-finished white dwellings. Like other plantations in the secondary zone some thirty to fifty miles from town, rice-focused Wambaw was specialized rather than diversified, but it resembled Mepkin in its relatively high levels of material refinement and social stability. Laurens referred to Broughton Island, Wright's Savannah, and New Hope as his "out" or "southern" plantations.[27] Slaves built all three into highly productive tidal rice plantations from scratch on undeveloped riverside tracts. These new plantations along the southern coastal frontier featured constant infusions of male, "new Negro" slaves, isolation from markets and neighbors, and comparatively crude material conditions. Focused almost entirely on the production of rice for export, these "remote frontier Settlements" were labor camps whose slaves depended on imported corn for their survival.[28] Living within an urban, core, or frontier household on this enterprise shaped, at a basic material level, the character of opportunity, work, suffering, family life, and access to goods for approximately 325 enslaved people.

Laurens's frontier plantations specialized in the production of rice for export. Given the expense of transporting goods to and from the southern coast and the productivity advantage of irrigating rice by the tides, this focus made economic sense. The extreme to which this logic was put into practice, however, reveals the new tidal rice plantations as a departure from earlier plantation forms. Typically built after 1760 in the southern- and northernmost reaches of the Lowcountry, frontier rice plantations were the much-altered offspring of the smaller inland rice plantations of the early eighteenth century and the diversified rice and indigo plantations of the 1740s and 1750s. On each of Laurens's three frontier plantations, rice accounted for more than 98 percent of all commodity sales during the period 1766–1773. Nonrice sales were so paltry that each can be explained as an exceptional event. Almost all of New Hope's nonrice "sales," for example, were amounts charged to the account of its overseer, William Barham, for goods he "took out of my barn without leave & sold" in 1771.[29] This severe tilt toward rice monoculture is surprising because Laurens imagined that his southern plantations would, in time, grow enough provisions to feed the slaves who lived there, as well as a diverse range of commodities for sale. As slaves excavated irrigation channels that watered Broughton Island's rice fields from the overflowing Altamaha, Laurens speculated on the prospects for making hemp, cotton, and indigo along with rice. Although "Rice, to be sure, must be the principal Article," Laurens expected "full Crops of provision after this Year 1771." Despite these hopes for self-sufficiency, the frontier plantations' focus on rice trapped them in a perpetual state of provisions deficit.

None managed to generate meaningful surpluses of corn that could be marketed for profit.[30] Beguiled by the promise of new commodities, Laurens dreamt of the future of plantation society within the idioms of crop diversification and agricultural innovation. His frontier plantations, however, realized their economic potential through an intensive specialization in rice.

Mepkin Plantation, by contrast, produced enough corn and "peas" (beans) to feed its own slaves, supply the frontier plantations with food they lacked, and still generate a substantial maize surplus (7,482 bushels in the period 1766–1773) that was sold at market.[31] Instead of specializing in the production of a single commodity, Mepkin slaves produced huge quantities of firewood, rice, corn, indigo, and lumber for sale, each of which contributed at least 10 percent to overall plantation earnings. Mepkin's slave population, about 70 strong, produced goods that sold for more than the combined efforts of more than 200 slaves on the three frontier plantations. Laurens took advantage of Mepkin's prime commercial location to gear slave labor toward transatlantic as well as local markets of consumption. On its high bluff overlooking the Cooper River's continuous water traffic, Mepkin was precisely the kind of diversified plantation that planters sought to create after the economic catastrophe of King George's War in the 1740s exposed the risks of depending on rice alone. With its multiple salable staples and regular corn surpluses, Mepkin was the enterprise's most productive unit, as well as its most reliable supplier of provisions.

Mepkin's most valuable commodity was neither rice nor indigo, but commonplace firewood, which accounted for a third of total commodity sales from 1766 to 1773. Turning riverside woodlands into more than £15,000 worth of fuel demonstrated the advantage that cheap access to Charlestown conferred on plantations within easy navigation of the city. Nearly a century of intensive agricultural use in the core plantation zone had deforested lands closest to navigable waterways. As a source of firewood, Mepkin's undeveloped land had "become so valuable as to be well worth preserving for Market" instead of clearing to plant crops.[32] Abundant forests and inexpensive transportation allowed Laurens to profit from the sale of 4,189 cords of cheap, bulky, and badly needed firewood.

Mepkin's sawmill produced tens of thousands of board feet of pine and oak plank, masts and yards for ships, cedar posts for fencing, and, on one occasion, an entire house frame shipped in pieces to Grenada in the

Windward Islands. Slave sawyers cut the lumber for their own "Negro Houses," constructed canoes and rafts, and cut the pieces for a schooner Laurens ordered built to ship even more lumber across the Lowcountry.[33] Wambaw produced thousands of shingles to avoid a total dependence on its rice crops. Unlike the frontier plantations, with their tidally flooded fields that could be replanted in perpetuity, Wambaw's inland swamp fields grew too grassy to cultivate forever. As Wambaw slaves cleared new rice fields to take their place, they turned swamp woods into waterproof shingles that protected houses in the Lowcountry and Caribbean from the elements. Two of Laurens's schooners, the *Baker* and the *Wambaw,* plied the inland waterways between these two plantations and Charlestown, and Laurens regularly requested that his boats be loaded with wood for their return trips to town.[34]

Plantations as diversified as Mepkin could change to suit the market. In 1765, three years after buying Mepkin, Laurens shifted plantation production from rice to indigo. He purchased pumps and built vats to process the plant into cakes of dye. Thinking that indigo's strong price performance would continue, he made the change to better "discharge the heavy expences" of refurbishing and expanding the plantation. For the next five years the seasonal rhythms of indigo cultivation and processing governed slave labor on Mepkin, so much so that Laurens asked that the slaves on what he called "my Indigo Plantation" be exempted from mandatory parish road work during the labor-intensive "making season." The price of rice, not indigo, surged in the second half of the 1760s just after he made the switch. Realizing that he had mistimed the market, Laurens abruptly halted indigo production in 1769 and again made Mepkin a rice plantation.[35] It took only a single transition year, 1769–1770, in which the plantation sold very little of either commodity, to end indigo production, repair irrigation works, and replant Mepkin's rice fields. Laurens sent his slaves to the sawmill to compensate, increasing lumber sales by 60 percent as indigo sales fell by 83 percent. Despite this wrenching change, plantation income remained above £6,000 for the season, actually increasing from the year before.

Mepkin was a creature of the market, a place of production in which changes in the price current for any of the commodities it produced altered the character of slave work. Such changes undermined slaves' expectations. When it was an indigo plantation, the dye's processing schedule moved slaves decisively between indigo and nonindigo work: in

1766–1767 monthly sales accounts show that slave workers chopped fire-wood exclusively and intensively in the months of October, December, and March, when indigo's labor demands were lightest. When Mepkin focused again on rice, its slaves engaged in rice, corn, firewood, and lumber production simultaneously.[36] As Laurens changed the staple-crop orientation of the plantation to capture price advantages, every transition disrupted labor practices and nullified previous agreements over work. Agricultural change undermined work customs that set limits to the expropriation of labor; it dismantled privileged positions in labor hierarchies that slaves turned to their material advantage while their skilled jobs lasted. When Mepkin slaves were not occupied hoeing rice, cutting indigo, chopping wood, or sawing planks, they stripped red-oak bark destined for Charlestown's tanneries, mowed hay for the town's stables, and grew extra peas, potatoes, and peanuts for sale to neighboring planters and Charlestown consumers. Although all these minor commodities together generated only 1 percent of total earnings, they suggest that Mepkin slaves had few waking hours that were not devoted to making goods for Laurens to sell. The "hands upon that Plantation," he wrote, "may be imployed in various ways to advantage."[37]

Compared with the range of tasks undertaken by Mepkin's slaves, work on the frontier plantations was numbingly uniform. When trunk minders opened irrigation channels to the ebbing tide, emptying rice fields of water, slaves spread out over the muddy fields to attack weeds with their hoes. Throughout the winter and between bouts of hoeing, harvesting, and processing rice, they excavated clogged drains and trenches and repaired earthen embankments eroded by the constant scouring of water against soil. The first contingents of Laurens's slaves cleared the land and carved it into rectangular fields; those who followed worked to maintain and expand these irrigated plots. Overseer James Bailey directed slaves in building a "Bank round Broughton Island Plantation" in 1771 that permitted fresh water to spread across every one of the plantation's 175 acres of rice land every time the Altamaha rose with the flowing tide. Because water released across its flat expanse covered the whole, the plantation was said to be "fully in the tide's-way." Even when the river surged to its highest level with the spring tides of every new and full moon, Broughton Island's banks kept it "free from any Damage by Freshes," or destructive floods. Such advantageously located land occupied, in the planters' argot, the "pitch of the tide," an ideal place for rice agriculture. Laurens drew a map of less developed New Hope Plantation, "improved upon Paper as I could wish to see it improved upon the spot." His lost sketch almost certainly imposed a tidal rice plantation's distinctively geometric grid of banks and channels on New Hope's portion of the Altamaha's flood plain.[38]

When Laurens purchased the 2,000-acre tract of flat, grassy land that Charles and Jermyn Wright had begun to clear for rice production, he sought above all else to ensure that Wright's Savannah Plantation would command its own water. He was certain that the "Tides" on his third frontier plantation were "indisputable" for making rice. Laurens bought the land (seized and sold at auction after the Wrights defaulted on a debt secured by the property) cheaply, but wondered whether neighbors' claims on the water that flowed around the plantation might compromise his ability to plant it. If the plantation were to become "dependant" on another's water, its location at the pitch of the tide meant nothing. His slaves shored up two critical dams along the property's borders, protecting new rice fields from natural floods, as well as the runoff from adjoining plantations. When neighbor James Brisbane gained a legal right to cut one of these dams, releasing an inland swamp to drain across Wright's Savannah's fields, Laurens prepared to sell the plantation as "unimprovable." Effective "Banking & Ditching" were essential prerequisites for a tidal rice plantation. Laurens expected his overseers at the frontier plantations, as their single most important duty, to "improve my land" and keep it in "good order" by maintaining the "Crop Banks" that made tidal irrigation possible. Slaves spent most of their working lives knee-deep in mud and water, maintaining the irrigation systems that nourished and protected growing rice even as the rigors of this labor impaired their own health.[39]

Developed to produce commodities in strikingly different ways, these diversified core and specialized frontier plantations developed distinctive material and demographic profiles. Investments in core plantation buildings, families, and refinement created households that were meant to persist and reproduce. On the frontier, by contrast, material life was stripped to its barest functional foundations. Laurens sent his team of skilled slave builders led by Samuel Massey, a literate mulatto slave, along with James Russell, a hired white carpenter who traveled with his own slave assistants, to reconstruct Mepkin. These workers expanded the Laurens family's country home, Mepkin House, installed floors "of the very best Yellow pine without blemishes," and performed the "piecing and patching" required to bring an aging residence up to his standards. They built sheds complete with glass windows, restored existing "Negro Houses," and built new ones from planks sawed from Mepkin's own trees. Laurens hired another white carpenter, William Yate, to build slave houses, in which he considered installing brick chimneys, at Wambaw. In the end, Massey and "his boys," Mercutio and Jack, built more conventional and less expensive clay and wood chimneys to make hearths for Wambaw's black households.[40]

Such rough-hewn "huts" were built to deteriorate, but even the most disposable buildings on Mepkin and Wambaw were paragons of refinement compared with the crudely built structures on the out plantations. To bring white artisans to the frontier, Laurens persuaded recent European immigrants to earn claims on his future patronage by paying their dues overseeing his distant holdings on the southern coast. Matthias Zopfi, "who seems to be a careful fellow," worked for more than fifteen months as a carpenter on the Georgia plantations. The same could not be said for Wright's Savannah's American-born artisan, John Morgan. Instead of repairing the main white residence, plagued by leaky windows and cracking floors, Morgan colluded with the overseer, William Godfrey, to spend his days building pieces for Godfrey's nearby indigo vats and his nights "dancing & drinking" with the "Overseers in the Neighborhood." The resident carpenter was discovered "in Liqueur" by John Lewis Gervais, a trusted Laurens associate sent to inspect the place. Wright's Savannah's decrepit house lacked a bed, and Gervais "did not chuse to accept" the overseer's offer to sleep on its "one Matress." So wanting in hospitality was the plantation that Gervais stayed at a neighbor's house during his six-day investigation into fraud and disorder on Wright's Savannah. It was a place of "dreadful Poverty" that lacked even the basic rudiments of a working farmstead, such as livestock pens. Its slaves survived on imported provisions.[41] Massey, Laurens's enslaved bricklayer and carpenter, avoided venturing south of the Savannah River, and Laurens only sent him to Georgia as a punishment when he behaved "foolishly." Laurens rarely mentioned the state of his Georgia plantations' houses and buildings, leaving overseers and slaves there largely to fend for themselves. Broughton Island Plantation lacked even a barn in which to store its rice during its first few years of existence.[42] Overseer James Rossel, a Huguenot raised in Germany, saw his life on this "remote" island as "almost a state of exile." Concerned with the isolated plantation's vulnerability to attack, Laurens armed it with at least six swivel guns, the kind of small cannon typically mounted on a ship's rail to repel invaders.[43]

Along with crude material conditions, the frontier plantations' slave population was skewed to increase rice production at the expense of family formation. Between 1766 and 1773 the account book records the purchase of sixty-five slaves, only six of whom were sent to Mepkin. The fifty-nine others destined for the frontier included almost twice as many men as women. Laurens also sent more than three times as many "new Negroes" as "country born" African Americans to the frontier.[44] Along with Laurens's decisions about what kinds of people to mobilize to settle his properties along the southern coast, the overwhelming numbers of adult, male Africans imported into South Carolina through the transatlantic slave trade reinforced the demographic imbalance that shaped black society on Broughton Island, New Hope, and Wright's Savannah. Drawing on his connections with London-based Richard Oswald and Company, a leading slave-trading firm that controlled the West African Bance Island factory, Laurens planned to send a ship on his own account to procure "prime Negroes" directly for the Altamaha River plantations.[45]

Throughout the rice-producing Lowcountry a "good Negro woman has the same day's work as the man in the planting and cultivating of the fields." Laurens suggested to an aspiring planter that an ideal plantation should be composed of "Men & Wives for the Field," with a few women performing specialized work "about the House" and a few men trained in sawing, building, and other craft work. On the newly established tidal rice plantations, however, tasks for which women were considered "weak hands," including cutting down trees, digging irrigation ditches, and processing rice by hand, loomed disproportionately large. Although men and women worked the same one-quarter or one-half acre daily tasks on inland fields, tidal "squares," surrounded by irrigation channels, were "proportioned to the strength of the negroes who work them." Laurens expected the young, male Africans who swelled the populations of the southern plantations to chop, dig, hoe, and pound more productively than a laboring population that featured greater demographic balance in terms of sex and age.[46] That these African- and male-leaning populations limited marriages and complicated the formation of African American families was a concern he subordinated to the imperatives of rice production.

Indifferent to families on the frontier, Laurens intervened personally in the social lives of slaves who lived on plantations closer to town. He sent a schooner to Wambaw with "Young Women" for men "who have lately lost their wives." Laurens dispatched a newly enslaved African woman, "My Lady being her country name," to Mepkin to "be a Wife to whome she shall like best amongst the single men." Even as Laurens removed fathers and husbands from Wambaw to become Broughton Island's first settlers, he recognized the family connections that thrived on his established plantations. Each conscript to the frontier was to have "the strongest assurances that each Man's property shall be safely deliver'd," a promise that was easy to keep for the "married Men" because "their Wives will give an eye to their respective goods."[47] The contrasts between Laurens's "settled" and "out" plantations began in the fields and extended into households. Slaves who lived closer to town cultivated bumper crops of corn, and with this self-sufficiency came the material foundations of a domestic economy that featured diverse jobs, sound buildings, and well-established slave families. The costs to community, family, and material life of reshaping wilderness tracts into working tidal plantations and specializing intensively on a single market crop made places like New Hope inversions of places like Mepkin. The all-encompassing drive for rice production on the frontier warped the plantation form against slaves' well-being, impoverishing it as a place in which to build families and elaborate social connections and simply to survive. As masters of multiple plantations extended their enterprises across the Lowcountry, they sorted their slaves, as if by a cruel lottery, into starkly different forums for life and work.

Providing and Consuming

Reconstructing consumption on the Laurens enterprise reveals a vital circuit of exchange in goods made to sustain life and assert authority. Laurens's double-entry bookkeeping, with credits confronting debits on every account-book page, illuminates consumption as a process that used up people, cloth, food, and tools to send out the staple commodities of transatlantic trade. For every barrel of rice sold and shipped eastward, imported articles of consumption moved in the opposite direction, logging charge after charge. In addition to their labor in the rice fields, slaves cultivated corn, raised livestock, and chopped down trees, the activities of a large internal domestic economy that a staples-focused view of trans-atlantic exchange obscures.[48] Accounting for this world of consumption makes apparent what planters, overseers, and slaves took for granted: that plantations were places that supported living (and dying), as well as making. More specifically, plantations were makeshift villages in which scores of black people lived and worked and to which a few white people sojourned to make sure that the work got done and that the value of what slaves produced exceeded, by an order of magnitude, the value of what they consumed.

Sheer distance between Laurens and his slaves obstructed in practice the formal mastery he exercised in law. Within Mepkin, Wambaw, and Wright's Savannah were widely spaced "settlements," separately planted fields in and around which distinct groups of slaves lived and worked under the command of individual overseers.[49] As working hands reckoned the constraints and opportunities of their narrowly circumscribed lives, they looked not to Laurens but to a hired overseer or a supervising driver who apportioned their rations of food and clothing, measured out their field tasks, and enforced order with a whip. The practical concerns of enslaved workers and free managers created local communities of interest and contest far removed from Laurens in Charlestown or London. To reconstruct patriarchal command from a distance, he reached into the intimate, material lives of those on the plantations by serving them as consumers.

In Laurens's view, as slaves and overseers made claims upon the re-sources of his household, they subjected themselves to his authority as its dependents, even though this "household" was one articulated across hundreds of miles into component plantations. Recognizing his physical absence from the plantations is important. Historians have used Laurens to epitomize both paternalism (linked to the domestic ideal of the modern nuclear family) and patriarchy (linked to the hierarchical ideal of the early modern extended family). Yet his extensive, multiple-plantation enterprise offered an unlikely setting for relations of power based on *any* familial model.[50] The fundamental, legitimating action for any male head of household was not to provide, to scrutinize, or to discipline, but to be present to do so. Laurens, however, like all planters who lived primarily in Charlestown or owned more than one plantation, did not live among his slaves. An occasional resident at Mepkin, Laurens visited his frontier plantations perhaps three times. Abroad for much of the early 1770s, he paid no more than cursory attention to his slaves from his Westminster lodgings. He idealized them as "poor Creatures who look up to their Master as their Father, their Guardian, & Protector, & to whom there is a reciprocal obligation upon their Master." Yet Laurens left the needy childlike creatures of his perception under the control of overseers whom he motivated with financial incentives—under the "shares" system they received a portion of the total proceeds—to drive workers to produce large crops.[51]

In 1764, a year after he obtained grants for more than 5,000 acres of land along Georgia's Altamaha River, Laurens settled a new residential seat from which he could better govern his expanding plantation enterprise. He was forty years old when he moved with his wife, Eleanor, their three young children, and perhaps a dozen slaves to this new property in the Ansonborough neighborhood on the outskirts of town. Occupying Rattray Green marked a formal retirement from the "hurry & bustle" of his commission firm with a move from the center of town to its sparsely settled environs. As much as this transition marked a withdrawal from commercial entanglements, Laurens in fact designed his suburban compound to be a nexus of exchange. More than a family residence, the property was a central household that served those who lived on each of the plantations. Its complex of buildings—including a residence, countinghouse, kitchen, stable, and smokehouse—drew together rural and urban forms and functions in ways that hinted at its role as a link between the plantation countryside and Charlestown's Atlantic-facing commerce with the world.[52]

He saw his family's new home as a "Cottage" retreat that offered a visitor to the port city "purer air than that which floats about the filthy moat & docks below." At the same time, he could describe this dwelling as a "large elegant brick House" outfitted with a staircase of imported mahogany and walls lined with oak wainscoting. Its expensive trappings (including two sets of china, silver, looking glasses, a harpsichord, a barometer, and "prints of birds") suggested the interior of a well-appointed town house, even if the exterior was meant to suggest a dwelling that was more rustic than refined.[53] He sought to enjoy a "quiet rural Life" here, even as he viewed the construction of his tenements from its parlor and watched the water traffic on the Cooper River from its adjoining wharf. "[W]hat should I have to do all the Summer?" he wondered, as he prepared to return from an extended trip abroad: "Eat Watermelon, Sleep after Dinner for want of Employment, and get the Fever and Ague," he concluded. The life of leisure he imagined was belied by an actual regimen of business activities guided by production and consumption on his plantations. Surrounded by glass-encased mahogany bookshelves in his library, he spent his mornings and evenings drafting the letters that kept his empire in motion. During his working days, when he was not called to attend the sessions of the Commons House of Assembly as one of its elected members, he greeted visitors and oversaw his clerks in a nearby countinghouse as they drew up accounts and copied his correspondence.[54] When one of his schooners arrived from the plantations, they tallied barrels of rice and casks of indigo and readied bolts of fabric and hogsheads of rum for a return voyage, entering costs and proceeds into the debit and credit columns of his master accounting ledger. Ansonborough afforded few moments of relaxation when the plantations were in need. For days at a time Laurens "was so busied in getting many articles to send into the Country for Plantation use" that he found few opportunities to write distant friends, much less break the seals on their waiting letters.[55]

On any day, before a slave performed a single daily task at a core, frontier, or urban site across the enterprise in the 1770s, Laurens needed to secure about 10 bushels (about 700 pounds) of corn and beans to feed approximately 340 "Negroes big & Small & the White people."[56] If purchased on the open market, the more than 3,500 bushels of provisions required annually to sustain this population at close to the caloric minimum would cost more than £2,000 for an enterprise that generated revenue on the order of £20,000 per year. Providing food for so many people living so far apart was the enterprise's principal undertaking after commodity production. Rather than making each plantation an autonomous farmstead responsible for feeding its slaves, Laurens circulated food throughout the enterprise, joining plantation food producers and consumers together in a single domestic economy.[57]

In times of dearth, planters who lacked provisions depended on an occasional "Neighbourly loan" to feed their slaves. For exchanging food, the enterprise took the form of a simulated neighborhood connected by long-distance schooner traffic rather than geographic proximity. Its provisions-rich core plantation, Mepkin, transferred massive quantities of food to its provisions-poor frontier plantations to make possible their specialization in rice. The three frontier plantations were each substantial net consumers of food. Broughton Island gained the most from this net-

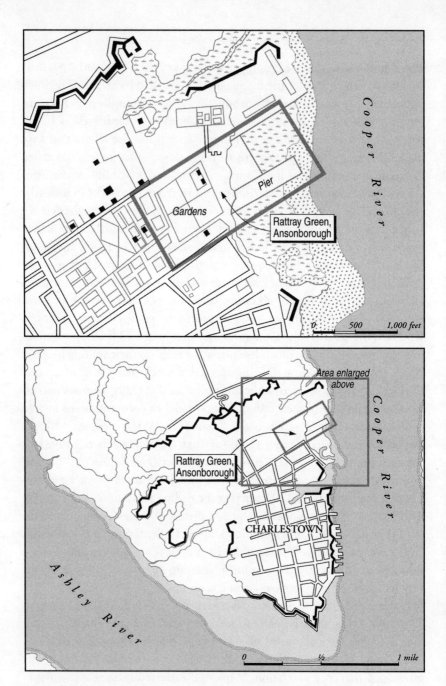

Map 6.2. Rattray Green: Henry Laurens's Ansonborough compound, Charlestown, c. 1780. Source: Joseph F. W. Des Barres, *A Sketch of the Operations before Charlestown, the Capital of South Carolina* (London, 1780). Map by Philip A. Schwartzberg.

work.[58] During the period 1766–1773 Mepkin surpluses provided the plantation with 207 bushels of rough rice, 209 bushels of beans, and 1,122 bushels of corn. Wambaw supplied it with smaller quantities of corn and some "small" rice (fit for the table but not for export to Europe), in addition to shingles for building construction. Broughton Island drew on Ansonborough's stores for imported consumption goods, including tea, pepper, sugar, herring, oil, butter, hams, and ale. In return, the Georgia plantation sent 5,498 pounds of small rice to town. This by-product of commodity production, worth less than £100, probably constituted the chief ration for black residents in Ansonborough.

No hard line separated the market and domestic economies in colonial South Carolina. In 1771, when corn fetched the extraordinary price of £1 per bushel, Wright's Savannah slaves, diverted from the rice fields, generated a onetime corn surplus, part of which went to Mepkin, which just the year before had provided it with 100 bushels, enough to feed its population for more than a month. Despite their primary orientation toward transatlantic markets, lowcountry plantations produced a staple commodity that was edible, as well as vendible. Because plantations were connected to local, interregional, and intercolonial markets for foodstuffs of all kinds, maize was likewise a subsistence staple and a potential commodity. Huge surpluses of corn at Mepkin, the enterprise's breadbasket, supplied slaves on the frontier plantations with bowls of hominy and, when sold at market, generated substantial returns. When Laurens believed that the price of corn would rise, he leveraged his role as a provisions producer and consumer to stake out a "long" position in the corn market more than a century before the advent of commodity futures offered a financial instrument for just such a maneuver. Nothing better illustrates the commercial orientation of the plantations than his order to prepare Mepkin's corn for shipment to town, where he planned to warehouse it until the price peaked. Laurens ordered his Mepkin overseer to keep only two months' provisions on hand, for corn could be purchased when slaves needed to eat.[59] Although the plantations together produced more than enough corn to feed everyone living within the enterprise, Laurens sold so much of it as a commodity that he was forced to buy 2,946 bushels to feed his slaves during the seven-year period covered by the account book. Because he sold corn, on average, for higher prices than he purchased it, foregoing self-sufficiency in food turned out to be a profitable form of market dependence.[60]

"Common prudence" dictated that colonists adapt to periodic corn shortages by making "a reserve of Rice." More frequently, rice planters withheld low-quality rice from transatlantic sale and used it to feed their slaves. During the first half of the eighteenth century, sloops destined for the West Indies filled unused space in their holds with shingles and staves. After midcentury these traders purchased unprocessed rice, a small part of which slaves produced independently. This "rough" rice was valuable as food, but its low quality made it not worth the labor to process for export. Broken or undersized "small" rice sold for about half the price of "large or whole" rice destined for European consumers. Rice was a familiar West African food to some slaves, and South Carolina slaves as a whole were "always desirous" of rations of small rice to supplement bland diets centered on maize.[61] The Laurens enterprise sold over 2 million pounds of rice between 1766 and 1773, a stream of grain so vast that its inevitable by-product of damaged, distressed, and discolored rice filled slaves' cooking pots on a regular basis.

This plantation enterprise was more than the sum of its parts. Integration within a common domestic economy supported the diversification of core plantations and the specialization of frontier plantations. The ways in which Laurens bought and sold provisions reveal the extent to which market exchange pervaded the plantation countryside. If the idea of the plantation as a place of genteel refuge is to have any meaning outside the fantasies of merchants seeking "retirement," we might expect a withdrawal from the world to be on display in the matter of making food. Instead of self-sufficient farmsteads, the Laurens plantations were places in which exchange shaped daily material life and the movement of rice and corn crossed the line between food and commodity as a matter of course. Beyond the opportunities for savings and profits that circulating provisions in this way made possible, Laurens demonstrated to slaves that he controlled a branch of commerce that guaranteed their survival. Slaves on Mepkin and Wambaw who produced more food than they could possibly eat found plantation barns emptied at his command. Every meal was a lesson in dependence on Laurens and the schooners that delivered provisions to the plantation landing and carried them away.

His Ansonborough household, by contrast, was a center of abundance. It consumed the bounty of the plantations, supplied imported food to the countryside, and was encircled by a vast and productive garden. Detachments of slaves from Mepkin and Wambaw turned skills in reshaping

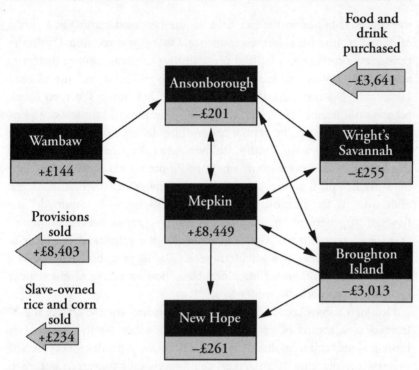

Figure 6.1. Food exchanges on Henry Laurens's plantation enterprise, 1766–1773. Frontier rice plantations depended on food surpluses from the core zone of settlement. This diagram shows the exchanges of food and alcohol among Henry Laurens's plantations and his central household in Ansonborough. The role each unit in the enterprise played in this network is represented in monetary terms as the net value, in South Carolina currency, of its production and consumption of food and alcohol. A positive number shows that the unit produced for sale or provided for the use of the other units goods of greater value than it consumed. A negative number shows that the value of what it consumed was greater than the value of what it produced for sale and exchange. Broughton Island and New Hope Plantations, located nearby one another on Georgia's Altamaha River, probably shared many of the expenses charged to Broughton Island alone. Diagram by Philip A. Schwartzberg.

the land first honed in the rice fields to the task of damming in a parcel of marsh around his suburban residence. Once it was reclaimed from the tides, slaves created an idealized plantation-in-miniature out of this four-acre plot.[62] Eleanor Laurens, Henry's wife, was its "Mistress." Just as Eliza Lucas initiated commercial indigo culture at her family's Wappo Creek plantation, Eleanor Laurens extended the conventional purview of an English "huswife" from the private realm of her family's domestic economy to the public sphere of South Carolina's agricultural economy. She made this garden both a place of ornament and a site for experiment. Enclosed by a brick wall, it re-created a flowering English ornamental landscape and, with it, the illusion of a rural idyll. Along with imported "hue flowers," it generated an abundance of fruits—grapes, nectarines, pomegranates, lemons, limes, figs, and melons—that mimicked the colorful orchards and arbors of a Mediterranean villa. Its greenhouse served as a tropical arboretum, protecting pineapples, "bonnana trees & other tender exoticks" from periodic winter frosts.[63]

Eleanor Laurens could "brag of her fine garden" for the service it performed as a means of gratifying and edifying her family's tastes. Her husband and children dined upon fresh country produce because she oversaw the planting of asparagus, cauliflower, cabbage, green peas, and other vegetables for the table. Such "moderate Fare" helped Laurens achieve an abstemious life in the shadow of a city known for its "barbarous dissipation." As he limited his consumption of meat, wine, and tobacco, he not only restored his sometimes-precarious health, but found that such moderation allowed him to "redeem . . . 3 to 7 Hours every Day after Dinner" for work. While Charlestown gluttons slept off their heavy evening meals, Laurens took "Command" of his "whole Time" for business.[64] The garden was also a nursery for a global range of potentially lucrative agricultural produce. These four intensively cultivated acres held out the promise that her husband's plantations, and plantations everywhere in the Lowcountry, might one day yield bumper crops of sugarcane, olives, and oranges for export. Bags of seed gathered through Henry's associations with merchants who conducted Britain's commerce with the world made possible the experimental planting of English rye, African grasses, and Chinese tallow together in "Mrs. Laurens's Garden."[65]

The garden was a node of intersection at which the rural, planting side of the Laurens enterprise met its urban, commercial counterpoint. Slaves from the countryside retired from long years of plantation labor to tend its trees, beds, and shrubs. In drawing together fruits, flowers, and crops from different continents and latitudes, it recapitulated seventeenth-century dreams of Carolina as a nursery for the world's lucrative flora. The transnational commerce that brought seeds and saplings to Anson-borough's experimental plots helped create a lush vision of what low-country plantations might yet become. After her death in 1770, Eleanor Laurens was remembered for the "great delight" she took in "cultivating & Ornamenting her Garden." It became a living memorial and an affec-tive center for the family's survivors. One of three sons in school abroad, John Laurens anticipated a tour of Holland "with great Pleasure" for the opportunity it offered to gather "Flower Roots and Garden seed" for a large addition to his late mother's garden.[66]

Supplementing the fruits and vegetables grown in this garden, the nearby plantations delivered both coarse fare and rural delicacies to Rattray Green in Ansonborough. From Wambaw came Christmas turkeys, wild geese, deer, and summer ducks. Hogs "bred & fattend" at Mepkin became hams that Eleanor Laurens cured. Consuming produce from the countryside began as a gratifying perquisite of plantation ownership, but it soon amounted to an internal trade of significant value. The account book records more than 100 transactions between the plantations and Laurens's family expense account. These exchanges detail the role of the Anson-borough compound as a central household that provisioned satellite households on the plantations with items of consumption as it consumed their surpluses. Ansonborough's hearths burned more than 100 cords of firewood that slaves chopped on the banks of the Cooper River; its horses ate through thousands of pounds of corn blades (maize leaves) after har-vest at Mepkin and Wambaw; and its black and white residents dined on meals of meat, bread, and hominy made possible by the labor of slaves who tended animals and cultivated provisions on the plantations. By virtue of the rural branch of his enterprise, Laurens saved nearly £1,000 in expenses incurred by its suburban center between 1766 and 1773.[67]

In contrast to the hundreds of slaves he knew as names on a tax list, if he knew them at all, Laurens was intimately acquainted with those who lived in Ansonborough and those who passed through Charlestown on their way from one plantation to another. There he played the patriarch convincingly, with equal parts of care and severity.[68] Laurens tended to a gravely ill "young Negro Man" along with his son Harry, who also suf-fered with "the epidemic Fever and Sore-Throat," in the "back Chambers" of his house. Another young slave, purchased to serve as an "occasional porter, Gardner, Scullian," and "running footman" about Rattray Green, received his censure and the threat of "some smart flogging" as the "Laziest Rascal that ever was in my service." When Laurens spoke of a rash of sickness that had overtaken "my family," he meant both "Blacks & Whites," but only those whites related to him and only those blacks who lived in Ansonborough.[69] This multiracial "family" included at times those mobile slaves, among them carpenters, shoemakers, bricklayers, and as many as ten sailors and boatmen, who, under the account-book heading "Handicraft Slaves," generated £329 in wage income. Builder "Mulatto Sam" Massey, perhaps the most privileged in this select group, received regular allotments of rum, sugar, and cash to secure his affiliation. Laurens authorized a payment of £25 to Massey's wife on one occasion "to add Some indulgencies to bare necessaries for him[s]elf." When Laurens bought him for £1,200, three times the going price for a field hand, this skilled slave's first task was to lay brick paths across his grounds at Ansonborough. Massey soon traveled to the plantations as the enterprise's master bricklayer and carpenter.[70]

After demonstrating their utility, "Town Negroes" on the Laurens enterprise were drawn from the anonymous population of plantation slaves into the intimate social orbit of Ansonborough. One of Mepkin's first field workers in 1762, Stepney worked as the "principal hand in the Garden" by the late 1760s. He returned from time to time to Mepkin, leading horses and carrying bags of sage he had grown, to supervise indigo production and aid the overseer in his campaign against theft by slaves. When he tired of plantation life, and perhaps the social ostracism that came with serving as Laurens's agent among other slaves, he returned to town. Laurens dispensed a "Drink of Grog" to him "upon the Occasion," although "too often he gets dead drunk." His sons said "how d'y'e to old Daddy Stepney" in letters from England. When Laurens returned from his three-year residence in England in 1774, Stepney, "weeping & Sobbing," embraced and kissed his master in gratitude for his return. For a small circle of skilled slaves, house servants, and "old Domestics" like Stepney who had long ago tied their prospects to a direct relationship with their master, Ansonborough was a functioning patriarchal household.[71]

Against the flow of farm produce to town, Laurens organized the delivery of vast quantities of cloth and provisions to the plantations worth more than £9,500. Orchestrated from Ansonborough, this commerce in the survival of plantation slaves affirmed his authority as master. Along with thousands of yards of textiles and thousands of bushels of corn, the material lifeblood of basic existence, special items of consumption worth about £400 were taken from Rattray Green's stores and charged against his family account. These goods played a disproportionately large role in constituting white and black households on the plantations and linking the individuals who received them to Laurens's largesse. Suits of clothes made to fit enslaved newborns, tea and pepper that distinguished overseers' tables, medicines that promised relief from suffering, and a virtual river of rum flowed from Ansonborough. Laurens compensated obedience, loyalty, and hard work every time a schooner arrived at a plantation's landing.[72]

White and black dependents who lived beyond Ansonborough's patriarchal household were connected to Laurens through constant acts of consumption. Laurens paid overseers a £200–300 annual salary and granted them right to work their own slaves for a share of the commodity proceeds. By allowing overseers to draw upon plantation stores and by supplying their tables with morsels from his own, Laurens helped constitute white authority on the plantations at a fraction of this cost. When it came to "a little eating & drinking," Laurens stifled a mercantile impulse to hold each overseer to precise account, provided he "eats only his Belly full" and did not engage in outright fraud by selling plantation goods. Having control over consumption in one's own household was a basic hallmark of patriarchal command that shored up overseers' sometimes-shaky authority over slaves. He did not begrudge an overseer "all that he reasonably can desire nor shall I differ with him about Rum, Sugar, & even Tea. I would have him to Live well to take good care of my Interest in general & particularly of my Negroes."[73]

Overseers expected regular supplies of rum and sugar to elevate their diets from the "plantation fare" of slaves, and Laurens further enhanced the variety and quality of their food by sending unexpected savories and sweets made at or imported through Ansonborough. Philadelphia cheeses, "fine" New York flour, kegs of butter, cured hams, cakes, barrels of fish, sugarcanes, pepper, oil, and, on one occasion, even a cypress table at which to make meals of this bounty offered "encouragement" to overseers to secure their allegiance. Laurens supplied the rudiments of polite households to young men who aspired to "make a pretty Livelihood" while they served him and "acquire an independence" as planters themselves in the future.[74] An extension of the custom of exchanging regional delicacies to affirm transatlantic friendships, these gifts to subordinates recreated patriarchy across space, yet also amended its tone. In setting overseers' households apart from those of slaves, granting them autonomy over eating, and conferring a mark of friendship with each edible token of esteem, Laurens diluted the stigma of their social inferiority as he negotiated for their loyalty. Overseers controlled two streams of goods, one "for the House" that they might use as they wished and one "for the Plantation" that it was their duty to ration conservatively to slaves. What fell beyond a basic provisions ration, overseers dispensed from their own household stores. At their discretion, slaves received the coarse sugar, cheap rum, and salted fish that Laurens sent for "Negroes use." When slaves fell ill, overseers were "not to be sparing of the Red wine," sour oranges, and bowls of rice to aid their recoveries.[75] Laurens gave overseers the materials with which to bestow comfort as caretakers. At these moments of vulnerability, slaves also knew that it was Laurens who ultimately supplied these special offerings of food, medicine, and alcohol.

Like enslaved workers throughout the Lowcountry, those on the Laurens plantations were "skillful and industrious" enough to "plant something for themselves after the day's work and buy trifles with the proceeds."[76] Laurens recorded their "several names" along with the "quantity of each ones Rice on the Credit side." In return, he sent up "sundry articles for the Negroes" they might claim in exchange, provided the overseers made them "Debtor for such goods as they take." In "Payment to the negroes" for "Rice & Corn of their own" he sent handkerchiefs, hats, and yards of cloth in different colors, patterns, and qualities, from the coarsest "Negro cloth" to indigo-printed calicos. New slaves received pipes "that they may be paid for, according to the Planter's custom," or perhaps that they could take away free of charge "as I shall think proper"; either way, his slaves would have to plant on their own accounts to fill these pipes with imported tobacco.[77] Laurens bought rice and corn from his slaves "at the lowest price that they will sell it for" and sent up goods for them to purchase with "the prices mark'd to each article." When they grumbled at the terms, he suggested that they take what he supplied at the prices he offered "without too much fuss & trouble that I may not be discouraged from being their Factor another Year." When Laurens served his slaves as consumers, he affirmed their ownership of the crops they cultivated on their own time, and he provided a means by which they could claim small luxuries as rightful earnings rather than as rewards for good behavior.[78]

These controlled experiences of exchange, far from eroding patriarchal relationships, strengthened them from a distance. A powerful inculcator of social discipline, the market offered a "framework of opportunity and affirmation" in which enslaved producers learned to count on fair dealing from Laurens and to invest the margin of their own labor that they controlled toward a predictable return in the future. Laurens gave workers a stake in plantation production that aligned their interests with his at a remarkably small cost. In the spring of 1769 Laurens sent £159 worth of goods that he "gave Wambaw Negroes for their Rice." During the 1768–1769 season Wambaw slaves also produced £3,884 worth of rice for the plantation.[79] The value of the Wambaw slaves' independent economy was thus about 4 percent of the market economy controlled by Henry Laurens on this single plantation during this year. Such discrepancies in the scale of economic endeavor allowed planters to sacrifice trivial amounts of labor time and consumption goods in order to provide slaves with non-coercive incentives to work within the plantation system. Such market activity, constrained in company-store fashion into a narrow channel of exchange between master and slaves, made manifest the patriarchal ethos of reciprocity based on station rather than sentiment. Unable to select the goods they purchased, slaves were consumers without the power of preference who were forced to accept Laurens's choices on their behalf. To Wambaw Laurens sent "15 very gay Wastcoats which some of the Negro Men may want at 10 Bushels per Wastcoat."[80] In doing so, he imagined what slaves might desire to own and provided it for them without asking if his selections suited their tastes. In return, he expected payment rather than gratitude. This internal commerce on the Laurens enterprise projected the cold calculation of mutual obligation that was a hallmark of household patriarchy across the distances that separated master and slaves.

Laurens involved himself directly in providing clothing, a basic patri-archal chore. New African slaves first encountered their master in An-sonborough, where Laurens himself often "named" them and gave each a blanket, handkerchief, cap, and three yards of cloth to be made into clothing on their arrival at a plantation.[81] His standing command to over-seers was to "cloth[e] them, warm, strong, and cheap as customary."

While he was in Britain, he purchased textiles directly from London ware-houses, opting for woolen flannels ("White plains" or "Walchit cloth") that were more expensive than the coarse South Carolina standard, cheap linen "oznabrigs." Absentee planter John Colleton, who sold Mepkin to Laurens in 1762, demonstrated that failing to provide adequate cloth un-dermined the patriarchal credentials of distant masters. He sent a parcel of "sorry Stuff" that was both "very unfit for the P[u]rpose" of making decent clothing and four months too late to distribute to his slaves before the winter cold set in. For next season, his agent urged, Colleton should "employ a Carolina Merchant that knows what is proper." Intimately familiar with the logistics of importing British dry goods to the colonies, Laurens took pains to supply his slaves in a timely fashion with durable plains and the "best duffil Blankets" at competitive prices. Others might settle for blankets "of inferior Weight," but because "my poor Negroes will feel the difference," he insisted on "real Whitney London Blankets." He wanted them to know that his expertise accounted for what comfort they enjoyed. From England he wrote New Hope's overseer, ordering him to tell the slaves: "I intend to send the best Cloth next year that ever they wore ... for such as shall have behaved well." Despite his distance from them, providing clothes fulfilled an essential patriarchal duty.[82]

Because clothing was tailored and shoes cobbled to fit the specific people who wore them, supplying these goods to slaves created an op-portunity for Laurens to mimic the face-to-face encounters by which a British head of household typically ruled an extended family of depend-ents. At the close of each summer overseers made a "measure" of the feet of each enslaved man and woman, perhaps tracing an outline on paper, and sent these to Ansonborough. By late autumn finished shoes "with measures in them" (and "their several names marked on the measure") arrived at the plantations. Laurens sent hired tailors, tape measures in hand, to Mepkin and Wambaw before "cutting the Negro Cloths" in town.[83] In exchange for their bodies' unique dimensions, Laurens re-turned garments and shoes custom-made to fit the person, whether he knew each individual or not. Such commerce personalized the imper-sonal character of mastery on this multiple-plantation enterprise.

Although patriarchs were to provide clothing, making it fell to women on the plantations, as it did in northwestern European households gen-erally. The production and consumption of clothing bound women, white and black, together in ways that mirrored patriarchal exchanges that connected Laurens, his overseers, and leading male slaves. When a mother gave birth on the plantations, Eleanor Laurens made up a suit of "Baby Cloaths" with her own hands for the infant. Daughter Martha studied arithmetic and English history, but, alongside the "finer Branches of a Carolina Ladies Education," her father hoped that she would emulate her mother as a seamstress by learning to "make up a Piece of Linnen, and even a Piece of white or blue Woolen for her Negroes." Hired women and the wives of overseers helped "make the Negro Cloth[e]s," dispense medicines, and provide "female help" when enslaved women's pregnancies came to term. Sheets for the bed of Mepkin's overseer and his wife were dyed at Ansonborough, from which Eleanor Laurens also sent a "parcel of rags," probably the odds and ends left over from her own household use. From these snippets came the raw material for the plantation's "Negro Women" to make and mend clothes. As surrogate heads who enforced "diligence in the field," overseers represented Laurens first and foremost in terms of production; their wives were also connected by the exchange of textiles with Eleanor Laurens and female slaves as they facilitated "frugality at home" in terms of consumption.[84]

When Laurens sat for a 1782 portrait, he displayed simple, but elegant, apparel. Wearing a plain wig and a dark-colored suit of monochrome velvet that lacked embroidery or patterned buttons, Laurens projected a self-image centered on the values of frugality and industry. He was known throughout the Atlantic world as past president of the Second Continental Congress, and his attire was consistent with the patriotic rejection of imported fashions during the era of the American Revolution. Laurens advocated a "masculine renunciation" of excessive finery in his own dress that suited his role as a master of slaves as much as it spoke to a patriot's opposition to tyranny.[85] His restrained dress also projected the sartorial standards of a father who feared that his sons were susceptible to the enervating luxuries of the metropolis. He instructed his son's English headmaster that Harry "be clad in plain decent Apparel, unmix'd with any kind of Foppery." Six-year-old James began his education at a Shropshire boarding school with sixty-seven items of clothing. The only splashes of color in his wardrobe came from two silk waistcoats amid prevailing blacks and browns (even a pair of "homespun breeches") that set a more somber tone. Since the boy was "fond of a little Cambrick or Lawn about his knuckles," however, he was to be allowed the indulgence of "Ruffles to his Holiday Shirts." Entering plantership was, for Laurens, a means of

Figure 6.2. John Singleton Copley, *Henry Laurens*, 1782. Oil on canvas. Courtesy of the National Portrait Gallery, Smithsonian Institution, gift of Andrew W. Mellon.

amassing productive wealth for his sons to inherit. A gentleman brought up to command others and provide for them, he believed, should demonstrate restraint in his own adornment, avoiding "meanness on one hand & profusion on the other." Like other self-made colonial elites, Laurens made the inconspicuous consumption of clothing a sign of patriarchal credibility. Committed to preserving his household's wealth, he would not play the role of the careless aristocrat, too busy squandering the resources of his estate to provide for dependents. His personal appearance served as an object lesson to his sons and his slaves in the relationship between legitimate power and consumption.[86]

When he installed Casper Springer as Wright's Savannah overseer, Laurens outfitted this impoverished German immigrant with a simpler, sturdier wardrobe, but one that included an important mark of distinction. His greatcoat, probably fastened with polished brass buttons, was a garment that displayed male authority in the Lowcountry. African American drivers also wore such coats as a sign of the coercive power they wielded over other slaves. As Laurens and his sons, "clad in a decent & neat manner," displayed a patriarchal aesthetic that restrained consumption, his slaves yearned for small reprieves from the yards of white cloth that bathed their material lives in neutral tones. In exchange for their rice, they bought the brightly colored handkerchiefs and "gay Wastcoats" that Laurens provided.[87]

Laurens used his power as a provider to do more than sustain workers and protect them from the elements. Against the backdrop of an early modern model of household governance, Laurens reconstructed patriarchy to make the lure of things compensate for the abstract quality of authority exercised in his absence. With his hand on the lever that controlled the circulation of goods throughout his multiple-plantation enterprise, he attempted to align the interests of his widely scattered dependents with his own through rituals of distribution. As part of a strategy of mastery, Laurens used this provisioning system to intervene in the lives of distant slaves and employees. He expected those who drew on Ansonborough's stores to acknowledge him as a figure who nourished, clothed, and gave comfort with every act of consumption. Supplying plantation consumers distinguished the different stations of a labor hierarchy—overseer, driver, artisan, and field hand—and made these visible through daily acts of wearing, eating, and drinking. Those who wore greatcoats, took white sugar with their tea, and possessed bottles of alcohol commanded those who draped themselves in blankets and received irregular rations of coarse muscovado and cheap rum. Catering to a few material wants eased off the potentially disruptive pressures of slaves who yearned for things without any means to satisfy their desires.

In the wake of his departure for a three-year sojourn in Europe in 1771, Laurens left behind networks of affiliation that connected every slave, overseer, and associate with a stake in his plantation enterprise to households that circulated its resources. Laurens was a true absentee in these years, but he had maintained a calculated distance from his plantations when he lived in South Carolina. The flow of goods that vitalized these households continued in his absence, and his clerks continued to take down the enterprise's expenses and sales in the ledger that remained open at his countinghouse table. When he returned to Charlestown aboard the packet *Le Despenser* in late 1774, Laurens resumed his role as the resident master and quartermaster to this enterprise from the *"pure air* which Ansonborough affords."[88]

Households in Competition

This strategy of long-distance patriarchy confronted a world of illicit exchange. Slaves and overseers used the goods within their reach to tangle the lines of affiliation that Laurens sought to keep separate. As they appropriated, embezzled, and traded, the single extended household he envisioned resolved into many clandestine households that worked against his interests and his authority. Laurens viewed the alliances among slaves and between slaves and overseers that formed a black market beyond his influence as so many small wildfires that, if not swiftly suppressed, might join to form a dangerous conflagration. At Broughton Island alcohol was kept under lock and key to deter its theft, but at Wambaw a more serious problem was a slave named Amos and his "great inclination to turn rum Merchant which I have strictly forbidden." Laurens saw his "Boat Negroes" as a mobile fencing ring, yet his empire depended on the frequent voyages of schooners between town and countryside that their labor made possible. Abram, the "sly & artful" slave captain of the schooner *Wambaw,* and his "gang" of boatmen engaged in any "trade or trick" that stood to turn the absence of white scrutiny over their activities to their own material advantage. Should Abram arrive there without permission to take on Amos's rum,

Laurens ordered Wambaw's overseer to "discipline him with 39 sound stripes," almost twice the number of "lashes" urged by the Negro Act of 1740 as a maximum for slave beatings. Abram's skills were simply too vital to the enterprise for Laurens to consider selling him.[89]

At fractious Wright's Savannah slaves and overseers bound to one another by kinship, sex, and mutual interest worked together to pillage the plantation during the 1770s. Overseer William Godfrey deprived Laurens's slaves of boots, caps, and blankets, forced them to work on his own nearby settlement, slaughtered plantation livestock for his table, and withheld from recently arrived "New Negroes" their "Belly full" of provisions. Although he robbed some slaves of clothes and food, he attempted to "make Friends" with others by measuring out smaller-than-average tasks, making for lighter workdays in the rice fields.[90] "What is become of Mary?" wrote Laurens several months before the overseer's fraud had been discovered. "Don't forget my Injunction, and your Promises relative to that Rebel." Godfrey had in fact "kept Mary in the house from the time she arrived," contrary to Laurens's orders. Perhaps the overseer was simply stealing the services of a house servant rather than keeping a concubine. At Mepkin Laurens dismissed overseer James Lawrence unambiguously for his "familiarity with Hagar" because the affair "must make a good deal of jealousy & disquiet amongst the Negroes." Three years after her sexual relationship with Lawrence ended with his termination and her forced departure, Hagar returned as a skilled indigo supervisor, displacing Amy, whom Laurens demoted to field labor as a degrading punishment for "the trouble she has lately occasioned on the plantation." As newcomers who stood outside enslaved communities on the plantations, Mary and Hagar became enmeshed in illicit households that Laurens believed were "very hurtful to my Interest." Even when overseers were not "keeping a Wench in the House in open Adultery," as did another Mepkin overseer, they often showed "partiality" to some slaves and "Cruelty and Inhumanity" to others.[91]

Mary resurfaces in the Laurens correspondence at the center of a new wave of subversion at Wright's Savannah in the late 1770s. When overseer Casper Springer confronted her husband, the enslaved driver March, for "stealing rice out of the Machine House," the two men fought, "but the Negro proved to be the Strongest & threw him." When Springer ordered "the negroes to Seize him, they would not do it." In a desperate frenzy March apparently turned a knife on himself, severing his "left hand above the Thumb" and brandishing this weapon in his right as he approached the overseer. Only then did slaves who were watching this violent scene unfold in the Negro yard restrain and disarm their driver. March was "ever a Man of a placid & obliging disposition," reflected Laurens, until his union with Mary "corrupted & ruined" him. Mary's son Cuffee, once a versatile skilled artisan at the top of the enterprise's labor hierarchy, had become a rebellious runaway "trading in the Steps of his Mother who had long been the bane of my Negro families." He derided this kinship network, which supplanted the loyalties of his most trusted slaves, as the "Noble family." Laurens considered selling Mary, "that wicked Devil," and others in the group, hoping that "the removal of Such leaven may Stop a contagion."[92]

Responding to the proliferation of these gangs, liaisons, and insubordinate families, Laurens identified slaves such as Mary who demonstrated their contempt for the patriarchal compact of goods for loyalty that he required all to accept. Although he claimed that he was "comfortable" in the belief that his slaves were "as happy as Slavery will admit," Laurens brought his considerable coercive powers as master to bear on subversive individuals. Their rejection of his authority seemed to prove the rule that the "rest of my slaves . . . are in general very orderly & give me but little trouble."[93] Just as he quarantined slaves during outbreaks of infectious disease, he aimed to break the networks that trafficked in stolen goods by ordering overseers to "prevent an intercourse" between plantation slaves and enslaved artisans and boatmen. The mobility these skilled specialists enjoyed gave them countless opportunities for illicit trade. Their conspicuous consumption of clothing and alcohol awakened material desires that few field hands could hope to satisfy by relying on Laurens alone.[94] When such efforts at segregation failed to suppress underground trade on the plantations, Laurens took the more drastic step of deporting slaves from more comfortable Mepkin and Wambaw to the southern frontier. Fearing that a malcontent might "corrupt" other slaves with his or her "bad example," he claimed that "the greatest punishment to a defaulter" was "to sell him" far from his kin and connections. Once he suppressed a contraband household by removing its leader, he hoped that a society of "happy orderly" families, their connections to Laurens refurbished, might again prevail.[95]

Not all slave theft threatened his authority. Laurens regarded pilfering as an endemic nuisance that required watchfulness rather than panic. He hoped to find "at least as many in number of my Cattle, Sheep, & Hogs as I left" at Mepkin, although he seems to have expected that a few animals would be barbequed on the sly. News of "Negroes stealing . . . Potatoes & Corn" left him indifferent.[96] To be hungry and to want meat was a reasonable desire that Laurens tolerated almost as if taking food was a perquisite of plantation life that could be discounted financially as wastage and written off as mild waywardness. To lead other slaves to conspire, steal, and sell food, however, infringed on Laurens's exclusive command over goods. However small the actual costs of the lost rice that March diverted from the Wright's Savannah machine house, the subterfuge with which he had marshaled slaves in his own criminal enterprise constituted a rebellion against properly constituted authority. In the same vein, overseers were expected to eat their fill without too much scrutiny on Laurens's part. He fired them, and did so often, when they kept their own "Interest rather too much in View," using his resources as if they headed the plantation households he worked to rule.[97]

Laurens deluded himself when he saw outbreaks of coordinated stealing more as isolated incidents than as the symptoms of endemic slave resistance. Although he relied on overseers, drivers, and the wardens of the Charlestown workhouse to administer the beatings, he sanctioned physical violence against slaves as a commonplace means of securing order on the plantations. When his letters instructed overseers privately instead of serving as semipublic platforms from which to put forward an appearance of compassionate mastery, Laurens did not mince words about brutalizing slaves. "[M]ake choice of the most stubborn one or two & chastise them severely," "punish him severely," and "take him down," he wrote without reservation or euphemism. In the case of Mary's son, Cuffee, he approved of applications of "that useful ointment . . . Stirrup Oil."[98] This was no medicine dispensed to comfort a sick dependent, but rather a vernacular term for a flogging. Laurens claimed to have ended his career as a slave trader on ethical grounds. He meditated on his slaves' well-being to other elites with a language of tender regard. He went so far as to declare, in a statement widely publicized in the nineteenth century, "I abhor Slavery."[99] Yet he brooked no dissent from field slaves and, unlike a few of his contemporaries who favored emotional negotiation over the strict enforcement of plantation rules, refused to entertain slaves' complaints against overseers. When his strategy of catering to material desires left slaves dissatisfied, he responded with violent discipline. Especially by claiming his goods as theirs, slaves undermined Laurens's monopoly on the role of provider and cast off the passivity he expected of them as consumers. Just as slaves undermined "designs for mastery" elsewhere with actions that ran the gamut from feigning illness to arson, slaves on the Laurens enterprise specialized in the organized appropriation of goods. When they ate rice they helped steal, slaves mocked the stance of submission that Laurens wanted them to assume with every bite.[100]

Profits and Losses

The thousands of exchanges that animated Henry Laurens's plantation empire survived it as the product of meticulous record keeping in a master account book. This ledger recounts how much Laurens invested in slaves, land, and durable machinery, how much he spent on clothes, food, tools, and wages, and how much the rice, corn, firewood, and indigo his slaves labored to produce sold for in Charlestown. Calculated with care, these figures yield a single number for each plantation at the end of each commercial year: the rate of return. This basic measure of profitability—a ratio of net earnings over the amount of total capital invested—compares Laurens's design for planting with his plantations' actual financial performance. It opens two views onto plantation agriculture in South Carolina at the close of the colonial period. From the outside, it begins an assessment of the economic vitality of the integrated plantation enterprises that expanded across the Lowcountry in the years leading up to the War for Independence. From the inside, it holds Laurens's commercial solutions to the problems of projecting authority across space up to scrutiny. Did the innovation of integrating very different kinds of plantations into a single enterprise breathe new life into a mode of production that some have seen as doomed by inherent structural inefficiencies? Were the mercantile strategies that Laurens used to knit far-flung lands and dependents together an effective system of control, or did these betray a hopelessly dilated vision of mastery? Turning to questions of profit and loss compares Laurens's dreams of systematic order with the disruptive realities of contending interests on the plantations.

Planters themselves measured successes and failures by citing rates of return, and their sense of good and bad returns offers numerical benchmarks that can place these figures in a meaningful context. A planter who borrowed all of his plantation capital paid 8 percent, the government-mandated interest rate, to service his loans every year. He would have to make a profit of more than 8 percent, reasoned Laurens, or "he is then but a labouring Overseer for his Creditors." Although Laurens did not borrow his £100,000 investment, he considered estates that returned "8 per Cent clear" as just minimally profitable. His friend Henry Gray, who planted in the 1750s and 1760s, "not only brought up a large family in a very decent & reputable way but has likewise added to his capital" on 10–12 percent returns. Laurens and his fellow planters would have welcomed a return in the range of 10–15 percent as the conclusion to a successful year of planting. By the close of the colonial era, when rising commodity prices created heady expectations for high profits, planters hoped that "Slaves will pay for themselves, in four or five Years," suggesting an optimum rate of return of 15–20 percent. A return of more than 15 percent signaled exceptionally strong markets and management, a credit to the planter who realized the potential of high rice and indigo prices. A planter who recouped more than 20 percent of his capital in any given year enjoyed an extraordinary windfall.[101]

Profitability on the Laurens enterprise varied from plantation to plantation. Wambaw was profitable, but not wildly so. A long-settled (and apparently well-managed) plantation that specialized in producing rice on a vast inland swamp, Wambaw did not post returns of more than 9 percent during the three years covered by the account book. If returns for this plantation were at all typical, then inland rice cultivation on lands within fifty miles of Charlestown possessed limited potential for growth. Using half-century-old agricultural methods and featuring a monocultural focus on rice, Wambaw was a throwback to the plantations of the early 1730s, and like them it strained to make "10 per cent. Profit on Land and Slaves."[102] Its lackluster returns and limited financial prospects encouraged Laurens to sell his one-half share in 1769. He transferred his capital, including as many as eighty Wambaw slaves, to build up his investment in the Altamaha River plantations (Broughton Island and New Hope) and create a new tidal rice settlement at Wright's Savannah plantation on the Savannah River.

Although long-settled areas of settlement offered few tidal floodplains capable of supporting advanced irrigation systems, Mepkin's remarkable rates of return proved that diversification was the key to making lands first occupied in the seventeenth century into highly profitable plantations in the eighteenth. Laurens led the way to the tidal frontier as the site of the plantation economy's lucrative future, but he also transformed Mepkin rather than abandoning Charlestown's hinterland as a relic of the past. What these lands lacked in hydrographic situation, namely, vast stretches of riverside land at the pitch of the tide, they made up for in commercial position. Mepkin resided in the economic heart of the Lowcountry. From the heights of its Cooper River bluff, Mepkin overlooked the waterway that connected a densely settled plantation region (St. John and St. Stephen parishes contained over 100 plantations and a 90 percent black-majority population) to more than 10,000 consumers in Charlestown.[103] Slaves from the countryside to the colonial capital subsisted on Mepkin corn, hundreds of urban hearths burned Mepkin firewood, and the plantation's sawmill cut the lumber from which indigo vats, mansions, and the "huts" of slaves were fashioned. Laurens's scheme for taking an old-fashioned rice plantation (with respectable returns of around 10 percent) and remaking it into a nimble provider of food, fuel, and export commodities proved wildly successful. By its third year the plantation posted a rate of return above 20 percent and surpassed that level for the next four seasons. Toward the end of 1771 Mepkin's cumulative profits exceeded the total value of its capital investments. Planters regarded this fiscal threshold, at which point they said one had "doubled his capital," as the most singular measure of accomplishment.[104] In less than six years Mepkin's slaves had paid for themselves and the land they worked.

With Mepkin yielding a "very satisfactory profit" and 700 barrels of rice expected from Wright's Savannah, Laurens looked to the prospects of Broughton Island and New Hope that were "but beginning to be at their best." Building tidal rice plantations along Georgia's isolated Altamaha River saddled his most distant plantations with heavy early expenses. Devoting labor to clearing, leveling, and embanking rice fields limited production and kept returns either negative or below 5 percent from 1766 to 1770. In the following season, however, Altamaha slaves had apparently completed the laborious process of field formation, and Laurens applied their labor fully to test the plantations' capacity for production. Revenue jumped fourfold on sales of more than 300,000 pounds of rice, compared with just over 100,000 pounds for the previous season. Although they were specialized rather than diversified, crude rather than comfortable, and positioned at the Lowcountry's periphery rather than entrenched at its center, "those delightful & profitable Plantations on Altamaha River" matched Mepkin's highest recorded rate of return in their first full-scale year of production.[105] With the same technology and comparable land, Wright's Savannah plantation posted a rate of return of 3.4 percent in the same season that the Altamaha plantations returned 24.8 percent of capital as earnings. It was puzzling that Wright's Savannah turned out to be "a very unprofitable part of [the] Estate." The land was "undoubtedly good," and the weather had been "as favourable as ever known," but still "they don't make 3 barrels Rice to a hand." Such low productivity, when slaves on tidal rice plantations elsewhere made more than 10 barrels per worker, hinted at hidden social dysfunctions. A 1772 inspection revealed the extent of fraud and theft on the plantation.[106] Wright's Savannah was a social and economic failure. Against their master's incessant attempts to bind them to his interests as consumers, slaves consumed the plantation's expected profits in the form of leisure time claimed from shirked field tasks and rice stolen from the barn to eat or sell. By firing Wright's Savannah's "mercenary" overseer and removing its driver and his wife from the top of a subversive slave kinship network, Laurens hoped to quell a culture of resistance that squandered the plantation's many material advantages. Even under these unruly conditions, the plantation still managed to post a positive, if low, rate of return.[107]

Taken as a whole, the Laurens plantation enterprise in 1766 returned a disappointing 4.6 percent. Despite Wambaw and Wright's Savannah's drag on profits, successful diversification at Mepkin and increasing production at the Altamaha plantations made the enterprise more profitable in each successive year, save one. By the close of the account book in 1773, just seven years later, total returns were over 15 percent and were poised to surpass 20 percent. Cost savings from integration—the constant swapping of goods among the plantations—and a commercial sensitivity to the costs of transportation reflected the stamp of a merchant's sensibility on the project of planting. Bringing together diversified plantations that served multiple markets and frontier plantations that produced rice exclusively for export with the best technologies available, Laurens's strategy of multiple-plantation expansion proved successful. By the mid-1770s he expected a rate of return above 20 percent, a profit level once considered exceptional, as the ordinary performance of his plantation investment.

As Laurens brought new lands on the Georgia frontier into production and made new uses for old lands in the core settlement zone, his profits rose. But this emphasis on land can be misleading. Approximately 300 plantation slaves, valued at more than £83,000, accounted for approximately 80 percent of Laurens's capital investment. Clothing slaves, paying white workers, and feeding both dominated the debit side of his ledger. In the breakdown of the enterprise's costs of nearly £25,000, human consumption and wages accounted for approximately 60 percent of total expenses.[108] Laurens converted a commercial fortune into an army of slave workers and a cadre of overseers, dispersed them across the Lowcountry in artificial communities of endeavor, and held them to account. In the specific language of early modern colonization, "to plant" meant "to settle (a person) in a place."[109] Finding the right land paled as a task beside the goal of enmeshing slaves within a single household that Laurens ruled. Every plantation was like a colony in miniature, a peripheral extension from a central core in which the problem of maintaining a connection to that center preoccupied the colonial planter. Much as South Carolina stood in relation to Britain, Wambaw, Mepkin, Broughton Island, Wright's Savannah, and New Hope stood in relation to Laurens at home in Ansonborough. Like British officials who were surveying the North American colonies from the metropolis in the period 1766–1773, Laurens had good reason to view his empire, even with its pockets of stagnation and resistance, as a thriving enterprise.

Wartime Contraction

As Britain lost its mainland colonies, Henry Laurens's empire contracted under catastrophic strains from within and without until only Mepkin remained as a viable plantation of those Laurens had ruled in the late 1760s and early 1770s. Before the war brought an army of occupation to South Carolina and Georgia, mortality devastated the Laurens family and undermined the enterprise's reason for being. Eleanor Laurens's death in 1770 shattered the central household Henry Laurens had lodged in Ansonborough six years earlier. Laurens was now "Father, Mother, Nurse, Tutor, and Companion" to five children. "[T]ied down to [his] melancholy Habitation" by the demands of parenting, he delayed a visit to the southern plantations so long that he feared that his "estate at Altamaha will be quite ruin'd." Overwhelmed and grief-stricken, Laurens disbanded the only household he ruled directly as a real father. He sent Henry and

James, both under ten years of age, to join their brother, teenage student John, at English boarding schools, writing pages of instruction to arrange for their transportation, education, and maintenance. As he left Charlestown, he installed his brother and sister-in-law in the Ansonborough house as surrogate parents to care for eleven-year-old Martha (called Patsy) and infant Mary Eleanor (called Polly). In short, he used his skills as a long-distance merchant to run his family, as well as his plantations, after 1770. As "mortifying" as it was to "disperse my Children & lodge them with Strangers," Laurens could not "get another Mother for them" and refused to marry again. He departed South Carolina for three years in Europe in 1771, settling his boys in their places at school and living as an absentee planter and father.[110]

On his return Laurens entered immediately into time-consuming positions of political leadership in revolutionary South Carolina (from 1774 to 1776) and in the Second Continental Congress (from 1777 to 1785), serving away from the state during this period as a congressional delegate, president and emissary and becoming a British political prisoner.[111] When he had lived at Rattray Green, he had scrutinized overseers and managers through letters and occasional visits, but when he left South Carolina in 1771 Laurens largely removed himself from the details of planting. He believed that if his "affairs would admit of my residence" at Altamaha, the plantations would return over 25 percent per year "& increasing, clear of all plantation charges." But "under the management of Hirelings the Lord knows what I may make." Because he was not there to manage his plantations directly, the best he might do was to live as frugally as possible off his income and bequeath an empire that "will deserve the attention of my sons if they live." Along with "burning droughts, devastating Tempests, [and] destructive Rice Birds," the "worthless Overseers" and "faithless friends" to whom he entrusted the management of the enterprise ensured that it would never be as profitable as it could be. With self-abnegating Christian humility, Laurens feigned a lack of concern with "a few Barrels of Rice more or less in my Estate which may be made or not made, saved or lost." As profitable as the enterprise was in fact, Laurens was keenly aware of the distance between its financial potential and its actual performance. What redeemed this margin of failure was the thought that his plantations, despite "all the bad effects of carelessness & dishonesty of Overseers," provided for his children and that his sons might realize the enterprise's true promise as planters themselves.[112]

He used to tell his oldest son, John, "how well I should improve

Broughton Island and other Plantations for him and his Brothers, if I was excused from serving in Assembly." Two of his three sons, including John, died before the war's end. Of thirteen children born to Henry and Eleanor Laurens, only five survived their mother, and only three outlived their father. One of the few to enter adulthood, Martha was a toddler when her sister Eleanor died in 1764 and her portrait was hung besides other images of dead relatives and friends on the wainscoted walls of the Ansonborough house. Martha burst into tears so often "because sister Nelly's dead" that the explanation *She is crying for sister Nelly*" gained the status of a catchphrase among the children of the Charlestown elite "when any one cried without knowing exactly for what." At seventeen Martha penned the emotionally raw "A Supplication for a Beloved Relative" as her aunt, to whom her father had turned over her care years before, lay dying. She claimed a clairvoyant awareness of her uncle James and brother John's distant deaths made plausible by her passionate engagement with Christian spirituality. Growing up a Laurens meant coming to intimate terms with death. Henry railed against fortune as mortality took its toll on his family and imperiled the reproduction of a second generation of Laurens planters. "Strip the Man who is honestly giving his daily Labour to the public for the good of rising generations, of his future prospects" he ruminated, "& you leave him the most miserable of all Men, doom'd to Labour in the Planting & Watering, without hopes of reaping the Harvest."[113] Laurens recorded the deaths of slaves, by contrast, in terse, dispassionate prose. He might consider them to be dependent members of a patriarchal "family," but, like other masters in plantation America, he kept almost all of them beyond the circle of sympathy reserved for blood kin, other whites, and a few select Ansonborough slaves.[114]

As death dispersed the Laurens household, the War for Independence exposed the vulnerabilities of an enterprise built on integrating far-flung plantations. His "remote frontier Settlements" fell first. Laurens spent more than a month at Broughton Island and New Hope in the spring of 1775, his longest and final visit to these "Southward Plantations." A year later Broughton Island yielded a record rice harvest. "[B]ut what of that?" Laurens asked when he learned of this agricultural milestone. With "Picaroons from St. Augustine" cruising the coastline, Florida raiders "all over the Country," British men-of-war "sweeping" plantations along the Savannah River of their slaves, and "a Number of Indians . . . coming against the Frontiers of Georgia," the "whole will either be destroyed stolen or lye . . . to perish by time & Vermin[,] no small sacrifice to the shrine of Liberty." He estimated the value of rice languishing at his three frontier plantations after the 1776 harvest at more than £30,000, more than twice what they had earned in any single year before, which in real terms amounted to "nought because I cannot remove it." Regular and irregular military forces menaced the frontier plantations, effectively cutting them off from Laurens's control. These isolated outposts, connected to the wider world for more than a decade by the periodic arrivals of coasting schooners, became busy sites of destructive military traffic as Britain launched its "southern campaign" to conquer Georgia and the Carolinas in the late 1770s.[115] After dispensing 3,000 bushels of rough rice to feed Continental forces (for which he was never paid), his overseers abandoned Broughton Island, New Hope, and Wright's Savannah and transported more than 200 slaves to the core plantations. "[E]xposed to the plunder and ravage of the Enemy" by land and sea, Georgia's revolutionary government further loosened Laurens's grip on his Altamaha River plantations by threatening to confiscate them under an act designed to deprive Loyalist absentees of their property. "Ben the boat negro," who took part in a last, dangerous voyage in the summer of 1778 to salvage abandoned New Hope's rice, returned with the news that its buildings "were all burnt down."[116]

As the enterprise contracted with the loss of his holdings on the southern frontier, Laurens bought new South Carolina lands to put displaced slaves to work. At a cost of £25,000 he purchased Mount Tacitus Plantation in 1777. This "large Indigo Plantation" was situated on the upper reaches of the Santee River, seventy-two miles from town.[117] Like the frontier plantations, sheer distance from port shaped Mount Tacitus's productive specialization. The costs of transporting casks of indigo by wagon across forty miles of roadways to the landings of the Cooper River could be borne at a profit because the cakes of dye packed a great deal of value in a small space compared with rice. Unlike the frontier plantations, Laurens imagined Mount Tacitus as a rustic rural retreat that he or his surviving son, Henry Laurens Jr., might someday inhabit. The plantation was named in homage to its previous owner, Tacitus Gaillard, but Laurens also evoked his predecessor's namesake, the classical historian who praised the simple virtue of Germanic tribesmen in their confrontation with a corrupt imperial Rome. In Pennsylvania, as Laurens served the cause of independence from imperial Britain as a delegate to the Continental Congress, he pictured Mount Tacitus "situated most delightfully on the River" and instructed his overseers to build a "neat, whol[e]some, durable" log house out of the tract's abundant stands of cypress and pine where, "weary of the dainties of York Town," he might dine on "excellent Trout & Bream" caught from the banks of the Santee.[118] With more mundane regard for settling slaves on land that was safe, for the moment, from British depredations, he bought Small's Field, adding 120 acres of rice land to enlarge nearby Mepkin's productive capacity.[119]

As a British invasion of South Carolina loomed, Laurens contemplated "what's to come" with the realization that years of work settling distant lands, enslaving hundreds to work them, and orchestrating thousands of plantation transactions to make them yield a profit had culminated most importantly in his "Spacious pretty Garden" in Ansonborough. "[I]f you could See me," he wrote to longtime friend William Manning, "three or four hours hence walking in my Garden, . . . you would Say I was one of the happiest Men in the World." The creation of his wife, these elaborately cultivated four acres survived her to serve as a sanctuary for family leisure and consumption, a center for elite hospitality where guests enjoyed "good Madeira Wine," and a site of emotionally gratifying mastery, where handpicked enslaved favorites tended the grounds. As he emptied his house of furniture in preparation for a threatened British attack, he waited for invasion "day by day improving my Garden," although he feared that it would soon become "the parading Ground of Some Scots Regiment."[120]

During the five-week siege of Charlestown in 1780, British cannonballs exploded through the roof of the Ansonborough house, splintering its mahogany staircase and peppering the compound's outbuildings and garden wall with more shots than could be counted. What this bombardment did not destroy, others "pilfered and wrecked," stripping the house of "Sashes, doors, Windows, Chimney Backs, wainscoting & even cutt[ing] up [a] great part of the Flooring" and leaving the "mansion . . . uninhabitable." Hessian soldiers converted his nearby brick tenements into their barracks, and marauders "entirely destroyed" Eleanor Laurens's garden.[121] After Charlestown's capitulation soldiers and militiamen descended on Mepkin, Mount Tacitus, and Small's Field seeking provisions, slaves, and plunder. They looted Mepkin House, breaking open trunks, robbing the overseer of his watch, and stealing "his Wife's shoes from her feet." After they laid waste to the buildings that gave Mepkin the appearance of a long-settled and refined place, raiders "carried off all they could carry" of the goods—food, alcohol, furniture, and clothing—crucial to the extension of household patriarchy to the plantations.[122]

In 1780 the British frigate *Vestal* captured Laurens en route to the Netherlands, to which Congress had dispatched him as its emissary to negotiate a vital loan. For the next year Laurens pondered the linked fates of the war effort and his plantation enterprise from behind a barred window in the Tower of London. In recollection of the Ansonborough garden, he "Garnish[ed]" his view with "Honeysuckles, & a Grape Vine."[123] Forbidden the use of pen and ink, Laurens could no longer project the role of protector and provider to his slaves from a distance. The last letters he received from South Carolina left him with images of his urban and rural properties in ruins. As Henry Laurens's world stood still, those who lived on his plantations had been on the move for several years. He sent part of Wright's Savannah's population to settle Mount Tacitus in 1776. The following year overseers scattered Broughton Island slaves to Mepkin, Mount Tacitus, and Wright's Savannah, whose remaining slaves were, in turn, uprooted and dispersed when that plantation was abandoned in 1779. Disbanding the southern plantations meant sailing and marching slaves in a series of forced migrations that shattered the customary arrangements by which Laurens had sought to stabilize their dependency.[124] Along with rice, slaves had cultivated expectations for how much labor they were to perform and the goods they might receive in return for their "good behavior." In law their bodies, which made up the bulk of the enterprise's capital, were a moveable species of personal (as opposed to real) property. Although slaves could be transplanted during the disruptions of wartime and made to labor on newly purchased tracts, the customs that grounded master-slave relations on the enterprise remained inscribed on the plantation landscapes they were forced to leave behind. Like shoes made to measure, overseers proportioned the tidal "squares" slaves hoed to their individual capacities for field labor; their participation in a master-controlled market for consumer goods depended on cultivating provisions patches they were also forced to abandon. Thomas, a slave at Wright's Savannah, was "very unwilling to go to Mepkin and be obliged to leave his Crop of Rice." Most displaced frontier slaves ended up working in the indigo fields at Mount Tacitus, where their intimate familiarity with water, land, and rice on the banks of the Altamaha and Savannah rivers meant nothing. The demands of dye processing organized field hands who were used to the independent pace of rice labor under the task system into supervised gangs for much of the season. Social and familial bonds forged under the harsh material conditions of the frontier fragmented as overseers dispersed slaves as strangers into new communities at Mount Tacitus, Mepkin, and nearby Small's Field. Several of the overseers with whom slaves had negotiated the details of their enslavement died, went over to the British, or disappeared into military service. Forced "removal" from the land sheltered the enterprise's essential human property from pillaging forces, but it also stripped the enslaved of their negotiated stakes in practices of production and consumption.[125] What Laurens saw as his slaves' rescue, they experienced as a series of betrayals.

When the war came to South Carolina in 1780, slaves moved on their own accord out of the path of danger and toward security and, some hoped, freedom. Laurens's self-perception as a benevolent master rested on a belief that his "Negroes . . . are to a Man attach'd to me," so much so that "not one has attempted to desert." By the early 1770s it was impossible for him to declare, as he had in 1768, that "none run away."[126] At least twenty-seven slaves, approximately 8 percent of his labor force, used the rising disorders that war brought to the enterprise to attempt to leave it in the period 1773–1778.[127] Chief builder Samuel Massey narrated the migrations of his fellow slaves from the plantations during the summer of 1780. His letter to Laurens (which begins with the salutation "My hounerable master" and closes with the compliment "your Ever humble Slave") offers the only account of the enterprise by an African American observer. Although no slave was more closely affiliated with Laurens, Massey's report of the slaves who "whent of[f] with the kings people" betrays a detailed social knowledge of their communities that Laurens rarely acknowledged in his correspondence. Poland and Lewis had fled Mepkin. Stepney left Small's Field but "has Returnd a gain." The list of the other runaways linked individuals to one another in bonds of kinship and connection: "Simon mary Old Cuffeys daughter ougen Stine [Augustine] and his wife and child fillis and hamlet and her 3 children Fredrick and his wife fullow prince and Binah tom Savage and antelope" all "whent from Smalls field."

Many of the slaves who ran away during the 1770s were single, male "New Negroes" who were resisting their initial enslavement on the plantations. Massey's list, by contrast, included husbands, wives, and children, many of whom had lived, in Laurens's words, "comfortably together in families" for years. Augustine, Stepney (Ansonborough's gardener), and Phillis, then a child, appeared among the first slaves sent to settle Mepkin seventeen years earlier. Mary, the head of the subversive "Noble family" at Wright's Savannah, avoided a punitive sale in 1777 long enough to be moved with other frontier migrants and escape with British forces. For at least a decade Prince, Poland, and Tom Savage had endured as Laurens's slaves. Dissatisfaction with life at Small's Field, probably little more than a refugee camp for those relocated from the frontier and occupied town, gave slaves little reason to stay. Its hated overseer, Andrew Campbell, pushed them to leave. At Mepkin, despite two departures, all others were "for Staying at home as Both your f[ie]ld and th[ie]r o[w]n are in a flourishing way." When the escapees from Small's Field reached Charlestown, where smallpox raged, several "deserted from the English" and proved "willing to go home."

Beneath a veneer of studied courtesy, Massey's letter to Laurens conveyed the sufferings of slave families under extraordinary pressures. Pushed to the brink of disintegration, the enterprise held together largely because slaves found a measure of security in remaining on its lands. They depended on Mepkin's provisions and continued to cultivate independent plots there. The alternative to remaining Laurens's slaves was uncertain refuge under British protection in a city plagued by an outbreak of infectious disease that had brought Massey's own children close to death. With a knack for understatement that softened this litany of disorder of any edge of grievance, Massey hoped that his "few lines" would "find you in as good State of he[a]lth as the times Sir will admit of. [A]s for our Selves master hear are but indiffren[t] as the times but Indiffrent Since the besidgement of charles Town . . . w[e] are all ways in the dreding w[a]y."[128] In addition to the eighteen runaways from Small's Field that Massey enumerated, nineteen left Mount Tacitus, all of whom returned by 1784. Some Mount Tactitus slaves "emigrated to Mepkin" before British troops "carried all [Laurens's] Negroes to Charles Town" sometime before the fall of 1782.[129]

When Laurens returned to South Carolina in 1785, he labored over metaphors of disintegration to describe the "shattered remains of a once great Estate." He estimated his wartime losses in town and country at £250,000. The prewar enterprise had encompassed, at one time or another, "Eight fine Plantations." Before his death in 1792, Laurens offered

his frontier lands for sale, presented Mount Tacitus to his son, and re-
signed himself to living in "dependence . . . upon Mepkin Plantation"
alone.[130] Vanished income, destroyed houses, and missing slaves surfaced
occasionally in the catalogue of losses he compiled. He fixated on the
image of British soldiers "scattering my Papers before the Wind, burning
them, tearing and destroying my Books" as the leading symbol and cause
of his "deranged and entangled" affairs. In practical terms he required
title deeds, bonds, and accounts to reassert legal and financial control
over his plantation enterprise. The act of "poring for Months over Fragments and disunited Parts, incapable of ascertaining Points of great Moment," also represented a profound loss of command for a planter who
had employed a merchant's control over information to keep this empire
in motion.[131] The fate of his papers during the war cast a harsh light on
the characters of white associates entrusted with his letter books and
ledgers, and who had returned his "Confidence" by plundering his property. But he looked to his slaves with new gratitude on the discovery of
"Six Small Trunks of Papers which some of my black Servants had hid
& saved from destruction." After years of separation, he sat side by side
with his sole male heir, Henry Laurens Jr., to "collect arrange & settle
our scattered fragments," a project that required the "utmost diligence of
Father & Son."[132]

Schemes to reconstruct his devastated Ansonborough compound accompanied Laurens's plan to reassert his authority over his "Plantation
Affairs" from his enterprise's long-standing administrative center. He
gathered "the remains of [his] family," scattered during the war in France
and America, together "all with me under the same roof, the Brick Tenements opposite to my old habitation [,] now a pile of Ruins." He imagined the reunited family moving into "a much better house than stood
upon the old Spot." Aided by his son, who pruned its surviving trees, he
was "determined to put the Garden in as good Condition as ever it was."
He shipped a damaged portrait of "my once dear Mrs. Laurens" to
London for repair so that it might hang on the house's renovated walls.[133]
Plans to rebuild the Ansonborough house, however, confronted his shaky
finances in "these days of humiliation" in postwar South Carolina.
Lacking the "means for living in my former Stile in the City" by 1786,
he settled his family at Mepkin in an "Overseer's ordinary House" until
his "own Workmen with Materials taken from the spot" constructed a
nine-room dwelling at the plantation. He decorated its walls with "new

invented paper hangings" from London and bragged that the "Duke of Richmond would upon a pinch be glad to lie in" one of its rooms. Necessary economies such as settling for cheap Pennsylvania marble when he would have preferred Italian, however, tarred the new Mepkin House with the brush of lowered expectations compared with the standard of his once richly appointed "old Mansion" in Ansonborough.[134]

After South Carolina ratified the U.S. Constitution in 1788, pro-federalist citizens marked the event like those in other states, with a parade. First among the "genteel people who formed the cavalcade" were the "Gentlemen Planters," and leading them was "that venerable, steady patriot, Col. Laurens . . . in a characteristic style of dress." Bringing up the rear were tradesmen, ministers, officers of the state, and the Fusilier Company. At Federal Green, just north of Laurens's Ansonborough home, this "great number of persons sat down to dinner, in a truly republican style."[135] What was it about his clothes that made the sixty-four-year-old Laurens stand out from the crowd? Were they too plain, too elaborate, or simply out of fashion by twenty years? Laurens began his career as a merchant and ended it, unequivocally, as a planter. In pursuit of productive rice lands, he led a quarter-century expansion to the farthest reaches of the Lowcountry. This move to incorporate new rice lands transformed the estates of South Carolina's wealthiest men from individually managed sites of production into integrated multiple-plantation enterprises. At the close of a war that fractured such expansive ventures, he and other planters at the end of their careers disowned their prewar experiment in extending planting across space.

"Once I was engaged in a very large and extensive Commerce," reflected Laurens in 1786; "at present I export the Produce of my own Plantation, and very little more." Plantation households, like households elsewhere in the early modern world, were units of "residence and of authority" that were "geared for work."[136] Above the enterprise as a whole, Laurens played the role of patriarch, whose authority to command slaves' labor rested on his ability to provide for their support. Among the many social changes slavery initiated, the creation of new-world households in which European masters ruled over African slaves "produced the greatest increase in dependency in colonial America."[137] Spreading such large, productive households across the Lowcountry meant finding solutions to the political problems of enforcing authority over subjects along with logistical problems of supply. Commerce offered Laurens a stockpile of strategies for building an expansive system of household governance. Schooners connected households across great distances, and the imperatives of exchange and consumption linked master and slaves. In contrast to the idea of paternalistic stasis that appeared to legitimize white rule and attach black slaves to the soil, the Laurens plantations operated, for the better part of two decades, under the banner of commercial circulation.

Conclusion: Into the American South

Through the profound disruptions of the War for Independence, South Carolina was transformed from a British colony into an American state. After the invasion and occupation of the Lowcountry in 1780, disorders in town and countryside intensified. An already-faltering economy, cut off for much of the 1770s from European and Caribbean markets, was devastated by forces that descended on plantations to seize crops, burn buildings, and bring production and consumption to a grinding halt. Slave flight, an ever-present threat to masters in peacetime, intensified into chaotic evacuations that drew thousands from the vulnerable countryside into the city and back again. These crises, "marked by social and economic upheaval and loosening of the fabric of community life," unraveled planters' prosperity and undermined their sense of security.[1] After the last British troops departed Charlestown in 1782, South Carolina's planter-citizens worked to pick up the pieces of their shattered economy and reconstitute plantation slavery within an emerging U.S. South.

As they surveyed their devastated landscape after the war, lowcountry planters wondered whether the economic culture they had fashioned over the course of a century had a viable future. More was at stake than determining whether slavery could be reconciled with modernity in the long run. Pervasive changes, already under way, were laying a course for development that made the quest to extend plantation agriculture a matter of urgent political and material interest. After 1750 the surge of immigration into South Carolina's immense Backcountry created a society of poor whites who eked out livings on small farms. American independence wrenched the Lowcountry from its Atlantic plantation world and fused it to the American South. In South Carolina as part of the

255

United States, the geographic scope for plantation enterprise shifted. Once focused on cultivating the coastal plain, planters intensified efforts to settle the South Carolina interior. Into the early nineteenth century, how the Lowcountry would fare seemed to rest on what the Backcountry would become.

Until the 1730s the Cherokees and Catawbas inhabited much of the territory within the province's official boundaries. Backed by a government plan to reserve inland townships for expanding white settlement in 1731, new settlers bypassed the shrinking supply of good rice swamps to stake claims to river bottoms, pine lands, and rich, red clay soil. Some fifty miles inland from Charlestown, beyond the reach of Atlantic Ocean tides, wetlands contracted as elevations rose. Settlers took up large tracts of conventional arable land that were always scarce in the Lowcountry.[2] British critics of rice agriculture praised the Backcountry's environmental potential compared with the coastal plain, singling out the region as a far more desirable place in which to transplant European agriculture than was the sandy, swampy, intemperate, and disease-ridden Lowcountry. But it was unclear whether colonists who had forged a collective identity around meeting the specific challenges of cultivating lowcountry land could refashion their plantation culture to develop the Backcountry.

Committed to the proposition that their swamp fields were "the Richest in the world," planters questioned whether a "Backwoods" peopled by "Northern stragglers and Irish Emigrants" would ever become a prosperous, stable society.[3] During the Cherokee War of 1758–1760, Indian fighters attacked nascent settlements across the colony's most distant frontier, plunging the third of the colony that lay above the fall line, 150 miles from the coast, into disorder.[4] Propertied vigilantes known as Regulators hunted mounted bands of poor "banditti" during the 1760s. Their campaigns against these so-called Crackers cemented the reputation of the Backcountry as a place where "economic backwardness" might be a permanent symptom of a place sick with the "social dangers of idleness." During the War for Independence irregular bands of patriot and Loyalist partisans squared off in bloody campaigns of extermination.[5]

A decade before independence, about three out of every four white people in South Carolina lived above its coastal plain. Although it had been a black-majority province for much of the eighteenth century, this influx created an overall white majority during the third quarter of the eighteenth century. Backcountry residents, however, owned less than 15 percent of the colony's taxable wealth and less than one in ten of its slaves. Only very late in the colonial period did lowcountry elites take seriously the promise of these distant lands. News of the scale of its rising white population often took them by surprise.[6] By the late 1760s many of the Lowcountry's "opulent people . . . turn'd their attention to the Lands in the back parts of the Province." Charles Woodmason, a former indigo planter who traveled the new region as an itinerant minister, viewed its people as a crude rabble, the "Off Scouring of America." He nevertheless invested in the potential of a new plantation frontier "Capable of vast improvement," taking up more than 2,000 acres for himself. Advertisements for backcountry lands published in the *South-Carolina Gazette* surged in the late colonial period. Sellers introduced more than 135,000 acres on the market in the five years before independence, almost three times as many acres as had been put up for sale over the previous forty years.[7]

Backcountry landowners discovered pockets of "good rice swamp" and actually cultivated small crops of the staple commodity on these lands. Such finds made it possible to imagine rice moving inland as it had up and down the Atlantic coast. Rice was an expensive commodity to transport, and overland journeys to Charlestown were notoriously expensive and time consuming. Because these promising lands were so "remote from Water carriage," in the final analysis they "would never answer to plant Rice in." When planted in indigo, however, which concentrated value into small cakes of dye, they could "turn to good Account."[8] Lowcountry indigo growers always found it difficult to make high-quality dye, but a "hundred miles backwards" their backcountry counterparts produced it extensively and "in great perfection." The lowcountry mantra that land was good for "rice, corn, and indigo" changed to "grain, indigo, or hemp" to promote the Backcountry.[9] This new mix of market crops suggested a profitable future for plantation slavery from the mountains to the coast, but one that would force planters to adapt commercial agriculture to the demands of a different environment,

In his 1778 Fourth of July oration, lowcountry planter, politician, and historian David Ramsay dreamt that the opportunities presented by so much backcountry wilderness would unify all of its citizens. Joined in a common, progressive project of improvement and scientific exploration, they could together change the "face of our interior country," turning the "remotest depths of our western frontiers" from a "barren wilderness, into the hospitable abodes of peace and plenty." Once limited to the mundane tasks of colonial regulation—"yoking hogs, branding cattle, or marking rice"—South Carolina's independent government now commanded part of a "wide extended empire" that it was free to develop. Convinced that the "industrious American planter received no more for his produce than the pittance the British merchant" allowed within the empire, planters and merchants looked forward to a time when "Whole forests" harvested in the Backcountry could be fashioned into "vessels of commerce" launched from Charlestown. Energized by commanding the resources of "this great continent" and no longer "sacrificed to the interests of a selfish European island," South Carolina could take its place with the other independent states as equals in an expanding "free trade with all the world."[10]

Just as they played critical roles in reshaping lowcountry plantation enterprises, Charlestown merchants helped organize the settlement of the Backcountry. In addition to settling their own plantations, they sent junior partners inland to organize the provisions market, financed stores that sold tools and supplies, and helped establish the city of Camden as a hub for immigration and exchange. The growth of a second major urban center in South Carolina's interior showed the importance of an "urban process" in developing the supposedly rural South. The surest sign that plantation agriculture was possible in the Backcountry was the rising demand for slaves there and the "Extravagent Price of negroes" this caused. "Upwards of two thirds" of slaves imported into South Carolina, Peter Manigault estimated in 1772, "have gone backwards."[11]

Although its future as a plantation society was still a matter of speculation in the late colonial period, the Backcountry became an important adjunct to the Lowcountry's expanding rice regime as it developed commercial farming. As planters settled slaves to clear and plant their coastal frontiers, backcountry settlers "employed their negroes," themselves, and their families in growing food crops to satisfy the rising demand for slave provisions. Lowcountry planters who could not supply slaves working on new tidal rice plantations with maize, beans, and sweet potatoes from their own core plantations purchased the surpluses sold by recently established farms in Charlestown's active provisions market.[12] Colonists still struggled to produce wheat bread and beer in the Lowcountry, depending on imports from the northern colonies for these staples of the English diet.[13] Rising numbers of backcountry settlers, "intent upon Cultivating their farms & making great quantities of produce," began feeding white and black alike, in town and country, after midcentury. This flow of provisions converged on Monck's Corner, a Cooper River trading village, where it awaited shipment to Charlestown. There the Backcountry's capacity to feed the Lowcountry was put on display as "great numbers of wagons Crowded the roads travelling in every direction."[14]

Before the war disrupted his own backcountry speculations, Henry Laurens envisioned "good Silk, fine Indigo, large herds of Cattle, a valuable breed of Horses, abundance of Hemp," but "no Cotton worth notice." Although he was as wrong about cotton as he was about silk, Laurens was convinced that the region could become a plantation society. Yet even as he invested in a 13,000-acre property at Long Canes—located an arduous two-week journey from town—he did not know what to call his new venture. Whether it would become a "Farm," "Farm & Plantation," or "Farm, Vinyards, & Plantations," it seemed unlikely to resemble any of his settlements in lowcountry South Carolina and Georgia.[15]

Since they had "but few or no slaves," the colony's "back settlers" seemed more like "farmers" than planters. In 1769 Charlestown merchant, planter, and revolutionary leader Christopher Gadsden anticipated that these small-scale landowners would find the few slaves they had to be "an incumbrance to them," just as colonists "to the northward" were beginning to abandon their limited stake in human property. The articulation of South Carolina into a society that was half slave and half free could be interpreted as a "clear gain" to lowcountry planters. That South Carolina's rice growers profited from slavery at the expense of the common security of the province was a long-standing criticism. Buying more slaves "year after year," they undermined the stability of white rule with every addition of "such very precarious property." Gadsden argued that with a burgeoning population of arms-bearing settlers behind them, the same acquisitive behavior, even though it added to a growing enslaved majority on the coast, could now seem "prudent and reasonable." Even the most "selfish rich planter" could bring more rice under cultivation without incurring the censure of those who worried about an impending slave rebellion.[16]

Such logic provided cold comfort to those who saw the divergence of Lowcountry and Backcountry by political economy as a recipe for the regional isolation of plantation slavery. Without a new frontier to expand into, planters feared that a limit to their ambitions would be set at the

[handwritten margin note: worried about the growth & import of more slaves]

Lowcountry's last uncultivated rice swamp. The provision in the proposed federal constitution to end the legal slave trade in 1808 raised the specter of widespread economic decline. While "there remained one acre of swamp-land uncleared of South Carolina," planter Charles Cotesworth Pinckney declared during South Carolina's constitutional convention, "I would raise my voice against restricting the importation of negroes." The coming ban also imperiled the reproduction of plantation slavery in the interior. Slaves were in a sense the state's "only natural resource," argued lowcountry political leader Rawlins Lowndes. "Without negroes" to clear the land and turn swamps and forests into fields, South Carolina would "degenerate into one of the most contemptible [states] in the Union."[17]

James Madison, in the course of framing the Constitution in 1787, articulated what was still a new cultural geography of a United States divided by section. Identifying two divergent and potentially antagonistic cultures distinguished by "their having or not having slaves," he helped create a "South" that was born in antithesis to a "North." Madison's "frank invocation of the danger of sectionalism" suggests that the seeds of disunion were sown in the very creation of the federal republic.[18] When white South Carolinians debated ratification in 1788, however, they were not yet crouched in a defensive posture against the North that they assumed in the decades before the Civil War. Not all took Madison's North-South distinction for granted. Pinckney compared the South with what he called the East, not the North. When he looked at a map of the early United States, Pinckney saw a diminutive New England that jutted eastward into the Atlantic and a vast South angled into the interior. He spoke of South and East to make the point that the South was better positioned to dominate future territorial expansion. The East, by contrast, seemed cut off by geography from taking part in the settlement of what he called "this growing and extensive country." "In fifty years," Ramsay concurred, "it is probable that the Southern states, will have a great ascendancy over the Eastern." The economy of New England, with its "eastern" orientation toward fishing, shipping, and shipbuilding, was poised for recession. When it came to drawing the bulk of new immigrants to settle the Southwest, commentators on American growth throughout the nation agreed that the South held a decisive edge.[19]

Making good on South Carolina's share of these geographic advantages depended on successfully extending plantation slavery into the state's immense interior. How to reconcile a "state divided into two great and distinct countries remarkably distinguished, the one for its possession of great wealth . . . the other for its superior population," became an intense political question during the 1790s. A politics of geographic division threatened to split South Carolina into "backcountry, or lowcountry," as it set the United States against itself "into a northern and southern, or into an eastern and western interest."[20] Planters were used to governing as a class of like-minded elites, many related by blood and all linked by their shared interests in the rice and indigo plantation economy. How this sociopolitical "harmony" could be reconstituted across the state's diverse regions obsessed political leaders as they framed new governments. The state's 1778 constitution defined the qualifications for highest political leadership in terms of planting wealth, namely, the possession of a "settled plantation or freehold" worth at least £10,000. Its terms also kept political power disproportionately in the hands of the lowcountry elite.[21]

The revised state constitution of 1790, although it shifted the capital inland from Charleston (as the newly incorporated city was renamed) to Columbia, did little to address backcountry demands for more equitable representation. Attacking this arrangement as "the very definition of aristocracy," Robert Goodloe Harper and other members of the Representative Reform Association urged immediate change. They attacked the Lowcountry as a place in which disease and dissipation had whittled down an old ruling class that now monopolized the "small spots on land" on which rice could grow. With its healthy climate and ample stores of good farmland, the Backcountry by the 1790s had become, in Harper's view, an ideal agrarian democracy supported by the wide distribution of productive land. As South Carolina's old region stagnated, its new region would grow along with its "frugal" yeomanry. "One wishes for slaves; the other will be better without them." Grounded on bedrock differences in environmental potential, these diverging regions seemed irreconcilably at odds.[22]

For their part, lowcountry planters claimed that this regional divergence entitled them to their disproportionate political power. "Nature has decreed," wrote Charleston politician Timothy Ford, "that the race of white people shall not labor in the fertile swamps," but they did so safely "in the up lands, particularly above the falls of the rivers." Without the political power to maintain slavery, the "swamp planter . . . is a planter no more." The coastal elites who dominated the legislature defeated the reformers' proposal to amend the constitution and "place the wealth of the low country, and all its interests and concerns, under the immediate administration of the backcountry." "To you who are settling a different country," the state's lowcountry rulers promised fair dealing but not political equality.[23] With arguments that foreshadowed antebellum fears of political marginalization, they saw the rhetoric of equalitarian democracy as a threat to slavery in principle. With the "awful catastrophe" of the recent Haitian Revolution in mind, they imagined the politics of the state sliding down a slippery slope until "this fine country would be deluged with blood, and desolated by fire and sword" in a general rebellion of black against white.[24]

The heated rhetoric of constitutional debate that set Lowcountry and Backcountry against one another in the 1790s took place alongside a process of economic integration that was binding the economies of the state's sections more firmly together. The state's major postwar economic initiative was chartering the Santee Canal Company. Charged with linking backcountry farms and plantations directly to Charleston, the canal project sought nothing less than to integrate the state's commercial landscape. The construction of roadways after 1730 had linked Santee River plantations to the Cooper River's central thoroughfare. This critical investment in the eighteenth-century plantation economy secured its expansion into a secondary zone of settlement. Farther west, the Santee's branches and tributaries fanned out across the length and breadth of the South Carolina interior, unifying the state as a common "commercial highway." Diverting this river into the transportation network of the old colonial core became an overriding imperative for the wealthy planters and merchants who bought the company's shares and directed its operations.

In the short term, wages paid to masters for the labor of thousands of slaves employed on the canal financed local plantations through the economic depression of the 1790s. Once the canal was completed in 1800, it also acted as the largest artificial drain ever built in the Lowcountry, protecting rice fields from the Santee's dangerous tendency to overflow its banks. Far more enduring benefits were expected from linking the Backcountry's natural resources with the Lowcountry's access to the Atlantic economy. Robert Mills, South Carolina's early nineteenth-century cartographer and tireless economic promoter, placed it at the center of an 1822 scheme to extend Charleston's grasp on inland navigation to the Mississippi River.[25] One of the earliest and most ambitious internal improvement projects undertaken in the eighteenth-century United States, the canal integrated South Carolina territory far beyond the zones of colonial settlement, bringing the "superabounding productions of the upper country" into an "easy intercourse" with Charleston. The low-country elites who stood behind it served as equally active entrepreneurs in building later turnpikes and railroads. As bales of cotton began to replace provisions in the vessels that plied its route, the canal helped secure South Carolina's place in the South's cotton revolution.[26]

Before the war intervened to cut short his schemes, Henry Laurens was set to extend his plantation enterprise by developing new tracts in Georgia and the Carolina Backcountry. Laurens has served as an exemplar planter for the late colonial Lowcountry. His extensive enterprise demonstrated how commercial strategies worked to integrate far-flung people and lands into a single system of production and consumption. Venturing success-fully into the distant reaches of the tidal rice frontier made clear how planting on such a scale could drive territorial colonization. But with his empire in ruins, Laurens traded ceaseless movement across the land in favor of an idealized stasis on it. After years of mobilizing people across this landscape, he reconstructed Mepkin, the one remaining plantation left in his hands, as an isolated retreat. In this respect he no longer rep-resented the capacity for plantation expansion within the Lowcountry or the dynamic possibilities for plantation enterprise that a new generation was realizing across the expanding American Southwest. Other, younger men, not "content to live . . . privately & frugally" on the income of a single plantation, passed him by in their quest to acquire planting for-tunes. They clamored for new slaves in Charleston as the transatlantic slave trade resumed briefly from 1783 to 1785. They took their share of the thousands of captives imported into South Carolina, alone among the United States in opening its port to new slave cargoes from 1804 to 1808.[27]

Cotton's beginnings as a wartime crop, grown to make slave clothing that could no longer be imported, demonstrated the flexibility of plan-tations in the face of destabilizing change.[28] The new staple's rise trans-formed the Backcountry into a plantation society. In 1810 there were almost three times as many slaves in the Backcountry as there had been in 1790. African American majorities emerged in districts where cotton was grown most intensively, joining the Lowcountry as part of an ex-panding "Black Belt."[29]

As plantation development intensified in the Lowcountry and expanded to the Backcountry, the material culture of slavery changed. Workers transported into the interior struggled with masters, with some documented success, to preserve the task labor system into the nineteenth century.[30] The daily task held in the rice fields, but came under pressure on new cotton plantations. Abolitionist memoirist and ex-slave Charles Ball bore witness to the imposition of gang labor and its impact on slave material autonomy. Slave traders brought him in chains from Maryland to labor on South Carolina's expanding cotton frontier sometime between 1800 and 1810. As he entered the state, he saw a landscape in which "Every thing betrayed a scarcity of the means of supplying the slaves, who cultivated the vast cotton-fields, with a sufficiency of food." Ball worked for three years on a plantation near the Congaree River, an inland branch of the Santee. Its small crops of rice and indigo re-created the the colonial Lowcountry in miniature, but cotton dominated this landscape and dictated the rhythms of work and life for the 260 slaves with whom Ball worked. With no weekday, daylight hours in which to cultivate independent crops on a larger scale, they worked on small garden "patches," trapped animals in the woods at night, and made brooms to sell at a nearby store.[31]

On this plantation in the midst of productive transition, there was no "smoke-house, nor any place for curing meat," and "no food was ever salted for the use of slaves." As other planters imposed gang labor and cotton agriculture later in the nineteenth century, however, they offered "stronger guarantees of subsistence to slaves."[32] The introduction of rice a century earlier had destabilized plantations by making it harder for slaves to get enough to eat. To resolve this subsistence crisis, colonial masters and slaves agreed to the terms of the task system. Planters first added meat to rations during the chaos of the War for Independence to entice slaves to remain at work. Bacon became the "universal article of slave-food" on cotton-belt plantations after 1800, when most slaves could count on three and a half pounds of pork per week.[33] This temporary practice hardened into a new customary expectation, taking root in old and new plantation regions alike. Slaves who grew rice along the Waccamaw River received ham, chicken, and molasses along with their corn. As masters burnished their credentials as paternalists, slaves in the cotton South enjoyed better and more varied rations, but their ability to pursue independent production and trade contracted.[34]

As he settled into retirement at Mepkin in 1786, Laurens envisioned slavery becoming a more settled institution over time. But the drive to plant cotton stimulated an internal slave trade that stretched from the Chesapeake Bay to the Mississippi Delta. Someday, Laurens speculated, African Americans might be "freed from the Tyranny & arbitrary power of Individuals." The model of benevolent paternalism that he vowed to institute broke ideological ground as South Carolina's masters worked to secure their hold on slaves after the war. In practical terms, however, the huge rice plantation enterprises of the antebellum Lowcountry condemned thousands to early deaths working in tidal swamps. Slave life on the unsettled cotton frontier was notorious for its brutality.[35] As lowcountry plantations became entrenched places of occupation, planters and slaves recapitulated the disruptive transformations that had defined colonial South Carolina's plantation landscape to plant the new cotton lands of the American Southwest.

A postrevolutionary elite rebuilt the irrigation infrastructure of the tidal frontier on a massive scale, putting in place the most advanced technologies on the most productive lands and abandoning overgrown inland swamp fields. The sheer scale of nineteenth-century plantation estates made the Laurens enterprise seem small by comparison. Joshua John Ward owned 1,121 slaves, all of whom lived on settlements within All Saints Parish on the northern coast. Nathaniel Heyward, perhaps the antebellum South's wealthiest planter, owned as many as 2,340 people on seventeen plantations between Charleston and the Savannah River. By 1860, twenty-two lowcountry families owned more than 20,000 slaves, about 40 percent of the entire labor force devoted to rice. The entire crop was grown on about 320 plantations, a remarkable concentration compared with colonial rice plantations, which probably numbered well over 1,000.[36]

Unlike the interdependence that Laurens maintained between core and frontier plantations, these new rice enterprises were weighted, in terms of slaves and acres, heavily toward the frontier. In the nineteenth century South Carolina's northern and southern coasts no longer merited the name. They were settled places, no longer outposts within an immense wilderness that seemed to offer a limitless scope for development. As opportunities to bring new land into production diminished, few newcomers could set themselves up as lowcountry planters. Even many of the children of this rice-planting elite could not establish themselves as masters and planters in their own right. Many awaited their inheritances and lived as dependent members of their fathers' households until they were middle aged. Those who ventured from the coastal plain into the interior helped extend plantation slavery into the South's expanding cotton frontier. As young men migrated in search of their own plantations, they often strained or broke ties with the families they left behind.[37]

The wealthiest plantation estates of the nineteenth-century South resembled Laurens's enterprise at its most extensive, not as he idealized it after independence. As Laurens retired to Mepkin after the war, the first Wade Hampton moved from trade to planting. He put together an extensive multiplantation empire that stretched from the Atlantic Ocean to the Mississippi River. It included Woodlands, the Congaree River plantation probably described by Charles Ball, as well as Ball himself for a few years. Men who owned at least 500 slaves on the eve of the Civil War settled them on "multiple holdings, frequently extending across both county and state boundaries." Colonists like Laurens established elaborate managerial hierarchies and depended on mercantile expertise to colonize the eighteenth-century Lowcountry. Their nineteenth-century successors extended these tactics to make plantation slavery profitable in the antebellum South.[38]

From their position within it, lowcountry planters did not see clearly how long-term structural vulnerabilities made their plantation economy "a tenuous one from the start." Over the course of a century, slave-owning colonists remade the coastal plain into a secure, productive, and lucrative place to grow rice and other commodities. This process of environmental adaptation, well calculated to generate wealth out of slave labor and improved swampland during the colonial period, was poorly calibrated to sustain economic growth in the long term. The impact of civil war and emancipation "exacerbated rather than initiated" the Lowcountry's "economic downfall." As it lost its comparative advantage as a rice-producing place in an increasingly global commodities market, it proved difficult to reorient this thoroughly modified plantation landscape toward other, more promising, enterprises.[39]

To reconstruct the Carolina Lowcountry on its own terms as an early American region means letting go of the idea that it was always part of "the South," locked into a trajectory of decline from its inception. From this perspective the introduction of African slaves menaced the futures of the Chesapeake and Lowcountry like a fatal flaw. As the first planters put

they didn't perceive themselves as part of a col. South

in place an archaic economic and social system, its rulers began a struggle to reconcile the incompatible principles of slavery and freedom that would lead, with seeming inevitability, to the slave South's collapse. Only in retrospect, however, was South Carolina bound together with Virginia as the lower and upper poles of a single "colonial South." From London, the colonial Lowcountry seemed to be "part of the West Indies."[40] Few colonists would have recognized this faltering South as the place in which they engaged in plantation enterprises that drove relentless economic growth and territorial expansion. Until 1776 the idea that its inhabitants were Southerners was still a novelty. Once bound like other colonial American regions into a primary, transatlantic relationship with metropolitan Britain, the Lowcountry was redefined in relation to the rest of mainland North America only in the last quarter of the eighteenth century.

A century before South Carolina joined the South, England unleashed a powerful model for colonization that established its empire in America. It granted colonists dominion over American land and left them to transform it through agriculture.[41] Settlers came to Carolina's coastal plain to claim its natural abundance. They enslaved thousands to convert swamps into productive fields, changing culture and agriculture as they occupied new territory. The dynamic tension at the heart of colonial plantation enterprise began with this expansion into new lands. With every extension, planters continually worked to bring plantations back into connection with established points of order. To harness the environmental complexity of unfamiliar lands, they discarded fundamental principles of European agriculture, from the hierarchies for valuing land to the methods considered the best practices for cultivating it. At the same time, they embraced the culture of British agricultural improvement to plant rice in swamps and linked every new site for production back to Charlestown and, through it, to the wider Anglo-Atlantic world. The economic culture they created to adapt to the novelty of their subtropical environment worked to reconcile the innovations of planting with the standards of the metropolitan center. As they cultivated an American brand of agricultural expertise to shape this colonial landscape, they modified their own identities as colonists, masters, and planters. Lowcountry planter Henry Laurens observed to Chesapeake planter George Washington in 1778 that white Southerners, regardless of region, shared a defining "versatility." This "habitual if not almost constitutional" characteristic was revealed in their "almost irresistible" compulsion "to Change."[42] Large-scale rice agriculture was profitable and productive in the Lowcountry into the Civil War, but the last critical innovations in its culture had been made decades before. As South Carolina joined an expanding South committed to plantation slavery by the 1820s, planters could put to rest fears that their region might be isolated on the Atlantic coast as a relic of the colonial era. As the Lowcountry became one of many settled, prosperous, and repressive places within the South, however, these dynamics relaxed, and the economic culture they animated began eroding from within.

To those who have idealized it, the plantation represented an isolated refuge from the passage of time. It evoked a rustic retreat on the eve of the American Revolution, a European feudal order reclaimed during the antebellum era, and an object of nostalgia for fading bucolic charm and lost racial order in twentieth-century America. The image of a rural mansion, dominating prospects of slaves and fields below, pictures the plantation landscape as a place of deep-rooted occupation. On the showplace estates of the South Carolina Lowcountry, Spanish moss dangled from live oak trees, encasing such scenes in an air of stillness that has become emblematic of a mythic Old South. Colonial planters who watched hungry cattle devour that "long sort of green Moss, which the Win[d] shakes off the Trees," however, inhabited a world in which such views of nature had not yet hardened into symbols.[43] These persistent images of stasis can be scraped away to reveal colonial plantations as sites of transformation rather than as places that seem to exist outside the currents of historical time.

plantations were sites of transformation

Abbreviations

Appendix

Notes

Index

Abbreviations

BPRO	Records in the British Public Record Office Relating to South Carolina, South Carolina Department of Archives and History, Columbia
ECCO	Eighteenth-Century Collections Online, Gale Group, galenet.galegroup.com
EEBO	Early English Books Online, Chadwyck-Healey, eebo.chadwyck.com
Hist. Coll.	*Historical Collections of South Carolina,* ed. B. R. Carroll, 2 vols. (New York, 1836)
HL	Henry Laurens
LC	Library of Congress, Manuscripts Division, Washington, D.C.
OED Online	*Oxford English Dictionary Online,* dictionary.oed.com
PHL	*The Papers of Henry Laurens,* ed. Philip M. Hamer et al., 16 vols. (Columbia: University of South Carolina Press, 1968–2003)
SCDAH	South Carolina Department of Archives and History, Columbia
SCG	*South-Carolina Gazette*
SCHM	*South Carolina Historical and Genealogical Magazine* and *South Carolina Historical Magazine*
SCHS	South Carolina Historical Society, Charleston
SCL	South Caroliniana Library, University of South Carolina, Columbia
S.C. Memorials	Records of the Auditor General, Memorials of Land Titles (Copies), vols. 1–5, Microcopy Number 12, South Carolina Department of Archives and History, Columbia
SHC	Southern Historical Collection, University of North Carolina, Chapel Hill
SP	*The Shaftesbury Papers and Other Records Relating to Carolina* (1897; repr., Charleston, S.C.: Tempus, 2000)
WMQ	*William and Mary Quarterly,* 3rd ser.

Appendix: Statistical Tables

South Carolina Memorials of Land Titles, 1731–1739

Under South Carolina's Quit Rent Act of 1731, landowners were required to register lands with the provincial government to secure their titles to real property. Lowcountry landowners had strong incentives to comply. The fees charged for entering a memorial (which stood at £20 South Carolina currency during the 1760s) posed a modest disincentive to register land, but those who did not submit memorials were deemed liable for unpaid quitrents when they later attempted to sell property. Unlike warrants and grants, through which landowners entered claims for land for the future, the memorials consist of claims to present occupation and past ownership of land. The largest group of memorials was registered in the first few years after the passage of the Quit Rent Act. Before 1756, land grants issued by the royal government were not required to be registered in memorials. After 1756 however, all grants required subsequent memorials, which typically consisted of a brief record summarizing the terms of the grant. These memorials, registered directly by the grantee, have been excluded from this sample. The 1,415 memorials included were filed in the period 1731–1739. The lands registered in them were granted during the period 1673–1724. See Judith M. Brimlowe and Joel A. Shirley, *Pamphlet Accompanying South Carolina Archives Microcopy Number 12: Memorials of Seventeenth- and Eighteenth-Century South Carolina Land Titles* (Columbia: South Carolina Department of Archives and History, 1984).

Colonial South Carolina Lowcountry Zones of Settlement, 1673–1775

Lands registered in the memorials and advertised in the *South-Carolina Gazette* were located, where possible, in one of three settlement zones.

271

The rivers and other geographic place names used to categorize them are listed in Table A.4.

A Chronology of Crop Seasons for South Carolina, 1717–1795

Table A.5 lists sources for 317 contemporary observations that support my characterizations in Chapter 3 about how rice, indigo, and provisions crops weathered the Lowcountry's climate. Observations have been collected for fifty-three years within the period 1717–1795. Years not covered in this sample include 1718–1719, 1721, 1723–1727, 1729–1732, 1734–1736, 1745–1746, 1750–1751, 1758, 1761, 1780, 1787–1789, and 1791.

Lands Advertised in the South-Carolina Gazette, 1732–1775

Advertisements for 3,330 tracts of land were collected and analyzed. Every extant, distinct advertisement in the *South-Carolina Gazette* during the period 1732–1775 was included, drawn from the microfilm series: Charleston Library Society, *South Carolina Newspapers, 1732–1782* (Charleston, S.C., 1956). When individuals of the same name advertised a tract of land on the same river and of the same acreage, I assumed that this was the same tract of land unless thirty years or more separated the two advertisements. Issues of the *Gazette* reproduced in this series contain several omissions during the period 1732–1775, including much of the period 1747–1751. On the publication history of this newspaper, see Hennig Cohen, *The South Carolina Gazette, 1732–1775* (Columbia: University of South Carolina Press, 1953). Urban lots and subsequent advertisements by which already-advertised tracts were offered for sale or lease by the same individual were excluded. Lands were considered to be "settled" or "plantation" lands only when evidence of actual settlement was included in the text of the advertisement. All other lands were assumed to be "undeveloped."

The Henry Laurens Account Book, 1766–1773

The account book records the balance of individual accounts, which contain single and multiple transactions. Calculations from the account book draw on the accounts of individuals in relation to the plantations, for the plantations themselves, as well as the account heading "Expenses," which

Laurens used to record the costs of and supplies from his Ansonborough residence. Accounts for January and part of February 1768 are missing. It appears that expenses and revenue for Broughton Island and New Hope plantations were combined at times. Where this seems to be the case, I have considered these together as "Altamaha River Plantations."

Table A.1 Means of land acquisition, 1731–1739

How acquired	Number of Tracts	Percentage of all tracts	Number of Acres	Mean acres
Purchase	632	45.9	274,024	434
Inheritance	457	33.2	218,631	478
Grant	158	11.5	57,407	363
Marriage	100	7.3	28,565	286
Gift	25	1.8	7,448	298
Patent	4	0.3	18,338	4,585
Total	1,376	100.0	604,413	

Source: Records of Auditor General, Memorials of Land Titles (Copies), vols. 1–5, Microcopy Number 12, SCDAH.

Note: Acreage and mean acreage figures have been rounded to the nearest whole unit. This subset of the memorials includes records that list the means by which the memorialist obtained the tract claimed. These 1,376 tracts comprise 97.2 percent of all tracts filed in this period among the 1,415 analyzed memorials.

Table A.2 Size and distribution of individual landholdings, 1731–1739

Size of landholding (acres)	Land claimed				Individuals claiming land	
	Median number of tracts per landholding	Total acres	Percentage of all land		Number	Percentage of all individuals
≤500	1	64,891	10.5		233	47.7
501–2,000	2	187,078	30.3		184	37.7
2,001–8,000	7	210,151	34.0		61	12.5
8,001+	12	155,650	25.2		10	2.0
	2	617,770	100.0		488	99.9

Source: Records of Auditor General, Memorials of Land Titles (Copies), vols. 1–5, Microcopy Number 12, SCDAH.

Note: Acreage figures have been rounded to the nearest whole unit. Errors in percentage totals are due to rounding.

Table A.3 Dispersion of land claims, 1673–1724

Settlement zone	Date granted		
	1673–1699	1700–1724	Total
Core			
Number of tracts	165	307	472
Number of acres	88,503	118,555	207,058
Percentage of acres	68.2	43.5	51.5
Secondary			
Number of tracts	35	205	240
Number of acres	19,181	79,280	98,461
Percentage of acres	14.8	29.1	24.5
Frontier			
Number of tracts	30	148	178
Number of acres	22,167	74,487	96,654
Percentage of acres	17.1	27.4	24.0
Total			
Number of tracts	230	660	890
Number of acres	129,851	272,322	402,173
Percentage of acres	100.1	100.0	100.0

Source: Records of the Auditor General, Memorials of Land Titles (Copies), vols. 1–5, Microcopy Number 12, SCDAH.

Note: Acreage figures have been rounded to the nearest whole unit; percentage errors are due to rounding. This subset of the memorials includes records that provide both an initial grant date and geographic information that allows for the location of the tract within one of the above zones of settlement. These 890 tracts comprise 62.9 percent of all tracts filed in this period among the 1,415 analyzed memorials.

Table A.4 Geography of lowcountry settlement zones

Settlement zone	Place name
Core	
Major waterways	Ashley River, Back River, Cooper River, Goose Creek, Stono River, Wando River, Wappo Creek
Other	Ashley Ferry Town, Bacon's Bridge, Beech Hill, Cainhoy, Cainhoy Swamp, Captain's Creek, Caw Caw Swamp, Childsbury, Cypress Swamp, Daniel's Island, Dorchester, Dorchester Creek, Eagles's Creek, Foster's Creek, Gray's Ferry, James Island, Log Bridge Creek, Long Savannah Swamp, Lynch[e]'s Creek, Monck's Corner, Moonham's Creek, Newington Creek, Newington Swamp, Newton Creek, Parris's Creek, The Quarter House, Quelche's Creek, Rantowle's, Red Bank, Shem Town, Slann's Bridge, Spoon Savannah, Steven's Bridge, Stone Landing, Stone Savannah, Stono Landing, Strawberry Ferry, Timothy's Creek, Toogoodoo, Wallace's Bridge, Wampee, Wassamsaw Swamp, Wadboo/Watboo, Wiskenboo Swamp, Yeshoe
Secondary	
Major waterways	Bohicket Creek, Edisto River, Kiawah River, Pon Pon River, Santee River, Wadmalaw River
Other	Awendaw Creek, Baracada Swamp, Bear Island, Bob Savannah, Cane Acre, Echaw Creek, Four Hole Swamp, Hell Hole Swamp, Horseshoe Savannah, Indian Field Swamp, Jacksonborough, Leading Way Creek, Pon Pon, Sewee Bay, Steed's Creek, Tooboodoo, Wambaw Creek, Wambaw Swamp
Frontier	
Major waterways	Northern coast: Black River, Pee Dee River, Sampit Creek, Waccamaw River, Winyah River; southern coast: Ashepoo River, Chehaw River, Combahee River, Coosawhatchie River, Port Royal/St. Helena River, Savannah River
Other	Northern coast: Black Mingo Creek, Bull's River, Gravelly Gulley Creek, Indian Town Creek, Indian Town Swamp, Little River, Muddy Creek, Peter's Creek, Simpson's Creek, Thorn Tree; southern coast: Backal's Creek, Bear Island, Black Creek, Broad River, Chulafinny Creek, Coosaw River, Cuckhold's Creek, Dafuskie Island, Day's Creek, Deer's Creek, Euhaw Creek, Euhaws, Godfrey's Savannah, Indian Land, New River, Okatee Creek, Paramenter's Creek, Pocotaligo Creek, Radnor, Saltketcher (Salkehatchie) River, Wannell's Creek

Table A.5 Sources for weather and crop observations, 1717–1795

Year	Source
1717	Lewis C. Gray, *History of Agriculture in the Southern United States to 1860*, 2 vols. (1933; repr., Gloucester, Mass.: Peter Smith, 1958), 1: 175–176.
1720	Gray, *History of Agriculture*, 1:175–176.
1722	M. Eugene Sirmans, *Colonial South Carolina: A Political History, 1663–1763* (Chapel Hill: University of North Carolina Press, 1966), 138; *The Journal of the Commons House of Assembly, November 10, 1736–June 7, 1739*, ed. J. H. Easterby (Columbia: University of South Carolina Press, 1951), 308.
1728	Alexander Hewit, *An Historical Account of the Rise and Progress of the Colonies of South Carolina and Georgia* (1779), in *Historical Collections of South Carolina*, ed. B. R. Carroll, 2 vols. (New York, 1836), 1:273.
1733	*South-Carolina Gazette*, 8 September 1733 (hereafter cited as *SCG*).
1737	*The Letterbook of Robert Pringle*, ed. Walter B. Edgar, 2 vols. (Columbia: University of South Carolina Press, 1972), 1:3, 24; *SCG*, 14 May 1737; Gray, *History of Agriculture*, 1:175–176; *Commons Journal, 1736–1739*, 308.
1738	*SCG*, 29 June 1738, 31 August 1738; *Pringle Letterbook*, 1:16, 26, 28, 30, 34.
1739	*SCG*, 15 February 1739; *Pringle Letterbook*, 1:73, 103–104, 136, 138, 143, 145, 210.
1740	*Pringle Letterbook*, 1:216, 228, 238, 247–248, 251, 257.
1741	Ibid., 1:300, 316, 401; *SCG*, 11 June 1741.
1742	*Pringle Letterbook*, 1:393, 410, 411–412, 2:430; *SCG*, 6 December 1742.
1743	Hill and Guerard Manuscripts, 16 June 1743, South Caroliniana Library, University of South Carolina, Columbia (hereafter cited as SCL); *Pringle Letterbook*, 2:582, 590, 601, 630; *SCG*, 12 September 1743; Richard Hill Letterbook, 29 September 1743, 27 October 1743, Special Collections, William R. Perkins Library, Duke University, Durham, N.C. (hereafter cited as Duke).
1744	*Pringle Letterbook*, 2:700, 719, 729, 733–734, 738, 750.
1747	*The Papers of Henry Laurens*, ed. Philip M. Hamer et al., 16 vols. (Columbia: University of South Carolina Press, 1968–2003), 1:11, 26, 37 (hereafter cited as *PHL*).
1748	Ibid., 1:145, 161.
1749	*The Colonial South Carolina Scene: Contemporary Views, 1697–1774*, ed. H. Roy Merrens (Columbia: University of South Carolina Press, 1977), 173.

Table A.5 (continued)

Year	Source
1752	John Guerard Letterbook, 20 June 1752, 18 July 1752, 25 July 1752, 29 July 1752, 30 July 1752, 12 August 1752, 27 August 1752, 20 September 1752, 17 October 1752, 21 October 1752, 6 November 1752, 1 January 1753, South Carolina Historical Society, Charleston (hereafter cited as SCHS); Diary-Account of Rene and Henry Ravenel, Thomas Porcher Ravenel Family Papers, folder 1, SCHS; Manigault Family Papers, 28 August 1752, box I, folder 1, SCL.
1753	Ravenel Diary-Account; Guerard Letterbook, 9 July 1753, 30 July 1753, 25 August 1753.
1754	Guerard Letterbook, 16 May 1754, 31 May 1754, 17 June 1754.
1755	*PHL*, 1:252, 268, 271, 296, 297, 310, 334, 337, 339, 346, 362, 364, 2:1, 7, 12, 27, 183.
1756	Ravenel Diary-Account; *PHL*, 2:183, 192, 198, 244, 264–265, 269, 275, 278, 280, 288, 299–300, 302, 333, 345, 402.
1757	*PHL*, 2:423, 488.
1759	Robert Raper Letterbook (photocopy of original in West Sussex Record Office), SCHS, 1 August 1759, 4 August 1759, 23 September 1759, 20 October 1759, 27 October 1759.
1760	*The Letterbook of Eliza Lucas Pinckney, 1739–1762*, ed. Elise Pinckney (Chapel Hill: University of North Carolina Press, 1972), 143; Raper Letterbook, 19 March 1760, 17 June 1760, 10 July 1760, 12 July 1760, 30 October 1760; Ravenel Diary-Account; James Glen Papers, 11 October 1761, SCL.
1762	Baker Family Correspondence, 1 June 1762 (folder 1), 30 September 1762 (folder 4), SCHS; *PHL*, 3:105, 115, 118, 119, 126, 128, 129, 134, 197, 260; Raper Letterbook, 14 August 1762.
1763	*PHL*, 3:260, 441, 486, 488, 489, 496, 499, 527, 538, 541, 4:3, 15, 24, 31; Ravenel Diary-Account.
1764	*PHL*, 4:265, 283, 286, 327, 328, 330, 357, 373, 377, 419, 460; Peter Manigault Letterbook, 18 June 1764, SCHS; John Bartram, "Diary of a Journey through the Carolinas, Georgia and Florida from July 1, 1765, to April 10, 1766," *Transactions of the American Philosophical Society* 33 (1942): 13.
1765	Raper Letterbook, 13 May 1765, 2 February 1766; Bartram, "Diary of a Journey," 14–15, 16; *The Correspondence of John Bartram, 1734–1777*, ed. Edmund Berkeley and Dorothy Smith Berkeley (Gainesville: University Press of Florida, 1992), 653; Manigault Letterbook, 14 September 1765.

Table A.5 (continued)

Year	Source
1766	*Bartram Correspondence,* 664; Manigault Letterbook, 14 May 1766, 12 August 1766; Raper Letterbook, 19 May 1766, 25 July 1766; Gray, *History of Agriculture,* 1:289; *PHL,* 5:144.
1767	Raper Letterbook, 22 June 1767, 11 July 1767, 1 August 1767, 2 October 1767; Manigault Letterbook, 31 July 1767, 8 October 1767.
1768	Ralph Izard Papers, 1 June 1768 (box: originals and photostats), SCL; Manigault Letterbook, 3 June 1768, 1 July 1768, 21 October 1768, 21 December 1768; Glen Papers, 23 June 1768; Raper Letterbook, 10 September 1768; *PHL,* 5:749, 6:80, 91, 135.
1769	Manigault Letterbook, 1 May 1769, 29 July 1769, 6 September 1769, 31 October 1769; Raper Letterbook, 29 September 1769; *PHL,* 6: 595, 7:140.
1770	Ravenel Diary-Account; Raper Letterbook, 3 July 1770, 15 October 1770.
1771	Manigault Letterbook, 10 March 1771, 18 June 1771; Letterbook 1771–1773, Henry Laurens Papers, 28 May 1771, 23 July 1771, SCHS (hereafter cited as HL Papers); Ravenel Diary-Account; Josiah Smith Jr. Letterbook, 15 June 1771, 17 June 1771, Southern Historical Collection, University of North Carolina, Chapel Hill; Palmer Family Papers, Palmer Family Account Book, 9 August 1784, SCL.
1772	Smith Letterbook, 28 July 1772, 30 July 1772, 3 September 1772, 5 September 1772; Letters 1772–1780, HL Papers, 18 August 1772; Gray, *History of Agriculture,* 1:175–176.
1773	Smith Letterbook, 8 June 1773, 10 June 1773, 22 July 1773, 31 January 1774; Letters 1767–1783, HL Papers, Piercy Letterbook, 5 July 1773.
1774	Smith Letterbook, 10 May 1774, 22 September 1774, 4 October 1774; Ja[me]s Jamieson Manuscript, SCL.
1775	HL Papers, Piercy Letterbook, 25 March 1775, 25 June 1775, 28 July 1775; Manigault Family Papers, 12 April 1775, box (legal), folder 2, SCL; Smith Letterbook, 16 June 1775, 19 October 1775; Edward Telfair Papers, 20 June 1775, Duke; Gray, *History of Agriculture,* 1: 175–176.
1776	Daniel Elliott Huger Smith Papers, 7 February 1776, SCHS.
1777	William Ancrum Letterbook, 15 August 1777, SCL.
1778	Letters 1777–1785, HL Papers, 16 July 1778; Ravenel Diary-Account; Gervais and Laurens Correspondence, HL Papers, 21 October 1778.

Table A.5 (continued)

Year	Source
1779	Ravenel Diary-Account; William Allston Jr. Manuscript, SCL; Ancrum Letterbook, 26 July 1779, 27 September 1779, 16 October 1779; Smith Letterbook, 10 October 1779.
1781	Ravenel Diary-Account.
1782	Ravenel Diary-Account.
1783	Thomas Morris Papers, 24 August 1783, SCL; Manigault Family Papers, 10 September 1783, box I (letter), folder 12, SCL; Sarah R. Gibbes Letters, 15 September 1783 (folder 6), SCHS; Smith Letterbook, 28 April 1784; William Gibbons Jr. Papers, 1 September 1784, Duke.
1784	Palmer Family Account Book, 9 August 1784, SCL; John Lewis Gervais Papers, 25 August 1784 (folder 2), SCL; Smith Letterbook, 27 September 1784.
1785	Letterbook 1785–1787, HL Papers, 7 July 1785, 15 September 1785; Palmer Account Book, 1 October 1785; Samuel Dubose, "Address Delivered at the Seventeenth Anniversary of the Black Oak Agricultural Society," in *A Contribution to the History of the Huguenots of South Carolina,* by Samuel Dubose and Frederick A. Porcher, ed. T. Gaillard Thomas (1887; repr., Columbia: University of South Carolina Press, 1972), 10.
1786	Elias Ball XIV Family Papers, 29 May 1786 (folder 7), SCHS; John Chesnut Papers, 10 August 1786, SCHS; Phillip Porcher Sr. Receipts and Miscellaneous, 25 November 1786, SCHS.
1790	Elias Ball XIV Family Papers, 10 February 1790, 6 June 1790 (folder 7).
1792	Pinckney Family Papers (ser. 1, box 4), 25 May 1792, 1 July 1792, 14 July 1792, 28 July 1792, 14 September 1792, Manuscripts Division, Library of Congress, Washington, D.C.
1793	Ibid., 17 July 1793.
1794	Ibid., 13 September 1794, 5 October 1794.
1795	Benjamin Pittman Papers (microfilm from originals in the State Historical Society of Wisconsin), 13 August 1795, SCHS.

Table A.6 Settled and undeveloped lands, 1732–1775

| Decade | Settled tracts | | Undeveloped tracts | | Ratio of settled tracts to undeveloped tracts |
	Number of tracts	Number of acres	Number of tracts	Number of acres	
1730s	236	130,454	254	231,407	0.9
1740s	183	93,566	197	136,222	0.9
1750s	262	156,725	412	253,750	0.6
1760s	415	256,238	637	440,541	0.7
1770s	245	179,935	489	341,346	0.5
	1,341	816,918	1,989	1,403,266	0.7

Source: South-Carolina Gazette.

Note: The newspaper's start of publication in January 1732, missing issues for the period 1747–1751 and other periods, and the end date for the study in December 1775 affected results for those decades. For 270 advertised tracts included here acreage information was not provided.

Table A.7 Suggested productions for advertised lands, 1732–1775

| Decade | Percentage of advertisements with suggested productions | | | | | | |
	Rice	Indigo	Corn	Livestock	Wood	Naval stores	N
1730s	66.4	0.0	28.5	29.8	27.1	13.4	295
1740s	71.0	10.1	27.6	21.2	20.7	6.5	217
1750s	75.7	69.6	34.1	9.9	23.0	3.4	384
1760s	67.5	48.8	27.9	16.1	32.8	4.0	553
1770s	63.9	40.9	21.8	6.6	30.2	3.1	393

Source: South-Carolina Gazette.

Note: These percentages are based on the number of advertisements that suggested any use. Of 3,330 advertisements, 1,827 (54.9 percent) suggested a productive use for the land. The newspaper's start of publication in January 1732, missing issues for the period 1747–1751 and other periods, and the end date for the study in December 1775 affected results for those decades.

Table A.8 Dispersion of plantation material refinement, 1732–1775

Indicator of refinement	Refinement evidence by settlement zone (percent)		
	Core	Secondary	Frontier
Dwellings			
Mentioned (*n* = 717)	58.2	20.5	21.3
Brick (*n* = 59)	89.8	5.1	5.1
Two-story (*n* = 71)	57.7	21.1	21.1
Four or more rooms (*n* = 50)	72.0	14.0	14.0
Piazzas (*n* = 22)	72.7	4.5	22.7
Grounds			
Orchards (*n* = 130)	70.8	13.8	15.4
Gardens (*n* = 103)	77.7	7.8	14.6
Fish and game (*n* = 54)	66.7	14.8	18.5

Source: South-Carolina Gazette.

Note: Tracts located in Georgia and North Carolina's Lower Cape Fear region are included in the frontier zone.

Table A.9 Size, dispersion, and development of land, 1732–1775

	Settlement zone		
	Core	Secondary	Frontier
Settled plantations			
Mean acres	508	825	924
Median acres	374	600	700
Percentage of acres (*n* = 726,125)	37.6	25.9	36.5
Percentage of tracts (*n* = 1,052)	51.0	21.7	27.3
Undeveloped land			
Mean acres	480	685	915
Median acres	331	500	500
Percentage of acres (*n* = 1,107,242)	15.2	18.6	66.2
Percentage of tracts (*n* = 1,452)	24.2	20.7	55.1

Table A.9 (continued)

	Settlement zone		
	Core	Secondary	Frontier
Smallest and largest tracts			
Bottom decile (percentage ≤140 acres)	71.9	10.3	17.8
Top decile (percentage ≥1,400 acres)	17.0	22.5	60.5
Ratio of settled/undeveloped tracts	1.5	0.8	0.4

Source: South-Carolina Gazette.

Note: Acre figures are rounded to the nearest whole unit. This sample excludes advertisements without listed tract size and those without sufficient geographic information to locate the tract within one of the above settlement zones. Tracts located in Georgia and North Carolina's Lower Cape Fear region are included in the frontier zone.

Table A.10 Capacity of land for rice agriculture, 1732–1775

Features of the tract	Core	Secondary	Frontier
Contains tidal rice land (percent; $n = 141$)	7.1	23.4	69.5
Average percentage of tract rice land ($n = 332$)	32.1	39.5	44.5
Average size of rice land (in acres; $n = 341$)	204	349	372
Average percentage of tract cleared ($n = 276$)	28.0	14.3	14.5
Average number of working hands suggested ($n = 22$)	25.4	39.0	39.2

Source: South-Carolina Gazette.

Note: Acreage figures are rounded to the nearest whole unit. Three estimates of the number of working hands of 100 or greater were omitted.

Table A.11 Size of plantations in proximity to Charlestown, 1732–1775

Miles from town	Mean tract size (acres)	N
<1–5	267	64
6–10	438	42
11–20	619	73
21–50	844	57

Source: *South-Carolina Gazette.*

Note: Acreage figures are rounded to the nearest whole unit. This sample includes advertised lands with some sign of development.

Table A.12 Commodity sales, Henry Laurens's frontier plantations, 1766–1773

Plantation	Commodity	Quantity	Units	Value (SC£)	Percentage of total
Broughton Island	Rice	658,954	Pounds	19,947	98.4
	All other sales			317	1.5
	Subtotal			*20,264*	*99.9*
Wright's Savannah	Rice	417,511	Pounds	11,462	99.1
	All other sales			104	0.9
	Subtotal			*11,566*	*100.0*
New Hope	Rice	324,176	Pounds	11,182	99.6
	All other sales			44	0.4
	Subtotal			*11,226*	*100.0*
Total				43,056	

Source: Henry Laurens Account Book, Robert Scott Small Library, Special Collections, College of Charleston, Charleston, S.C.

Note: The account book begins in January 1766 and ends in September 1773. January and part of February 1768 accounts are missing. Quantities and values are rounded to the nearest whole unit, and some values have been estimated on the basis of values for the same items elsewhere in the account book. Figures do not include items exchanged among plantations or between plantations and Laurens-owned schooners.

Table A.13 Commodity sales, Henry Laurens's core and secondary plantations, 1766–1773

Plantation	Commodity	Quantity	Units	Value (SC£)	Percentage of total
Mepkin	Firewood	4,189	Cords	15,777	34.2
	Rice	370,041	Pounds	11,950	25.9
	Corn	7,482	Bushels	5,804	12.6
	Indigo	3,985	Pounds	5,089	11.0
	Lumber	47,273	Feet	4,783	10.4
	Rice, rough	3,252	Bushels	1,875	4.1
	All other sales			863	1.9
	Subtotal			*46,141*	*100.1*
Wambaw	Rice	280,625	Pounds	8,309	93.6
	Shingles	74,980	Shingles	375	4.2
	Corn	198	Bushels	160	1.8
	All other sales			37	0.4
	Subtotal			*8,881*	*100.0*
Total				55,022	

Source: Henry Laurens Account Book, Robert Scott Small Library, Special Collections, College of Charleston, Charleston, S.C.

Note: Laurens sold Wambaw Plantation in 1769; earnings are for the period 1766–1769. The account book begins in January 1766 and ends in September 1773. January and part of February 1768 accounts are missing. Quantities and values are rounded to the nearest whole unit, and some values have been estimated on the basis of values for the same items elsewhere in the account book. Figures do not include items exchanged among plantations or between plantations and Laurens-owned schooners. Lumber figures exclude pieces not measured in feet.

Table A.14 Estimated slave populations, Henry Laurens's plantation enterprise, 1766–c. 1785

Location	Dates operated	Recorded slave population, 1766–1773	Estimated slave population, c. 1772	Estimated slave population, c. 1785
Wambaw	1756–1769	79	—	—
Mepkin	1762–1792	71	70	100
Wright's Savannah	1766–1779	24	102	—
Broughton Island	1766–1778	105	85	—
New Hope	1768–1778	2	35	—
Mount Tacitus	1776–1792	—	—	75
Small's Field	1777–1792	—	—	75
Rattray Green, Ansonborough	1764–1792	14	33	15
Total		295	325	265

Note: The account book records slaves owned in 1766 and slaves purchased in the period 1766–1773, as noted in column 3. Laurens (hereafter cited as HL) sold Wambaw Plantation in 1769 and distributed its slaves to other plantations. For Wright's Savannah Plantation in 1772, 102 slaves were recorded, *The Papers of Henry Laurens*, ed. Philip M. Hamer et al., 16 vols. (Columbia: University of South Carolina Press, 1968–2003), 8:288 (hereafter cited as *PHL*). Estimates for the other plantations are based on the size of annual cloth shipments at 4.5 yards per slave, as suggested in *PHL*, 14:181. Wright's Savannah's 10 suits of baby clothes plus 414 yards of white plains for 1771 confirm the observation of 102 slaves "big & Small" ("Journal of the Proceedings at Wright Savannah 1772," HL Papers). Mepkin shipments for 1769–1770 of 312 yards suggest a slave population of 69. Debits for 547 yards of white plains were charged to Broughton Island and New Hope Plantations equally, suggesting 121 slaves on both plantations. During the 1771–1772 season New Hope sold £7 for every £10 sold by Broughton Island, suggesting a 7:10 ratio of working hands, HL Account Book. In addition to the 14 skilled or urban-based slaves who I assigned to Rattray Green, Ansonborough, and who were listed in the account book in 1766, 19 others are mentioned elsewhere in the account book, suggesting a total of 33 c. 1770. In 1785 HL estimated the total at "near or upwards of 250" and noted that "about three fourths of my Negroes remain," a comment that suggests a prewar population of about 333, *PHL*, 16:545, 558. In 1785 HL estimated Mepkin's population at "upwards of a hundred Negroes" and his "two other Plantations" (Mount Tacitus and Small's Field) "with a much greater number of Negroes," *PHL*, 15:551. A shoe order for 1785 puts the total population at 250 with fifteen pairs ordered separately; I assume for skilled or urban-based slaves, *PHL*, 16:545. A 1786 cloth order of 1,200 yards of plains suggests a total population of 266, *PHL*, 16:655.

Table A.15 Return on investment, Henry Laurens's plantation enterprise, 1766–1773

Year	Mepkin	Wambaw	Wright's Savannah	Altamaha River plantations	Total rate of return
1766–1767	10.0	8.0	—	−2.6	4.6
1767–1768	13.3	3.3	—	−0.3	4.6
1768–1769	20.5	8.5	−9.6	3.7	8.1
1769–1770	21.5	—	5.9	0.9	8.2
1770–1771	24.2	—	9.7	4.3	11.6
1771–1772	25.0	—	3.4	24.8	18.3
1772–1773	23.9	—	6.5	19.2	16.4
Total	138.4	19.7	22.2	50.2	70.9

Source: Henry Laurens Account Book, Robert Scott Small Library, Special Collections, College of Charleston, Charleston, S.C.

Note: The account book begins in January 1766 and ends in September 1773; January and part of February 1768 accounts are missing. Years in the table run from June 1 to May 31. Calculations for Wright's Savannah are estimates; Broughton Island and New Hope, which shared many expenses, are calculated together as "Altamaha River plantations." Total rates of return were calculated as a ratio of net earnings to total capital invested for the whole period; annual rates of return were calculated based on a running total of capital up to and including that invested in each annual period.

Notes

Introduction

1. Henry Laurens to James Laurens, 15 April 1774, in *The Papers of Henry Laurens*, ed. Philip M. Hamer et al., 16 vols. (Columbia: University of South Carolina Press, 1968–2003), 9:409 (hereafter cited as HL and *PHL*). See also ibid., 9:409, 10:217.
2. HL to Duncan Rose, 5 June 1785, ibid., 16:565; HL to William Lee, 8 January 1783, ibid., 16:126.
3. HL to John Ettwein, 19 March 1763, ibid., 3:373–374.
4. Joyce E. Chaplin, *Subject Matter: Technology, the Body, and Science on the Anglo-American Frontier, 1500–1676* (Cambridge, Mass.: Harvard University Press, 2001), 116–117; Donna Merwick, *Possessing Albany, 1630–1710: The Dutch and English Experiences* (New York: Cambridge University Press, 1990), chap. 4.
5. Robert Olwell, *Masters, Slaves, and Subjects: The Culture of Power in the South Carolina Low Country, 1740–1790* (Ithaca, N.Y.: Cornell University Press, 1998), 184–187; John Norris, *Profitable Advice for Rich and Poor . . .* (1712), in *Selling a New World: Two Colonial South Carolina Promotional Pamphlets,* ed. Jack P. Greene (Columbia: University of South Carolina Press, 1989), 87, 91.
6. Peter H. Wood, *Black Majority: Negroes in Colonial South Carolina from 1670 through the Stono Rebellion* (New York: W. W. Norton, 1974); Daniel C. Littlefield, *Rice and Slaves: Ethnicity and the Slave Trade in Colonial South Carolina* (Baton Rouge: Louisiana State University Press, 1981); Philip D. Morgan, *Slave Counterpoint: Black Culture in the Eighteenth-Century Chesapeake and Lowcountry* (Chapel Hill: University of North Carolina Press, 1998).
7. Peter A. Coclanis, *The Shadow of a Dream: Economic Life and Death in the*

South Carolina Low Country, 1670–1920 (New York: Oxford University Press, 1989); Joyce E. Chaplin, *An Anxious Pursuit: Agricultural Innovation and Modernity in the Lower South, 1730–1815* (Chapel Hill: University of North Carolina Press, 1993); Olwell, *Masters, Slaves, and Subjects.*

8. Robin Blackburn, *The Making of New World Slavery: From the Baroque to the Modern, 1492–1800* (New York: Verso, 1997); Dale Tomich, *Through the Prism of Slavery: Labor, Capital, and the World Economy* (Lanham, Md.: Rowman & Littlefield, 2004).

9. John Ogilby, *America: Being the Latest, and Most Accurate Description of the New World* (London, 1671), 206, Early English Books Online, Chadwyck-Healey, eebo.chadwyck.com; William Stephens, *The Journal of William Stephens, 1743–1745*, ed. E. Merton Coulter, 2 vols. (Athens: University of Georgia Press, 1958–1959), 2:245; *Oxford English Dictionary Online*, s.v. "swamp," dictionary.oed.com (accessed 11 November 2005).

10. [George Milligen-Johnston], *Short Description of the Province of South Carolina, with an Account of the Air, Weather, and Diseases, at Charles-Town* (1763), facsimile repr. in *Colonial South Carolina: Two Contemporary Descriptions*, ed. Chapman J. Milling (Columbia: University of South Carolina Press, 1951), 118–119.

11. James Glen, *A Description of South Carolina* (1761), in ibid., 14.

12. Stephens, *Journal*, 2:245, 248.

13. François-Alexandre-Frédéric, duc de La Rochefoucauld-Liancourt, *Travels through the United States of North America, the Country of the Iroquois, and Upper Canada, in the Years 1795, 1796, and 1797*, 2 vols. (London, 1799), 1:558, Eighteenth-Century Collections Online, Gale Group, galenet .galegroup.com.

14. T. H. Breen, *Tobacco Culture: The Mentality of the Great Tidewater Planters on the Eve of Revolution* (Princeton, N.J.: Princeton University Press, 1985), 86; Kathleen Brown, *Good Wives, Nasty Wenches, and Anxious Patriarchs: Gender, Race, and Power in Colonial Virginia* (Chapel Hill: University of North Carolina Press, 1996), 266–267.

15. *The Shaftesbury Papers and Other Records Relating to Carolina* (1897; repr., Charleston, S.C.: Tempus, 2000), 469; Norris, *Profitable Advice*, 83; on the "secularization of the calling," see J. E. Crowley, *This Sheba, Self: The Conceptualization of Economic Life in Eighteenth-Century America* (Baltimore: Johns Hopkins University Press, 1974), chap. 2.

16. *American Husbandry: Containing an Account of the Soil, Climate, Production and Agriculture, of the British Colonies in North America*, ed. Harry J. Carman (1775; repr., New York: Columbia University Press, 1939), 275; [John Mitchell], *The Present State of Great Britain and North America with Regard to Agriculture, Population, Trade, and Manufactures* (London, 1767), 149–150, 198.

17. Brown, *Good Wives*, chap. 8; Michal J. Rozbicki, *The Complete Colonial Gentleman: Cultural Legitimacy in Plantation America* (Charlottesville: University Press of Virginia, 1998), 157–161.

18. Lord Adam Gordon, "Journal of an Officer Who Travelled in America and the West Indies in 1764 and 1765," in *Travels in the American Colonies*, ed. Newton D. Mereness (New York: Macmillan, 1916), 397–398.

19. Paul Langford, *A Polite and Commercial People: England, 1727–1783* (Oxford: Oxford University Press, 1989).

20. S. Max Edelson, "Carolinians Abroad: Cultivating English Identities from the Colonial Lower South," in *Britain and the American South: From Colonialism to Rock and Roll*, ed. Joseph P. Ward (Jackson: University Press of Mississippi, 2003), 81–105.

21. Peter H. Wood, "Slave Labor Camps in Early America: Overcoming Denial and Discovering the Gulag," in *Inequality in Early America*, ed. Carla Gardina Pestana and Sharon V. Salinger (Hanover, N.H.: University Press of New England, 1999), 227.

22. Coclanis, *Shadow of a Dream*, chap. 3.

23. S. Max Edelson, "The Nature of Slavery: Environmental Disorder and Slave Agency in Colonial South Carolina," in *Cultures and Identities in Colonial British America*, ed. Robert Olwell and Alan Tully (Baltimore: Johns Hopkins University Press, 2005), 21–44.

24. George Ogilvie to [Margaret] Ogilvie, February 1770, in "The Letters of George Ogilvie," ed. David S. Shields, *Southern Literary Journal*, special issue (1986): 130; William Butler, "Observations on the Culture of Rice" (1786), South Carolina Historical Society, Charleston (hereafter cited as SCHS); John Martin to John Martin, 1 July 1788, John Martin Estate Papers, SCHS.

25. S. Max Edelson, "The Planter's Stock: Employing Slave Labor in the Colonial Lower South" (paper presented at the Institute for Southern Studies conference on "Slavery in Early South Carolina," Columbia, S.C., 12–13 February 1999); Glen, *Description of South Carolina*, 16; Robert Raper to John Colleton, 13 May 1761, Robert Raper Letterbook (photocopy of original in West Sussex Record Office), SCHS.

26. John Drayton, *A View of South-Carolina, as Respects Her Natural and Civil Concerns* (Charleston, S.C., 1802), 20; Mrs. A. Capers to Mrs. Russell, 25 March 1791, Edith Mitchell Dabbs Papers, Southern Historical Collection, University of North Carolina, Chapel Hill.

1. Laying Claim to the Land

1. Harry Roy Merrens, *Colonial North Carolina in the Eighteenth Century: A Study in Historical Geography* (Chapel Hill: University of North Carolina Press, 1964), 18.

2. L. H. Roper, *Conceiving Carolina: Proprietors, Planters, and Plots, 1662–1729* (New York: Palgrave Macmillan, 2004), 15–16.

3. Lord Ashley to Henry Woodward, 10 April 1671, in *The Shaftesbury Papers and Other Records Relating to Carolina* (1897; repr., Charleston, S.C.: Tempus, 2000), 316–317 (hereafter cited as *SP*).

4. Peter Hulme, *Colonial Encounters: Europe and the Native Caribbean, 1492–1797* (London: Routledge, 1992), 35.

5. John Dryden (1682), quoted in David Armitage, "John Locke, Carolina, and the *Two Treatises of Government*," *Political Theory* 32 (2004): 613.

6. Joyce E. Chaplin, *Subject Matter: Technology, the Body, and Science on the Anglo-American Frontier, 1500–1676* (Cambridge, Mass.: Harvard University Press, 2001), 12–18.

7. Samuel Wilson, *An Account of the Province of Carolina, in America . . .* (1682), in *Historical Collections of South Carolina . . .*, ed. B. R. Carroll, 2 vols. (New York, 1836), 2:33 (hereafter cited as *Hist. Coll.*); T. A. [Thomas Amy], *Carolina; or, A Description of the Present State of That Country and the Natural Excellencies Thereof* (1682), ibid., 2:61; [Edward Ward], *A Trip to Jamaica: With a True Character of the People and Island*, 3rd ed. (London, 1698), 13–16, Early English Books Online, Chadwyck-Healey, eebo .chadwyck.com (hereafter cited as EEBO).

8. John Archdale, *A New Description of that Fertile and Pleasant Province of Carolina . . .* (1707), in *Narratives of Early Carolina, 1650–1708*, ed. Alexander Salley Jr. (New York: C. Scribner's Sons, 1911), 308.

9. *Carolina Described More Fully Then [sic] Heretofore . . .* (Dublin, 1684), 3–5, EEBO.

10. Robert Allen, "Agriculture during the Industrial Revolution," in *The Economic History of Britain since 1700*, ed. Roderick Floud and Donald McClosky, 2nd ed. (Cambridge: Cambridge University Press, 1994), 103–104.

11. William Hilton, "Relation of a Discovery" (1664), in *SP*, 24; Nicholas Carteret, "Mr. Carteret's Relations of Their Planting at Ashley River '70," in *Narratives of Early Carolina*, 119–120.

12. William Sayle and Council to Lords Proprietors, 1670, in *SP*, 175; John Ogilby, *America: Being the Latest, and Most Accurate Description of the New World* (London, 1671), 207, EEBO.

13. R. F. [Robert Ferguson], *The Present State of Carolina with Advice to the Settlers* (London, 1682), 18, EEBO; *The Agrarian History of England and Wales*, vol. 4, *1500–1640*, ed. Joan Thirsk (Cambridge: Cambridge University Press, 1967), 195–197; Hilton, "Relation of a Discovery," 24; Archdale, *New Description*, 288; Ogilby, *America*, 207.

14. Robert Sandford, "A Relation of a Voyage on the Coast of the Province of Carolina, 1666," in *Narratives of Early Carolina*, ed. Salley, 100, 90–91; Wallace E. McMullen Jr., *English Topographic Terms in Florida, 1563–1874*

(Gainesville: University of Florida Press, 1953), 21, 191; Ogilby, *America*, 206; Thirsk, *Agrarian History*, 179–180; Ferguson, *Present State of Carolina*, 16, 9; Robert Morden, *Geography Rectified; or, A Description of the World* . . . (London, 1688), 560, EEBO.

15. Wilson, *Account of the Province*, 33; Ferguson, *Present State of Carolina*, 5.

16. Wilson, *Account of the Province*, 29; Ferguson, *Present State of Carolina*, 7–9, 12; Peter Purry, *Proposals by Mr. Peter Purry of Newfchatel, for Encouragement of Such Swiss Protestants . . .*, in *Hist. Coll.*, 2:133.

17. Sandford, "Relation of a Voyage," 93; Ogilby, *America*, 208; Amy, *Carolina*, 61; Robert Horne, *A Brief Description of the Province of Carolina, on the Coasts of Floreda . . .* (1666), in *Hist. Coll.*, 2:6.

18. "An Old Letter" (c. 1671), in *SP*, 308; Archdale, *New Description*, 290; Ferguson, *Present State of Carolina*, 12.

19. Amy, *Carolina*, 79; Purry, *Proposals*, 2:136–137; "An Old Letter," 308.

20. Richard Blome, *A Description of the Island of Jamaica with the Other Isles and Territories in America to Which the English Are Related . . .* (1672; London, 1678), 57, EEBO; Archdale, *New Description*, 288.

21. Joyce E. Chaplin, "Natural Philosophy and an Early Racial Idiom in North America: Comparing English and Indian Bodies," *William and Mary Quarterly*, 3rd ser., 54 (1997): 234 (hereafter cited as *WMQ*); Ferguson, *Present State of Carolina*, 9. Fruits: Purry, *Proposals*, 131; Blome, *Description of Jamaica*, 57; Amy, *Carolina*, 69; Ogilby, *America*, 205; "An Old Letter," 308; Maurice Mathews to Lord Ashley, 30 August 1671, in *SP*, 333.

22. Ogilby, *America*, 208; [Nathaniel Crouch], *The English Empire in America; or, A Prospect of His Majesties Dominions in the West-Indies . . .* (London, 1685), 141, EEBO; Wilson, *Account of the Province*, 25–26; Sandford, "Relation of a Voyage," 100; Horne, *Brief Description*, 1. Ice and sun: "An Old Letter," 309; Maurice Mathews to Lord Ashley, 30 August 1671, in *SP*, 336; *Carolina Described*, 9. On Carolina's comparative temperance, see also Jack P. Greene, *Imperatives, Behaviors, and Identities: Essays in Early American Cultural History* (Charlottesville: University Press of Virginia, 1992), chap. 4.

23. Ogilby, *America*, 207–208; [John Peachi], *Some Observations Made upon the Herb Cassiny; Imported from Carolina* (London, 1695), 4–5, EEBO; Amy, *Carolina*, 69–70; Wilson, *Account of the Province*, 27; "An Old Letter," 308.

24. Robert Montgomery (1717), quoted in Greene, *Imperatives, Behaviors, and Identities*, 92; Archdale, *New Description*, 288 (amiable country/paradise); "An Old Letter," 309 (Canaan). Florida: Amy, *Carolina*, 62; "Letters from John Stewart to William Dunlop," *South Carolina Historical and Genealogical Magazine* 32 (1931): 4 (hereafter cited as *SCHM*); Ferguson, *Present State of Carolina*, 3; "Proposealls [*sic*] of Severall Gentlemen of Barbadoes," in *SP*, 10; Thomas Scanlan, *Colonial Writing and the New World, 1583–1671*:

Allegories of Desire (Cambridge: Cambridge University Press, 1999), 32–37; *Carolina Described*, 5–7; Amy, *Carolina*, 79.

25. *The English Pilot* . . . (London, 1698), 23, EEBO; Archdale, *New Description*, 93; Horne, *Brief Description*, 5; [George Milligen-Johnston], *Short Description of the Province of South Carolina, with an Account of the Air, Weather, and Diseases, at Charles-Town* (1763), facsimile repr. in *Colonial South Carolina: Two Contemporary Descriptions*, ed. Chapman J. Milling (Columbia: University of South Carolina Press, 1951), 140; *Carolina Described*, 4; Ferguson, *Present State of Carolina*, 27. See Karen Ordahl Kupperman, "The Puzzle of the American Climate in the Early Colonial Period," *American Historical Review* 87 (1982): 1262–1289; see also Chaplin, *Subject Matter*, 43–44.

26. Ferguson, *Present State of Carolina*, 4; *Carolina Described*, 2; Purry, *Proposals*, 2:138; Wilson, *Account of the Province*, 35.

27. Versions of the phrase appear in "An Old Letter," 307, 308; Horne, *Brief Description*, title; Blome, *Description of Jamaica*, 57; see also "Instructions for Mr. Andrew Percivall," 23 May 1674, in *SP*, 440.

28. Robert Matz, *Defending Literature in Early Modern England: Renaissance Literary Theory in Social Context* (Cambridge: Cambridge University Press, 2000), 1.

29. Wayne Franklin, *Discoverers, Explorers, Settlers: The Diligent Writers of Early America* (Chicago: University of Chicago Press, 1979), 77–79.

30. "Mr. Mathews'[s] Relation" (1670), in *SP*, 169; John Lawson, *A New Voyage to Carolina*, ed. Hugh Talmage Lefler (1709; repr., Chapel Hill: University of North Carolina Press, 1967), 24–25; Council Journals, 4 March 167[3], in *SP*, 420.

31. Sandford, "Relation of a Voyage," 88; *SP*, 168; Hilton, "Relation of a Discovery," 21; *Carolina Described*, 10; Joseph Dalton to Lord Ashley, 20 January 167[2] in *SP*, 380; *Carolina Described*, 4; Hilton, "Relation of a Discovery," 24. On the importance of Indian bodies in early English understandings of race, see Chaplin, *Subject Matter*.

32. Sandford, "Relation of a Voyage," 88, 90–91, 102–103, 93.

33. Gene Waddell, "Cusabo," in *Handbook of North American Indians*, vol. 14, *Southeast*, ed. Raymond D. Fogelson (Washington, D.C.: Smithsonian Institution, 2004), 254–264; Waddell, *Indians of the South Carolina Lowcountry, 1562–1751* (Spartanburg, S.C.: Reprint Company, 1980), 3–15.

34. "Cassique" was an Arawak term used by the Spanish and later by the English to refer to Indian leaders. Among the coastal Indians of Carolina, these figures probably served as *cockawases* who provided primary leadership as advisors to a group of elders; elsewhere *cockawases* were paired with *werowances* (war leaders). John T. Juricek, "The Westo Indians," *Ethnohistory* 11 (1964): 147–148.

35. Sandford, "Relation of a Voyage," 93–94, 105–106; Ogilby, *America,* 210.

36. Richard Hakluyt, "Discourse of Western Planting" (1584), in *The Original Writings & Correspondence of the Two Richard Hakluyts,* ed. E. G. R. Taylor, 2 vols. (London: Hakluyt Society, 1935), 2:254–255.

37. Hilton, "Relation of a Discovery," 19; Letter to Col. Tho[mas] Modyford and Petter Colleton, 30 August 1663, in *SP,* 13–14; Sandford, "Relation of a Voyage," 84.

38. Sandford, "Relation of a Voyage," 93–94, 104, 106–107.

39. Lord Ashley to John Yeamans, c. May 1670, in *SP,* 164; "Mr. Carteret's Relation" (1670), ibid., 166–168; Capt. Brayne to the Proprietors, 20 November 1670, ibid., 226–227. Brayne noted that "one of the two Indians of our Country" initiated contact with this apparently hostile party, one of whom was the Kiawah leader.

40. "Mr. Mathews'[s] Relation," 170–171.

41. *SP,* 201, 223.

42. On Columbus and charges of cannibalism among the Caribs, see Hulme, *Colonial Encounters,* chaps. 1–2; Juricek, "Westo Indians," 137–139, 150, 155–156; James H. Merrell, *The Indians' New World: Catawbas and Their Neighbors from European Contact through the Era of Removal* (Chapel Hill: University of North Carolina Press, 1989), 40–42; Stephen Bull to Lord Ashley, 12 September 1670, in *SP,* 194; William Owen to Lord Ashley, 15 September 1670, ibid., 200–201.

43. William Owen to Lord Ashley, ibid., 198; Morden, *Geography Rectified,* 560; Horne, *Brief Description,* 5; Blome, *Description of Jamaica,* 58; *SP,* 346; Maurice Mathews to Lord Ashley, 30 August 1671, ibid., 335; ibid., 348–349.

44. Stephen Bull to Lord Ashley, 12 September 1670, in *SP,* 193; William Owen to Lord Ashley, 15 September 1670, ibid., 197; see also Archdale, *New Description,* 96.

45. Joseph Dalton to Lord Ashley, 20 January 167[2], in *SP,* 378–379; M. Eugene Sirmans, *Colonial South Carolina: A Political History, 1663–1763* (Chapel Hill: University of North Carolina Press, 1966), 44.

46. "Woodward[']s Westo Discovery," 31 December 1674, in *SP,* 456–462.

47. On the coastal Indians allied with the English, see ibid., 334; Verner W. Crane, *The Southern Frontier, 1670–1732* (Durham, N.C.: Duke University Press, 1928), 14–21. On Anglo-Westo relations, see Alan Gallay, *The Indian Slave Trade: The Rise of the English Empire in the American South, 1670–1717* (New Haven, Conn.: Yale University Press, 2002), chap. 2. For examples of coastal Indians who rejected this status, see ibid., 44, 51–52; see also Merrell, *Indians' New World,* 67–68, 75–76, 90.

48. Waddell, *Indians of the Lowcountry,* 12–13; *SP,* 187 ("Petty Cassekas"); ibid., 343 (peaceably).

49. Joseph West to Lord Ashley, June 1670, in *SP,* 174; Stephen Bull to Lord

Ashley, 2 March 167[1], ibid., 275; [Florence] O'Sulliva[n] to Lord Ashley, 10 September 1670, ibid., 189; Council to Lords Proprietors, 12 September 1670, ibid., 191.

50. Ibid., 173n (Indian village). Archaeological excavations have unearthed Native American structures near Old Charlestown's fortified boundary. Stanley South, *Archaeological Pathways to Historic Site Development* (New York: Kluwer Academic/Plenum Publishers, 2002), 8–14; "Barbados Proclamation," 4 November 1670, in *SP*, 211 (Indian labor); Ferguson, *Present State of Carolina*, 16; Russell R. Menard, "Slave Demography in the Lowcountry, 1670–1740: From Frontier Society to Plantation Regime," *SCHM* 96 (1995): 281–289, 290–296; hired Indian hunters: *Carolina Described*, 2, 9; Archdale, *New Description*, 94; Wilson, *Account of the Province*, 28.

51. "Co[p]y of Instruc[ti]ons for Mr. West about [Our] Planta[ti]on," c. 1669, in *SP*, 126; ibid., 349; Maurice Mathews to Lord Ashley, 30 August 1671, ibid., 333–334.

52. Capt. West to John Locke, n.d., ibid., 425; Carl Sauer, "The Settlement of the Humid East," in *Climate and Man: Yearbook of Agriculture, 1941*, by U.S. Department of Agriculture (1941; repr., Detroit: Gale Group, 1974), 160; *SP*, 348. Despite an early request for a plow as well as horses capable of pulling it, the Proprietors equipped the Carolina expedition with dozens of hoes, some of which were earmarked for the Indian trade, ibid., 350, 286, 148, 19, 150, 199.

53. Joseph West to Lord Ashley, September 1670, in *SP*, 204; Lord Ashley to Joseph West, 1 November 1670, ibid., 209–210. Native American names used for the Ashley River were "Kiawah" and "Acabe," for the Cooper, "Wando" or "Ettiwan," ibid., 307, 397n, 400. On the influence of Native American "geographies" in early Virginia, see April Lee Hatfield, *Atlantic Virginia: Intercolonial Relations in the Seventeenth Century* (Philadelphia: University of Pennsylvania Press, 2003), chap. 1.

54. James Glen, *A Description of South Carolina . . .* (1761), in *South Carolina: Contemporary Descriptions*, 14.

55. Shaftesbury to Sir Peter Colleton, 27 November 1672, in *SP*, 416; Shaftesbury to Joseph West, 20 June 1672, ibid., 403. On the changing meaning of "plantation," see also Robert Olwell, *Masters, Slaves, and Subjects: The Culture of Power in the South Carolina Low Country, 1740–1790* (Ithaca, N.Y.: Cornell University Press, 1998), 184.

56. Joan Thirsk, *Economic Policy and Projects: The Development of a Consumer Society in Early Modern England* (Oxford: Oxford University Press, 1978), 2–3, 11, 139, 106; on specific commodities, see ibid., 4–7, 13–14, 26; on merchants, projecting, and colonization, see ibid., 75–77, 101–102; on Ireland as a colonial project see Nicholas Canny, *Kingdom and Colony: Ireland*

in the Atlantic World, 1560–1800 (Baltimore: Johns Hopkins University Press, 1988), 16, 79–93.

57. Thirsk, *Economic Policy and Projects,* 32, 47; Karen Ordahl Kupperman, "Colonization and Fen Drainings as English Projects: A Comparative Analysis" (conference paper, Seventh Annual Conference of the Omohundro Institute of Early American History and Culture, Glasgow, Scotland, 10–16 July 2001); Proprietors to the Governor and Council, 18 May 1674, in *SP,* 437; Amy, *Carolina,* 65; Wilson, *Account of the Province,* 33; experiments: Thirsk, *Economic Policy and Projects,* 140–141; Joseph West to Sir P[eter] Colleton, 2 March 167[1], in *SP,* 272; "Instruc[ti]ons for Mr. West," ibid., 125–126.

58. Thirsk, *Economic Policy and Projects,* 140–143, 189.

59. See Jean-Christophe Agnew, *Worlds Apart: The Market and the Theater in Anglo-American Thought, 1550–1750* (New York: Cambridge University Press, 1986), chap. 2; Richard Drayton, *Nature's Government: Science, Imperial Britain, and the "Improvement" of the World* (New Haven, Conn.: Yale University Press, 2000), 53.

60. Proprietors to the Governor and Council, 18 May 1674, in *SP,* 437.

61. Jos[eph] Dalton to Proprietors, 16 March 1670, in *SP,* 287; Walter Edgar, *South Carolina: A History* (Columbia: University of South Carolina Press, 1998), 41; Proprietors to the Governor and Council, 18 May 1674, in *SP,* 436–437; Nic[h]olas Blake to [Joseph Williamson], 12 November 1669, ibid., 158; Council to Proprietors, c. 1670, ibid., 175–176.

62. Jack P. Greene, *The Intellectual Construction of America: Exceptionalism and Identity from 1492 to 1800* (Chapel Hill: University of North Carolina Press, 1993), 47–50, 56; Roper, *Conceiving Carolina,* chap. 2.

63. Ashley to Sir J[ohn] Yeamans, 18 September 1671, in *SP,* 343–344; "Instructions to Mr. Andrew Percivall," 23 May 1674, ibid., 439–450; ibid., 103–104.

64. Ashley to Sir J[ohn] Yeamans, 18 September 1671, ibid., 343–344; Ashley to Gov[ernor] Sayle, 10 April 1671, ibid., 311; "Temporary Laws, Carolina," c. May 1671, ibid., 325; Ashley to Sir J[ohn] Y[ea]mans, 10 April 1671, ibid., 315.

65. Ashley to Sir J[ohn] Yeamans, 18 September 1671, ibid., 344; "First Meeting of the Proprietors," 23 May 1663, ibid., 5; "First Set of the Constitutions for the Government of Carolina," ibid., 93–94. On large-scale grants, see also Robert K. Ackerman, *South Carolina Colonial Land Policies* (Columbia: University of South Carolina Press, 1977), 11–19.

66. "Co[p]y of Instruc[ti]ons Annexed to [th]e Com[m]ission for [th]e Govern[or] and Councell," 27 July 1669, in *SP,* 121–122; "Instruc[ti]ons for Mr. West," ibid., 126; Robert Southwell to Lord Ashley, 31 August 1669, ibid., 152; Meaghan N. Duff, "Creating a Plantation Province: Proprietary

Land Policies and Early Settlement Patterns," in *Money, Trade, and Power: The Evolution of Colonial South Carolina's Plantation Society*, ed. Jack P. Greene, Rosemary Brana-Shute, and Randy J. Sparks (Columbia: University of South Carolina Press, 2001), 12; quoted in ibid., 4.

67. Stewart, "Letters," 4.

68. Proprietors to the Governor and Council, 18 May 1674, in *SP*, 437; Amy, *Carolina*, 65; Joseph Dalton to Lord Ashley, 20 January 167[2], in *SP*, 377–378, 382.

69. On the hacienda, see William B. Taylor, "Landed Society in New Spain: A View from the South," in *Readings in Latin American History*, vol. 1, *The Formative Centuries*, ed. Peter J. Bakewell, John J. Johnson, and Meredith D. Dodge (Durham, N.C.: Duke University Press, 1985), 105–128. Ferguson, *Present State of Carolina*, 32; Proprietors to Shaftesbury, 20 November 1674, in *SP*, 455; "Instructions for Mr. Andrew Percivall," 23 May 1674, ibid., 444; Shaftesbury to Sir Thomas Lynch, 29 October 1672, ibid., 414–415; Sir Peter Colleton to John Locke, 28 May 1673, ibid., 423.

70. Letter to Col. Tho[mas] Modyford and Peter Colleton, 30 August 1663, in *SP*, 14; Capt. West to John Locke, 28 June 1673, ibid., 425; Joseph Dalton to Lord Ashley, 20 January 167[2], ibid., 376–378; Maurice Mathews to Lord Ashley, 30 August 1671, ibid., 334.

71. "Captain Halsted[']s Instructions," 1 May 1671, in *SP*, 321; ibid., 352; on ginger, see also ibid., 127, 267, 309, 377; on the various ports of call of early voyages to Carolina, see ibid., 129–130, 175, 232–235, 242, 304; on the secondary staples of Barbados, see Richard Ligon, *A True & Exact History of the Island of Barbados . . .* (London, 1657), 22–23, EEBO.

72. "Instruc[ti]ons for Mr. West," in *SP*, 125–126; ibid., 348, 127n.

73. Stewart, "Letters," 82, 6, 16, 98.

74. Shaftesbury to Joseph West, 2 May 1674, in *SP*, 447; *Carolina Described*, 2, 8–9; Stephen Bull to Lord Ashley, 12 September 1670, in *SP*, 193; Ferguson, *Present State of Carolina*, 18; Amy, *Carolina*, 69.

75. Ferguson, *Present State of Carolina*, 32–33; Maurice Mathews to Lord Ashley, 30 August 1671, in *SP*, 333; Councell to L[ords] Proprietors, 21 March 167[1], ibid., 284.

76. Eric H. Ash, *Power, Knowledge, and Expertise in Elizabethan England* (Baltimore: Johns Hopkins University Press, 2004), 213, 9.

77. Joseph West to Sir P[eter] Colleton, 2 March 167[1], in *SP*, 272; ibid., 349; Maurice Mathews to Lord Ashley, 30 August 1671, ibid., 333; Joseph Dalton to Lord Ashley, 20 January 167[2], ibid., 376; Stephen Bull to Lord Ashley, 2 March 167[1], ibid., 275.

78. Daniel Vickers, "Competency and Competition: Economic Culture in Early America," *WMQ* 47 (1990): 3.

79. Amy, *Carolina*, 82. Agnes Leland Baldwin has identified 3,300 individual land claimants recorded in the period 1670–1700, although some may not have settled in South Carolina, *First Settlers of South Carolina, 1670–1700* (Easley, S.C.: Southern Historical Press, 1985). The total white population was reported as 4,220 in 1703, Sirmans, *Colonial South Carolina*, 60; Robert M. Weir estimates the total white immigration at approximately 6,000 before 1700; see *Colonial South Carolina: A History* (Millwood, N.Y.: KTO Press, 1983), 205–206. See also Peter H. Wood, *Black Majority: Negroes in Colonial South Carolina from 1670 through the Stono Rebellion* (New York: W. W. Norton, 1974), 24–28.

80. Capt. Brayne to the Proprietors, 20 November 1670, in *SP*, 231; E. A. Wrigley, "A Simple Model of London's Importance in Changing English Society and Economy, 1650–1750," *Past and Present* 37 (1967): 44–70; James Horn, "Servant Emigration to the Chesapeake in the Seventeenth Century," in *The Chesapeake in the Seventeenth Century*, ed. Thad W. Tate and David L. Ammerman (New York: W. W. Norton, 1979), 69–74.

81. On sailors as settlers, see *SP*, 229, 241, 331; Ann Kussmaul, *Servants in Husbandry in Early Modern England* (Cambridge: Cambridge University Press, 1981), 2–3, 49, 51, 55, 68–69; Joan Thirsk, *Agricultural Regions and Agrarian History in England, 1500–1750* (Houndmills, U.K.: Macmillan Education, 1987), 1–18; Richard Waterhouse, "England, the Caribbean, and the Settlement of Carolina," *Journal of American Studies* 9 (1975): 260–261.

82. On the diversity of the English agricultural landscape, see Ann Kussmaul, *A General View of the Rural Economy of England, 1538–1840* (Cambridge: Cambridge University Press, 1990), 2–3. The mobility of the servant labor force, she has argued, set general standards for agricultural practice, but also promoted technical change as "best practices" and innovations diffused along with migrating laborers. See Kussmaul, *Servants in Husbandry*, 68–69.

83. Much of this literature codified the agricultural practices of working farmers. On the widespread reach of agricultural projects such as tobacco growing, see Thirsk, *Economic Policy and Projects*, 8, 73, 77, 88, 132, 136, 141.

84. Jack P. Greene has concluded that more than half of identifiable settlers in the period 1670–1690 came from Barbados; see Greene, *Imperatives, Behaviors, and Identities*, 73. Kinloch Bull has revised estimates of 500 or more early Barbadian settlers downward to 200–300, "Barbadian Settlers in Early Carolina: Historiographical Notes," *SCHM* 96 (1995): 336–339.

85. *Carolina Described*, 3; Richard Grove, *Green Imperialism: Colonial Expansion, Tropical Island Edens, and the Origins of Environmentalism, 1600–1860* (Cambridge: Cambridge University Press, 1995), 276–277; Samuel Clarke,

A True and Faithful Account of the Four Chiefest Plantations of the English in America (London, 1670), 61, EEBO; Greene, *Imperatives, Behaviors, and Identities,* 82–83.

86. Capt. Brayne to Proprietors, 20 November 1670, in *SP,* 230; ibid., 412n.
87. "Barbados Proclamation," 4 November 1670, ibid., 210–211; Gov. West to Lord Ashley, 21 March 1671, ibid., 297; Waterhouse, "Settlement of Carolina," 278–279, 264–267.
88. [Florence] O'Sullivan to Lord Ashley, 10 September 1670, ibid., 189; Gov. West to Lord Ashley, 21 March 1671, ibid., 299; "The Clarendon Address," 1666, ibid., 84–85; Councell to L[ords] Proprietors, 21 March 1671, ibid., 284; Edward Waterhouse, "A Declaration of the State of the Colony and Affaires in Virginia . . ." (1622), in *The Records of the Virginia Company of London,* ed. Susan Myra Kingsbury, 4 vols. (Washington, D.C.: Government Printing Office, 1906–1935), 3:550.
89. Stephen Bull to Lord Ashley, 2 March 167[1], in *SP,* 274.
90. Barbadians issued a series of "Proposals" (1663) that paved the way for the "Concessions" (1664). At the Clarendon settlement, the Barbadian-dominated Assembly issued the "Clarendon Address" (1666) that made specific objections to Proprietary policies based on the scarcity of good contiguous planting land. In 1670 the "Barbados Proclamation" forced new concessions from the Proprietors. See *SP,* 10–12, 29–49, 84–88, 210–213. On the "Concessions" accorded the status of a customary constitution, see ibid., 195, 301.
91. "Culpeper's Draught of Ashley River," ibid., 339–340; Thomas Newe, "Letters of Thomas Newe from South Carolina, 1682," *American Historical Review* 12 (1907): 325; Samuel Thomas, "Letters of Rev. Samuel Thomas, 1702–1710," *SCHM* 4 (1903): 279.
92. Ackerman, *Land Policies,* 3–47; Sirmans, *Political History,* 31; Wesley Frank Craven, *The Southern Colonies in the Seventeenth Century, 1607–1689* (Baton Rouge: Louisiana State University Press, 1970), 338–342. On the practice of honoring squatters' rights regardless of the law throughout the British colonial periphery, see Peter A. Karsten, *Between Law and Custom: "High" and "Low" Legal Cultures in the Lands of the British Diaspora—The United States, Canada, Australia, and New Zealand, 1600–1900* (Cambridge: Cambridge University Press, 2002), 146–149.
93. Stewart, "Letters," 6.
94. Ashley to W[illiam] Saile, 13 May 1671, in *SP,* 327; Amy, *Carolina,* 67; John R. Stilgoe, *Common Landscape of America, 1580 to 1845* (New Haven, Conn.: Yale University Press, 1982), 63; John S. Otto, "Livestock-Raising in Early South Carolina, 1670–1700: Prelude to the Rice Plantation Economy," *Agricultural History* 61 (1987): 15–23.

95. Proprietors to the Governor and Council, 18 May 1674, in *SP*, 437; *Oxford English Dictionary Online*, s.v. "grazier," dictionary.oed.com (accessed 11 September 2003).

96. Amy, *Carolina*, 67–68; Thirsk, *Agrarian History in England*, 1–18; Eric Kerridge, *The Agricultural Revolution* (London: George Allen & Unwin, 1967), 181–222; Will[iam] Dunlop to [James Montgomerie], 21 October 1686, 21 November 1686, n.d. [c. 1687], Dunlop Letters, Papers of the Lords Proprietors in the Malmsbury Collection (photocopies of originals in the Scottish Record Office), South Carolina Department of Archives and History, Columbia (hereafter cited as SCDAH).

97. Wilson, *Account of the Province*, 30; John Norris, *Profitable Advice for Rich and Poor* ... (1712), in *Selling a New World: Two Colonial South Carolina Promotional Pamphlets*, ed. Jack P. Greene (Columbia: University of South Carolina Press, 1989), 102–104; John S. Otto and Nain E. Anderson, "The Origins of Southern Cattle-Grazing: A Problem in West Indian History," *Journal of Caribbean History* 21 (1988): 139, 146–147.

98. Timothy Silver, *A New Face on the Countryside: Indians, Colonists, and Slaves in South Atlantic Forests, 1500–1800* (New York: Cambridge University Press, 1990), 59–64; Otto and Anderson, "Origins," 142–144; Wood, *Black Majority*, 28–34, 105–106.

99. Otto, "Livestock-Raising," 21; Aaron M. Shatzman, *Servants into Planters: The Origin of an American Image: Land Acquisition and Status Mobility in 17th-Century South Carolina* (New York: Garland, 1989), 45, 51–52, 115, 131.

100. On this "mixed farming tradition," see Gordon G. Whitney, *From Coastal Wilderness to Fruited Plain: A History of Environmental Change in Temperate North America, 1500 to the Present* (New York: Cambridge University Press, 1994), 126–130. Provincial legislation supported open pastures in the last decade of the seventeenth century, mandating the enclosure of fields, as well as a register of brands to identify livestock ownership. Otto, "Livestock-Raising," 16. On the move to grazing lands in the interior in the eighteenth century, see "Report of Mr. Ettwein's Journey to Georgia and South Carolina, 1765," ed. George F. Jones, *SCHM* 91 (1990): 259–260; Robert L. Meriwether, *The Expansion of South Carolina, 1729–1765* (Kingsport, Tenn.: Southern Publishers, 1940), 75.

101. Newe, "Letters," 322–327.

102. "Bacon's 'Manifesto,'" in *The Old Dominion in the Seventeenth Century: A Documentary History of Virginia*, ed. Warren M. Billings (Chapel Hill: University of North Carolina Press, 1975), 278; Shaftesbury to Governor and Council, 10 June 1675, in *SP*, 468. On the Clarendon settlers as a "Rude Rable ... dayly ready to mutany," see ibid., 89.

103. "Proposalls of Severall Gentlemen of Barbadoes," 12 August 1663, in *SP*, 11; Henry Brayne to Sir P[eter] Colleton, 20 November 1670, ibid., 235–236; Sirmans, *Political History*, 19–54; for a critique of this characterization, see Roper, *Conceiving Carolina*, chaps. 3–4.

104. On the Yamassee land scheme, see Gary L. Hewitt, "Expansion and Improvement: Land, People, and Politics in South Carolina and Georgia, 1690–1745" (Ph.D. dissertation, Princeton University, 1996), 106–129; Sirmans, *Political History*, 115; Proprietors to Governor and Council, 3 March 1716, Records in the British Public Record Office Relating to South Carolina, SCDAH, 6:151 (hereafter cited as BPRO); see also letter of 6 August 1716, ibid., 6:237–238.

105. Franklin, *Discoverers, Explorers, Settlers*, 81; "A Memorandum of [the] Product and Trade of Carolina . . ." (1706), in BPRO, 5:152–153.

2. Rice Culture Origins

1. Duncan Clinch Heyward, *Seed from Madagascar* (1937; repr., Columbia: University of South Carolina Press, 1993), 40.

2. "Governor William Bull's Representation of the Colony, 1770," in *The Colonial South Carolina Scene: Contemporary Views, 1697–1774*, ed. H. Roy Merrens (Columbia: University of South Carolina Press, 1977), 264; Heyward, *Seed from Madagascar*, 9–10; *South-Carolina Gazette*, 8 October 1744 (hereafter cited as *SCG*); P[eter] Collinson, "An Account of the Introduction of Rice and Tar into Our Colonies," *Gentleman's Magazine* 36 (1766): 278–280; Alexander Hewit, *An Historical Account of the Rise and Progress of the Colonies of South Carolina and Georgia* (1779), in *Historical Collections of South Carolina*, ed. B. R. Carroll, 2 vols. (New York, 1836), 1:108–109 (hereafter cited as *Hist. Coll.*); John Drayton, *A View of South-Carolina, as Respects Her Natural and Civil Concerns* (Charleston, S.C., 1802), 115; Mark Catesby, *The Natural History of Carolina, Florida, and the Bahama Islands* . . . , 2 vols. (London, 1771), 1:xvii, Eighteenth-Century Collections Online, Gale Group, galenet.galegroup.com (hereafter cited as ECCO).

3. Collinson, "Introduction of Rice"; Madagascar ship dates: Heyward, *Seed from Madagascar*, 4 (1685); Catesby, *Natural History*, 1:xvii (1696); Collinson, "Introduction of Rice" (1713). Letter of Agricola [Charles Pinckney], *SCG*, 8 October 1744 (Barbary vessel).

4. Jean Watt (1726), quoted in Peter H. Wood, *Black Majority: Negroes in Colonial South Carolina from 1670 through the Stono Rebellion* (New York: W. W. Norton, 1974), 36 ("by a woman"). Abbé Raynal, *A Philosophical and Political History of the British Settlements and Trade in North America* . . . (Edinburgh, 1779), 137, ECCO.

5. Drayton, *View of South-Carolina*, 115; Catesby, *Natural History*, 1:xvii; Hewit, *Historical Account*, 109. For the claim that planters began "with only one Bushell," see Richard Hall to Board of Trade, 8 November 1734, Records in the British Public Record Office Relating to South Carolina, South Carolina Department of Archives and History, Columbia, 17:165 (hereafter cited as SCDAH).

6. Drayton, *View of South-Carolina*, 115; Hewit, *Historical Account*, 141.

7. Fayrer Hall, *The Importance of the British Plantations in America to This Kingdom* . . . (London, 1731), 18–19, ECCO. On similarities between Carolina "gold" rice and "varieties from Madagascar and South Asia," see Judith A. Carney, *Black Rice: The African Origins of Rice Cultivation in the Americas* (Cambridge, Mass.: Harvard University Press, 2001), 145.

8. Collinson, "Introduction of Rice."

9. David Ramsay, *Ramsay's History of South Carolina, from Its First Settlement in 1670 to the Year 1808*, 2 vols. (1809; repr., Newberry, S.C., 1858), 2:113–114, 264.

10. Catesby, *Natural History*, 1:xvii (Johnson); Fayrer Hall, *British Plantations*, 18 (Woodward); Collinson, "Introduction of Rice" (Du Bose); Ramsay, *Ramsay's History*, 2:113–114 (Smith). On inconsistencies, see A. S. Salley Jr., *The Introduction of Rice Culture in South Carolina*, Bulletins of the Historical Commission of South Carolina, no. 6 (Columbia: Historical Commission of South Carolina, 1919), 20.

11. Jack P. Greene, *Imperatives, Behaviors, and Identities: Essays in Early American Cultural History* (Charlottesville: University Press of Virginia, 1992), 154; Drayton, *View of South-Carolina*, 115; Hewit, *Historical Account*, 1:75–76, 420–421, 122–123.

12. Letter of Agricola [Charles Pinckney], *SCG*, 8 October 1744.

13. David S. Shields, *Oracles of Empire: Poetry, Politics, and Commerce in British America, 1690–1750* (Chicago: University of Chicago Press, 1990), 83 and chap. 4; Shields, "George Ogilvie's *Carolina; Or, The Planter* (1776)," *Southern Literary Journal*, special issue (1986): 7–8.

14. R.F.W. Allston, *Essay on Sea Coast Crops* (Charleston, S.C., 1854), 28.

15. Salley, *Introduction of Rice*, 11; Lewis C. Gray, *History of Agriculture in the Southern United States to 1860*, 2 vols. (1933; repr., Gloucester, Mass.: Peter Smith, 1958), 1:277–279; see also Converse D. Clowse, *Economic Beginnings in Colonial United South Carolina, 1670–1730* (Columbia: University of South Carolina Press, 1971), 61, 68, 81–82.

16. Peter A. Coclanis has explained the shift to rice in terms of changes in the factors of production in *The Shadow of a Dream: Economic Life and Death in the South Carolina Low Country, 1670–1920* (New York: Oxford University Press, 1989), 59–62. R. C. Nash has emphasized the pull of European

demand in "South Carolina and the Atlantic Economy in the Late Seventeenth and Eighteenth Centuries," *Economic History Review* 45 (1992): 677–702.

17. Shields, *Oracles of Empire*, 92; Shields, "Ogilvie's *Carolina*," 7; James Glen (1761), quoted in Salley, *Introduction of Rice*, 14 ("lucky accident").

18. Wood, *Black Majority*, chap. 2.

19. Daniel C. Littlefield, *Rice and Slaves: Ethnicity and the Slave Trade in Colonial South Carolina* (Baton Rouge: Louisiana State University Press, 1981), 98, 80, 113, and chap. 4.

20. Ibid., 48, 154.

21. Beauchamp Plantagenet (1648), quoted in Littlefield, *Rice and Slaves*, 100.

22. Abbé Raynal, *A Philosophical and Political History of the Settlements and Trade of the Europeans in the East and West Indies . . .* , 2nd ed., 6 vols. (London, 1798), 6:59, ECCO; "Bull's Representation," 264. On beliefs in the Asian origins of rice, see also Ramsay, *Ramsay's History*, 119–120; Heyward, *Seed from Madagascar*, 9–10.

23. Wood, *Black Majority*, 34; Carney, *Black Rice*, 103, 81. See also Peter H. Wood, " 'It was a Negro Taught Them': A New Look at African Labor in Early Carolina," *Journal of Asian and African Studies* 9 (1974): 175; Littlefield, *Rice and Slaves*, 99; Charles Joyner, *Down by the Riverside: A South Carolina Slave Community* (Urbana: University of Illinois Press, 1984), 13–14.

24. Carney, *Black Rice*, 32.

25. Littlefield mentions the "composite" character of economic culture in slave societies in *Rice and Slaves*, 177. Carney acknowledges that rice culture "bore the hybridized imprimatur of both African and European influences" as it developed technically in *Black Rice*, 162.

26. David Grigg, "The Starchy Staples in World Food Consumption," *Annals of the Association of American Geographers* 86 (1996): 412–413; Philip D. Morgan, "Work and Culture: The Task System and the World of Lowcountry Blacks, 1700–1880," *William and Mary Quarterly*, 3rd ser., 39 (1982): 597 (hereafter cited as *WMQ*).

27. See Sidney W. Mintz, *Sweetness and Power: The Place of Sugar in Modern History* (New York: Penguin, 1985), chap. 3.

28. Joseph Dalton to Lord Ashley, 20 January 167[2], in *The Shaftesbury Papers and Other Records Relating to Carolina* (1897; repr., Charleston, S.C.: Tempus, 2000), 377 (hereafter cited as *SP*).

29. An example of this literature of critique is *American Husbandry*, ed. Harry J. Carman (1775; repr., New York: Columbia University Press, 1939), 261–277.

30. Harry Roy Merrens, *Colonial North Carolina in the Eighteenth Century: A*

Study in Historical Geography (Chapel Hill: University of North Carolina Press, 1964), chap. 3.

31. Wood, " 'Negro Taught Them,' " 175.

32. Carney, *Black Rice,* 140, 162.

33. Ibid., 153–154; Judith A. Carney, " 'With Grains in Her Hair': Rice in Colonial Brazil," *Slavery & Abolition* 25 (2004): 21.

34. See Richard I. Groening Jr., "The Rice Landscape in South Carolina: Valuation, Technology, and Historical Periodization" (M.A. thesis, University of South Carolina, 1998), 45–46; Great Britain, Parliament, House of Commons, *Report of the Lords of the Committee of Council . . .* (London, 1789), n.p., image 123, ECCO.

35. José Miguel Gallardo, "The Spaniards and the English Settlement in Charles Town," *South Carolina Historical and Genealogical Magazine* 37 (1936): 85–86, 95, 96, 98–99 (hereafter cited as *SCHM*).

36. Henry Brayne to Lord Ashley, 9 November 1670, in *SP,* 215–216.

37. Robert Horne, *A Brief Description of the Province of Carolina, on the Coasts of Floreda . . .* (1666), in *Hist. Coll.,* 2:4; see *SP,* 442, 178, 288–289, 333–334.

38. Richard Ligon, *A True & Exact History of the Island of Barbados . . .* (London, 1657), 31, Early English Books Online, Chadwyck-Healey, eebo.chadwyck .com (hereafter cited as EEBO); Gervase Markham, *Markhams Farwell to Husbandry . . .* (London, 1620), 131, EEBO; N[athan] Bailey, *An Universal Etymological English Dictionary . . . ,* 3rd ed. (London, 1726), ECCO, s.v. "loblolly"; Leland Ferguson, *Uncommon Ground: Archaeology and Early African America, 1650–1800* (Washington, D.C.: Smithsonian Institution Press, 1992), 96–97.

39. Ligon, *True & Exact History,* 31; Hilary McD. Beckles, "An Economic Life of Their Own: Slaves as Commodity Producers and Distributors in Barbados," in *The Slaves' Economy: Independent Production by Slaves in the Americas,* ed. Ira Berlin and Philip D. Morgan (London: Frank Cass, 1991), 33 (Guinea corn); Thomas Tryon, *Friendly Advice to the Gentlemen-Planters of the East and West Indies* (London, 1684), 97–98, EEBO ("miserable fare"). James La Fleur suggests that slaves probably considered sorghum an inferior grain, especially compared with millet or rice. La Fleur, e-mail message to author, 12 June 2004.

40. Grigg, "Starchy Staples," 413–414.

41. Mintz, *Sweetness and Power,* 8–14.

42. John Campbell, *A Political Survey of Britain . . . ,* 2nd ed., 4 vols. (Dublin, 1775), 4:668, ECCO; Ligon, *True & Exact History,* 81–82, 43–44.

43. John Fransham, *The World in Miniature; or, The Entertaining Traveller,* 2 vols. (London, 1741), 2:298, ECCO; Ligon, *True & Exact History,* 22–23, 37–38, 43, 113–114. On Guinea corn, see Jerome Handler and Frederick

W. Lange, *Plantation Slavery in Barbados: An Archaeological and Historical Investigation* (Cambridge, Mass.: Harvard University Press, 1978), 86–87; see also William Douglass, *A Summary, History and Political, of the First Planting, Progressive Improvements, and Present State of the British Settlements in North America* (London, 1760), 118, ECCO; and Griffith Hughes, *The Natural History of Barbados* (London, 1650), 254, ECCO.

44. Ligon, *True & Exact History,* 99–100, 75, 66.

45. Philip D. Morgan, "Slaves and Livestock in Eighteenth-Century Jamaica: Vineyard Pen, 1750–1751," *WMQ* 52 (1995): 69–70; Hans Sloane, *A Voyage to the Islands Madera, Barbados, Nieves, S. Christophers and Jamaica . . . ,* 2 vols. (London, 1707–1725), 1:xix, ECCO. This linguistic comment is James La Fleur's, who also notes that such grain/bean mixtures had no African precedents and were thus probably American innovations. La Fleur, e-mail message to author, 12 June 2004.

46. James La Fleur, "Fusion Foodways of the Gold Coast and Atlantic World" (conference paper, Forty-sixth Annual Meeting of the African Studies Association, Boston, Mass., 31 October 2003).

47. David Watts, "Early Hispanic New World Agriculture, 1492 to 1509," in *Caribbean Slavery in the Atlantic World: A Student Reader,* ed. Verene Shepherd and Hilary McD. Beckles (Princeton, N.J.: Marcus Wiener, 2000), 144; Sloane, *Voyage to the Islands,* 1:xix.

48. *The Natural History of Birds . . . ,* 2 vols. (London, 1791), 1:19, ECCO; Carney, *Black Rice,* 151–154; *A Collection of Voyages . . . ,* 4 vols. (London, 1729), 1:175, ECCO.

49. Sidney W. Mintz, "Tasting Food, Tasting Freedom," in *Slavery in the Americas,* ed. Wolfgang Binder (Würzburg, Germany: Königshausen & Neumann, 1993), 261–268.

50. S. Max Edelson, "The Nature of Slavery: Environmental Disorder and Slave Agency in Colonial South Carolina," in *Cultures and Identities in Colonial British America,* ed. Robert Olwell and Alan Tully (Baltimore: Johns Hopkins University Press, 2005), chap. 1.

51. John Lawson, *A New Voyage to Carolina,* ed. Hugh Talmage Lefler (1709; repr., Chapel Hill: University of North Carolina Press, 1967), 16; *Luigi Castiglioni's Viaggio: Travels in the United States of North America, 1785–87,* ed. and trans. Antonio Pace (1824; repr., Syracuse, N.Y.: Syracuse University Press, 1983), 171–172; Catesby, *Natural History,* 1:xvii, xviii.

52. Drayton, *View of South-Carolina,* 125; David Doar, *Rice and Rice Planting in the South Carolina Low Country,* Contributions from the Charleston Museum 8 (Charleston, S.C.: Charleston Museum, 1936), 23–24. Carney asserts that this "red rice undoubtedly came from Africa," but this conclusion is by no means certain. Carney, *Black Rice,* 144–152. On the "slight morpho-

logical differences" that separate the two species, "making them difficult to tell apart in the field" or by reading contemporary descriptions, see Olga Linares, "African Rice (*Oryza glaberrima*): History and Future Potential," *PNAS* 99 (2002): 16361.

53. On the slave population, see Wood, *Black Majority*, 24–26; see also Coclanis, *Shadow of a Dream*, 64–66.

54. William James Rivers, *A Sketch of the History of South Carolina to the Close of the Proprietary Government by the Revolution of 1719* (Charleston, S.C., 1856), 382; Lord Ashley to [Joseph] West, 15 January 1672, in *SP*, 375; Carney, *Black Rice*, 142 (germination). Rice was not included on a 1699 list of intended experimental crops that featured indigo, ginger, olives, grapes, sugar, and cotton. *SP*, 125–127. In 1674 runaway servant Thomas Jibe reported that this plantation was established "for the purpose of introducing cattle raising." Gallardo, "Spaniards and English Settlement," 135–136.

55. Hannah Woolley, *The Accomplish'd Lady's Delight in Preserving, Physick, Beautifying, and Cookery* (London, 1675), 242, 320, 285, EEBO.

56. Markham, *Markhams Farwell to Husbandry*, 130–132. See also Peter A. Coclanis, "The Poetics of American Agriculture: The United States Rice Industry in International Perspective," *Agricultural History* 69 (1995): 148–149.

57. Maurice Mathews to Lord Ashley, 30 August 1671, in *SP*, 333.

58. Roy Porter, preface to *Bread of Dreams: Food and Fantasy in Early Modern Europe*, by Piero Camporesi (Chicago: University of Chicago Press, 1989), 10–13; William Ashely, *The Bread of Our Forefathers: An Inquiry in Economic History* (Oxford: Clarendon Press, 1928), 1–2 and chap. 1. By the early seventeenth century even the poorest consumers refused to buy rye or barley, even as an additive to wheat flour. Ibid., 44–47.

59. R. F. [Robert Ferguson], *The Present State of Carolina with Advice to the Settlers* (London, 1682), 8, EEBO.

60. Joseph Dalton to Lord Ashley, 20 January 167[2], in *SP*, 376; Johann Martin Bolzius, "Johann Martin Bolzius Answers a Questionnaire on Carolina and Georgia," ed. and trans. Klaus G. Loewald et al., *WMQ* 14 (1957): 238; Catesby, *Natural History*, 1:xviii. On wheat as a poor crop for "pioneer communities," see Lois Green Carr, Russell R. Menard, and Lorena S. Walsh, *Robert Cole's World: Agriculture and Society in Early Maryland* (Chapel Hill: University of North Carolina Press, 1991), 34.

61. John Stewart, "Letters from John Stewart to William Dunlop," *SCHM* 32 (1931): 22; Trudy A. Eden, " 'Makes Like, Makes Unlike': Food, Health, and Identity in the Early Chesapeake" (Ph.D. dissertation, Johns Hopkins University, 1999), 104–106 (assimilation). On maize aversion in Virginia, see ibid., 128, 135–142, 161. See also Joyce E. Chaplin, *Subject Matter: Tech-*

nology, the Body, and Science on the Anglo-American Frontier, 1500–1676 (Cambridge, Mass.: Harvard University Press, 2001), 149–150.

62. *SP*, 350. Maize eating was blamed for dysentery in Virginia in 1620 as well. Eden, " 'Makes Like, Makes Unlike,' " 142, 144. Mary Stafford, "A Letter Written in 1711 by Mary Stafford to Her Kinswoman in England," *SCHM* 81 (1980): 3–4.

63. Gallardo, "Spaniards and English Settlement," 133, 135; Council Journals, 4 June 1672, in *SP*, 394.

64. Henry Pitman, *A Relation of the Great Sufferings and Strange Adventures of Henry Pitman*... (London, 1689), 11–12, EEBO. John Smith, quoted in Eden, " 'Makes Like, Makes Unlike,' " 130 ("trash"). Maize terms: *Carolina Described More Fully Then [sic] Heretofore*... (Dublin, 1684), 9, EEBO; John Norris, *Profitable Advice for Rich and Poor*... (1712), in *Selling a New World: Two Colonial South Carolina Promotional Pamphlets*, ed. Jack P. Greene (Columbia: University of South Carolina Press, 1989), 89.

65. Norris, *Profitable Advice*, 90. On the role of the "huswife" in the English household economy, see Keith Wrightson, *Earthly Necessities: Economic Lives in Early Modern Britain* (New Haven, Conn.: Yale University Press, 2000), 45–48, 296–300.

66. Dairy production: Thomas Newe, "Letters of Thomas Newe from South Carolina, 1682," *American Historical Review* 12 (1907): 323; Norris, *Profitable Advice*, 103–104. Gardens: *SP*, 203, 250; Newe, "Letters," 324; T. A. [Thomas Amy], *Carolina; or, A Description of the Present State of that Country and the Natural Excellencies Thereof* (1682), in *Hist. Coll.*, 2:67. Drinks: ibid., 92, 100; Newe, "Letters," 323; Amy, *Carolina*, 64–65; Stafford, "Letter," 4. On the perceived dangers of drinking water, see Chaplin, *Subject Matter*, 149.

67. Alexander Moore, "Daniel Axtell's Account Book and the Economy of Early South Carolina," *SCHM* 95 (1994): 300. Newington Plantation debited rice sold by the hundredweight, the standard measure for processed rice, and by the bushel, which indicated that it was also sold in the "rough" for seed or later processing.

68. Norris, *Profitable Advice*, 92–93.

69. [John Mitchell], *The Present State of Great Britain and North America with Regard to Agriculture, Population, Trade, and Manufactures* (London, 1767), 153.

70. Ashely, *Bread of Our Forefathers*, 15–20; Ligon, *True & Exact History*, 29–31; William Byrd, *William Byrd's Natural History of Virginia; or, The Newly Discovered Eden*, ed. and trans. Richmond Croom Beatty and William J. Mulloy (1737; repr., Richmond, Va.: Dietz Press, 1940), 20–21.

71. Wood, *Black Majority*, 61.

72. Beth Preston, "The Functions of Things: A Philosophical Perspective on Material Culture," in *Matter, Materiality and Modern Culture,* ed. P. M. Graves-Brown (London: Routledge, 2000), 42–43.

73. Located on the eastern shore of the Cooper River, this plantation was first known by its Native American name, Makkean, which was later anglicized to "Mepkin."

74. Stewart, "Letters," 1–2, 6–7, 29.

75. Ibid., 15, 6, 19.

76. Ibid., 85–86, 16.

77. Ibid., 22.

78. Ibid., 85.

79. Hartlib, quoted in Littlefield, *Rice and Slaves,* 104. On Hartlib, see Chaplin, *Subject Matter,* 235–236.

80. Letter to Col. Tho[mas] Modyford and Peter Colleton, 30 August 1663, in *SP,* 14; Horne, *Brief Description,* 2:13; Coclanis, "Poetics of Agriculture," 148; John R. Stilgoe, *Common Landscape of America, 1580 to 1845* (New Haven, Conn.: Yale University Press, 1982), 33 (Crusoe). By the end of the colonial period, starch makers consumed thousands of barrels of rice every year. Josiah Smith Jr. to George Austin, 30 January 1773, Josiah Smith Jr. Letterbook, Southern Historical Collection, University of North Carolina, Chapel Hill (hereafter cited as SHC).

81. E. L. Jones, "The European Background," in *The Cambridge Economic History of the United States,* vol. 1, *The Colonial Era,* ed. Stanley L. Engerman and Robert E. Gallman (Cambridge: Cambridge University Press, 1996), 133.

82. Groening, "Rice Landscape," 45–46, 55n–56n; Edward Williams, *Virginia, More Especially the South Part Thereof, Richly and Truly Valued* (London, 1650), 3–4, EEBO; William Berkeley, *A Discourse and View of Virginia* (1663; repr., Norwalk, Conn.: William H. Smith Jr., 1914), 2; Beauchamp Plantagenet, *A Description of the Province of New Albion . . .* (London, 1648), 10–11, EEBO.

83. Samuel B. Hilliard, "Antebellum Tidewater Rice Culture in South Carolina and Georgia," in *European Settlement and Development in North America: Essays on Geographic Change in Honour and Memory of Andrew Hill Clark,* ed. James R. Gibson (Toronto: University of Toronto Press, 1978), 96–97; David L. Coon, *The Development of Market Agriculture in South Carolina, 1670–1785* (New York: Garland, 1989), 181; Eric Kerridge, *The Agricultural Revolution* (London: George Allen & Unwin, 1967), 250–266; *American Husbandry,* 275. See also Groening, "Rice Landscape," 23–26.

84. Kerridge, *Agricultural Revolution,* 222–223, 88, 120–122, 128, 134; Joan Thirsk, *Fenland Farming in the Sixteenth Century* (Leicester, U.K.: University

College, 1953), 13–24; *The Agrarian History of England and Wales,* vol. 5, *1640–1750,* ed. Joan Thirsk (Cambridge: Cambridge University Press, 1985), 44–46, 54–55.

85. Walter Blith (1649), quoted in Groening, "Rice Landscape," 24; Karen Ordahl Kupperman, "Colonization and Fen Drainings as English Projects: A Comparative Analysis" (conference paper, Seventh Annual Conference of the Omohundro Institute of Early American History and Culture, Glasgow, Scotland, 10–16 July 2001).

86. Moore, "Axtell's Account Book," 292–296; Lubbock, *SCG,* 13 May 1745; Lining, ibid., 12 June 1763; William Bartram, *The Travels of William Bartram: Naturalist's Edition,* ed. Francis Harper (1791; repr., New Haven, Conn.: Yale University Press, 1958), 7.

87. For an example of a tide mill in use in 1410, see Peter Barfoot, *A Candid Review of Facts, in the Litigation between Peter Barfoot, Esq. and Richard Bargus* (London, 1788), 117–118, ECCO. On the workings of early modern tide mills, see William Marshall, *The Rural Economy of the West of England . . . ,* 2 vols. (London, 1796), 2:63–64, ECCO; Marshall, *The Rural Economy of the Southern Counties . . . ,* 2 vols. (London, 1798), 2:262–263, ECCO. See also Johann Beckmann, *A History of Inventions and Discoveries,* 3 vols. (London, 1797), 1:245, 245n, ECCO. On tide mills in use in eighteenth-century New England, see *Collections of the Massachusetts Historical Society* 3 (1794): 121, ECCO.

88. William Bailey, *One Hundred and Six Copper Plates of Mechanical Machines, and Implements of Husbandry . . . ,* 2 vols. (London, 1782), 1:179–180, ECCO; *The Annual Register; or, A View of the History, Politicks, and Literature, for the Year 1759,* 7th ed. (London, 1783), 159–160, ECCO. The Society for the Encouragement of the Arts and Commerce made awards for advances in tide-mill designs in 1759, 1762, and 1764. See also John Banks, *A Treatise on Mills, in Four Parts . . .* (London, 1795), ECCO.

89. Karl W. Butzer, "French Wetland Agriculture in Atlantic Canada and Its European Roots: Different Avenues to Historical Diffusion," *Annals of the Association of American Geographers* 92 (2002): 464–466.

90. Philip D. Morgan, e-mail message to the author, 21 November 2003.

91. Carr, Menard, and Walsh, *Robert Cole's World,* xvi.

92. Carney, *Black Rice,* 92, 95–97. For a discussion of English "trunks," see Groening, "Rice Landscape," 158–159.

93. "The Fundamental Constitutions (1669)," in *SP,* 103–104; *Carolina Described,* 9.

94. James Glen, *A Description of South Carolina . . .* (1761), facsimile repr. in *Colonial South Carolina: Two Contemporary Descriptions,* ed. Chapman J. Milling (Columbia: University of South Carolina Press, 1951), 95.

95. John J. McCusker and Russell R. Menard, "The Sugar Industry in the Seventeenth Century: A New Perspective on the Barbadian 'Sugar Revolution,'" in *Tropical Babylons: Sugar and the Making of the Atlantic World, 1450–1680,* ed. Stuart B. Schwartz (Chapel Hill: University of North Carolina Press, 2004), 292–294, 301.

96. Stewart, "Letters," 94; Carney, *Black Rice,* 83.

97. Stewart, "Letters," 7.

98. See, for example, Sidney W. Mintz, *Caribbean Transformations* (Chicago: Aldine Publishing, 1974), chap. 7.

99. Wood, *Black Majority,* 61.

100. Yi-Fu Tuan, *Topophilia: A Study of Environmental Perception, Attitudes, and Values* (Englewood Cliffs, N.J.: Prentice-Hall, 1974), 78–79.

101. Elizabeth Donnan, *Documents Illustrative of the History of the Slave Trade to America,* 4 vols. (Washington, D.C.: Carnegie Institution, 1935), 4:375, 377–380, 413, 428, 438, 442, 625. For a reproduction of one such advertisement, see Daniel P. Mannix in collaboration with Malcolm Cowley, *Black Cargoes: A History of the Atlantic Slave Trade, 1518–1865* (New York: Viking Press, 1962), unnumbered page following 146. James M. Clifton erred when he quoted Mannix's caption to this advertisement ("from the Windward Coast, valued for their knowledge of rice culture") as if it were the text of the advertisement itself in "The Rice Industry in Colonial America," *Agricultural History* 55 (1981): 273. Judith A. Carney repeats this mistake in *Black Rice,* 90.

102. Henry Laurens to Corsley Rogers & Son, 31 July 1755, in *The Papers of Henry Laurens,* ed. Philip M. Hamer et al., 16 vols. (Columbia: University of South Carolina Press, 1968–2003), 1:308 (competition for slaves) (hereafter cited as HL and *PHL*); *Evening Gazette* (1785), quoted in Wood, "'Negro Taught Them,'" 171 ("accustomed"). On planters' preference for Gambian slaves, see Littlefield, *Rice and Slaves,* chap. 1. For a succinct critique of preferences as an explanation for the ethnic composition of black populations in American slave societies, see introduction to *Cultivation and Culture: Labor and the Shaping of Slave Life in the Americas,* ed. Ira Berlin and Philip D. Morgan (Charlottesville: University Press of Virginia, 1993), 12–14.

103. Richard Oswald, quoted in David Eltis, Philip Morgan, and David Richardson, "The African Contribution to Rice Cultivation in the Americas" (unpublished manuscript), 21; James Glen, quoted in Marcus W. Jernegan, *Laboring and Dependent Classes in Colonial America, 1607–1783* (1931; repr., New York: Frederick Ungar Publishing, 1960), 19–20.

104. Samuel Dubose, "Address Delivered at the Seventeenth Anniversary of the Black Oak Agricultural Society," in *A Contribution to the History of the*

Huguenots of South Carolina, by Samuel Dubose and Frederick A. Porcher, ed. T. Gaillard Thomas (1887; repr., Columbia: University of South Carolina Press, 1972), 9–10. On drivers, see Philip D. Morgan, *Slave Counterpoint: Black Culture in the Eighteenth-Century Chesapeake and Lowcountry* (Chapel Hill: University of North Carolina Press, 1998), 222–225.

105. HL to John Owen, 15 February 1785, in *PHL,* 16:540; Elias Ball to John Ball, 27 August 1786, Elias Ball XIV Family Papers, South Carolina Historical Society, Charleston (hereafter cited as SCHS).

106. John Rutledge to Jonathan Bryan, 17 August 1777, John Rutledge Jr. Papers, Special Collections, William R. Perkins Library, Duke University, Durham, N.C.; HL to Isaac Peace, 21 September 1767, in *PHL,* 5:306–307.

107. Marguerite B. Hamer, "The Fate of the Exiled Acadians in South Carolina," *Journal of Southern History* 4 (1938): 199–208; Ruth Allison Hudnut and Hayes Baker-Crothers, "Acadian Transients in South Carolina," *American Historical Review* 43 (1938): 500–513. On Acadian wetland agriculture, see Andrew Hill Clark, *Acadia: The Geography of Early Nova Scotia to 1760* (Madison: University of Wisconsin Press, 1968), chap. 6; see also Butzer, "French Wetland Agriculture." On Acadian rice growing in Louisiana, see Daniel Jacobson, "The Origin of the Koasati Community of Louisiana," *Ethnohistory* 7 (1960): 109; Carl A. Brasseaux, *The Founding of New Acadia: The Beginnings of Acadian Life in Louisiana, 1765–1803* (Baton Rouge: Louisiana State University Press, 1987), 128–129. M. Eugene Sirmans, *Colonial South Carolina: A Political History, 1663–1763* (Chapel Hill: University of North Carolina Press, 1966), 317; quoted in Hamer, "Exiled Acadians," 204 ("well acquainted"). "Extract of a Letter from Charles-Town, South Carolina, July 22, 1763," Items Pertaining to the Carolinas in the Belfast [Ireland] Newspapers, 1729–1776, South Caroliniana Library, University of South Carolina, Columbia ("bigoted") (hereafter cited as SCL).

108. Littlefield, *Rice and Slaves,* 109, 114; Carney, "From Hands to Tutors: African Expertise in the South Carolina Rice Economy," *Agricultural History* 67 (1993): 1–30.

109. Edward Randolph, "Letter of Edward Randolph to the Board of Trade, 1699," in *Narratives of Early Carolina, 1650–1708,* ed. Alexander S. Salley Jr. (New York: C. Scribner's Sons, 1911), 204–210; Coon, *Development of Market Agriculture,* 167, 173–174; quoted in Salley, *Introduction of Rice,* 6–7 ("Ships").

110. Governor James Glen reported that 2,225 pounds of clean rice per field hand was the standard c. 1748, when rice was produced largely on inland swamp fields equipped with reservoirs, Coclanis, *Shadow of a Dream,* 97. An early eighteenth-century ton contained 20 hundredweights (2,240 pounds). At this rate, 332 slaves (13.6 percent of the estimated black pop-

ulation of 2,444 in 1700) could have produced Randolph's reported 330 tons. Many more slaves would have been required at the lower rates of productivity that probably prevailed during rice's first commercial season. Ibid., table 3-13, 82. On rice exports for the period 1698–1752, see ibid., table 3-13, 82.

111. See Carney, *Black Rice*, 132.

112. Catesby, *Natural History*, 1:xvii; *SCG*, 28 July 1733. Several others attributed high slave mortality to the rigors of hand rice processing. See "Correspondence between Alexander Garden, M.D., and the Royal Society of Arts," *SCHM* 64 (1963): 17; Peter Manigault to Ralph Izard, 18 June 1764, Peter Manigault Letterbook, SCHS; John Bartram to William Bartram, 5 April 1766, in *The Correspondence of John Bartram, 1734–1777*, ed. Edmund Berkeley and Dorothy Smith Berkeley (Gainesville: University Press of Florida, 1992), 662.

113. Josiah Smith Jr. to George Austin, 31 January 1774, Smith Letterbook; *SCG*, 14 October 1732.

114. Wood, *Black Majority*, 106, 159–166, and esp. table 7, 162–163; ibid., 97, 105.

115. Stafford, "Letter," 4.

116. Carney, *Black Rice*, 98–101. On the operation of the task system, see Morgan, "Work and Culture," and Philip D. Morgan, "Task and Gang Systems: The Organization of Labor on New World Plantations," in *Work and Labor in Early America*, ed. Stephen Innes (Chapel Hill: University of North Carolina Press, 1988), 189–220; on the historiography of the task system, see Daniel C. Littlefield, "Continuity and Change in Slave Culture: South Carolina and the West Indies," *Southern Studies* 26 (1987): 203, 203n; see also Peter A. Coclanis, "How the Low Country Was Taken to Task: Slave-Labor Organization in Coastal South Carolina and Georgia," in *Slavery, Secession, and Southern History*, ed. Robert Louis Paquette and Louis A. Ferleger (Charlottesville: University Press of Virginia, 2000), 59–78.

117. Anon. (1806), quoted in Morgan, "Task and Gang Systems," 191.

118. William Butler, "Observations on the Culture of Rice" (1786), SCHS.

119. Carney, *Black Rice*, 81.

120. To answer this question, Peter A. Coclanis has offered a "principal-agent" approach that stresses information asymmetries. His model rests on the assumption that slaves "possessed private information about risiculture unavailable or only partially available to Europeans," "Taken to Task," 67–68.

121. Russell R. Menard and Stuart B. Schwartz, "Why African Slavery? Labor Force Transitions in Brazil, Mexico, and the Carolina Lowcountry," in *Slavery in the Americas*, 104.

122. Robert Ferguson, *Present State of Carolina*, 20.

123. Edward Hyrne to unknown addressee, 1 February 1708, in "Hyrne Family Letters, 1701–10," in *Colonial South Carolina Scene,* 26. On the export and internal consumption of provisions, c. 1712, see Norris, *Profitable Advice,* 91.

124. Brian Hunt (1727), quoted in Frank J. Klingberg, *An Appraisal of the Negro in Colonial South Carolina* (Washington, D.C.: Associated Publishers, 1941), 52.

125. Coclanis, *Shadow of a Dream,* 42. On farm building and diversified agriculture in early South Carolina, see Russell R. Menard, "Financing the Lowcountry Export Boom: Capital and Growth in Early South Carolina," *WMQ* 51 (1994): 659–676. On concerns for reducing costs on newly settled plantations, see Robert Ferguson, *Present State of Carolina,* 10. On the low costs of slave maintenance compared with that of white servants, see Will[iam] Dunlop to [James Montgomerie], 21 October 1686, Letters from William Dunlop, Papers of the Lords Proprietors in the Malmsbury Collection (photocopy of originals in the Scottish Record Office), SCDAH.

126. Gideon Johnston (1713), quoted in Klingberg, *Appraisal of the Negro,* 7; Francis Le Jau to the Secretary, 20 February 1712, in *The Carolina Chronicle of Dr. Francis Le Jau, 1706–1717,* ed. Frank J. Klingberg (Berkeley: University of California Press, 1956), 108. On commonplace tortures, see ibid., 108, 129–130; see also "An Act for the Better Ordering and Governing Negroes and Other Slaves in This Province," in *Statutes at Large of the State of South Carolina,* ed. Thomas Cooper and David J. McCord, 10 vols. (Columbia, S.C., 1836–1841), 7:411.

127. Gideon Johnston (1713), quoted in Klingberg, *Appraisal of the Negro,* 7. On weekend work, see also "Documents Concerning Rev. Samuel Thomas, 1702–1707," *SCHM* 4 (1903): 26, 42. George Fenwick Jones, "John Martin Boltzius' Trip to Charelston, October 1742," *SCHM* 82 (1981): 102 ("old rags"). See also Norris, *Profitable Advice,* 107.

128. Moore, "Axtell's Account Book," 285, 290. Planters later imported and distributed cotton and linen "Negro cloth" as a matter of course, but cotton was grown c. 1690 as an experimental crop. Axtell's record of slaveproduced cotton suggests that early slaves may have produced their own clothes, as well as their own food. For Caribbean examples of slave selfprovisioning and weekend work, see Ligon, *True & Exact History,* 48; Chaplin, *Subject Matter,* 220; Michael Mullin, *Africa in America: Slave Acculturation and Resistance in the American South and the British Caribbean* (Urbana: University of Illinois Press, 1992), 140–141.

129. Le Jau to Henry Compton, 27 May 1712, in *Carolina Chronicle . . . Le Jau,* 116; Le Jau to the Secretary, 13 June 1710, ibid., 76.

130. On resistance in this period, see Wood, *Black Majority,* chap. 8; Gideon Johnston (1713), quoted in Klingberg, *Appraisal of the Negro,* 7.

131. Quoted in Mullin, *Africa in America*, 141.

132. Catesby, *Natural History*, 2:xix; Morgan, *Slave Counterpoint*, 179–180; John Lewis Gervais to HL, 5–10 May 1772, in *PHL*, 8:291.

133. Mullin, *Africa in America*, 129–130.

134. On slave housing, see Bolzius, "Questionnaire on Carolina," 257; Morgan, *Slave Counterpoint*, 104–124; Kenneth E. Lewis, "Plantation Layout and Function in the South Carolina Lowcountry," in *The Archaeology of Slavery and Plantation Life*, ed. Teresa Singleton (Orlando, Fla.: Academic Press, 1985), 46, 59; J. W. Joseph, "Building to Grow: Agrarian Adaptations to South Carolina's Historical Landscapes," in *Carolina's Historical Landscapes: Archaeological Perspectives*, ed. Linda F. Stine et al. (Knoxville: University of Tennessee Press, 1997), 46.

135. Alexander Garden (1740), quoted in Klingberg, *Appraisal of the Negro*, 106.

136. Leland Ferguson, *Uncommon Ground*, 63–82, 96–98, 105.

137. Bolzius, "Questionnaire on Carolina," 256, 259–260.

138. ["Scotus Americanus"] (1773), quoted in "Some North Carolina Tracts of the Eighteenth Century," ed. William K. Boyd, *North Carolina Historical Review* 3 (1926): 616.

139. Morgan, *Slave Counterpoint*, chap. 10.

140. Sidney W. Mintz, "Tasting Food, Tasting Freedom."

141. Robert Ferguson, *Present State of Carolina*, 20; Horne, *Brief Description*, 7; James Wright, quoted in Mart Stewart, " 'Whether Wast, Deodand, or Stray': Cattle, Culture, and the Environment in Early Georgia," *Agricultural History* 65 (1991): 22 ("Calculated"). On customary rights in Britain, see E. P. Thompson, *Customs in Common: Studies in Traditional Popular Culture* (New York: New Press, 1993), 1–12, 128–129. On the common-law-like status of customs of slavery in the antebellum United States, see Peter Karsten, *Between Law and Custom: "High" and "Low" Legal Cultures in the Lands of the British Diaspora—The United States, Canada, Australia, and New Zealand, 1600–1900* (Cambridge: Cambridge University Press, 2002), 298.

142. Lauren Benton, *Law and Colonial Cultures: Legal Regimes in World History, 1400–1900* (Cambridge: Cambridge University Press, 2002), 262. On "legal pluralism" and the space it created for cross-cultural interaction in American slave societies, see ibid., 5, 60–78.

143. For a survey of Africans' experiences of dependency, see John Thornton, *Africa and Africans in the Making of the Atlantic World, 1400–1680* (New York: Cambridge University Press, 1992), 76–85. For old-world examples of tasked labor, see Carney, *Black Rice*, 100; see also Eona Karakacili, "Peasants, Productivity and Profit in the Open Fields of England: A Study of Economic and Social Development" (Ph.D. dissertation, University of Toronto, 2001), 36–38; see also Ann Kussmaul, *Servants in Husbandry in Early Modern En-*

gland (Cambridge: Cambridge University Press, 1981), 6–7; see also Carr, Menard, and Walsh, *Robert Cole's World,* 110, 312n.

144. John Stuart Mill, *Principles of Political Economy,* 8th ed., 2 vols. (London, 1878), 1:299.

145. Mintz, *Caribbean Transformations,* 193.

146. Christopher Morris has referred to this dynamic as the "articulation" of capitalist and traditional practices within American slave societies generally, and in specific reference to the task system. "The Articulation of Two Worlds: The Master-Slave Relationship Reconsidered," *Journal of American History* 85 (1998): 996–999. See also S. Max Edelson, "Affiliation without Affinity: Skilled Slaves in Eighteenth-Century South Carolina," in *Money, Trade, and Power: The Evolution of South Carolina's Plantation Society,* ed. Jack P. Greene, Rosemary Brana-Shute, and Randy J. Sparks (Columbia: University of South Carolina Press, 2001), chap. 9.

147. Catesby, *Natural History,* 1:xvii; Leland Ferguson, *Uncommon Ground,* 95; *Castiglioni's Viaggio,* 169. Like modern West Africans who grow small quantities of *glaberrima* for ritual uses and large quantities of *sativa* for sale, slaves may have retained this variety as an independent provision crop. Linares, "African Rice," 16363–16365. On late colonial African American preferences for maize, see Ramsay, *Ramsay's History,* 123.

148. Eliza Lucas Pinckney to Mr. Gerard, [c. August 1758?], in *The Letterbook of Eliza Lucas Pinckney, 1739–1762,* ed. Elise Pinckney (Chapel Hill: University of North Carolina Press, 1972), 97; Elias Ball to Elias Ball Jr., 6 September 1785, Ball Family Papers, SCL; Drayton, *View of South-Carolina,* 143; *Castiglioni's Viaggio,* 169, 171. Bernard Romans also mentioned a "wafer-like bread called journey cakes in Carolina" made from rice in *A Concise Natural History of East and West Florida,* ed. Kathryn E. Holland Braund (1775; repr., Tuscaloosa: University of Alabama Press, 1999), 164.

149. Lord Adam Gordon, "Journal of an Officer Who Travelled in America and the West Indies in 1764 and 1765," in *Travels in the American Colonies,* ed. Newton D. Mereness (New York: Macmillan, 1916), 400. See also Ramsay, *Ramsay's History,* 115. Imported flour from New England and the Middle Colonies gave way to supplies by farmers in the interior by the early 1760s. Robert L. Meriwether, *The Expansion of South Carolina, 1729–1765* (Kingsport, Tenn.: Southern Publishers, 1940), 106.

150. *Castiglioni's Viaggio,* 171–172; Josiah Quincy Jr., "Journal of Josiah Quincy, Junior, 1773," in Massachusetts Historical Society *Proceedings* 49 (1915–1916), 445–456; "Diary of William Dillwyn during a Visit to Charles Town in 1772," ed. A. S. Salley Jr., *SCHM* 36 (1935): 31.

3. Transforming the Plantation Landscape

1. John Lewis Gervais to Henry Laurens, 15 April 1784, Henry Laurens Manuscripts, South Caroliniana Library, University of South Carolina, Columbia (hereafter cited as SCL). Details on the creation of Ball family plantations can be found in Wills of Charleston County, 22 (1786–1793): 387–390, South Carolina Department of Archives and History, Columbia (hereafter cited as SCDAH); Records of the Court of Common Pleas, Writs of Partition, Book A (1754–1777): 161–164, SCDAH; *The Papers of Henry Laurens*, ed. Philip M. Hamer et al., 16 vols. (Columbia: University of South Carolina Press, 1968–2003), 2:180, 4:493n (hereafter cited as HL and *PHL*). On the Ball family, see also Edward Ball, *Slaves in the Family* (New York: Farrar, Straus and Giroux, 1998).

2. Judith M. Brimlowe and Joel A. Shirley, *Pamphlet Accompanying South Carolina Archives Microcopy Number 12: Memorials of Seventeenth- and Eighteenth-Century South Carolina Land Titles* (Columbia: SCDAH, 1984), 1–5. The Quit Rent Act of 1731 is included in *The Statutes at Large of South Carolina*, ed. Thomas Cooper and David J. McCord, 10 vols. (Columbia, S.C., 1836–1841), 3:289–304.

3. Approximately 715,000 acres were granted through 1730, and 619,043 acres were memorialized, suggesting that something on the order of 87 percent of grants were later claimed. Meaghan N. Duff, "Designing Carolina: The Construction of an Early American Social and Geographical Landscape, 1670–1719" (Ph.D. dissertation, College of William and Mary, 1998), 91.

4. Fire: Records of the Auditor General, Memorials of Land Titles (Copies), vols. 1–5, Microcopy Number 12, SCDAH, 4:16 (hereafter cited as S.C. Memorials); failure: ibid., 1:87, 2:162; geographic terms: ibid., 3:520, 5:327, 2:133; Yamassee War: ibid., 3:234, 5:190, 176–177.

5. Ibid., 1:174, 4:176, 3:305–306, 23.

6. Russell R. Menard, "Financing the Lowcountry Export Boom: Capital and Growth in Early South Carolina," *William and Mary Quarterly*, 3rd ser., 51 (1994): 661–665 (hereafter cited as *WMQ*).

7. Edward T. Price, *Dividing the Land: Early American Beginnings of Our Private Property Mosaic* (Chicago: University of Chicago Press, 1996), 136–139. On the sale of patents, see George C. Rogers Jr., *History of Georgetown County* (Columbia: University of South Carolina Press, 1970), 22–23; see also Julia S. Bolick, *Waccamaw Plantations* (Clinton, S.C.: Jacobs Press, 1946), 1–2, 4–11.

8. S.C. Memorials, 4:170; *Wadboo Barony: Its Fate as Told in Colleton Family*

Papers, 1773–1793, ed. J. H. Easterby (Columbia: University of South Carolina Press, 1952), vii.

9. Of the 1,415 registered tracts 159 (11.2 percent) were subject to a single transaction; 623 (44.0 percent) were subject to two transactions; 419 (29.6 percent) were subject to three transactions; and 214 (15.1 percent) were subject to four to thirteen transactions, proportions that should be regarded as minimums because of incomplete reporting. S.C. Memorials.

10. Memorialists registered 159 (11.2 percent) tracts that they had themselves been granted; 265 (18.7 percent) tracts were bequeathed directly by the grantee to heirs who registered them; together, these amounted to 29.9 percent of the total. Conveyances (purchases or sales) totalled 1,150 recorded transactions; 756 were inheritances, a ratio of 1.5/1. For 334 tracts both a grant date and a date for the second transaction was recorded; 146 were registered by the grantee and included a grant date. Of these 480, 143 (29.8 percent) had changed hands within ten years. Ibid.

11. Individuals registered 392 tracts (27.7 percent) adjacent to lands also owned by the individual; 298 (21.1 percent) tracts had been portions of a larger grant; and 25 (1.8 percent) were larger than the initial grant. Counting each tract that featured one or more of these alterations only once, 642 (45.4 percent) were altered from the original grant. Ibid.

12. Linda M. Pett-Conklin, "The Evolution of Colonial South Carolina's Cadastral Landscape" (paper presented at the conference on "New Directions in South Carolina Lowcountry Studies," Program in the Carolina Lowcountry and the Atlantic World, College of Charleston, Charleston, S.C., 16–19 May 1995); Stanley South and Michael Hartley, *Deep Water and High Ground: Seventeenth Century Low Country Settlement* (Columbia, S.C.: Institution of Archaeology and Anthropology, n.d.), 24. Evidence of marsh exclusion can be found in Thomas Butler Plats (1696), Richard B. Baker Business and Legal Papers, folder 2, South Carolina Historical Society, Charleston (hereafter cited as SCHS); *The Shaftesbury Papers and Other Records Relating to Carolina* (1897; repr., Charleston, S.C.: Tempus, 2000), 357 (hereafter cited as *SP*); Agnes Leland Baldwin, *Marsh Granting Practices in South Carolina* (Summerville, S.C.: Committee for Preservation of Privately Owned Marshlands, 1976), 6, 11–12.

13. Baldwin, *Marsh Granting Practices*, 11. For additional examples of wetland acquisition and how surveying practices affected this process, see ibid., 13–23.

14. Allien, quoted in ibid., 18–19; S.C. Memorials, 2:90, 3:4. For other examples of wetland acquisitions, see ibid., 1:159, 268, 481, 3:279, 323, 458, 515, 524, 5:11, 164. For examples of how this practice continued after 1740, see Welshuysen, *South-Carolina Gazette*, 19 November 1744 (hereafter cited as *SCG*); Guerard, ibid., 21 January 1772.

15. Pett-Conklin, "South Carolina's Cadastral Landscape."

16. S.C. Memorials, 3:174, 222–224 (town lots); Henry A. M. Smith, "The Town of Dorchester in South Carolina: A Sketch of Its History," *South Carolina Historical and Genealogical Magazine* 6 (1905): 72 (hereafter cited as *SCHM*); Bullock, *SCG,* 23 March 1734.

17. Alexander Hewit, *An Historical Account of the Rise and Progress of the Colonies of South Carolina and Georgia* (1779), in *Historical Collections of South Carolina,* ed. B. R. Carroll, 2 vols. (New York, 1836), 1:101 (hereafter cited as *Hist. Coll.*); David Ramsay, *Ramsay's History of South Carolina, from Its First Settlement in 1670 to the Year 1808,* 2 vols. (1809; repr. Newberry, S.C., 1858), 2:116.

18. Peter A. Coclanis, *The Shadow of a Dream: Economic Life and Death in the South Carolina Low Country, 1670–1920* (New York: Oxford University Press, 1989), 82–83, 66.

19. For a contrasting view of the Chesapeake, see Holly Brewer, "Entailing Aristocracy in Colonial Virginia: 'Ancient Feudal Restraints' and Revolutionary Reform," *WMQ* 54 (1997): 304–346.

20. Eliza Lucas to [Thomas Lucas], 22 May 1742, in *The Letterbook of Eliza Lucas Pinckney, 1739–1762,* ed. Elise Pinckney (Chapel Hill: University of North Carolina Press, 1972), 39. Examples of such polite exchange can be found in Robert Raper to James Crokatt, 20 October 1759, 24 May 1760, Robert Raper Letterbook (photocopy of original in West Sussex Record Office), SCHS; Edward Fenwicke to John Fenwicke, 30 September 1726, Edward Fenwicke Letterbook, SCHS; HL to William Bull, 28 February 1786, Letterbook 1785–1787, HL Papers, SCHS.

21. For examples of the rising scale of orange growing, see Daniel, *SCG,* 18 January 1735; Daniel, ibid., 19 November 1744; Saxby, ibid., 30 June 1746; Lake, ibid., 8 November 1745. On orange exports, see Robert Pringle to Thomas Hutchinson and Thomas Goldthwait, 18 August 1744, in *The Letterbook of Robert Pringle,* ed. Walter B. Edgar, 2 vols. (Columbia: University of South Carolina Press, 1972), 2:732; ibid., 2:732n; see also *SCG,* 14 October 1745.

22. James Glen, *A Description of South Carolina . . .* (1761), facsimile repr. in *Colonial South Carolina: Two Contemporary Descriptions,* ed. Chapman J. Milling (Columbia: University of South Carolina Press, 1951), 36–37; HL to John Lewis Gervais, 29 January 1766, in *PHL,* 5:55; HL to James Grant, 22 December 1768, ibid., 6:231.

23. Hewit, *Historical Account,* 1:75; John Drayton, *A View of South-Carolina, as Respects Her Natural and Civil Concerns* (Charleston, S.C., 1802), 26–27.

24. HL to James and Catherine Futterell, 4 June 1785, in *PHL,* 16:565; William Stephens, *The Journal of William Stephens, 1743–1745,* ed. E. Merton

Coulter, 2 vols. (Athens: University of Georgia Press, 1958–1959), 1:251; Charles Cotesworth Pinckney to Thomas Pinckney, 1 July 1792, Pinckney Family Papers, ser. 1, box 4, Manuscripts Division, Library of Congress, Washington, D.C. (hereafter cited as LC).

25. [George Milligen-Johnston], *Short Description of the Province of South Carolina, with an Account of the Air, Weather, and Diseases, at Charles-Town* (1763), facsimile repr. in *South Carolina: Contemporary Descriptions,* 124–125; Peter Collinson to John Bartram, 25 December 1767, in *The Correspondence of John Bartram, 1734–1777,* ed. Edmund Berkeley and Dorothy Smith Berkeley (Gainesville: University Press of Florida, 1992), 694; HL to William Cowles & Co., 12 August 1769, in *PHL,* 7:123.

26. George Ogilvie, *Carolina; Or, The Planter* (1776), repr. in *Southern Literary Journal,* special issue (1986): 47; Hewit, *Historical Account,* 77–78.

27. Entries for 20 July 1752 and 15 August 1752, Diary-Account of Rene and Henry Ravenel, Thomas Porcher Ravenel Family Papers, folder 1, SCHS; John Guerard to Thomas Rock, 20 September 1752, John Guerard Letterbook, SCHS; Milligen-Johnston, *Short Description,* 130. On responses to this hurricane and other natural disasters, see Matthew Mulcahy, " 'Melancholy and Fatal Calamities': Disaster and Society in Eighteenth-Century South Carolina," in *Money, Trade, and Power: The Evolution of South Carolina's Plantation Society,* ed. Jack P. Greene, Rosemary Brana-Shute, and Randy J. Sparks (Columbia: University of South Carolina Press, 2001), 278–298.

28. John Bartram, "Diary of a Journey through the Carolinas, Georgia and Florida from July 1, 1765, to April 10, 1766," *Transactions of the American Philosophical Society* 33 (1942): 20.

29. Joy Tivy, *Agricultural Ecology* (Harlow, Essex, U.K.: Longman Scientific, 1990), 184–185; Peter Manigault to Ben Stead, 1 May 1769, Peter Manigault Letterbook, SCHS; Manigault to [Benjamin Stead], 3 June 1768, ibid.

30. HL to William Fisher, 20 September 1762, in *PHL,* 3:126; HL to Henry Bright, 9 September 1762, ibid., 3:118; Robert Pringle to John Erving, 21 July 1738, in *Pringle Letterbook,* 1:22; Robert Raper to John Colleton, 23 September 1759, Raper Letterbook.

31. Peter Manigault to [Benjamin Stead], 3 June 1768, Manigault Letterbook; HL to Smith & Baillies, 25 August 1763, in *PHL,* 3:538; HL to Henry Byrne, 14 July 1763, ibid., 3:488.

32. Robert Pringle to James Humphrey, 3 July 1738, in *Pringle Letterbook,* 1:16; Robert Raper to Margaret Colleton, 11 July 1767, Raper Letterbook; HL to Cowles & Harford, 5 July 1762, in *PHL,* 3:105; HL to William Bell, 15 September 1785, Letterbook 1785–1787, HL Papers.

33. E. L. Jones, *Seasons and Prices: The Role of the Weather in English Agricultural*

History (London: Allen & Unwin, 1964), 46–47, 50, 56; HL to James Cowles, 16 October 1765, in *PHL*, 2:341.

34. Comparative climates: Carl Sauer, "The Settlement of the Humid East," in *Climate and Man: Yearbook of Agriculture, 1941*, by U.S. Department of Agriculture (1941; repr., Detroit: Gale Group, 1974), 158; Gordon G. Whitney, *From Coastal Wilderness to Fruited Plain: A History of Environmental Change in Temperate North America, 1500 to the Present* (New York: Cambridge University Press, 1994), 47–48. Jones, *Seasons and Prices*, 49; Robert Pringle to John Keith, 4 November 1743, in *Pringle Letterbook*, 2: 597; John Guerard to Thomas Rock, 30 July 1753, Guerard Letterbook; HL to Devonsheir & Reeve, 12 September 1764, in *PHL*, 4:419.

35. On weather lore, see Jones, *Seasons and Prices*, 54–55; M. G. Wurtele, "Some Thoughts on Weather Lore," *Folklore* 82 (1971): 292–303; Jon Gjerde, *From Peasants to Farmers: The Migration from Balestrand, Norway, to the Upper Middle West* (New York: Cambridge University Press, 1985), 28–45.

36. Violent weather: Stephens, *Journal*, 1:251; *American Husbandry*, ed. Harry J. Carman (1775; repr., New York: Columbia University Press, 1939), 264; Josiah Smith Jr. to J. K. Livingston, 28 April 1784, Josiah Smith Jr. Letterbook, Southern Historical Collection, University of North Carolina, Chapel Hill (hereafter cited as SHC); Drayton, *View of South-Carolina*, 9; remembered weather: Peter Manigault to W[illiam] Blake, 10 March 1771, Manigault Letterbook; entry for 19 October 1771, Ravenel Diary-Account; John Lewis Gervais to HL, 11 October 1784, in *PHL*, 16:511. On New England colonists' reliance on Indian environmental knowledge, see Karen Ordahl Kupperman, "Climate and Mastery of the Wilderness in Seventeenth-Century New England," in *Seventeenth-Century New England*, ed. David D. Hall and David Grayson Allen (Boston: Colonial Society of Massachusetts, 1984), 7–8.

37. For a list of sources used to construct this sample, see the appendix, table 5.

38. HL to Devonsheir & Reeve, 12 September 1764, in *PHL*, 4:419.

39. Jonathan Cocran to unknown addressee, 20 June 1775, Edward Telfair Papers, Special Collections, William R. Perkins Library, Duke University, Durham, N.C. (hereafter cited as Duke); entry for November 1771, Ravenel Diary-Account; HL to James Cowles, 16 October 1755, in *PHL*, 1:362; HL to Grubb & Watson, 18 August 1764, ibid., 4:373.

40. HL to Giles Heysham, 11 August 1756, in *PHL*, 2:288; HL to Devonsheir, Reeve, & Lloyd, 18 November 1756, ibid., 2:354. On indigo quality, see S. Max Edelson, "The Characters of Commodities: The Reputations of South Carolina Rice and Indigo in the Atlantic World," in *The Atlantic Economy*

during the Seventeenth and Eighteenth Centuries: Organization, Operation, Practice, and Personnel, ed. Peter A. Coclanis (Columbia: University of South Carolina Press, 2005), 344–360.

41. E. L. Jones, "Creative Disruptions in American Agriculture, 1620–1820," *Agricultural History* 48 (1974): 510–528.

42. Hewit, *Historical Account,* 141.

43. Thomas Nairne, *A Letter from South Carolina . . .* (1710), in *Selling a New World: Two Colonial South Carolina Promotional Pamphlets,* ed. Jack P. Greene (Columbia: University of South Carolina Press, 1989), 40; Mark Catesby, *The Natural History of Carolina, Florida, and the Bahama Islands . . . ,* 2 vols. (London, 1771), 1:xvii, Eighteenth-Century Collections Online. Gale Group, galenet.galegroup.com.

44. George Ogilvie to Pegie Ogilvie, 25 June 1774, in "The Letters of George Ogilvie," ed. David S. Shields, *Southern Literary Journal,* special issue (1986): 119.

45. Swinton, *SCG,* 22 February 1772.

46. Starns, ibid., 19 March 1737.

47. Walter, ibid., 3 November 1758 (stream); "convenient": Keating, ibid., 9 February 1739; Hamilton, ibid., 29 January 1737. Gaillard, ibid., 2 July 1741; Morris, ibid., 4 May 1738 ("moderate Charge").

48. George Ogilvie to Pegie Ogilvie, 25 June 1774, in "Letters," 120 ("dead levels"); *Luigi Castiglioni's Viaggio: Travels in the United States of North America, 1785–87,* ed. and trans. Antonio Pace (1824; repr., Syracuse, N.Y.: Syracuse University Press, 1983), 167; Marion, *SCG,* 19 July 1739; Young, ibid., 25 January 1772; Hyrne, ibid., 28 November 1741; Rutledge, ibid., 21 January 1772.

49. Waring, *SCG,* 1 March 1773; Fenwicke, ibid., 25 November 1756; Mullins, ibid., 13 June 1774; George Ogilvie to Pegie Ogilvie, 25 June 1774, in "Letters," 120; George Ogilvie, *Carolina; Or, The Planter* (1776), *Southern Literary Journal,* special issue (1986): 62, 58.

50. Before ditching and draining, water flows over such wetlands intermittently, and they drain slowly. Their conversion to agriculture lowers the water table, promotes drainage, and encourages the continuous flow of water over the surface of the land. Gregory L. Bruland, Matthew F. Hanchey, and Curtis J. Richarson, "Effects of Agriculture and Wetland Restoration on Hydrology, Soils, and Water Quality of a Carolina Bay Complex," *Wetlands Ecology and Management* 11 (2003): 141.

51. Osgood, *SCG,* 30 November 1734; Lining, ibid., 12 June 1753.

52. Examples of such hybrid rice plantations include Jordan, ibid., 17 July 1762; Neyle, ibid., 10 August 1767; Hutson, ibid., 6 June 1768; and Foissin, ibid., 5 January 1769.

53. Jones, *Seasons and Prices,* 107, 119–120; see also David L. Coon, *The Development of Market Agriculture in South Carolina, 1670–1785* (New York: Garland, 1989), 181; Richard I. Groening Jr., "The Rice Landscape in South Carolina: Valuation, Technology, and Historical Periodization" (M.A. thesis, University of South Carolina, 1998), 22–26.

54. Satur, *SCG,* 17 December 1744; Mazyck, ibid., 23 January 1744.

55. Robert Raper to James Michie, 17 June 1760, Raper Letterbook; Elias Ball to [Elias Ball], 6 June 1790, Elias Ball XIV Family Papers, folder 7, SCHS; Elias Ball, "Plan of a Plantation Called Limerick . . ." (1796), surveyed by John Hardwick, McCrady Plat Collection, 4:227, SCDAH.

56. Robert Barnwell Rhett (1841), quoted in William W. Freehling, *Prelude to Civil War: The Nullification Controversy in South Carolina, 1816–1836* (New York: Harper and Row, 1966), 28; Robert Raper to Thomas Boone, 17 June 1760, Raper Letterbook; HL to Henry Bright, 9 September 1762, in *PHL,* 3:118.

57. Villepontoux, *SCG,* 20 September 1770; Swinton, ibid., 19 January 1738; Johnston, ibid., 7 February 1761; Simmons, ibid., 10 July 1755; George Ogilvie to Pegie Ogilvie, 25 June 1774, in "Letters," 120 ("Tedious").

58. Bernard Romans, *A Concise Natural History of East and West Florida,* ed. Kathryn E. Holland Braund (1775; repr., Tuscaloosa: University of Alabama Press, 1999), 165.

59. Drayton, *View of South-Carolina,* 116; Adam Davis, e-mail message to the author, 20 April 2006; [Richard Hutson] to Mr. Croll, 22 August 1767, Charles Woodward Hutson Papers, SHC; Josiah Smith Jr. to George Austin, 22 July 1774, Smith Letterbook.

60. Johann Martin Bolzius, "Johann Martin Bolzius Answers a Questionnaire on Carolina and Georgia," ed. and trans. Klaus G. Loewald et al., *WMQ* 14 (1957): 233; Drayton, *View of South-Carolina,* 116–117; George Ogilvie to Pegie Ogilvie, 25 June 1774, in "Letters," 120; *American Husbandry,* 276.

61. Philip D. Morgan, *Slave Counterpoint: Black Culture in the Eighteenth-Century Chesapeake and Lowcountry* (Chapel Hill: University of North Carolina Press, 1998), 153–155; see also Joyce E. Chaplin, *An Anxious Pursuit: Agricultural Innovation and Modernity in the Lower South, 1730–1815* (Chapel Hill: University of North Carolina Press, 1993), 252–262.

62. O'Neal, *SCG,* 27 January 1752; Wright, ibid., 16 July 1763.

63. Deveaux, ibid., 9 March 1752; Wilkinson, ibid., 13 February 1775. For other examples of irrigation systems powering mills see Nisbitt, ibid., 1 January 1752; Lining, ibid., 12 June 1763. Johnston, ibid., 14 October 1756 (first tidal mill).

64. Romans, *Concise Natural History,* 165; "Correspondence between Alexander Garden, M.D., and the Royal Society of Arts," *SCHM* 64 (1963): 16–17.

Contemporary descriptions of rice processing present a confusing picture of the kind of work machines performed. Judith A. Carney has argued that colonial-era processing equipment removed the hull of the grains, but that hand processing was used to "polish" them by removing their inner cuticle of germ and bran, Carney, "Rice Milling, Gender and Slave Labour in Colonial South Carolina," *Past and Present* 153 (1996): 116–120. My own reading of these sources is that hand processing was employed on plantations without machines and to supplement mechanized processing. Those planters who invested in the best machines first put their rough rice through hand-cranked mills that ground the grains between pine blocks to remove the hull. They turned to the machines discussed here, in my view, to polish the rice mechanically. HL wrote that "nothing but the Pestle will take off the Inside Coat, & shew the neat whiteness of the Grain." I believe that he was referring not to manual polishing exclusively, but to less-than-perfect mechanical polishing that the "People in Carolina are acquainted with." HL to Peter LePoole, 14 August 1772, in *PHL*, 8:409. Planters described their machines producing "barrels of clean rice," indicating that once rice had passed under mechanical pestles, it required no additional processing aside from screening to remove broken grains before it was packed. Sacheverall, *SCG*, 24 September 1763.

65. These calculations use a ratio of 1 unprocessed bushel of "rough" rice to 25 pounds of clean rice, as reported in Bartram, "Diary of a Journey," 15n. The daily rice-processing task stood at 21 pecks (5.25 bushels) of rough rice in 1755. The daily product of hand labor at this rate would be 131.25 pounds. If this figure is multiplied by 16, the horse-powered mills cited by Garden would yield 2,100 pounds of clean rice per day. Garden, "Correspondence," 16–17. Advertisers reported daily processing rates for water mills of 2,500 and 3,400 pounds: Elliott, *SCG*, 5 July 1770; Keith, ibid., 29 September 1768. Advertisers cited rates of 4, 5, 6, and 8 barrels per day: Akin, ibid., 21 September 1769; Johnston, ibid., 14 October 1756; Williamson, ibid., 13 December 1770; Crokatt, ibid., 19 December 1761. Average barrel size for the period 1758–1773 was 530 pounds. Stephen G. Hardy, "Colonial South Carolina's Rice Industry and the Atlantic Economy: Patterns of Trade, Shipping, and Growth, 1715–1775," in *Money, Trade, and Power*, table 5.13, 139–140.

66. Sacheverall, *SCG*, 24 September 1763; Shubrick, ibid., 17 August 1769; *Castiglioni's Viaggio*, 169; Josiah Smith Jr. to George Austin, 17 June 1771, Smith Letterbook.

67. Lewis C. Gray, *History of Agriculture in the Southern United States to 1860*, 2 vols. (1933; repr., Gloucester, Mass.: Peter Smith, 1958), 2:729–730; Ferguson, *SCG*, 19 January 1767.

68. Ogilvie, *Carolina; Or, The Planter,* 13; George Ogilvie to Pegie Ogilvie, 25 June 1774, "Letters," 120.

69. HL to Devonsheir, Reeve, & Lloyd, 4 July 1755, in *PHL,* 1:285; *SCG,* 2 March 1747. On the "low price of Rice" as a factor that led planters to experiment with indigo, see Records in the British Public Record Office Relating to South Carolina, 23:13, SCDAH.

70. HL to James Cowles, 16 October 1755, in *PHL,* 1:362; Gracia, *SCG,* 20 February 1755; Guerard, ibid., 21 January 1772; Yonge, ibid., 5 May 1759; Green, ibid., 1 January 1756.

71. Gibbons, *SCG,* 5 March 1763; see also Eveleigh, ibid., 17 December 1753; Walter, ibid., 11 December 1752; Garner, ibid., 26 July 1770.

72. HL to Devonsheir, Reeve, & Lloyd, 4 July 1755, in *PHL,* 1:285. Loyalist compensation claims indicate that the "hybrid rice/indigo plantation was very rare." R. C. Nash, "South Carolina and the Atlantic Economy in the Late Seventeenth and Eighteenth Centuries," *Economic History Review* 45 (1992): 695. Estate inventories, however, indicate that just over one-fourth of probated estates produced both crops. Virginia Gail Jelatis, "Tangled Up in Blue: Indigo Culture and Economy in South Carolina, 1747–1800" (Ph.D. dissertation, University of Minnesota, 1999), table 10, 80. Inventories indicate production at a single moment, the death of the owner, and thus may underrepresent plantations that shifted between the crops over time.

73. Lord Adam Gordon, "Journal of an Officer Who Travelled in America and the West Indies in 1764 and 1765," in *Travels in the American Colonies,* ed. Newton D. Mereness (New York: Macmillan, 1916), 400. For other examples of swampland indigo growing, see *Castiglioni's Viaggio,* 121; Josiah Smith Jr. to J. K. Livingston, 28 April 1784, Smith Letterbook; Davidson, *SCG,* 16 May 1774.

74. John Channing to [William Gibbons], 20 December 1769, William Gibbons Jr. Papers, Duke; Channing to Gibbons, 4 June 1770, ibid.; Josiah Smith Jr. to George Austin, 31 January 1774, Smith Letterbook; Drayton, *View of South-Carolina,* 130. For other examples of swampland corn growing, see Ramsay, *Ramsay's History,* 2:123; Cordes, *SCG,* 1 August 1743.

75. Foisson, *SCG,* 15 June 1767; Dutarque, ibid., 17 October 1771; Screven, ibid., 5 May 1759; Evance, ibid., 14 November 1771; Elliott, ibid., 12 January 1759.

76. *SP,* 225; Samuel Wilson, *An Account of the Province of Carolina, in America* . . . (1682), in *Hist. Coll.,* 2:35.

77. Russell R. Menard, "Slavery, Economic Growth, and Revolutionary Ideology in the South Carolina Lowcountry," in *The Economy of Early America: The Revolutionary Period, 1763–1790,* ed. Ronald Hoffman et al. (Charlottesville: University Press of Virginia, 1993), 254.

78. Mart A. Stewart, *"What Nature Suffers to Groe": Life, Labor, and Landscape on the Georgia Coast, 1680–1920* (Athens: University of Georgia Press, 1996), chap. 3 and epilogue; Drew Gilpin Faust, *James Henry Hammond and the Old South: A Design for Mastery* (Baton Rouge: Louisiana State University Press, 1983), 3.

79. Five hundred acres was a common tract size in part because the colony granted land in increments of 50 to 150 acres. It was the median value for 3,060 tracts advertised in the *SCG* for the period 1732–1775 that listed acreage. The mean tract size was 725.5 acres.

80. Philip J. Greven Jr., *Four Generations: Population, Land, and Family in Colonial Andover, Massachusetts* (Ithaca, N.Y.: Cornell University Press, 1970), 223–224; Keith Wrightson, *English Society, 1580–1680* (New Brunswick, N.J.: Rutgers University Press, 1982), 31–32.

81. Land laws limited the river frontage of grants. This encouraged topographical diversity because it forced grantees to include land at a distance from waterways that had different elevations. Robert K. Ackerman, *South Carolina Colonial Land Policies* (Columbia: University of South Carolina Press, 1977), 30–31; see also Meaghan N. Duff, "Creating a Plantation Province: Proprietary Land Policies and Early Settlement Patterns," in *Money, Trade, and Power*, 17.

82. Rebecca R. Sharitz and William J. Mitsch, "Southern Floodplain Forests," in *Biodiversity of the Southeastern United States: Lowland Terrestrial Communities*, ed. William H. Martin, Stephen G. Boyce, and Arthur C. Echternacht (New York: John Wiley & Sons, 1993), 316–337.

83. In 360 advertisements acres suited for rice were listed, as well as total acres. The mean percentage of rice acres compared with total tract size was 40.1 percent; the median was 36.8 percent. *SCG*.

84. Sanders, *SCG*, 22 January 1752; Smith & Nutt, ibid., 18 July 1761. For an example of a tract featuring cleared uplands and lowlands, see Welshuysen, ibid., 12 March 1741.

85. "Settlements" within plantation tracts: Gibbons, ibid., 28 January 1764; Deveaux, ibid., 26 November 1763; entry for 7 March 1780, John Peebles Diary, SCL.

86. Robert Raper to John Colleton, 23 September 1759, Raper Letterbook; HL to William Yate, 5 February 1766, in *PHL*, 5:70; Kenneth E. Lewis, "Plantation Layout and Function in the South Carolina Lowcountry," in *The Archaeology of Slavery and Plantation Life*, ed. Theresa A. Singleton (Orlando, Fla.: Academic Press, 1985), 46, 59; J. W. Joseph, "Building to Grow: Agrarian Adaptations to South Carolina's Historical Landscapes," in *Carolina's Historical Landscapes: Archaeological Perspectives*, ed. Linda F. Stine et

al. (Knoxville: University of Tennessee Press, 1997), 46. On the location of slave housing, see also Bolzius, "Questionnaire on Carolina," 257; Bartram, "Diary of a Journey," 21.

87. S. Max Edelson, "The Nature of Slavery: Environmental Disorder and Slave Agency in Colonial South Carolina," in *Cultures and Identities in Colonial British America,* ed. Robert Olwell and Alan Tully (Baltimore: Johns Hopkins University Press, 2005), chap. 1.

88. In 295 advertisements sellers listed the number of acres cleared, as well as total acres. The mean percentage of acres cleared compared to total tract size was 19.8 percent, the median percentage was 14.0 percent. *SCG.*

89. John Solomon Otto, "Livestock-Raising in Early South Carolina, 1670–1700: Prelude to the Rice Plantation Economy," *Agricultural History* 61 (1987): 16–20; John R. Stilgoe, *Common Landscape of America, 1580 to 1845* (New Haven, Conn.: Yale University Press, 1982), 188–190; *Carolina Described More Fully Then [sic] Heretofore . . .* (Dublin, 1684), 9, Early English Books Online, Chadwyck-Healey, eebo.chadwyck.com.

90. William Gerhard De Brahm, "Philosophico-Historico-Hydrogeography of South Carolina, Georgia, and East Florida" (c. 1772), in *Documents Connected with the History of South Carolina,* ed. P. C. J. Weston (London, 1856), 197; Catesby, *Natural History,* 1:xvi; Hewit, *Historical Account,* 514.

91. *SCG,* 9 March 1738; Morgan, *Slave Counterpoint,* 58–60, table 9. Contemporaries estimated that a slave could cultivate between 3 and 5 acres of rice per season, excluding provisions. *SCG,* 3 February 1733; Bolzius, "Questionnaire on Carolina," 257; De Brahm, "Philosophico-Historico-Hydrogeography," 197; William Butler, "Observations on the Culture of Rice" (1786), SCHS; John Martin to John Martin, 17 February 1788, John Martin Estate Papers, SCHS.

92. Morgan, *Slave Counterpoint,* 39–40, table 1. Slave-buying practices: HL to Wells, Wharton, & Doran, 27 May 1755, in *PHL,* 1:257; Peter Manigault to Ralph Izard, 7 July 1764, [July or August] 1765, Manigault Letterbook; J[ohn] Channing to [Edward Telfair], 10 August 1786, Telfair Papers; William Piercy to Lady Huntingdon, 23 March 1773, William Piercy Letterbook, HL Papers; Peter Manigault to Daniel Blake, 10 March 1771, Manigault Letterbook; Charles Cotesworth Pinckney to Thomas Pinckney, 29 October 1793, Pinckney Family Papers, series 1, box 4, LC.

93. Peter Manigault to Ralph Izard, [July or August] 1765, Manigault Letterbook; Lining, *SCG,* 15 March 1760.

94. William Bartram, *The Travels of William Bartram: Naturalist's Edition,* ed. Francis Harper (1791; repr., New Haven, Conn.: Yale University Press, 1958), 298–299.

95. Cater, *SCG*, 10 November 1766; Johnston, ibid., 7 February 1761. One Georgia tract included a swamp that extended nearly three miles in length and up to a quarter mile across. Milledge, ibid., 29 February 1768.

96. Wright, ibid., 16 July 1763; Deveaux, ibid., 1 October 1764. See also Dunn, ibid., 9 February 1765; Dwight, ibid., 5 January 1769.

97. See Lois Green Carr, Russell R. Menard, and Lorena S. Walsh, *Robert Cole's World: Agriculture and Society in Early Maryland* (Chapel Hill: University of North Carolina Press, 1991), 88–90. On farm building in early South Carolina, see Menard, "Lowcountry Export Boom," 664–665.

98. James L. Michie, "Impermanent Architecture at the Oaks Plantation: The Colonial House of William Allston, Georgetown County, South Carolina," *South Carolina Antiquities* 27 (1995): 42–51.

99. Richard Ludlum (1725), quoted in Frank J. Klingberg, *An Appraisal of the Negro in Colonial South Carolina* (Washington, D.C.: Associated Publishers, 1941), 47.

100. Hewit, *Historical Account,* 297, 285–286. For examples of land appreciation, see J[oseph] Manigault to G[abriel] Manigault, 11 December 1785, Manigault Family Papers, box II, folder 13, SCL; HL in Account with Josiah Smith, October 1769, HL Account Book, Robert Scott Small Library, Special Collections, College of Charleston, S.C.; Josiah Smith Jr. to George Austin, 17 June 1771, Smith Letterbook; Stephen Mazyck to [Paul Mazyck], 7 February 1776, Daniel Elliott Huger Smith Papers, SCHS.

101. David B. Ryden and Russell R. Menard, "South Carolina's Colonial Land Market: An Analysis of Rural Property Sales, 1720–1775," *Social Science History* 29 (2005): 602, 617–619; Coclanis, *Shadow of a Dream,* 96–97, 106–109; Nash, "South Carolina and the Atlantic Economy," 685–687, 694–696.

102. Wright, *SCG*, 7 March 1768; Lowndes, ibid., 13 October 1757; Gendron, ibid., 25 December 1755; Sanders, ibid., 12 February 1756; Goddard, ibid., 27 June 1744. For sale with crops: Crouch, ibid., 12 September 1741; Hutson, ibid., 6 June 1768. For sale with slaves: Brisbane, ibid., 15 December 1759; Hunt, ibid., 3 July 1755.

103. Josiah Smith Jr. to George Austin, 25 February 1772, Smith Letterbook.

104. [William] Blake to Peter Manigault, 2 October 1769, Manigault Letterbook. For examples of such migrations, see Lowndes, *SCG*, 18 January 1735; Bulloch, ibid., 28 November 1761.

105. Credit terms were reported for 1,528 tracts (45.9 percent). Of these, 929 (60.8 percent) were sold at a year's credit; 372 (24.3 percent) at less than a year; and 227 (14.9 percent) at more than a year. Waites, *SCG*, 6 September 1760 (eighteen years).

106. Migration out of South Carolina (particularly to England, but also on occasion to New England and the Caribbean) was a common listed reason

for selling land. See, for example, Cripps, ibid., 8 December 1737; Hopton, ibid., 4 February 1764. Health as a reason for migration: Simpson, ibid., 26 October 1734; Govan, ibid., 1 June 1767; leaving planting: Lowndes, ibid., 13 October 1757; [William] Blake to Peter Manigault, 2 October 1769, Manigault Letterbook.

107. "Complete" plantations: Walter, *SCG*, 17 October 1771; see also Johnston, ibid., 26 February 1756; Crokatt, ibid., 19 December 1761. Assembling tracts: Singleton, ibid., 8 August 1771; see also Wright, ibid., 17 July 1763; Valk, ibid., 24 May 1773.

108. Ainger, ibid., 30 March 1767; Chiffelle, ibid., 4 July 1768.

109. Reservoirs: DuTargue, ibid., 12 January 1767; Valk, ibid., 22 March 1773. Pineland: McPherson, ibid., 17 November 1766; Elliott, ibid., 7 December 1762.

110. Pouncey, ibid., 2 November 1769; Robert Raper to John Colleton, 16 June 1761, Raper Letterbook.

111. Farrol, *SCG*, 4 December 1755; Stevens, ibid., 26 December 1761.

112. See appendix, table 7. Sellers suggested productive uses for 1,827 tracts in the period 1732–1775. Of these, rice was listed as a commodity for 1,257 (68.8 percent). Indigo, first mentioned in 1742, was listed in 713 (48.8 percent) of the 1,461 tracts advertised in the period 1742–1775. Glen, *Description of South Carolina*, 18. On the complementarity of indigo and rice, see also Josiah Smith Jr. to George Appleby, 2 December 1780, 30 March 1784, Smith Letterbook; George D. Terry, " 'Champaign Country': A Social History of an Eighteenth Century Lowcountry Parish in South Carolina, St. Johns Berkeley County" (Ph.D. dissertation, University of South Carolina, Columbia, 1981), 182–183; J. F. D. Smyth, *A Tour of the United States of America*, 2 vols. (Dublin, 1784), 2:37.

113. Otto, "Livestock-Raising," 19–23; naval stores: Robert Pringle to John Erving, 17 May 1744, in *Pringle Letterbook*, 2:694; *PHL*, 4:247–251.

114. Beaird, *SCG*, 6 May 1745; *American Husbandry*, 272. See also *Castiglioni's Viaggio*, 143, 170.

115. Middleton, *SCG*, 7 February 1771; Colleton, ibid., 20 March 1762; Nisbett, ibid., 1 January 1752. For examples of the range of wood products, see Thradcreaft, ibid., 24 March 1746; Gibbons, ibid., 5 March 1763.

116. William Byrd II to Charles Boyle, Earl of Orrey, 5 July 1726, in *The Correspondence of the Three William Byrds of Westover, Virginia, 1684–1776*, ed. Marion Tinling, 2 vols. (Charlottesville: University Press of Virginia, 1977), 1:355.

117. Wells, *SCG*, 17 December 1764; Stevens, ibid., 6 October 1766; Faucherea[ud], ibid., 4 December 1752.

118. Smyth, *Tour of America*, 1:132; Robert M. Weir, *Colonial South Carolina: A*

History (Millwood, N.Y.: KTO Press, 1983), 149; David C. Crass and Richard D. Brooks, "Settlement Patterning on an Agriculturally Marginal Landscape," in *Carolina's Historical Landscapes,* 75, 80.

119. De Brahm, "Philosophico-Historico-Hydrogeography," 170.

4. City, Hinterland, and Frontier

1. William Dillwyn, "Diary of William Dillwyn during a Visit to Charles Town in 1772," *South Carolina Historical and Genealogical Magazine* 36 (1935): 5–6 (hereafter cited as *SCHM*); Miles Mark Fisher, "Friends of Humanity: A Quaker Anti-slavery Influence," *Church History* 4 (1935): 187. On Dillwyn, see also David Brion Davis, *The Problem of Slavery in the Age of Revolution, 1770–1823* (Ithaca, N.Y.: Cornell University Press, 1975), 219–224, 227–236.

2. Dillwyn, "Diary," 35, 109–110.

3. Alexander Hewit, *An Historical Account of the Rise and Progress of the Colonies of South Carolina and Georgia,* in *Historical Collections of South Carolina,* ed. B. R. Carroll, 2 vols. (New York, 1836), 1:75–76, 420–421 (hereafter cited as *Hist. Coll.*); Robert Olwell, *Masters, Slaves, and Subjects: The Culture of Power in the South Carolina Low Country, 1740–1790* (Ithaca, N.Y.: Cornell University Press, 1998), 10.

4. Thomas Newe, "Letters of Thomas Newe from South Carolina, 1682," *American Historical Review* 12 (1907): 325; *Carolina Described More Fully Then [sic] Heretofore . . .* (Dublin, 1684), 11, Early English Books Online, Chadwyck-Healey, eebo.chadwyck.com.

5. Lord Adam Gordon, "Journal of an Officer Who Travelled in America and the West Indies in 1764 and 1765," in *Travels in the American Colonies,* ed. Newton D. Mereness (New York: Macmillan, 1916), 398; *Carolina Described,* 1; *The Shaftesbury Papers and Other Records Relating to Carolina* (1897; repr., Charleston, S.C.: Tempus, 2000), 340.

6. T. A. [Thomas Amy], *Carolina; or, A Description of the Present State of That Country and the Natural Excellencies Thereof* (1682), in *Hist. Coll.,* 2:82; Newe, "Letters," 325.

7. John Norris, *Profitable Advice for Rich and Poor . . .* (1712), in *Selling a New World: Two Colonial South Carolina Promotional Pamphlets,* ed. Jack P. Greene (Columbia: University of South Carolina Press, 1989), 110–111; Sanders, *South-Carolina Gazette,* 15 November 1760 (hereafter cited as *SCG*); time: Hutchinson, ibid., 23 April 1741; see also Spencer, ibid., 25 January 1735.

8. John Archdale, *A New Description of That Fertile and Pleasant Province of*

Carolina (1707), in *Narratives of Early Carolina, 1650–1708,* ed. Alexander S. Salley Jr. (New York: C. Scribner's Sons, 1911), 291.

9. Hewit, *Historical Account,* 361–362; William Gerhard De Brahm, "Philosophico-Historico-Hydrogeography of South Carolina, Georgia, and East Florida" (c. 1772), in *Documents Connected with the History of South Carolina,* ed. P. C. J. Weston (London, 1856), 177–178.

10. "A Gentleman's Account of His Travels, 1733–34," in *The Colonial South Carolina Scene: Contemporary Views, 1697–1774,* ed. H. Roy Merrens (Columbia: University of South Carolina Press, 1977), 118.

11. Mark Catesby, *The Natural History of Carolina, Florida, and the Bahama Islands . . . ,* 2 vols. (London, 1771), 1:iii, Eighteenth-Century Collections Online, Gale Group, galenet.galegroup.com (hereafter cited as ECCO).

12. John Lawson, *A New Voyage to Carolina,* ed. Hugh Talmage Lefler (1709; repr., Chapel Hill: University of North Carolina Press, 1967), 9. On the administration of road construction, see M. Eugene Sirmans, *Colonial South Carolina: A Political History, 1663–1763* (Chapel Hill: University of North Carolina Press, 1966), 143. For regional examples of internal improvements, see Lawrence S. Rowland, "Eighteenth Century Beaufort: A Study of South Carolina's Parishes to 1800" (Ph.D. dissertation, University of South Carolina, Columbia, 1978), 125–126; George D. Terry, " 'Champaign Country': A Social History of an Eighteenth Century Lowcountry Parish in South Carolina, St. Johns Berkeley County" (Ph.D. dissertation, University of South Carolina, Columbia, 1981), 188, 191, 196; George C. Rogers Jr., *History of Georgetown County* (Columbia: University of South Carolina Press, 1970), 40–44.

13. Johann Martin Bolzius, "Johann Martin Bolzius Answers a Questionnaire on Carolina and Georgia," ed. and trans. Klaus G. Loewald et al., *William and Mary Quarterly,* 3rd ser., 14 (1957): 232–233 (hereafter cited as *WMQ*); De Brahm, "Philosophico-Historico-Hydrogeography," 177–178.

14. Williams, *SCG,* 16 November 1769.

15. Will[iam] Dunlop to [James Montgomerie], 21 October 1686, Letters from William Dunlop, Papers of the Lords Proprietors in the Malmsbury Collection (photocopy of originals in the Scottish Record Office), South Carolina Department of Archives and History, Columbia (hereafter cited as SCDAH); "Address to the Lords Commissioners for Trade" (1719), Coe Papers, South Carolina Historical Society, Charleston (hereafter cited as SCHS); Records in the British Public Record Office Relating to South Carolina, 6:140–141, 129, SCDAH.

16. *Statutes at Large of the State of South Carolina,* ed. Thomas Cooper and David J. McCord, 10 vols. (Columbia, S.C., 1836–1841), 2:641–645; "Gen-

tleman's Account," 118; Hill and Guerard to James Pearce, 16 June 1743, 8 July 1743, Hill and Guerard ALS, South Caroliniana Library, University of South Carolina, Columbia (hereafter cited as SCL).

17. Catesby, *Natural History*, 1:iv; "Gentleman's Account," 112, 114, 115–116.

18. William Stephens, *The Journal of William Stephens, 1743–1745*, ed. E. Merton Coulter, 2 vols. (Athens: University of Georgia Press, 1958–1959), 1:236, 249–250, 252.

19. *Luigi Castiglioni's Viaggio: Travels in the United States of North America, 1785–87*, ed. and trans. Antonio Pace (1824; repr., Syracuse, N.Y.: Syracuse University Press, 1983), 122; Stevens, *SCG*, 6 October 1766.

20. Livingston, *SCG*, 29 March 1735; Cart, ibid., 1 January 1753; Michie, ibid., 26 April 1740. On water access to Savannah River plantations, see David Colin Crass and Richard D. Brooks, "Settlement Patterning on an Agriculturally Marginal Landscape," in *Carolina's Historical Landscapes: Archaeological Perspectives*, ed. Linda F. Stine et al. (Knoxville: University of Tennessee Press, 1997), 75, 80.

21. "Documents Concerning Rev. Samuel Thomas, 1702–1707," *SCHM* 4 (1903): 32.

22. Morris, *SCG*, 25 July 1743; see also *The Journal of the Commons House of Assembly, May 18, 1741–July 10, 1742*, ed. J. H. Easterby (Columbia: Historical Commission of South Carolina, 1953), 83.

23. McGregor, *SCG*, 23 January 1755; Coachman, ibid., 10 November 1764; Shubrick, ibid., 17 August 1769.

24. Out-settlements: Norris, *Profitable Advice*, 109; John Stewart, "Letters from John Stewart to William Dunlop," *SCHM* 32 (1931): 29; *Colonial South Carolina Scene*, 119; northward/southward: *Statutes of South Carolina*, 7: 351; Lawson, *Voyage to Carolina*, 11; Wright, *SCG*, 22 January 1756. Guerard, ibid., 5 April 1773 (distance from town).

25. Carville Earle and Ronald Hoffman, "Staple Crops and Urban Development in the Eighteenth-Century South," *Perspectives in American History* 10 (1976): 7, 14–19, 66–67; Joseph A. Ernst and H. Roy Merrens, " 'Camden's Turrets Pierce the Skies!' The Urban Process in the Southern Colonies during the Eighteenth Century," *WMQ* 30 (1973): 551, 552–557; D. A. Smith, "Dependent Urbanization in Colonial America: The Case of Charleston, South Carolina," *Social Forces* 1 (1987): 1–28.

26. R. C. Nash, "Urbanization in the Colonial South: Charleston, South Carolina, as a Case Study," *Journal of Urban History* 19 (1992): 15–16; Rogers, *History of Georgetown County*, 38–39, 52. Despite its role as Georgia's capital, Savannah was another satellite port. Prices there tracked those in Charlestown, to which it shipped commodities for export. Robert Raper to James Crokatt, 15 January 1760, Robert Raper Letterbook (photocopy of original

in West Sussex Record Office), SCHS; see also Julia Floyd Smith, *Slavery and Rice Culture in Low Country Georgia* (Knoxville: University of Tennessee Press, 1985), 22–24. Hewit, *Historical Account*, 501 ("villages").

27. Gordon, "Journal of an Officer," 397.

28. J. F. D. Smyth, *A Tour of the United States of America*, 2 vols. (Dublin, 1784), 2:52–53; Peter A. Coclanis, *The Shadow of a Dream: Economic Life and Death in the South Carolina Low Country, 1670–1920* (New York: Oxford University Press, 1989), chap. 4; Frederick Cople Jaher, *The Urban Establishment: Upper Strata in Boston, New York, Charleston, Chicago, and Los Angeles* (Urbana: University of Illinois Press, 1982), 9, 320–336; Robert M. Weir, " 'The Harmony We Were Famous For': An Interpretation of Pre-Revolutionary South Carolina Politics," *WMQ* 26 (1969): 473–501.

29. Coclanis, *Shadow of a Dream*, 113–114, 116.

30. Robert Raper to William Vanderspeigel, 16 July 1760, Raper Letterbook; see also Daniel, *SCG*, 30 June 1746; Lloyd, ibid., 13 May 1732.

31. On the high prices offered for specialty lumber, see Gray, *SCG*, 19 April 1773; Parker, ibid., 25 April 1761. Lucy B. Wayne, " 'Burning Brick and Making a Large Fortune at It Too': Landscape Archaeology and Lowcountry Brickmaking," in *Carolina's Historical Landscapes*, 97–111; Walter, *SCG*, 3 November 1758.

32. Woodward, *SCG*, 10 February 1746; Nickleson, Shubrick & Co., ibid., 30 September 1742; Brailsford, ibid., 11 July 1761. Sellers recommended 320 tracts for nonstaple economic uses. The core zone accounted for 75.0 percent of tracts suited for materials and manufacturing (excluding general lumber), 61.3 percent of those suited for providing services (such as warehousing and tavern and innkeeping), and 84.8 percent of those suited for urban market agriculture, ibid. Odingsell, ibid., 30 April 1763 ("truck"); Parker, ibid., 23 May 1771 ("Vicinity").

33. Peter Manigault to Miles Brewton, [June or July] 1768, Peter Manigault Letterbook, SCHS.

34. Dillwyn, "Diary," 110; Alexander, *SCG*, 5 February 1754.

35. *Castiglioni's Viaggio*, 167; Valk, *SCG*, 19 September 1774; famous: Dwight, ibid., 20 February 1762; Hasell, ibid., 20 February 1755. Of the twenty-six advertisements mentioning tidal rice lands before 1750, eighteen mentioned lands that were located in the frontier and none in the core, ibid.

36. On tidal rice productivity, see Coclanis, *Shadow of a Dream*, 96–98; see also R. C. Nash, "South Carolina and the Atlantic Economy in the Late Seventeenth and Eighteenth Centuries," *Economic History Review* 45 (1992): 695–696; 3 barrels: Peter Manigault to Daniel Blake, 6 September 1769, Manigault Letterbook; Parker, *SCG*, 23 May 1771. Elliott, ibid., 28 January 1773 (6 barrels).

37. Valk, ibid., 19 September 1774; on landholding size and slave labor capacity, see Philip D. Morgan, *Slave Counterpoint: Black Culture in the Eighteenth-Century Chesapeake and Lowcountry* (Chapel Hill: University of North Carolina Press, 1998), 42–43; Henry Laurens to W[illiam] Piercy, 19 March 1773, Henry Laurens Papers, SCHS (hereafter cited as HL Papers); Henry Laurens to John Holman, 8 September 1770, in *The Papers of Henry Laurens*, ed. Philip M. Hamer et al., 16 vols. (Columbia: University of South Carolina Press, 1968–2003), 7:344 (hereafter cited as HL and *PHL*). Pastures: Yonge, *SCG*, 22 February 1768; Elliott, ibid., 12 December 1774. Conditional praise for core land: Lake, ibid., 18 November 1745; Middleton, ibid., 22 September 1766. Quoted in William P. Baldwin Jr., *Plantations of the Low Country, South Carolina, 1697–1865* (Greensboro, N.C.: Legacy, 1985), 14 ("sorry undertaking").

38. Dillwyn, "Diary," 110; miles: Mayer, *SCG*, 9 March 1769; Milledge, ibid., 29 February 1768. Gordon, "Journal of an Officer," 396; Hyrne, *SCG*, 10 July 1755 ("for ever").

39. Sanders, *SCG*, 22 January 1752; Yonge, ibid., 22 February 1768; Miles, ibid., 14 September 1767; Guerard, ibid., 5 April 1773; Peter Manigault to Ben Stead, 12 March 1770, Manigault Letterbook.

40. Bulloch, *SCG*, 28 November 1761; Lowndes, ibid., 18 January 1735; Shelley Elizabeth Smith, "The Plantations of Colonial South Carolina: Transmission and Transformation in Provincial Culture" (Ph.D. dissertation, Columbia University, 1999), 305–306; Stone, *SCG*, 24 October 1768; Drayton, ibid., 14 March 1771.

41. C. Vann Woodward, *Origins of the New South, 1877–1913* (Baton Rouge: Louisiana State University Press, 1971), 154–161; Nisbett, *SCG*, 1 January 1752; Donning, ibid., 13 August 1737, 26 March 1744, 7 May 1744.

42. Fitch, *SCG*, 19 March 1741; Hill, ibid., 15 February 1735; Renato Rosaldo, *Culture and Truth: The Remaking of Social Analysis* (Boston: Beacon Press, 1989), chap. 3 ("imperialist nostalgia"); Samuel Gaillard Stoney, *Plantations of the Carolina Low Country* (Charleston, S.C.: Carolina Art Association, 1938).

43. Name examples: Crawford, *SCG*, 9 May 1768; Goddard, ibid., 22 February 1739; Michie, ibid., 16 January 1744; Wright, ibid., 31 January 1736. Of 1,341 settled plantations advertised, 132 (9.8 percent) were named. Of 61 "positively" named tracts, 38 (62.3 percent) were in the core zone, 7 (11.5 percent) in the secondary zone, and 14 (23.0 percent) in the frontier zone, ibid.

44. Shelley Smith, "Colonial South Carolina Plantations," 75–95, 126, 106–138; Baldwin, *Plantations of the Low Country*, 10–19; Bremar, *SCG*, 19 May 1746; Wright, ibid., 11 March 1745.

45. John E. Crowley, *The Invention of Comfort: Sensibilities and Design in Early Modern Britain and Early America* (Baltimore: Johns Hopkins University Press, 2001), 86; interiors: Caw, *SCG*, 24 September 1772; Welshuysen, ibid., 8 February 1735; Jones, ibid., 19 March 1744; Bremar, ibid., 19 May 1736. On rooms' social functions, see Bernard L. Herman, "Home and Hearth: The British Colonies," in *Encyclopedia of the North American Colonies,* ed. Jacob Ernest Cooke (New York: Charles Scribner's Sons, 1993), 573–576. For a survey of scholarship on race and plantation layout, see J. W. Joseph, "Building to Grow: Agrarian Adaptations to South Carolina's Historical Landscapes," in *Carolina's Historical Landscapes,* 47–48.

46. Middleton, *SCG*, 7 February 1771; Ladson, ibid., 31 January 1774; out-buildings: Martini, ibid., 12 September 1741; Welshuysen, ibid., 8 February 1735; Fauchereaud, ibid., 15 December 1758; Keith, ibid., 26 September 1768.

47. Shelley Smith, "Colonial South Carolina Plantations," 205, 208, 217; Valk, *SCG*, 13 June 1774; Dell Upton, *Holy Things and Profane: Anglican Parish Churches in Colonial Virginia* (New Haven, Conn.: Yale University Press, 1997), 110.

48. Norris, *Profitable Advice,* 86; Crowley, *Invention of Comfort,* 84; Gordon, "Journal of an Officer," 398. On the "rectangularity" of "carpentered" spaces, see Yi-Fu Tuan, *Topophilia: A Study of Environmental Perception, Attitudes, and Values* (Englewood Cliffs, N.J.: Prentice-Hall, 1974), 75–76.

49. Louisa Susannah Wells, *The Journal of a Voyage from Charlestown, S.C., to London Undertaken during the American Revolution by a Daughter of an Eminent Loyalist in the Year 1778 and Written from Memory Only in 1779* (1779; repr., New York: New York Historical Society, 1906), 43.

50. Sellers advertised 1,180 developed plantations in these three zones (including those without acreage information). Of these, core tracts accounted for 616 (52.2 percent), secondary tracts 253 (21.4 percent), and frontier tracts 311 (26.4 percent). *SCG.*

51. George Ogilvie to [Margaret] Ogilvie, 25 June 1774, in "The Letters of George Ogilvie," ed. David S. Shields, *Southern Literary Journal,* special issue 19 (1986): 118; Ogilvie to Ogilvie, 22 November 1774, ibid., 122.

52. Ibid., 121–124; George Ogilvie, *Carolina; Or, The Planter* (1776), repr. in *Southern Literary Journal,* special issue (1986): 11 ("aguish vapours"); on "muschata curtains," see John Bartram, "Diary of a Journey through the Carolinas, Georgia and Florida from July 1, 1765, to April 10, 1766," *Transactions of the American Philosophical Society* 33 (1942): 21.

53. David S. Shields, "George Ogilvie's *Carolina; Or, The Planter* (1776)," *Southern Literary Journal,* special issue (1986): 7; Ogilvie, *Carolina; Or, The Planter,* iii; Shields, *Oracles of Empire: Poetry, Politics, and Commerce in*

British America, 1690–1750 (Chicago: University of Chicago Press, 1990), 68–72; George Ogilvie to Margaret Ogilvie, 22 November 1774, "Ogilvie Letters," 122–123.

54. Quoted in Baldwin, *Plantations of the Low Country,* 117–118 ("wilderness"); Raines, *SCG,* 6 September 1773; Richard Hill to John Herman, 8 September 1743, Richard Hill Letterbook, Special Collections, William R. Perkins Library, Manuscripts Department, Duke University, Durham, N.C. ("watertite") (hereafter cited as Duke); Bossard, *SCG,* 11 October 1735 ("huts"). On African elements in slave housing, see Leland Ferguson, *Uncommon Ground: Archaeology and Early African America, 1650–1800* (Washington, D.C.: Smithsonian Institution Press, 1992), 81, 63–82; Bolzius, "Questionnaire on Carolina," 257 (nails). HL calculated that slave huts usually lasted about four years, HL to Peter Broughton, 1 October 1765, in *PHL,* 5:14.

55. Mackay, *SCG,* 13 October 1759; Mullins, ibid., 13 June 1774; see also Williamson, ibid., 22 August 1768; Williams, ibid., 17 March 1759.

56. [Ill.], ibid., 26 January 1765; Josiah Smith Jr. to George Austin, 31 January 1774, Josiah Smith Jr. Letterbook, Southern Historical Collection, University of North Carolina, Chapel Hill (hereafter cited as SHC); Elliott, *SCG,* 28 January 1773; see also Maybank, ibid., 4 January 1770; Joor, ibid., 5 November 1772.

57. George C. Rogers Jr., "Changes in Taste in the Eighteenth Century: A Shift from the Useful to the Ornamental," *Journal of Early Southern Decorative Arts* 8 (1982): 16–18.

58. Hewit, *Historical Account,* 1:377–378; Guerard, *SCG,* 5 April 1773. On merchant-planters, see also R. C. Nash, "The Organization of Trade and Finance in the Atlantic Economy: Britain and South Carolina, 1670–1775," in *Money, Trade, and Power: The Evolution of South Carolina's Plantation Society,* ed. Jack P. Greene, Rosemary Brana-Shute, and Randy J. Sparks (Columbia: University of South Carolina Press, 2001), 95–96.

59. Crowley, *Invention of Comfort,* chap. 7, 143; Rivers, *SCG,* 11 September 1762; Guerard, ibid., 5 April 1773; Logan, ibid., 2 April 1763.

60. Joor, *SCG,* 12 July 1773; Shubrick, ibid., 11 September 1762; Palthasar, ibid., 3 September 1753; Welshuysen, ibid., 8 February 1735; Gray, ibid., 15 October 1763. On piazzas, see Crowley, *Invention of Comfort,* 234 and chap. 8; Shelley Smith, "Colonial South Carolina Plantations," 255–271.

61. Norris, *Profitable Advice,* 98, 103–105.

62. Smith, *SCG,* 28 November 1771; Vicaridge, ibid., 6 April 1734; wheat and grain: Elliott, ibid., 18 July 1771; Evans, ibid., 24 March 1759; Mazick, ibid., 28 February 1736; S[k?]eed, ibid., 25 December 1762; plowing: Pendarvis, ibid., 30 June 1759; Creighton, ibid., 6 August 1763. For another example

of a hinterland "farm," see *Gazette of the State of South Carolina*, 13 October 1779.

63. Pastures: Guerard, *SCG*, 5 April 1773; Butler, ibid., 31 January 1736; Saxby, ibid., 30 June 1746; Coachman, ibid., 19 November 1764. Mary Stafford, "A Letter Written in 1711 by Mary Stafford to Her Kinswoman in England," *SCHM* 81 (1980): 3–4; English livestock: Elliott, *SCG*, 22 August 1771; Haskins, ibid., 22 August 1771; HL to Frederick Wiggins, 31 July 1766, in *PHL*, 5:145. On beer imports and production, see [Anon.], *SCG*, 24 December 1759; Morgan, ibid., 26 September 1754; James Glen, *A Description of South Carolina . . .* (1761), facsimile repr. in *Colonial South Carolina: Two Contemporary Descriptions*, ed. Chapman J. Milling (Columbia: University of South Carolina Press, 1951), 36–37; on the use of rice malt to make beer, see Slide, *SCG*, 29 March 1739.

64. McDoual, *SCG*, 12 January 1759; Creighton, ibid., 6 August 1763; Wells, *Journal of a Voyage*, 43.

65. Lake, *SCG*, 14 July 1739; Bullock, ibid., 23 March 1734; paled fences: Por[care?], ibid., 2 February 1767; Caw, ibid., 24 September 1772.

66. Wright, ibid., 25 January 1746; Middleton, ibid., 22 September 1766; Martha Daniell Logan, *A Gardener's Kalendar: Done by a Colonial Lady*, ed. Alice Logan Wright (Charleston: National Society of the Colonial Dames of America in the State of South Carolina, 1976); Robert Squibb, *The Gardener's Calendar for South-Carolina, Georgia, and North-Carolina* (1787; repr., Athens: University of Georgia Press, 1980); Robert Blair St. George, *Conversing by Signs: Poetics of Implication in Colonial New England Culture* (Chapel Hill: University of North Carolina Press, 1998), 18 (rosemary).

67. HL to Gabriel Manigault, 2 March 1772, in *PHL*, 8:207; Shepherd, *SCG*, 12 September 1754; Perkins, ibid., 1 December 1755; Williamson, ibid., 15 February 1770.

68. Jones, *SCG*, 19 March 1744; Vicaridge, ibid., 6 April 1734; Dandridge, ibid., 15 August 1768; Dry, ibid., 4 August 1733; Smith, ibid., 28 November 1771; Blake, ibid., 7 August 1736.

69. David Ramsay, *Ramsay's History of South Carolina, from Its First Settlement in 1670 to the Year 1808*, 2 vols. (1809; repr., Newberry, S.C., 1858), 2:130, 127–128; Shelley Smith, "Colonial South Carolina Plantations," 130, 154–155.

70. Rhys Isaac, *The Transformation of Virginia, 1740–1790* (New York: W. W. Norton, 1982), 34–42; Upton, *Holy Things and Profane*, 206–207; Fuller, *SCG*, 5 January 1738; town: Jordan, ibid., 2 March 1767; Nickleson, Shubrick, & Co., ibid., 30 September 1742; neighborhood: Fauchereaud, ibid., 15 December 1758; Drayton, ibid., 14 March 1771.

71. Hearst, *SCG,* 18 October 1773; Butler, ibid., 2 June 1739; Barbara Novak, *Nature and Culture: American Landscape Painting, 1825–1875* (New York: Oxford University Press, 1980), 40–41.

72. HL to Richard Shubrick, 12 October 1756, in *PHL,* 2:335; Barnard Elliott to Richard Bohun Baker, 10 May 1764, Baker Family Correspondence, SCHS.

73. Elliott, *SCG,* 18 July 1771; Deveaux, ibid., 9 March 1752; Ward, ibid., 24 July 1774.

74. Hyrne, ibid., 28 November 1741; Letter of "The Stranger," ibid., 17 September and 24 September 1772; Ferguson, *Uncommon Ground,* xxi; Alexander Garden (1740), quoted in Frank J. Klingberg, *An Appraisal of the Negro in Colonial South Carolina* (Washington, D.C.: Associated Publishers, 1941), 106.

75. "The 1780 Siege of Charleston as Experienced by a Hessian Officer," ed. and trans. George Fenwick Jones, *SCHM* 88 (1987): 63, 64, 67; on white wartime migrations, see also Josiah Smith Jr. to James Poyas, 21 September 1775, Smith Letterbook.

76. Gordon, "Journal of an Officer," 397–398.

77. John Channing to William Gibbons Jr., 4 June 1770, William Gibbons Jr. Papers, Duke; Sirmans, *Colonial South Carolina,* 227; HL to Lachlan McIntosh, 29 December 1763, in *PHL,* 4:114; Peter Manigault to Ralph Izard, 2 August 1770, Manigault Letterbook; Shelley Smith, "Colonial South Carolina Plantations," 326; David Duncan Wallace, *The Life of Henry Laurens, with a Sketch of the Life of Lieutenant-Colonel John Laurens* (New York: G. P. Putnam's Sons, 1915), 45; unknown author to Ralph Izard, November 1788, Ralph Izard Papers, box 1, folder 2, SCL.

78. Norris, *Profitable Advice,* 107–108. Of 2,052 distinct individuals who advertised tracts, 602 (29.3 percent) had more than one to sell; of 1,113 individuals who were selling developed plantations, 124 (11.1 percent) had more than one to sell. *SCG.*

79. Josiah Quincy Jr., "Journal of Josiah Quincy, Junior, 1773," Massachusetts Historical Society, *Proceedings* 49 (1915–1916): 453; entry for 28 March 1780, John Peebles Diary, SCL. On "wealthy young Planters" as avid slave buyers, see HL to Ross & Mill, 31 March 1769, in *PHL,* 6:422.

80. Eliza Pinckney to [Mr. Morley], 14 March 1760, in *The Letterbook of Eliza Lucas Pinckney, 1739–1762,* ed. Elise Pinckney (Chapel Hill: University of North Carolina Press, 1972), 144.

81. Josiah Smith Jr. to George Smith, 28 February 1781, Smith Letterbook; HL to James Marion, 25 February 1765, in *PHL,* 4:585; see also Robert Raper to James Michie, 17 June 1760, Raper Letterbook.

82. Peter Manigault to Ralph Izard, 10 August 1772, Manigault Letterbook; Manigault to Ben Stead, 12 March 1770, ibid.

83. HL to John Ettwein, 19 March 1763, in *PHL*, 3:373–374.

84. Richard Hutson to Sam Smith, 12 March 1766, Charles Woodward Hutson Papers, SHC; Hutson to I[saac] Hayne, 11 May 1767, ibid.; Hutson to William Schank, 14 June 1766, ibid.; Hutson to Mr. Croll, 22 August 1767, ibid.

85. Samuel Dubose, "Address Delivered at the Seventeenth Anniversary of the Black Oak Agricultural Society," in *A Contribution to the History of the Huguenots of South Carolina,* by Samuel Dubose and Frederick A. Porcher, ed. T. Gaillard Thomas (1887; repr., Columbia: University of South Carolina Press, 1972), 9–10.

86. Bartram, "Diary of a Journey," 22; James Habersham to HL, 3 June 1771, in *PHL*, 7:516.

87. *SCG,* 15 February 1770.

88. See *Rural Images: Estate Maps in the Old and New Worlds,* ed. David Buisseret (Chicago: University of Chicago Press, 1996).

89. Davis, *SCG,* 25 June 1772; Guerard, ibid., 5 April 1773.

90. John Martin to John Martin, 17 February 1788, John Martin Estate Papers, SCHS; John Drayton to James Glen, 11 October 1761, James Glen Papers, SCL; James Grant (1769), cited in Daniel C. Littlefield, *Rice and Slaves: Ethnicity and the Slave Trade in Colonial South Carolina* (Baton Rouge: Louisiana State University Press, 1981), 70.

91. John Drayton, *A View of South-Carolina, as Respects Her Natural and Civil Concerns* (Charleston, S.C., 1802), 116–117, 147; Hewit, *Historical Account,* 141–142; *American Husbandry,* ed. Harry J. Carman (1775; repr., New York: Columbia University Press, 1939), 277; Philip D. Morgan, "Black Society in the Lowcountry, 1760–1810," in *Slavery and Freedom in the Age of the American Revolution,* ed. Ira Berlin and Ronald Hoffman (Charlottesville: University Press of Virginia, 1983), 98, 105; Morgan, *Slave Counterpoint,* 156–157.

92. Entries for May–July 1792, Allard Belin Plantation Journal, SCHS.

93. HL to Elias Ball, 28 February 1766, in *PHL,* 5:81–82.

94. Quoted in Jeffrey Robert Young, *Domesticating Slavery: The Master Class in Georgia and South Carolina, 1670–1837* (Chapel Hill: University of North Carolina Press, 1999), 121; Bartram, "Diary of a Journey," 22; John Scott Strickland, "Traditional Culture and Moral Economy: Social and Economic Change in the South Carolina Low Country, 1865–1910," in *The Countryside in the Age of Capitalist Transformation,* ed. Steven Hahn and Jonathan Prude (Chapel Hill: University of North Carolina Press, 1985), 149.

95. Morgan, "Black Society," 98, 105; E. P. Thompson, "Time, Work-Discipline, and Industrial Capitalism," *Past and Present* 38 (1967): 59–97; Eugene D. Genovese, *Roll, Jordan, Roll: The World the Slaves Made* (New York: Pan-

theon, 1974), 285–294; Robert W. Fogel, *Without Consent or Contract: The Rise and Fall of American Slavery* (New York: W. W. Norton, 1989), 158, 160–162.

96. Bolzius, "Questionnaire on Carolina," 258–259; Edward McCrady, *The History of South Carolina under the Royal Government, 1719–1776* (New York: Macmillan, 1899), 387; Lewis C. Gray, *History of Agriculture in the Southern United States to 1860*, 2 vols. (1933; repr., Gloucester, Mass.: Peter Smith, 1958), 1:554; Philip D. Morgan, "Work and Culture: The Task System and the World of Lowcountry Blacks, 1700–1880," *WMQ* 39 (1982): 577; Josiah Smith Jr. to George Austin [Jr.], 14 June 1775, Smith Letterbook; [Joseph Clay?] to unknown addressee, 6 December [1785?], Edward Telfair Papers, Duke. Morgan argues that some of these irrigation-system tasks were completed using gang labor, "Black Society," 105.

97. *Statutes of South Carolina*, 7:413; quoted in Olwell, *Masters, Slaves, and Subjects*, 84; Alexander Garden, "Correspondence between Alexander Garden, M.D., and the Royal Society of Arts," *SCHM* 64 (1963): 17; *Castiglioni's Viaggio*, 165; Bolzius, "Questionnaire on Carolina," 258–259; on "night work," see also HL to Timothy Creamer, 25 January 1765, in *PHL*, 4:571.

98. HL to Richard Clarke, 25 August 1770, in *PHL*, 7:329; see also Charles Joyner, *Down by the Riverside: A South Carolina Slave Community* (Urbana: University of Illinois Press, 1984), 58–59; Julie Saville, *The Work of Reconstruction: From Slave to Wage Laborer in South Carolina, 1860–1870* (New York: Cambridge University Press, 1996), 51–52.

99. Quoted in Young, *Domesticating Slavery*, 128.

100. Entries for 31 May–2 June 1798, Belin Journal.

101. Philip D. Morgan, "Task and Gang Systems: The Organization of Labor on New World Plantations," in *Work and Labor in Early America*, ed. Stephen Innes (Chapel Hill: University of North Carolina Press, 1988), 220.

102. See, for example, Strickland, "Traditional Culture," 147; Joyce E. Chaplin, *An Anxious Pursuit: Agricultural Innovation and Modernity in the Lower South, 1730–1815* (Chapel Hill: University of North Carolina Press, 1993), 228, 326–327.

103. "Good order": Josiah Smith Jr. to George Austin, 17 June 1771, Smith Letterbook; John Lewis Gervais to HL, 5–10 May 1772, in *PHL*, 8:287. For other examples of "necessary" work, see Robert Raper to Margaret Colleton, 20 May 1768, Raper Letterbook; Drayton, *View of South-Carolina*, 117; James Laurens to HL, 21 June 1774, in *PHL*, 9:476; HL to Lachlan McIntosh, 24 December 1771, ibid., 8:114–115. For examples of the erosion of customary labor arrangements elsewhere, see Lois Green Carr, Russell R.

Menard, and Lorena S. Walsh, *Robert Cole's World: Agriculture and Society in Early Maryland* (Chapel Hill: University of North Carolina Press, 1991), 63; Dale W. Tomich, *Through the Prism of Slavery: Labor, Capital, and World Economy* (Lanham, Md.: Rowman & Littlefield, 2004), 169.

104. William Butler, "Observations on the Culture of Rice" (1786), SCHS; General Floyd, "On the Cultivation and Preparation of Indigo," *Southern Agriculturist* 2 (1829): 154. Floyd was identified as one of the "old Indigo Planters" who probably produced the crop in the late eighteenth century, ibid., 105.

105. Vats: Middleton, *SCG*, 26 August 1756; Fauchereaud, ibid., 15 December 1758; D. J. Huneycutt, "The Economics of the Indigo Industry in South Carolina" (M.A. thesis, University of South Carolina, Columbia, 1949), 21–22; Floyd, "Cultivation and Preparation of Indigo," 154.

106. Quoted in Klingberg, *Appraisal of the Negro*, 90; Dubose, "Black Oak Address," 9.

107. S. Max Edelson, "Affiliation without Affinity: Skilled Slaves in Eighteenth-Century South Carolina," in *Money, Trade, and Power*, 217–255.

108. Morgan, "Black Society," tables 13a, 13b, 14a, 14b, 101–104.

109. Letter of "The Stranger," *SCG*, 17 September and 24 September 1772; on slave marketing, see Olwell, *Masters, Slaves, and Subjects*, 166–178.

110. Morgan, "Black Society," 97–99.

111. Demotions: HL to John Smith, 9 May 1766, in *PHL*, 5:125; Josiah Smith Jr. to George Austin, 17 June 1771, Smith Letterbook; see also Chaplin, *Anxious Pursuit*, 125–126. Gourdin, quoted in Virginia Gail Jelatis, "Tangled Up in Blue: Indigo Culture and Economy in South Carolina, 1747–1800" (Ph.D. dissertation, University of Minnesota, 1999), 147; Smith to George Austin, 14 June 1775, Smith Letterbook.

112. Compare the age pyramids for the Ashepoo (frontier) plantation and the Ball Family plantations (core) in Morgan, *Slave Counterpoint*, figure 4, 91; Cheryll Ann Cody, "There Was No 'Absalom' on the Ball Plantations: Slave Naming Practices in the South Carolina Low Country, 1720–1865," *American Historical Review* 92 (1987): 579, 581; see also Russell R. Menard, "Slave Demography in the Lowcountry, 1670–1740: From Frontier Society to Plantation Regime," *SCHM* 96 (1995): 280–303.

113. Robinson, *SCG*, 15 November 1760; Hutson, ibid., 6 June 1768.

114. Letter of "The Stranger."

115. Olwell, *Masters, Slaves, and Subjects*, 37.

116. HL to James Grant, 23 March 1767, in *PHL*, 5:238; Wells, *Journal of a Voyage*, 28.

117. For an example of an illiterate overseer, see William Ancrum to [Mr.

Giving?], 17 October 1778, William Ancrum Letterbook, SCL; for an example of rough prose, see James Postell to Ralph Izard, 1 April 1769, Izard
Papers, SCL; *SCG*, 29 May 1762 (boards).

118. Josiah Smith Jr. to George Austin, 17 July 1771, Smith Letterbook; Hewit,
Historical Account, 350; Smith to Austin, 30 July [1772], Smith Letterbook.

119. John Laurens to James Laurens, 24 October 1776, HL Papers; Catherine
Piercy to Barnard Elliott, 5 October 1778, Baker Correspondence.

120. Richard Hutson to Isaac Hayne, 29 January 1767, Hutson Papers; Ralph
Izard to Peter Manigault, 23 April 1769, Izard Papers.

121. J. Hector St. John de Crèvecoeur, *Letters from an American Farmer and
Sketches of Eighteenth-Century America*, ed. Albert E. Stone (1782; repr.,
New York: Penguin, 1981), 168.

122. *SCG*, 27 June 1744; see also Reid, ibid., 2 November 1738.

123. Peter H. Wood, "Slave Labor Camps in Early America: Overcoming Denial
and Discovering the Gulag," in *Inequality in Early America*, ed. Carla Gardina Pestana and Sharon V. Salinger (Hanover, N.H.: University Press of
New England, 1999), 231.

5. Marketplace of Identity

1. Jack P. Greene, *Imperatives, Behaviors, and Identities: Essays in Early American Cultural History* (Charlottesville: University Press of Virginia, 1992),
164, 159, and chap. 8.

2. Trevor Burnard, *Creole Gentlemen: The Maryland Elite, 1691–1776* (New
York: Routledge, 2002), chap. 7; Joyce E. Chaplin, *An Anxious Pursuit: Ag-
ricultural Innovation and Modernity in the Lower South, 1730–1815* (Chapel
Hill: University of North Carolina Press, 1993).

3. Some of these ideas are developed in Jack P. Greene, "Dimensions of Identity" (unpublished paper, 1995, courtesy of the author).

4. S. Max Edelson, "Carolinians Abroad: Cultivating English Identities from
the Colonial Lower South," in *Britain and the American South: From Colonialism to Rock and Roll*, ed. Joseph P. Ward (Jackson: University Press of
Mississippi, 2003), 81–105.

5. Jean-Christophe Agnew, *Worlds Apart: The Market and the Theater in Anglo-
American Thought, 1550–1750* (New York: Cambridge University Press,
1986), chap. 2; Craig Muldrew, *The Economy of Obligation: The Culture of
Credit and Social Relations in Early Modern England* (Houndmills, U.K.:
Macmillan, 1998), 150–166.

6. Patrick Coleman, "The Idea of Character in the *Encylopédie*," *Eighteenth-
Century Studies* 13 (1979): 26.

7. Michal J. Rozbicki, *The Complete Colonial Gentleman: Cultural Legitimacy in Plantation America* (Charlottesville: University Press of Virginia, 1998).

8. The "TOURS" refers to the books of Arthur Young, a proponent of scientific agriculture who published accounts of regional farming methods and experiments used to improve them in the late 1760s and 1770s. Among these are *A Six Weeks Tour, through the Southern Counties of England and Wales* ... (London, 1769) and *The Farmer's Tour through the East of England* ... (London, 1771).

9. [William] Marshall, *Minutes of Agriculture, Made on a Farm of 300 Acres of Various Soils, Near Croydon, Surry* ... (London, 1778), 7–13, Eighteenth-Century Collections Online, Gale Group, galenet.galegroup.com (hereafter cited as ECCO). For another comment on this passage, see Ann Kussmaul, *Servants in Husbandry in Early Modern England* (Cambridge: Cambridge University Press, 1981), 45.

10. [John Mitchell], *The Present State of Great Britain and North America with Regard to Agriculture, Population, Trade, and Manufactures* (London, 1767), 133, 135; *American Husbandry*, ed. Harry J. Carman (1775; repr., New York: Columbia University Press, 1939), 393–394.

11. See Richard L. Kagan, "Prescott's Paradigm: American Historical Scholarship and the Decline of Spain," *American Historical Review* 101 (1996): 423–446.

12. On the "depravity" thesis that has depicted the West Indies as a social and cultural failure and its critics, see Jack P. Greene, "Society and Economy in the British Caribbean during the Seventeenth and Eighteenth Centuries," *American Historical Review* 79 (1974): 1499–1517; on negative characterizations of planters, see Greene, *Imperatives, Behaviors, and Identities*, 191, 268, 47–48, and chap. 2; see also Rozbicki, *Complete Colonial Gentleman*, chap. 3.

13. S. Max Edelson, "The Nature of Slavery: Environmental Disorder and Slave Agency in Colonial South Carolina," in *Cultures and Identities in Colonial British America*, ed. Robert Olwell and Alan Tully (Baltimore: Johns Hopkins University Press, 2005), 31–36; "A View of Coastal South Carolina in 1778: The Journal of Ebenezer Hazard," ed. H. Roy Merrens, *South Carolina Historical Magazine* 73 (1972): 190 (hereafter cited as *SCHM*); Josiah Smith Jr. to George Austin, 30 January 1773, Josiah Smith Jr. Letterbook, Southern Historical Collection, University of North Carolina, Chapel Hill (hereafter cited as SHC); Smith to James Caldwell, 24 March 1776, ibid.

14. Quoted in Jackson Turner Main, *The Social Structure of Revolutionary America* (Princeton, N.J.: Princeton University Press, 1965), 167 ("lowest

classes"); *Carolina Chronicle: The Papers of Commissary Gideon Johnston, 1707–1716*, ed. Frank J. Klingberg (Berkeley: University of California Press, 1946), 22; Johann Martin Bolzius, "Johann Martin Bolzius Answers a Questionnaire on Carolina and Georgia," ed. and trans. Klaus G. Loewald et al., *William and Mary Quarterly*, 3rd ser., 14 (1957): 244, 245 (hereafter cited as *WMQ*); Greene, *Imperatives, Behaviors, and Identities*, 40–41.

15. John Drayton, *A View of South-Carolina, as Respects Her Natural and Civil Concerns* (Charleston, S.C., 1802), 113. On this dynamic of colonial adaptation and metropolitan critique as it relates to livestock husbandry, see Virginia Dejohn Anderson, "Animals into the Wilderness: The Development of Livestock Husbandry in the Seventeenth-Century Chesapeake," *WMQ* 59 (2002): 377–408.

16. On the ways in which colonists conformed to and departed from an idealized model of spatial organization, see John R. Stilgoe, *Common Landscape of America, 1580 to 1845* (New Haven, Conn.: Yale University Press, 1982), 34, 46–47.

17. John J. McCusker and Russell R. Menard, *The Economy of British America, 1607–1789* (Chapel Hill: University of North Carolina Press, 1985), 305–306; see also Lois Green Carr, Russell R. Menard, and Lorena S. Walsh, *Robert Cole's World: Agriculture and Society in Early Maryland* (Chapel Hill: University of North Carolina Press, 1991), xvii–xviii, 151–152.

18. Jethro Tull (1674–1741) invented the mechanized seed drill. He advocated deep plowing and other methods of improved husbandry in *The New Horse-Houghing Husbandry; or, An Essay on the Principles of Tillage and Vegetation* . . . (London, 1731) and other books.

19. Henry Laurens to Lachlan McIntosh, 10 May 1769, in *The Papers of Henry Laurens*, ed. Philip M. Hamer et al., 16 vols. (Columbia: University of South Carolina Press, 1968–2003), 6:447 (hereafter cited as HL and *PHL*).

20. George Ogilvie, *Carolina; Or, The Planter* (1776), repr. in *Southern Literary Journal*, special issue (1986): 46, 7–8.

21. Land judges: William Hudson estate, *South-Carolina Gazette*, 6 June 1768 (hereafter cited as *SCG*); Samuel Eveleigh, ibid., 26 December 1754; Mr. Farrol, ibid., 4 December 1755. John Harvey, ibid., 9 March 1765 (viewing land). Known by reputation: Solomon M[ai?]zer estate, ibid., 28 January 1764; George Sheed, ibid., 15 November 1770.

22. John Bartram, "Diary of a Journey through the Carolinas, Georgia and Florida from July 1, 1765, to April 10, 1766," *Transactions of the American Philosophical Society* 33 (1942): 14; HL to John Bartram, 9 August 1766, in *PHL*, 5:152; John Lewis Gervais to HL, 5–10 May 1772, ibid., 8:287; "Diary of William Dillwyn during a Visit to Charles Town in 1772," ed. A. S. Salley Jr., *SCHM* 36 (1935): 110; George Ogilvie to Margaret Ogilvie, 22 November

1774, in "The Letters of George Ogilvie," ed. David S. Shields, *Southern Literary Journal,* special issue (1986): 122.

23. William Gibbons Jr. Papers, box 1728–1771, folder 1760–1764, William R. Perkins Library, Special Collections, Duke University, Durham, N.C. (hereafter cited as Duke).

24. Eliza Lucas Pinckney (1758), quoted in Cara Anzilotti, *In the Affairs of the World: Women, Patriarchy, and Power in Colonial South Carolina* (Westport, Conn.: Greenwood Press, 2002), 172; Pinckney to [Mr. Morley], 14 March 1760, in *The Letterbook of Eliza Lucas Pinckney, 1739–1762,* ed. Elise Pinckney (Chapel Hill: University of North Carolina Press, 1972), 144.

25. Josiah Smith Jr. to George Austin, 31 January 1774, Smith Letterbook.

26. M. Eugene Sirmans, *Colonial South Carolina: A Political History, 1663–1763* (Chapel Hill: University of North Carolina Press, 1966), 242; Mrs. A. Capers to Mrs. Russell, 25 March 1791, Edith Mitchell Dabbs Papers, SHC.

27. On prevailing standards for polite discourse that tended to exclude discussions of economic matters, see David S. Shields, *Civil Tongues and Polite Letters in British America* (Chapel Hill: University of North Carolina Press, 1997), 34–37.

28. Josiah Quincy Jr., "Journal of Josiah Quincy, Junior, 1773," Massachusetts Historical Society, *Proceedings* 49 (1915–1916): 450, 456; Ralph Izard to Gabriel Manigault, 9 June 1789, Ralph Izard Papers, box 1, folder 2, South Caroliniana Library, University of South Carolina, Columbia (hereafter cited as SCL); Alexander Hewit, *An Historical Account of the Rise and Progress of the Colonies of South Carolina and Georgia,* in *Historical Collections of South Carolina,* ed. B. R. Carroll, 2 vols. (New York, 1836), 1:415–416.

29. HL to Joseph Brown, 15 March 1764, in *PHL,* 4:210–211; Bolzius, "Questionnaire on Carolina," 240.

30. Bolzius, "Questionnaire on Carolina," 243; Drayton, *View of South-Carolina,* 116; *American Husbandry,* 392.

31. HL to John McCullough, 18 May 1772, in *PHL,* 8:316–317.

32. HL to John Coming Ball, 7 January 1763, ibid., 3:207; HL to Richard Oswald, 7 July 1764, ibid., 4:338; HL to James Marion, 25 February 1765, ibid., 4:585; Robert Raper to John Colleton, 14 January 1761, 16 June 1761, Robert Raper Letterbook (photocopy of original in West Sussex Record Office), South Carolina Historical Society, Charleston (hereafter cited as SCHS); Raper to Mr. Swainston, 25 February 1764, ibid.; HL to Foster Cunliffe & Sons, 5 November 1755, 24 February 1756, in *PHL,* 2:10, 106.

33. See Richard Drayton, *Nature's Government: Science, Imperial Britain, and the "Improvement" of the World* (New Haven, Conn.: Yale University Press, 2000), 51.

34. Lord Adam Gordon, "Journal of an Officer Who Travelled in America and the West Indies in 1764 and 1765," in *Travels in the American Colonies*, ed. Newton D. Mereness (New York: Macmillan, 1916), 397–398.

35. Jack P. Greene, "Social and Cultural Capital in Colonial America: A Case Study," *Journal of Interdisciplinary History* 29 (1999): 494.

36. Drayton, *View of South-Carolina*, 144, 146–147.

37. R. C. Nash, "The Organization of Trade and Finance in the Atlantic Economy: Britain and South Carolina, 1670–1775," in *Money, Trade, and Power: The Evolution of Colonial South Carolina's Plantation Society*, ed. Jack P. Greene, Rosemary Brana-Shute, and Randy J. Sparks (Columbia: University of South Carolina Press, 2001), 77–81; T. H. Breen, *Tobacco Culture: The Mentality of the Great Tidewater Planters on the Eve of Revolution* (Princeton, N.J.: Princeton University Press, 1985), 84, 116.

38. On Charlestown's vibrant theater scene, see Carl Bridenbaugh, *Myths and Realities: Societies of the Colonial South* (New York: Atheneum, 1970), 92–94.

39. Jeanne A. Calhoun, Martha A. Zierden, and Elizabeth A. Paysinger, "The Geographic Spread of Charleston's Merchant Community, 1732–1767," *SCHM* 86 (1985): 183, 188–189.

40. Ibid., 186–187 (merchants); Robert M. Weir, *Colonial South Carolina: A History* (Millwood, N.Y.: KTO Press, 1983), 217 (planters); Nash, "Organization of Trade," 79 (factors).

41. HL to William Cowles & Co., 15 April 1766, in *PHL*, 5:649.

42. Agnew, *Worlds Apart*, 40.

43. Peter A. Coclanis, *The Shadow of a Dream: Economic Life and Death in the South Carolina Lowcountry, 1670–1920* (New York: Oxford University Press, 1989), 107–110.

44. R. C. Nash, "South Carolina and the Atlantic Economy in the Late Seventeenth and Eighteenth Centuries," *Economic History Review* 45 (1992): 680–681; Peter A. Coclanis, "Rice Prices in the 1720s and the Evolution of the South Carolina Economy," *Journal of Southern History* 48 (1982): 536–541; Coclanis, *Shadow of a Dream*, 106–109; Henry C. Dethloff, "The Colonial Rice Trade," *Agricultural History* 56 (1982): 237.

45. Report of the Committee on the State of Paper Currency in the Province, 5 March 1737, in *The Journal of the Commons House of Assembly, November 10, 1736–June 7, 1739*, ed. James H. Easterby (Columbia: University of South Carolina Press, 1951), 311; HL to James Wright, 27 February 1768, in *PHL*, 5:610; Robert Pringle to John Erving, 17 May 1744, in *The Letterbook of Robert Pringle*, ed. Walter B. Edgar, 2 vols. (Columbia: University of South Carolina Press, 1972), 2:694; Pringle to William Cookson and William Welfitt, 25 September 1742, ibid., 1:423; Peter Manigault to Dan[iel] Blake, 10 March 1771, Peter Manigault Letterbook, SCHS. On

price volatility, see also R. C. Nash, "Trade and Business in Eighteenth-Century South Carolina: The Career of John Guerard, Merchant and Planter," *SCHM* 96 (1995): 23; Kenneth Morgan, "The Organization of the Colonial Rice Trade," *WMQ* 52 (1995): 445–456.

46. HL to Gidney Clarke, 21 February 1756, in *PHL*, 2:100. Extending credit to merchants: John Guerard to William Jolliff, 26 February 1754, John Guerard Letterbook, SCHS; Robert Raper to [Thomas] Boone, 2 May 1761, Raper Letterbook; Peter Manigault to Isaac King, 1 May 1769, Manigault Letterbook.

47. Nash, "Organization of Trade," 81–85; glutted dry-goods trade: Richard Splatt, "Richard Splatt's Letter and Invoice, 1726," in *The Colonial South Carolina Scene: Contemporary Views, 1697–1774*, ed. H. Roy Merrens (Columbia: University of South Carolina Press, 1977), 77, 80; Josiah Smith Jr. to James Poyas, [c. 31 January 1784], Smith Letterbook; HL to John Pagan, 6 July 1764, in *PHL*, 4:330.

48. Robert Raper to Messrs. Moses Nunes and Son, 17 September 1759, Raper Letterbook; Cowper and Telfair to Edward Telfair and Company, 17 March 1775, Edward Telfair Papers, Duke.

49. HL to Richard Grubb, 5 November 1747, in *PHL*, 1:69–70; John Guerard to William Jolliff, 6 May 1754, Guerard Letterbook; Guerard to John Nickleson, 14 November 1752, ibid. On merchant-planters, see Nash, "Trade and Business," 10–11, 22–23; see also Nash, "Organization of Trade," 94–97; see also Frederic Cople Jaher, *The Urban Establishment: Upper Strata in Boston, New York, Charleston, Chicago, and Los Angeles* (Urbana: University of Illinois Press, 1982), 322–327. William Pollard, "A Business Visit, 1774," in *Colonial South Carolina Scene*, 277 ("evil eye").

50. Ian K. Steele, *The English Atlantic, 1675–1740: An Exploration of Communication and Community* (New York: Oxford University Press, 1986), 34.

51. Robert Pringle to John Erving, 29 September 1738, in *Pringle Letterbook*, 1: 34; HL to Richard Baker, 25 January 1764, in *PHL*, 4:146–147.

52. Robert Raper to Francis and Jos. Van OuderKercks, 18 November 1760, Raper Letterbook; HL to Graham, Read, & Mossman, 7 December 1763, in *PHL*, 4:74.

53. *SCG*, 1 December 1737.

54. HL to Devonsheir, Reeve, & Lloyd, 24 February 1757, in *PHL*, 2:466.

55. Josiah Smith Jr. to Messrs. Wraxall and Hall, 7 December 1771, Smith Letterbook; HL to Smith & Baillies, 19 October 1763, in *PHL*, 4:31. For other examples of the impact of demand news on the local market, see *PHL*, 3:173; Thomas Morris to Nicholas Low, 3 January 1785, Thomas Morris Papers, SCL; John Guerard to Thomas Rock, 19 April 1753, Guerard Letterbook.

56. Robert Pringle to Edward and John Mayne and Company, 2 March 1739,

in *Pringle Letterbook*, 1:73 (Italian rice); HL to Samuel Munckley, 11 March 1757, in *PHL*, 2:489 (European grain); Smith to George Austin, 30 January 1773, Smith Letterbook (hurricane).

57. HL to Cox & Furman & Company, 18 November 1762, in *PHL*, 3:157; HL to Gidney Clarke, 13 January 1763, ibid., 3:213; see also Peter Manigault to Ben Stead, 29 April 1771, Manigault Letterbook.

58. Robert Pringle to Richard Thompson, 1 September 1738, in *Pringle Letterbook*, 1:30. The demands of rice processing and other factors governed the pace of rice shipments to town and delayed the bulk of the crop from arriving before mid-December. Thomas Morris to Messrs. Alexander Nesbett and Company, August 24, 1783, Morris Papers; *Pringle Letterbook*, 1: 102; *PHL*, 1:349. On late fall trade dynamics in which the last season's "old" rice was shipping along with the first "new" rice, see Josiah Smith Jr. to Joseph Clay, 5 November 1772, Smith Letterbook. On trade disruptions caused by toredo worms infesting ship hulls in summer and hurricanes in the fall, see *Pringle Letterbook*, 1:83.

59. HL to James Dennistoune, John Pagan & Company, 6 May 1763, *PHL*, 3: 441; HL to John Knight, 15 July 1763, ibid., 3:495. Other deceptions are documented in John Guerard to John Nickleson, 14 November 1752, Guerard Letterbook; Robert Raper to Messers Benj[amin] and Samuel Shoemaker, 20 November 1759, Raper Letterbook.

60. HL to James Dennistoune, 6 July 1764, in *PHL*, 4:327.

61. *Commons Journal 1736–1739*, 311.

62. John Guerard to William Jolliff, 14 November 1753, Guerard Letterbook; Thomas Morris to Nicholas Low, 20 November 1784, Morris Papers.

63. John Guerard to William Jolliff, 21 October 1752, Guerard Letterbook; HL to John Knight, 22 December 1763, in *PHL*, 4:95. On the increasing scale of Charlestown shipping, see Steele, *English Atlantic*, 32–35, 51, 55, 288–289; see also Quincy, "Journal," 441.

64. HL to Henry Bright, 12 November 1763, in *PHL*, 4:44; breaking the price: Josiah Smith Jr. to Messrs. Wraxall and Hall, 7 December 1771, Smith Letterbook; HL to Cox & Furman & Co., 4 December 1762, in *PHL*, 3:180; see also ibid., 2:15, 3:177, 187, 549. On price premiums given to the first indigo and rice sold, see ibid., 1:299, 4:39.

65. Richard Hill to John [Guerard], 9 June 1743, Richard Hill Letterbook, Duke; HL to John Knight & Thomas Mears, 11 February 1763, in *PHL*, 3:247.

66. HL to James Cowles, 22 September 1755, in *PHL*, 1:338; Guerard to William Jolliff, 14 November 1753, Guerard Letterbook.

67. Josiah Smith Jr. to John Ray Jr., 22 April 1774, Smith Letterbook; Robert Pringle to Andrew Pringle, 7 November 1740, in *Pringle Letterbook*, 1:269; *SCG*, 7 April 1733.

68. John Drayton to James Glen, 23 June 1768, 13 August 1772, James Glen Papers, SCL. Contemporary estimates suggest that 2–4 barrels per acre (compared with Drayton's .25 barrels in 1768) were typical. Bolzius, "Questionnaire on Carolina," 260; Peter Manigault to Daniel Blake, 6 September 1769, Manigault Letterbook; Lewis C. Gray, *History of Agriculture in the Southern United States to 1860,* 2 vols. (1933; repr., Gloucester, Mass.: Peter Smith, 1958), 2:730. HL to William Fisher, 26 November 1756, in *PHL,* 2: 363. For other examples of price demands motivated by crop damage, see John Guerard to Thomas Rock, 6 November 1752, Guerard Letterbook; *PHL,* 1:364, 337–338; *Pringle Letterbook,* 1:316.

69. S. Max Edelson, "The Characters of Commodities: The Reputations of South Carolina Rice and Indigo in the Atlantic World," in *The Atlantic Economy in the Seventeenth and Eighteenth Centuries: Organization, Operation, Practice, and Personnel,* ed. Peter A. Coclanis (Columbia: University of South Carolina Press, 2005), 344–360; John Norris, *Profitable Advice for Rich and Poor . . .* (1712), in *Selling a New World: Two Colonial South Carolina Promotional Pamphlets,* ed. Jack P. Greene (Columbia: University of South Carolina Press, 1989), 89–90; William Gerhard De Brahm, "Philosophico-Historico-Hydrogeography of South Carolina, Georgia, and East Florida," in *Documents Connected with the History of South Carolina,* ed. P. C. J. Weston (London, 1856), 199.

70. [James Crokatt], *Further Observations Intended for Improving the Culture and Curing of Indigo, &c. in South-Carolina* (London, 1747), 11, ECCO; Claude L. Berthollet and A. B. Berthollet, *Elements of the Art of Dyeing,* trans. and ed. A. Ure, 2nd ed., 2 vols. (London, 1824), 2:36; HL to George Austin, 27 December 1747, in *PHL,* 1:200.

71. HL to Augustus & John Boyd & Co., 23 September 1755, in *PHL,* 1:340; HL to Samuel Munckley, John Adlam, & Francis Rogers Jr., 11 March 1757, ibid., 2:489; Edelson, "Characters of Commodities," 344, 351–353.

72. HL to Gabriel Manigault, 20 March 1772, in *PHL,* 8:228; John Guerard to William Jolliff, 31 May 1754, Guerard Letterbook (adulteration); HL to Devonsheir, Reeve, & Lloyd, 22 March 1757, in *PHL,* 2:502.

73. Rice was enumerated in 1705. A twenty-year lobbying campaign followed that secured an exemption that permitted the direct shipment of rice to Spain and Portugal, an important secondary market. Only in the last decade of the colonial period could rice be shipped legally to the increasingly important West Indian markets and directly to Europe. Gray, *History of Agriculture,* 1:284–285.

74. HL to Richard Oswald, 26 May 1757, in *PHL,* 2:203; Great Britain, Parliament, House of Commons, *Journals of the House of Commons,* 90 vols. to date (London, 1803–), 25:619–625, 635; Hewit, *Historical Account,* 342.

75. HL to James Dennistoune, John Pagan & Co., 6 July 1764, in *PHL*, 4:327; John Guerard to John Nickleson, 13 December 1752, Guerard Letterbook. For an instance in which planters broke ranks at the close of the shipping season, see Guerard to William Jolliff, 8 December 1753, 3 January 1754, 23 May 1754, Guerard Letterbook.

76. R. F. W. Allston, *Essay on Sea Coast Crops* (Charleston, S.C., 1854), 7–8; HL to Lloyd & Borton, 24 December 1764, in *PHL*, 4:558. This particular response might have been exaggerated by the impending prospect of a new slave-duty act that would make slave imports prohibitively expensive for the following three years.

77. Francis Yonge, "A Narrative of the Proceedings of the People of South Carolina in the Year 1719," in *Tracts and Other Papers, Relating Principally to the Origin, Settlement, and Progress of the Colonies in North America,* comp. Peter Force (Washington, D.C., 1836), 1:144. On South Carolina as an imperial frontier see also John Lawson, *A New Voyage to Carolina,* ed. Hugh Talmage Lefler (1709; repr., Chapel Hill: University of North Carolina Press, 1967), 10; Gordon, "Journal of an Officer," 398.

78. "Swiss Settlers in South Carolina," ed. and trans. R. W. Kelsey, *SCHM* 23 (1922): 89–90; Letter of "The Stranger" (1772), quoted in Alex Bontemps, *The Punished Self: Surviving Slavery in the Colonial South* (Ithaca, N.Y.: Cornell University Press, 2001), 70; see Peter H. Wood, *Black Majority: Negroes in Colonial South Carolina from 1670 through the Stono Rebellion* (New York: W. W. Norton, 1974), 132.

79. Gary L. Hewitt, "Expansion and Improvement: Land, People, and Politics in South Carolina and Georgia, 1690–1745" (Ph.D. dissertation, Princeton University, 1996), 1–24, 106–129, 178–206, 274–277; Sirmans, *Political History,* 115.

80. Robert K. Ackerman, *South Carolina Colonial Land Policies* (Columbia: University of South Carolina Press, 1977), 86–88; Robert L. Meriwether, *The Expansion of South Carolina, 1729–1765* (Kingsport, Tenn.: Southern Publishers, 1940), 31–76; *SCG,* 15 February 1735.

81. Hewit, *Historical Account,* 215–227, 228; Chaplin, *Anxious Pursuit,* 38–39; J. E. Crowley, *This Sheba, Self: The Conceptualization of Economic Life in Eighteenth-Century America* (Baltimore: Johns Hopkins University Press, 1974), 32; Kenneth Coleman, *Colonial Georgia, a History* (New York: Scribner, 1976), 11–12; Gray, *History of Agriculture,* 1:186–187; Harold E. Davis, *The Fledgling Province: Social and Cultural Life in Colonial Georgia, 1733–1776* (Chapel Hill: University of North Carolina Press, 1976), 8–13.

82. Frank J. Klingberg, *An Appraisal of the Negro in Colonial South Carolina* (Washington, D.C.: Associated Publishers, 1941), 64. On initial positive views of Georgia, see also Crowley, *This Sheba, Self,* 32; *SCG,* 10 March 1733; Hewitt, "Expansion and Improvement," 308.

83. *SCG*, 27 June 1743.

84. Ibid., 12 November 1744; Hewit, *Historical Account*, 407.

85. Hewit, *Historical Account*, 482; John Gerar William De Brahm, *History of the Province of Georgia* (Wormsloe, Ga., 1849), 51; Hewit, *Historical Account*, 308–309; see also ibid., 323, 392–393, 407; Hewitt, "Expansion and Improvement," 280–281, 309–312; David R. Chesnutt, *South Carolina's Expansion into Colonial Georgia, 1720–1765* (New York: Garland, 1989).

86. *SCG*, 14 November 1754; South Carolina Grand Jury Presentments, ibid., 8 November 1742 ("insurrection").

87. *SCG*, 14 November 1754.

88. Edelson, "Nature of Slavery," 36–42.

89. Charles L. Mowat, *East Florida as a British Province, 1763–1784* (Berkeley: University of California Press, 1943), 6–7, 50–51, 61–64; Donna T. McCaffrey, "Charles Townshend and Plans for British East Florida," *Florida Historical Quarterly* 68 (1990): 324–340; Bernard Bailyn, *Voyagers to the West: A Passage in the Peopling of America on the Eve of the Revolution* (New York: Vintage, 1986), chap. 12; Gordon, quoted in George C. Rogers Jr., "The East Florida Society of London," *Florida Historical Quarterly* 54 (1976): 483.

90. Rolle, quoted in Mowat, *East Florida*, 51. Negative views of Florida land can be found in Mitchell, *State of Great Britain*, 198; *American Husbandry*, 360–363; Hewit, *Historical Account*, 482.

91. Peter Collinson to John Bartram, 28 May 1766, in *The Correspondence of John Bartram, 1734–1777*, ed. Edmund Berkeley and Dorothy Smith Berkeley (Gainesville: University Press of Florida, 1992), 666–667; Bartram to Peter Collinson, 26 August 1766, ibid., 675; Alexander Garden to Bartram, 12 February 1766, ibid., 658.

92. F. G. Mulcaster to unknown addressee, 3 September 1768, 6 November 1768, Manigault Family Papers, box 1 (letter), folder 4, SCL. For a different interpretation of this dream, see Chaplin, *Anxious Pursuit*, 1–2.

93. HL to James Grant, 1 May 1767, in *PHL*, 5:245; De Brahm, quoted in Bailyn, *Voyagers to the West*, 443; HL to Alexander Gray, 26 May 1769, in *PHL*, 6: 578 ("infected"); HL to Richard Oswald, 12 August 1766, ibid., 5:156; HL to James Grant, 10 January 1767, ibid., 5:225 ("died before"); HL to James Grant, 28 January 1768, ibid., 5:576.

94. HL to James Grant, 30 January 1767, in *PHL*, 5:226–228.

95. John Solomon Otto, "Cracker: The History of a Southern Ethnic, Economic, and Racial Epithet," *Names* 35 (1987): 28–30; James A. Lewis, "Cracker—Spanish Florida Style," *Florida Historical Quarterly* 63 (1984): 184–185; *The Adventures of a Hackney Coach*, 3rd ed. (London, 1781), 4, ECCO ("small capital"); Samuel Johnson, *A Dictionary of the English Language . . .* , 11th ed., 2 vols. (London, 1799), s.v. "cracker," ECCO ("boasting fellow");

Aesop, *Æsop's Fables: With His Life, and Morals and Remarks...* (London, 1754), 107, ECCO ("empty fellows"). Others have traced the term's origins to onomatopoeic associations with backcountry practices such as pounding or "cracking" corn into hominy and herdsmen's use of long cattle whips. Gray, *History of Agriculture,* 1:149, 484.

96. *Belfast News Letter,* 6 November 1767, Items Pertaining to the Carolinas in the Belfast [Ireland] Newspapers, folder 2, SCL; Charles Woodmason, *The Carolina Backcountry on the Eve of Revolution: The Journal and Other Writings of Charles Woodmason, Anglican Itinerant,* ed. Richard J. Hooker (Chapel Hill: University of North Carolina Press, 1953), 6. See Crowley, *This Sheba, Self,* 83; Rachel N. Klein, *Unification of a Slave State: The Rise of the Planter Class in the South Carolina Backcountry, 1760–1808* (Chapel Hill: University of North Carolina Press, 1990), 47–48, 58–61. On the problem of "vagrants" and "white Indians" in Georgia, see Mart A. Stewart, " 'Whether Wast, Deodand, or Stray': Cattle, Culture, and the Environment of Early Georgia," *Agricultural History* 65 (1991): 25–26.

97. Entry for 24 May 1780, John Peebles Diary, SCL. On white "barbarism" on the frontier, see *Colonial South Carolina Scene,* 234–235, 241; see also Klingberg, *Appraisal of the Negro,* 48.

98. Mowat, *East Florida,* 5; Lewis, "Cracker," 188–202. These characterizations were made by Spanish authorities c. 1790 about the poor settlers who remained after the British withdrawal.

99. Alexander Grant, quoted in Bailyn, *Voyagers to the West,* 440–441.

100. HL to James Grant, 30 January 1767, in *PHL,* 5:228; HL to James Grant, 22 December 1768, ibid., 6:233; *American Husbandry,* 366 ("dubious articles ... languor"); HL to Richard Oswald, 28 May 1771, in *PHL,* 7:501; HL to Andrew Turnbull, 14 November 1768, ibid., 6:155. On indigo exports from East Florida, see Mowat, *East Florida,* 77–78; see also *Colonial Plantations and Economy in Florida,* ed. Jane G. Landers (Gainesville: University Press of Florida, 2000), 39, 20–21, 48–52, 70.

101. Bailyn, *Voyagers to the West,* 453; HL to John Bartram, 9 August 1766, in *PHL,* 5:152; William Bartram, *The Travels of William Bartram: Naturalist's Edition,* ed. Francis Harper (1791; repr., New Haven, Conn.: Yale University Press, 1958), 60–61, 160. On Rolle, see Bailyn, *Voyagers to the West,* 447–451; see also Charles L. Mowat, "The Tribulations of Denys Rolle," *Florida Historical Quarterly* 23 (1944): 1–14.

102. *The Antislavery Debate: Capitalism and Abolitionism as a Problem in Historical Interpretation,* ed. Thomas Bender (Berkeley: University of California Press, 1992).

103. George Ogilvie, *Carolina; Or, The Planter* (1776), repr. in *Southern Literary Journal,* special issue (1986); David S. Shields argues that Ogilvie maintained

a critical, metropolitan view of Carolina rice farming's departures from British forms, however, in "George Ogilvie's *Carolina; Or, The Planter* (1776)," *Southern Literary Journal*, special issue (1986): 8–9. Jack P. Greene, "Creolean Despotism: The Humanitarian Critique of Slaveholders and the Reassessment of Empire in Metropolitan Britain during the Late Eighteenth Century" (paper presented at the Illinois Program for Research in the Humanities Conference on "The South," Urbana, Ill., 5 April 2003).

104. Samuel Martin, *An Essay upon Plantership, Humbly Inscrib'd to All the Planters of the British Sugar-Colonies in America*, 2nd ed. (Antigua, 1750), vii, 9, iii, 19–20, ECCO.

105. Ibid., vi–vii, 9, 10–14. On plantership, see also Richard B. Sheridan, *Sugar and Slavery: An Economic History of the British West Indies, 1623–1775* (Baltimore: Johns Hopkins University Press, 1974), chap. 7.

106. Chaplin, *Anxious Pursuit*, chap. 2.

107. *American Husbandry*, 272–273, 277.

108. Joan Thirsk, *Fenland Farming in the Sixteenth Century* (Leicester, U.K.: University College, 1953), 4–5, 9, 27–28; De Brahm, *History of Georgia*, 51 ("professed").

109. See, for example, J. G. A. Pocock, *The Machiavellian Moment: Florentine Political Thought in the Atlantic Republican Tradition* (Princeton, N.J.: Princeton University Press, 1975), 15–19.

110. Records in the British Public Record Office Relating to South Carolina, South Carolina Department of Archives and History, Columbia, 17:334. On positive early-eighteenth-century associations between slavery and improvement, see ibid., 5:206. On slaves serving in arms in the militia, see ibid., 5: 204.

111. Seymour Drescher, *The Mighty Experiment: Free Labor versus Slavery in British Emancipation* (New York: Oxford University Press, 2002).

112. On planters and provincialism, see Burnard, *Creole Gentlemen*, chap. 7; Rozbicki, *Complete Colonial Gentleman*, 120–126.

113. See J. G. A. Pocock, "British History: A Plea for a New Subject," *Journal of Modern History* 47 (1975): 601–621; see also Linda Colley, "Britishness and Otherness: An Argument," *Journal of British Studies* 31 (1992): 312–316.

114. On American exceptionalism and the environment, see Jack P. Greene, *The Intellectual Construction of America: Exceptionalism and Identity from 1492 to 1800* (Chapel Hill: University of North Carolina Press, 1993).

6. Henry Laurens's Empire

1. Quotations from Egerton Leigh, *The Man Unmasked; or, The World Undeceived . . .* (1769), in *The Papers of Henry Laurens*, ed. Philip M. Hamer

et al., 16 vols. (Columbia: University of South Carolina Press, 1968–2003), 6:457 (hereafter cited as *PHL*). In addition to his plantations, Henry Laurens (hereafter cited as HL) owned vessels, developed urban properties, and was a partner is a large backcountry farming venture. He continued to participate, on a limited basis, in transatlantic trade after 1765. In 1768 he claimed to have sold 10 percent of all South Carolina rice exported that season, HL to George Appleby, 24 May 1768, ibid., 5:688.

2. See Eugene D. Genovese, *The World the Slaveholders Made: Two Essays in Interpretation* (New York: Pantheon, 1969); Peter A. Coclanis, *The Shadow of a Dream: Economic Life and Death in the South Carolina Low Country, 1670–1920* (New York: Oxford University Press, 1989); see also Joyce E. Chaplin, *An Anxious Pursuit: Agricultural Innovation and Modernity in the Lower South, 1730–1815* (Chapel Hill: University of North Carolina Press, 1993), 11–17.

3. Henry Laurens Account Book, Robert Scott Small Library, Special Collections, College of Charleston, S.C. (hereafter HL Account Book).

4. John Michael Vlach, *The Planter's Prospect: Privilege and Slavery in Plantation Paintings* (Chapel Hill: University of North Carolina Press, 2002); Rhys Isaac, *The Transformation of Virginia, 1740–1790* (New York: W. W. Norton, 1982), 34–42.

5. HL to Richard Oswald, 27 April 1768, in *PHL*, 5:663; HL to James Grant, 22 January 1769, ibid., 6:251.

6. HL to Abraham Schad, 10 March 1766, ibid., 5:85–86; HL to Elias Ball, 28 February 1766, ibid., 5:81–82. Merchant Benjamin Perdrieau owned a one-third share in the *Wambaw* along with Ball and Laurens when it was built in 1760. Anne Baker Leland Bridges and Roy Williams III, *St. James Santee Plantation Parish: History and Records, 1685–1925* (Spartanburg, S.C.: Reprint Company, 1997), 49; *PHL*, 2:xvii; HL to Richard Oswald, 27 April 1768, ibid., 5:668; "Deed for Purchase of Wambaw Plantation," 11–12 May 1756, ibid., 2:180; "Purchase of 500 Acres of Wambaw Swamp," 13 February 1759, ibid., 3:2.

7. David Hancock, *Citizens of the World: London Merchants and the Integration of the British Atlantic Community, 1735–1785* (New York: Cambridge University Press, 1995), 105–107; William Watson, quoted in ibid., 106 ("communion"). Examples of plantation partnerships can be found in Alexander Moore, "Daniel Axtell's Account Book and the Economy of Early South Carolina," *South Carolina Historical Magazine* 95 (1994): 289 (hereafter cited as *SCHM*); Martin, *South-Carolina Gazette*, 9 October 1736 (hereafter cited as *SCG*); *PHL*, 3:81n; Entries relating to Brunswick Plantation, 1769, Henry Ravenel Day Book, South Carolina Historical Society, Charleston (hereafter cited as *SCHS*); Thomas Gullan to Edward Telfair, 12 March

1774, Edward Telfair Papers, William R. Perkins Library, Manuscripts Department, Duke University, Durham, N.C.

8. HL to John Coming Ball, 7 January 1763, in *PHL*, 3:207; HL to James Grant, 3 November 1763, ibid., 4:488; HL to Ball, 29 November 1763, ibid., 4:59 ("every loss"); HL to Ball, 27 December 1766, ibid., 4:112; HL to William Stork, 28 January 1768, ibid., 5:573 ("Axe to each"); HL to Cowles & Harford, 5 July 1762, ibid., 3:105 ("our crop"). HL's Wambaw activities: ibid., 3:208, 218–219.

9. "Purchase of Mepkin Plantation," 5 June 1762, ibid., 3:100; HL to Watson, Gregory, & Delmestre, 24 January 1763, ibid., 3:218–219; Robert Raper to John Colleton, 27 February 1762, Robert Raper Letterbook (photocopy of original in West Sussex Record Office), SCHS; HL to James Lawrence, 1 January 1763, in *PHL*, 3:203.

10. George D. Terry, " 'Champaign Country': A Social History of an Eighteenth Century Lowcountry Parish in South Carolina, St. Johns Berkeley County" (Ph.D. dissertation, University of South Carolina, Columbia, 1981), 20; HL to Taylor & Graham, 12 January 1770, in *PHL*, 7:218. For the period 1766–1773, transportation and marketing costs for Mepkin were equal to 1.1 percent of sales; costs for Wambaw were equal to 2.3 percent of sales, HL Account Book. On Mepkin transportation, see also *PHL*, 16:610n, 668, 723–724, 729.

11. HL to Richard Oswald, 26 May 1757, in *PHL*, 2:203; HL to Gidney Clarke, 21 February 1756, ibid., 2:100; HL to Oswald, 27 April 1768, ibid., 5:668.

12. HL to James Grant, 3 November 1763, ibid., 4:488; HL to John Coming Ball, 29 November 1763, ibid., 4:58–59.

13. HL to James Grant, 30 January 1767, ibid., 5:226; James Habersham to HL, 3 June 1771, ibid., 7:516.

14. HL to James Grant, 22 April 1766, ibid., 5:107–108; HL to Andrew Turnbull, 14 November 1768, ibid., 6:155–156; HL to John Holman, 8 September 1770, ibid., 7:345; see also David R. Chesnutt, "South Carolina's Penetration of Georgia in the 1760's: Henry Laurens as a Case Study," *SCHM* 73 (1972): 194–208.

15. Navigation: HL to Richard Oswald, 27 April 1768, in *PHL*, 5:667–668; HL to James Grant, 30 January 1767, ibid., 5:226. HL to John Holman, 8 September 1770, ibid., 7:345 ("my Barn"); HL to Jonathan Bryan, 4 September 1767, ibid., 5:289–291.

16. For the period 1766–1773, transportation and marketing costs for Broughton Island and New Hope were equal to 4.0 percent of sales; costs for Wright's Savannah were equal to 5.2 percent of sales, HL Account Book. HL to John Holman, 8 September 1770, in *PHL*, 7:345; HL to Jonathan Bryan, 4 September 1767, ibid., 5:290.

17. HL to Zachary Villepontoux, 11 May 1764, in *PHL*, 4:278; HL to Joseph Rainford, 17 December 1764, ibid., 4:536. On shipping tonnage departing Charlestown, see Stephen G. Hardy, "Colonial South Carolina's Rice Industry and the Atlantic Economy: Patterns of Trade, Shipping, and Growth, 1715–1775," in *Money, Trade, and Power: The Evolution of South Carolina's Plantation Society*, ed. Jack P. Greene, Rosemary Brana-Shute, and Randy J. Sparks (Columbia: University of South Carolina Press, 2001), table 5.4, 130.

18. "Remonstrance of Divers Inhabitants of the Province of South Carolina," November 1767, Charles Garth Papers, SCHS; "Seizure of the *Wambaw*," 17 July 1767, in *PHL*, 5:273; HL to James Grant, 12 August 1767, ibid., 5:278.

19. Thomas C. Barrow, *Trade and Empire: The British Customs Service in Colonial America, 1660–1775* (Cambridge, Mass.: Harvard University Press, 1967), 204–211; Daniel J. McDonough, *Christopher Gadsden and Henry Laurens: The Parallel Lives of Two American Patriots* (Selinsgrove, Penn.: Susquehanna University Press, 2000), 80–98; David Duncan Wallace, *The Life of Henry Laurens, with a Sketch of the Life of Lieutenant-Colonel John Laurens* (New York: G. P. Putnam's Sons, 1915), 137–149. On Laurens-owned vessels, see *PHL*, 6:610–611.

20. HL to James Habersham, 5 September 1767, in *PHL*, 5:294; McDonough, *Gadsden and Laurens*, chap. 5.

21. Leigh, *Man Unmasked*, 6:457, 465, 520, 472, 514, 492, 459, 517, 519. On the political and moral critique of early modern commerce, see J. G. A. Pocock, *Virtue, Commerce, and History: Essays on Political Thought and History, Chiefly in the Eighteenth Century* (Cambridge: Cambridge University Press, 1985), 103–123; Jean-Christophe Agnew, *Worlds Apart: The Market and the Theater in Anglo-American Thought, 1550–1750* (New York: Cambridge University Press, 1986); Michal J. Rozbicki, *The Complete Colonial Gentleman: Cultural Legitimacy in Plantation America* (Charlottesville: University Press of Virginia, 1998), 61–69.

22. Leigh, *Man Unmasked*, 6:503; responses to "mercantile patriots": *PHL*, 6:64–65, 106, 346, 363–364.

23. Laurens refuted Leigh in the appendix to a second edition of his *Extracts* in which he took issue with the charge that he was a "dabbler" at least twice, *PHL*, 7:11, 51.

24. HL to Devonsheir & Reeve, 12 September 1764, ibid., 4:419; HL to James Grant, 27 October 1765, ibid., 7:174.

25. On integration as an innovative feature of eighteenth-century transatlantic commerce, see Hancock, *Citizens of the World*, 171–172.

26. On arcadian impulses, see Jack P. Greene, *Imperatives, Behaviors, and Iden-*

tities: Essays in Early American Cultural History (Charlottesville: University Press of Virginia, 1992), 230–231.

27. HL to Joseph Brown, 4 October 1765, in *PHL,* 5:16–17; HL to George Appleby, 24 May 1768, ibid., 5:688; HL to James Laurens, 27 May 1772, ibid., 8:341.

28. This isolation was more a characteristic of New Hope and Broughton Island than it was of Wright's Savannah, which joined a neighborhood of tidal rice plantations and was within a day's canoe ride from Savannah. See HL to Richard Oswald, 27 April 1768, ibid., 5:668; "frontier": HL to Joseph Clay, 2 September 1777, ibid., 11:482; HL to William Brisbane, 6 September 1776, ibid., 11:264.

29. William Barham to New Hope Plantation, 25 May 1771, HL Account Book. Proceeds from onetime shipments of corn and beef, credited to the frontier plantations, seem to have been merely delivered there to a buyer rather than produced by slaves on-site. Richard Lamton to Broughton Island Plantation, 30 April 1767, ibid.; Lachlan McIntosh to Broughton Island Plantation, 4 August 1769, ibid.

30. HL to Richard Oswald, 27 April 1768, in *PHL,* 5:667; HL to Oswald, 28 May 1771, ibid., 7:502; HL to James Habersham, 3 June 1771, ibid., 7:513; HL to Lachlan McIntosh, 20 December 1771, ibid., 8:109.

31. HL Account Book; see also James Laurens to HL, 17 November 1772, in *PHL,* 8:498.

32. James Laurens to HL, 19 December 1772, in *PHL,* 8:504–505.

33. HL to John Smith, 17 September 1765, ibid., 5:6; HL to Smith, 8 March 1766, ibid., 5:84; HL to Samuel Wragg, 5 April 1766, ibid., 5:98–99.

34. HL to John Tarleton, 23 January 1768, ibid., 5:559; HL to Timothy Creamer, 25 January 1765, ibid., 4:571. The Colleton family's Wadboo Barony plantations also featured planter-owned schooners, sawmilling, and firewood production. Robert Raper to John Colleton, 10 May 1759, Raper Letterbook.

35. HL to James Marion, 10 July 1765, in *PHL,* 4:649; HL to Marion, 13 July 1765, ibid., 4:651; HL to Nathaniel Savineau, 15 August 1765, ibid., 4:660; HL to James Cordes Jr., 30 August 1765, ibid., 4:670; on prices, see Coclanis, *Shadow of a Dream,* 106–109.

36. Mepkin Plantation sold firewood between June 1766 and May 1767 during the following months: October (£889), December (£785), March (£602), April (£68), and May (£5); in 1771–1772 firewood sales of more than £100 occurred in each month from November through May. HL Account Book.

37. HL to James Laurens, 8 January 1773, in *PHL,* 8:525.

38. HL to James Laurens, 12 June 1772, ibid., 8:370–371; James Habersham to HL, 3 June 1771, ibid., 7:516; HL to Lachlan McIntosh, 15 January 1770, ibid., 7:219. In 1772 there were "about 300" acres planted in rice at both

Broughton Island and New Hope plantations, James Laurens to HL, 12 June 1772, ibid., 8:371. During the 1771–1772 season New Hope sold £7 of rice for every £10 sold by Broughton Island; on the basis of a 7:10 ratio, we can estimate rice acreage at approximately 125 and 175 acres, respectively, HL Account Book.

39. HL to Richard Oswald, 27 April 1768, in *PHL*, 5:668; HL to William Mayne, 20 August 1766, ibid., 5:169; HL to Lachlan McIntosh, 20 August 1772, ibid., 8:432; HL to McIntosh, 3 March 1769, ibid., 6:398; John Lewis Gervais to HL, 5–10 May 1772, ibid., 8:287. On Laurens's concerns for water on Wright's Savannah, see also ibid., 5:65, 8:291; on the legal battle over this dam, see ibid., 8:286, 11:361, 361n, 380–381, 407, 412; Laurens secured a memorandum that gave him the right to drain Wright's Savannah through an adjoining property's drains, ibid., 5:671. On disputes over water in general, see Chaplin, *Anxious Pursuit*, 244–247. Chaplin's reference to a dispute between Laurens and Christopher Gadsden refers to their bordering suburban, not plantation, properties, as is claimed, ibid., 245; see *PHL*, 16: 366n.

40. Mepkin House: HL to William Yate, 5 February 1766, in *PHL*, 5:69; HL to John Smith, 9 May 1766, ibid., 5:125. Sheds: HL to James Russell, 3 March 1766, ibid., 5:84; HL to Russell, 31 March 1766, ibid., 5:94–95. HL to Abraham Schad, 1 February 1766, ibid., 5:62 (chimneys); see also ibid., 5: 3, 6, 46–47. HL to James Laurens, 5 December 1771, ibid., 8:67 ("his boys").

41. Slave "huts": HL to Peter Broughton, 1 October 1765, ibid., 5:14; HL to Baron von Steuben, 14 January 1778, ibid., 12:304. HL to Lachlan McIntosh, 10 May 1769, ibid., 6:445, 445n (Zopfi); John Lewis Gervais to HL, 5–10 May 1772, ibid., 8:287–291; HL to James Laurens, 12 December 1771, ibid., 8:90 ("Poverty").

42. HL to James Laurens, 5 December 1771, ibid., 8:66–67. Laurens hired a single slave carpenter for seventeen months on Broughton Island and another for five weeks at Wright's Savannah, Broughton Island Plantation to William Hopton, 12 November 1766, HL Account Book; Wright's Savannah Plantation to James Moore, 28 September 1772, ibid. Broughton Island lacked a barn in 1768, but one had been built by 1770, *PHL* 5:667–668, 7: 345. Massey was present at Broughton Island in 1770, ibid., 7:234.

43. HL to John Lewis Gervais, 1 September 1766, in *PHL*, 5:181–182; HL to John Miller, 25 October 1770, ibid., 7:386.

44. Of 59 slaves sent to frontier plantations, 40 were identified by sex (68 percent); of those identified, 26 were male and 14 were female. Information regarding origin at time of purchase was recorded for 33 of these 59 (56 percent); 25 were identified as "new Negroes"; 8 were either purchased at auction or were previously the joint property of HL and other slave owners

in South Carolina subsequently purchased by him for the plantations. HL Account Book.

45. Philip D. Morgan, *Slave Counterpoint: Black Culture in the Eighteenth-Century Chesapeake and Lowcountry* (Chapel Hill: University of North Carolina Press, 1998), 70–71, table 14; see also Jennifer L. Morgan, *Laboring Women: Reproduction and Gender in New World Slavery* (Philadelphia: University of Pennsylvania Press, 2004), chap. 3; HL to Richard Oswald & Company, 3 March 1764, in *PHL,* 4:203–204.

46. Johann Martin Bolzius, "Johann Martin Bolzius Answers a Questionnaire on Carolina and Georgia," ed. and trans. Klaus G. Loewald et al., *William and Mary Quarterly,* 3rd ser., 14 (1957): 257; HL to John Holman, 8 September 1770, in *PHL,* 7:344; William Gerhard De Brahm, "Philosophico-Historico-Hydrogeography of South Carolina, Georgia, and East Florida," in *Documents Connected with the History of South Carolina,* ed. P. C. J. Weston (London, 1856), 197–198; John Drayton, *A View of South-Carolina, as Respects Her Natural and Civil Concerns* (Charleston, S.C., 1802), 116. On gender and rice milling, see Judith A. Carney, *Black Rice: The African Origins of Rice Cultivation in the Americas* (Cambridge, Mass.: Harvard University Press, 2001), 119–121; on lighter rice-pounding tasks for women, see Edward McCrady, *The History of South Carolina under the Royal Government, 1719–1776* (New York: Macmillan, 1899), 387.

47. HL to Abraham Schad, 16 May 1765, in *PHL,* 4:625; HL to Timothy Creamer, 26 January 1764, ibid., 4:148; HL to James Theodore Rossel, 8 April 1766, ibid., 5:99–100.

48. See Richard B. Sheridan, "The Domestic Economy," in *Colonial British America: Essays in the New History of the Early Modern Era,* ed. Jack P. Greene and J. R. Pole (Baltimore: Johns Hopkins University Press, 1984), 43–85.

49. HL to William Bell, 7 December 1785, in *PHL,* 16:610; HL to Abraham Schad, 30 April 1765, ibid., 4:616; HL to William Yate, 5 February 1766, ibid., 5:70; John Lewis Gervais to HL, 5–10 May 1772, ibid., 8:288; James Laurens to HL, 26 March 1773, ibid., 8:646.

50. On Laurens, patriarchy, and paternalism, see Philip D. Morgan, "Three Planters and Their Slaves: Perspectives on Slavery in Virginia, South Carolina, and Jamaica, 1750–1790," in *Race and Family in the Colonial South,* ed. Winthrop D. Jordan and Sheila Skemp (Jackson: University Press of Mississippi, 1987), 54–68; Robert Olwell, " 'A Reckoning of Accounts': Patriarchy, Market Relations, and Control on Henry Laurens's Lowcountry Plantations, 1762–1785," in *Working toward Freedom: Slave Society and Domestic Economy in the American South,* ed. Larry E. Hudson Jr. (Rochester, N.Y.: University of Rochester Press, 1994), 33–52; Jeffrey Robert Young,

Domesticating Slavery: The Master Class in Georgia and South Carolina, 1670–1837 (Chapel Hill: University of North Carolina Press, 1999), 38–54, 60–81, 87–88. On paternalism and patriarchy as categories applied to different slave societies, see Daniel C. Littlefield, *Rice and Slaves: Ethnicity and the Slave Trade in Colonial South Carolina* (Baton Rouge: Louisiana State University Press, 1981), 62–63.

51. HL to Lachlan McIntosh, 13 March 1773, in *PHL*, 8:618; HL to Peter Nephew, 20 December 1771, ibid., 8:111.

52. HL to William Keith, [June 1764], ibid., 4:297; Wallace, *Life of Laurens*, 62; James Custer to HL, June 1780, in *PHL*, 15:302.

53. HL to Lachlan McIntosh, 14–15 August 1764, in *PHL*, 4:368 ("Cottage"); HL to James Grant, 22 April 1766, ibid., 5:109 ("docks"); HL to Benjamin Addison, 26 May 1768, ibid., 5:702 ("brick House"). House interior and furnishings: HL to John Knight, 24 August 1764, ibid., 4:379; HL to McIntosh, 14–15 August 1764, ibid., 4:368; "Newspaper Account," 28 November 1771, ibid., 8:61–62; James Laurens to John Laurens, 5 December 1771, ibid., 8:81–84. On the cottage as a symbol of "picturesque comfort," see John E. Crowley, *The Invention of Comfort: Sensibilities and Design in Early Modern Britain and Early America* (Baltimore: Johns Hopkins University Press, 2001), 203–260.

54. HL to Benjamin Addison, 26 May 1768, in *PHL*, 5:702; Leigh, *Man Unmasked*, 6:238; HL to James Laurens, 6 February 1772, ibid., 8:174; Wallace, *Life of Laurens*, 46, 63; HL to John Lewis Gervais, 1 September 1766, in *PHL*, 5:181.

55. HL to John Gordon, 2 October 1765, in *PHL*, 5:15.

56. John Lewis Gervais to HL, 5–10 May 1772, ibid., 8:288.

57. HL Account Book. The heading "Expenses" details what the Ansonborough household supplied to the enterprise and consumed from it.

58. HL to William Yate, 24 February 1766, in *PHL*, 5:76. It seems likely that goods consumed by Broughton Island and New Hope plantations, located across the Altamaha River from one another, were debited from Broughton Island's account alone.

59. HL to John Smith, 7 February 1766, in *PHL*, 5:72–73; HL to Smith, 10 September 1766, ibid., 5:189; James Laurens to HL, 19 December 1772, ibid., 8:504; HL to Timothy Creamer, 25 January 1765, ibid., 4:571–572. On the emergence of the futures market, see William Cronon, *Nature's Metropolis: Chicago and the Great West* (New York: W. W. Norton, 1991), 120–132. Laurens's prediction that the price of corn would rise was validated when it rose by 100 percent in 1766, from 12 shillings 6 pence per bushel to 25 shillings. HL Account Book.

60. Corn accounted for the bulk of total food sold (7,830 bushels valued at £6,110) and about half of total food and alcohol purchased (2,946 bushels valued at £1,739). The average sale price of corn was £.78; the average purchase price was £.59. If Laurens had never purchased those 2,946 bushels, but instead had engaged in strict "safety-first" agriculture by marketing only the surplus after consumption, he would have foregone £560 in lost revenue at that price differential, approximately the cost of two adult field slaves. HL Account Book.

61. John Guerard to Thomas Rock, 21 February 1753, John Guerard Letterbook, SCHS; HL to Devonsheir & Reeve, 16 December 1762, in *PHL*, 3: 192; HL to John Tarleton, 20 February 1770, ibid., 7:236; Judith A. Carney, "Rice Milling, Gender and Slave Labour in Colonial South Carolina," *Past and Present* 153 (1996): 118n. Examples of low-quality rice sold "rough" or used as slave provisions can be found in Josiah Smith Jr. to George Smith, 14 January 1781, in Josiah Smith Jr. Letterbook, Southern Historical Collection, University of North Carolina, Chapel Hill; Smith to George Appleby, 30 March 1784, ibid.; John Lewis Gervais to HL, 21 October 1778, Gervais and Laurens Correspondence, Henry Laurens Papers (hereafter cited as HL Papers), SCHS.

62. HL to Benjamin Addison, 26 May 1768, in *PHL*, 5:702; HL to Timothy Creamer, 26 June 1764, ibid., 4:319; HL to John Coming Ball, [June 1764], ibid., 4:297–298; HL to James Grant, 1 November 1765, ibid., 5:35. John Bartram reported that the garden was "wal[l]ed with brick, 200 yards long & 150 broad," in "Diary of a Journey through the Carolinas, Georgia and Florida from July 1, 1765, to April 10, 1766," *Transactions of the American Philosophical Society* 33 (1942): 15n.

63. Garden products: HL to Peter Bachop, 10 September 1770, in *PHL*, 7:357; HL to James Grant, 13 November 1766, ibid., 5:212–213; John Laurens to HL, 6 January 1773, ibid., 8:524; Bartram, "Diary of a Journey," 15n; HL to Judith Ball, 5 September 1770, in *PHL*, 7:333. James Laurens to John Laurens, 5 December 1771, ibid., 8:84 (greenhouse); for another example of experimental gardening, see ibid., 6:587n.

64. HL to Elizabeth Baker, 2 February 1769, in *PHL*, 6:263 ("fine garden"). Food crops: HL to James Grant, 5 December 1771, ibid., 8:84; HL to James Laurens, 12 December 1771, ibid., 8:96. HL to Benjamin Addison, 26 May 1768, ibid., 5:702 ("moderate Fare"); HL to John Laurens, 1 July 1771, ibid., 8:388 ("dissipation"). HL's consumption: HL to John Lewis Gervais, 22 March 1773, ibid., 8:632–633; see also 8:518, 526, 601.

65. Experimental commodities: HL to James Laurens, 23 January 1773, ibid., 8:545; ibid., 8:611–612n; HL to Bright & Milward, 10 September 1770, ibid.,

7:356. HL to John Lewis Gervais, 29 January 1766, ibid., 5:55 ("Mrs. Laurens's Garden"). For a list of the plants and seeds HL requested "Sufficient for a Gentleman's private Kitchen Garden," see ibid., 9:629.

66. HL to James Laurens, 15 April 1772, ibid., 8:271; HL to John Augustus Shubart, 31 December 1763, ibid., 4:11.

67. Goods to Ansonborough: HL to James Brenard, 27 April 1763, ibid., 3:425–426; HL to Brenard, 6 January 1764, ibid., 4:121; HL to Abraham Schad, 1 October 1765, ibid., 5:11; HL to James Grant, 30 January 1767, ibid., 5:227. The plantations supplied £969 worth of goods debited from "Expenses," including 129 cords of firewood, nearly 2,500 pounds of corn blades, and supplies of corn, beef, turkeys, pigs, potatoes, and peas, HL Account Book.

68. See Morgan, "Three Planters," 55–58.

69. HL to William Carter, 28 December 1770, in *PHL*, 7:418; HL to Joseph Brown, 21 August 1766, ibid., 5:170–171; HL to John Knight, 22 December 1763, ibid., 4:94.

70. HL to John Lewis Gervais, 5 September 1777, ibid., 11:491–492; HL to Magnus Watson, 15 February 1770, ibid., 7:234; "Bill of Sale," 11 April 1764, ibid., 4:241; Joanna Bowen Gillespie, *The Life and Times of Martha Laurens Ramsay, 1759–1811* (Columbia: University of South Carolina Press, 2001), 25 (paths); S. Max Edelson, "Affiliation without Affinity: Skilled Slaves in Eighteenth-Century South Carolina," in *Money, Trade, and Power*, 237–238.

71. HL to James Laurens, 27 May 1772, in *PHL*, 8:341 ("Town Negroes"). Stepney at Mepkin: HL to James Lawrence, 1 January 1763, ibid., 3:203; HL to John Smith, 30 August 1766, ibid., 5:175–176; HL to Smith, 15 August 1765, ibid., 4:661. Stepney's work and drinking: HL to Benjamin Addison, 26 May 1768, ibid., 5:702; HL to James Laurens, 5 December 1771, ibid., 8:67–68. Stepney's relationship with HL: HL to James Laurens, 12 December 1771, ibid., 8:96; HL to John Laurens, 12 December 1774, ibid., 10:2–3. See also Morgan, "Three Planters," 57–58; Edelson, "Affiliation without Affinity," 236–238. On urban slaves assisting in trade, see *PHL*, 4:138.

72. For the period 1766–1773, total plantation expenses for cloth and related materials were £4,441; total plantation provisions expenses, including items purchased and exchanged among plantations, were £5,242. Total recorded alcohol purchases for the plantations included 482 gallons of rum in addition to dozens of bottles and barrels of wine, beer, and ale. HL Account Book.

73. HL to John Jackson, 19 March 1766, in *PHL*, 5:91; HL to Joseph Brown, 4 October 1765, ibid., 5:16–17.

74. HL to John Lewis Gervais, 17 August 1772, ibid., 8:421–422; HL to John

Smith, 1 October 1765, ibid., 5:11. On special foods to overseers, see ibid., 7:562, 574. For another example of overseer consumption, see Robert Raper to John Colleton, 3 April 1760, Raper Letterbook. On the overseer shares system on the Laurens enterprise, see *PHL,* 5:100, 7:513, 8:635.

75. HL to John Smith, 5 September 1765, in *PHL,* 5:4 ("House"); HL to James Brenard, 27 April 1763, ibid., 3:425 ("Plantation"). Goods for sick slaves: HL to Smith, 30 May 1765, ibid., 4:632–633; HL to Smith, 4 October 1765, ibid., 5:16; Mepkin Plantation to Expenses, 28 June 1771, HL Account Book; Mepkin Plantation to Joseph Turpin Jr., 30 December 1772, ibid. Rum and sugar were reserved for overseer use except when distributed to sick slaves on the Colleton plantations, Robert Raper to John Colleton, 3 April 1760, Raper Letterbook.

76. Bolzius, "Questionnaire on Carolina," 256.

77. HL to Abraham Schad, 30 April 1765, in *PHL,* 4:616; HL to Schad, 14 February 1766, ibid., 5:73; Wright's Savannah Plantation to Hawkins Petrie & Co., February and March 1773, HL Account Book; HL to John Smith, 29 January 1766, in *PHL,* 5:57.

78. HL to Frederick Wiggins, 30 November 1765, in *PHL,* 5:41; HL to Abraham Schad, 30 April 1765, ibid., 4:616.

79. Thomas L. Haskell, "Capitalism and the Origins of the Humanitarian Sensibility, Part 2," *American Historical Review* 90 (1985): 550–561; Wambaw Plantation to Alexander Gillon, 1 March 1769, HL Account Book.

80. HL to Abraham Schad, 7 October 1765, in *PHL,* 5:20.

81. HL to Timothy Creamer, 26 June 1764, ibid., 4:319. In this instance, Laurens gave caps to male slaves only, but in others, new slaves were to receive "each good Cloth[e]s and a good Blanket and Cap," HL to James Habersham, 3 June 1771, ibid., 7:513.

82. HL to Felix Warley, 10 October 1771, ibid., 8:6; HL to James Laurens, 22 January 1773, ibid., 8:534–535; Robert Raper to John Colleton, 2 March 1763, Raper Letterbook. Blankets: HL to William Cowles & Co., 9 May 1768, in *PHL,* 5:678, 678n; HL to William Manning, 5 November 1774, ibid., 9:627. HL to Peter Nephew, 20 December 1771, ibid., 8:111. On Laurens's concern for buying high-quality cloth, see also ibid., 9:24, 386. On contemporary English concerns for poverty and material comfort, see Crowley, *Invention of Comfort,* 216–223. For a different interpretation of these patriarchal exchanges, see Robert Olwell, *Masters, Slaves, and Subjects: The Culture of Power in the South Carolina Low Country, 1740–1790* (Ithaca, N.Y.: Cornell University Press, 1998), 203–205.

83. HL to John Smith, 10 September 1766, in *PHL,* 5:189; HL to Bridgen & Waller, 25 March 1785, ibid., 16:545; HL to Abraham Schad, 1 October 1765, ibid., 5:12.

84. Providing clothing: HL to Abraham Schad, 1 April 1765, ibid., 4:598; HL to James Laurens, 12 December 1771, ibid., 8:91; HL to Timothy Creamer, 18 August 1764, ibid., 4:369; HL to John Smith, 10 September 1766, ibid., 5:189 (sheets); HL to Smith, 17 September 1765, ibid., 5:7 ("rags"). Care for slaves: HL to Schad, 7 June 1765, ibid., 4:634; HL to John Bartram, 9 August 1766, ibid., 5:154. HL to Schad, 9 April 1766, ibid., 5:100–101 ("diligence . . . frugality").

85. J. C. Flugel, quoted in David Kuchta, "The Making of the Self-Made Man: Class, Clothing, and English Masculinity, 1688–1832," in *The Sex of Things: Gender and Consumption in Historical Perspective*, ed. Victoria de Grazia (Berkeley: University of California Press, 1996), 54.

86. HL to Thomas Corbett, 4 April 1771, in *PHL*, 7:474; HL to William Howell, 11 May 1772, ibid., 8:303; HL to James Laurens, 13 April 1774, ibid., 9:407; HL to Howell, 6 November 1774, ibid., 9:633–634.

87. Ibid., 8:89n; J[ohn] Channing to [Edward Telfair], 10 August 1786, Telfair Papers; on special clothing provided to "Boat Negroes," see *PHL*, 11:385–386.

88. *PHL*, 14:xxxi; Leigh, *Man Unmasked*, 6:489.

89. HL to John Lewis Gervais, 10 April 1766, in *PHL*, 10:105; HL to Abraham Schad, 30 April 1765, ibid., 4:616; HL to John Smith, 5 September 1765, ibid., 5:2–3; on Abram (also spelled Abraham), see also ibid., 3:207–208, 4:661, 5:11, 70. This limit of "twenty lashes" applied only to whippings by provincial officials. No limit applied to masters beating their own slaves, provided they were carried out with a "horse-whip, cow-skin, switch or small stick" and did not result in permanent maiming. *Statutes at Large of the State of South Carolina*, ed. Thomas Cooper and David J. McCord, 10 vols. (Columbia, S.C., 1836–1841), 7:403–406, 410–411.

90. John Lewis Gervais to HL, 5–10 May 1772, in *PHL*, 8:288–291; see also ibid., 9:167.

91. Mary: HL to William Godfrey, 16 December 1771, ibid., 8:101; John Lewis Gervais to HL, 5–10 May 1772, ibid., 8:290; HL to James Laurens, 12 December 1771, ibid., 8:89. Mary might have been the "Maria" who served Eleanor Laurens at Ansonborough. If so, Laurens apparently banished her to the rice frontier soon after his wife's death for an unrecorded act of insubordination, ibid., 7:299n. Overseer-slave relationships: HL to James Lawrence, 12 February 1763, ibid., 3:248; HL to John Smith, 9 May 1766, ibid., 5:125 (Hagar and Amy); HL to James Habersham, 1 October 1770, ibid., 7:376; HL to Abraham Schad, 1 March 1766, ibid., 5:83; HL to Lachlan McIntosh, 13 March 1773, in ibid., 8:617.

92. March: John Lewis Gervais to HL, 26 July 1777, ibid., 11:407; HL to John Lewis Gervais, 5 September 1777, ibid., 11:487. Cuffee and Mary:

HL to Gervais, 18 October 1777, ibid., 11:565; HL to Gervais, 5 September 1777, ibid., 11:492; HL to William Brisbane, 17 October 1777, ibid., 11:562.

93. HL to Richard Oswald, 27 April 1768, ibid., 5:668; HL to Joseph Brown, 28 June 1765, ibid., 4:645.

94. HL to John Smith, 4 June 1765, ibid., 4:633; see also ibid., 3:205, 4:319, 656.

95. HL to Joseph Brown, 28 June 1765, ibid., 4:645; HL to James Laurens, 5 December 1771, ibid., 8:67; HL to Jacob Read, 15 September 1785, ibid., 16:597; see also ibid., 4:298–299.

96. HL to John McCullough, 27 February 1774, ibid., 9:262; HL to John Smith, 1 October 1765, ibid., 5:11.

97. HL to James Habersham, 3 June 1771, ibid., 7:513.

98. HL to John Smith, 30 May 1765, ibid., 4:633; HL to Frederick Wiggins, 19 March 1766, ibid., 5:91; HL to James Lawrence, 1 January 1763, ibid., 3:203. "Stirrup Oil": HL to William Smith, 25 April 1766, ibid., 5:120; *Oxford English Dictionary Online*, s.v. "stirrup-oil," dictionary.oed.com (accessed 24 April 2004) (hereafter cited as *OED Online*).

99. HL to John Laurens, 14 August 1776, in *PHL*, 11:224.

100. See Drew Gilpin Faust, *James Henry Hammond and the Old South: A Design for Mastery* (Baton Rouge: Louisiana State University Press, 1982); Alex Lichtenstein, " 'That Disposition to Theft, With Which They Have Been Branded': Moral Economy, Slave Management, and the Law," *Journal of Social History* 21 (1988): 413–440.

101. HL to John Polson, 13 November 1770, in *PHL*, 7:401–402; HL to Cowles & Harford, 17 July 1764, ibid., 4:343; James Glen to Lords Commissioners for Trade and Plantations, [c. 1748], Letter Book of James Glen, Dalhousie Muniments: Papers Relating to America, in the Dalhousie Muniments (microfilm of original in the Scottish Record Office), Milton S. Eisenhower Library, Johns Hopkins University, Baltimore, 21. For other examples of plantation returns, see Chaplin, *Anxious Pursuit*, 9.

102. *SCG*, 7 April 1733.

103. Morgan, *Slave Counterpoint*, 97; John J. McCusker and Russell R. Menard, *The Economy of British America, 1607–1789* (Chapel Hill: University of North Carolina Press, 1985), 184–185.

104. James Glen to Lords Commissioners for Trade and Plantations, [c. 1748], Glen Letter Book, 21; Alexander Hewit, *An Historical Account of the Rise and Progress of the Colonies of South Carolina and Georgia*, in *Historical Collections of South Carolina*, ed. B. R. Carroll, 2 vols. (New York, 1836), 1:375–376, 386; R. F. W. Allston, *Essay on Sea Coast Crops* (Charleston, S.C., 1854), 9.

105. HL to George Appleby, 26 September 1769, in *PHL*, 7:151; HL Account Book; HL to John Laurens, 16 September 1776, in *PHL*, 11:268–269.

106. James Laurens to HL, 6 January 1773, in *PHL*, 8:522. Contemporary observers cited the following barrel per hand figures: 4.5 (1761), 7.3 (1762–1763), 8.8 (c. 1770s), 9.8 (1772). James Glen, *A Description of South Carolina . . .* (1761) facsimile repr. in *Colonial South Carolina: Two Contemporary Descriptions,* ed. Chapman J. Milling (Columbia: University of South Carolina Press, 1951), 16; Robert Raper to John Colleton, 2 March 1763, Raper Letterbook; John Gerar William De Brahm, *History of the Province of Georgia* (Wormsloe, Ga., 1849), 50–51; Josiah Smith Jr. to George Austin, 25 February 1772, Smith Letterbook. Average barrel weights for the 1760s remained roughly constant at 525–535 pounds, Hardy, "South Carolina's Rice Industry," table 5.13, 139–140. Planters in 1791 believed that 5–6 barrels per hand were average yields, 8–10 good, and 12–14 extraordinary, Lewis C. Gray, *History of Agriculture in the Southern United States to 1860,* 2 vols. (1933; repr., Gloucester, Mass.: Peter Smith, 1958), 2:730.

107. HL to William Godfrey, 16 December 1771, in *PHL*, 8:100.

108. HL Account Book.

109. *OED Online,* s.v. "plant" (accessed 26 April 2004).

110. HL to William Fisher, 2 November 1770, in *PHL*, 7:396; HL to Habersham, 15 April 1771, ibid., 7:491; HL to Daniel Grant, 27 April 1770, ibid., 7:286 ("with Strangers"); HL to Ann Foster, 24 October 1771, ibid., 8:16 ("another Mother"); HL to Messieurs and Madame Laurence, 25 February 1774, ibid., 9:311 (will not remarry). See also ibid., 7:xvii–xviii, 298, 375–376, 401, 463, 468, 473–474, 545–546, 15:578.

111. For the "Principal Dates of Laurens's Life," see ibid., 16:xliii–xlvi.

112. HL to Richard Oswald, 27 April 1768, ibid., 5:667–668; HL to James Laurens, 13 April 1774, ibid., 9:404; HL to James Laurens, 1 February 1773, ibid., 8:571–572.

113. HL to James Laurens, 13 May 1772, ibid., 8:305; on the Laurens children, see Gillespie, *Martha Laurens Ramsay,* xiii; James Laurens to John Laurens, 5 December 1771, in *PHL*, 8:82; David Ramsay, *Memoirs of Martha Laurens Ramsay* (Philadelphia, 1845), 16, 72–74, 77, 90–91; HL to Jonathan Bryan, 4 September 1767, in *PHL*, 5:289.

114. HL to James Laurens, 11 March 1773, in *PHL*, 8:612; HL to John Delagaye, 6 June 1783, ibid., 16:207. For examples of HL's comments on slave deaths, see ibid., 13:539, 14:39. On masters' emotional indifference to slave deaths, see also Trevor Burnard, *Mastery, Tyranny, and Desire: Thomas Thistlewood and His Slaves in the Anglo-Jamaican World* (Chapel Hill: University of North Carolina Press, 2004), 127–129.

115. HL to Joseph Clay, 2 September 1777, in *PHL*, 11:482 ("remote frontier");

HL to William Manning, 21 August 1775, ibid., 10:342 ("Southward"); HL to John Laurens, 14 August 1776, ibid., 11:223 (abandoned rice); HL to George Appleby, 10 April 1775, ibid., 10:97 (final visit); HL to John Laurens, 16 September 1776, ibid., 11:269 (abandoning the plantations). Threatening forces: HL to John Laurens, 14 August 1776, ibid., 11:223; John Lewis Gervais to HL, 21 September 1778, ibid., 14:333; HL to Martha Laurens, 14 March 1776, ibid., 11:160. See John S. Pancake, *This Destructive War: The British Campaign in the Carolinas, 1780–1782* (Tuscaloosa: University of Alabama Press, 1985), 20–35. Laurens estimated the value of lost rice at the three southern plantations at £5,000 sterling, worth £37,500 in South Carolina currency in 1775, *PHL*, 11:269; on currency conversion rates, see John J. McCusker, *Money and Exchange in Europe and America, 1600–1775: A Handbook* (Chapel Hill: University of North Carolina Press, 1978), 317.

116. HL to Joseph Clay, 2 September 1777, in *PHL*, 11:482; "Copy of Mr. James Baileys Letter," 2 June 1778, Letters 1778–1785, HL Papers; John Lewis Gervais to HL, 2 July 1778, in *PHL*, 13:541. On the legal status of the Georgia plantations during and after the war, see also ibid., 12:24n, 16:30n, 265, 584, 584n, 590n, 777.

117. HL to Babut & Labouchere, 29 March 1777, in *PHL*, 11:326; HL to Samuel Johnston, 4 August 1791, ibid., 16:770.

118. Ibid., 11:264n; HL to John Laurens, 16 September 1776, ibid., 11:268–269; HL to John Burnet, 24 July 1778, ibid., 14:65; HL to Francis Dana, 1 March 1778, ibid., 12:491. The Santee River was "for finny-tenants fam'd." George Ogilvie, *Carolina; Or, The Planter* (1776), repr. in *Southern Literary Journal*, special issue (1986): 13.

119. John Lewis Gervais to HL, 5 May 1784, in *PHL*, 16:449; ibid., 15:455n. A single overseer supervised Mepkin and Small's Field plantations in the 1780s, ibid., 16:388.

120. HL to William Manning, 20 October 1775, ibid., 10:485–486 ("what's to come"/"walking"); HL to John Laurens, 22 January 1775, ibid., 10:46 ("pretty Garden"); HL to John Laurens, 21 September 1779, ibid., 15:173 ("Madeira"); HL to William Manning, 14 November 1775, ibid., 10:510 ("improving"); HL to Robert Deans, 6 February 1775, ibid., 10:54 ("Scots Regiment"). See also ibid., 10:204–205.

121. James Custer to HL, June 1780, ibid., 15:301–302; ibid., 15:455n; HL to William Bell, 7 February 1785, ibid., 16:535–536; John Laurens to HL, 25 May 1780, ibid., 15:300.

122. John Lewis Gervais to HL, 22 July 1780, ibid., 15:317; HL to William Bell, 7 December 1785, ibid., 16:610–611.

123. Ibid., 15:xvi–xvii; "Journal and Narrative of Capture and Confinement to the Tower of London," 13 August 1780–4 April 1782, ibid., 15:343.

124. HL to John Laurens, 16 September 1776, ibid., 11:269; HL to Lachlan Mc-
Intosh, 12 May 1777, ibid., 11:337; Rawlins Lowndes to HL, 9 January 1779,
ibid., 15:32.

125. "Copy of Mr. James Baileys Letter," 2 June 1778, Letters 1778–1785, HL
Papers (Thomas). On HL's overseers during the war, see *PHL,* 11:264, 16:
30–31. HL to Lachlan Mcintosh, 24 March 1776, ibid., 11:189 ("removal").

126. John Laurens to James Laurens, 24 October 1776, Letters 1767–1783, Account Book of James Laurens, HL Papers; HL to Richard Oswald, 27 April
1768, in *PHL,* 5:668. Despite HL's statement, slaves had run away from his
plantations before 1773; see ibid., 4:656.

127. James Custer to HL, June 1780, in *PHL,* 15:303–304. Twelve slaves escaped
from Broughton Island in 1773, at least nine of whom were recaptured, HL
to Lachlan McIntosh, 13 March 1773, ibid., 8:617; James Laurens to HL,
26 March 1773, ibid., 8:646–647. A junior overseer at New Hope fled to
Florida with five slaves in 1776, HL to John Laurens, 16 September 1776,
ibid., 11:269. In 1777, four slaves "absconded from Mepkin" and four more
"are gone from Santé," including "Doctor Cuffee," John Lewis Gervais to
HL, 29 July 1777, ibid., 11:411–412. Two others ran away in 1778, Gervais
to HL, 19 April 1778, ibid., 13:155. HL sold Doctor Cuffee in 1778, ibid.,
14:180.

128. Samuel Massey to HL, 12 June 1780, ibid., 15:304–307, 305n. On Massey's
life as HL's slave, see ibid., 16:304–305n. On disease outbreaks in revolutionary South Carolina, see Elizabeth A. Fenn, *Pox Americana: The Great
Smallpox Epidemic of 1775–82* (New York: Hill and Wang, 2001), 110–123.

129. John Lewis Gervais to HL, 27 September 1782, in *PHL,* 16:30; Gervais to
HL, 12 February 1784, ibid., 16:389.

130. HL to Baron von Steuben, 5 January 1786, ibid., 16:625; HL to Duncan
Rose, 5 June 1785, ibid., 16:565; HL to Lachlan McIntosh, 10 September
1785, ibid., 16:592. Laurens probably included in this number his Turtle
River lumber camp in Georgia, and perhaps Wambaw, sold in 1769. HL
estimated that he had "lost 30 or 40 thousand Pounds sterling," worth
between £227,700 and £303,600 in South Carolina currency in 1775. HL to
George Appleby, 18 February 1783, ibid., 16:150–151; for conversion rates,
see McCusker, *Money and Exchange,* 317. On HL's wartime losses, see also
PHL, 16:404, 446–447.

131. HL to Baron von Steuben, 5 January 1786, ibid., 16:625; HL to James C.
Fisher and Samuel W. Fisher, 31 May 1786, ibid., 16:664; HL to John Boyd,
14 February 1786, Letterbook 1785–1787, HL Papers; HL to Babut, Fils &
Labouchere, 22 February 1786, ibid.

132. HL to James Bourdieu, 6 May 1785, in *PHL,* 16:558; HL to Samuel Johnston, 4 August 1791, ibid., 16:770; HL to Daniel Roberdeau, 1 July 1785,
ibid., 16:569–570; see also ibid., 16:208, 394, 404, 547, 550–551, 558.

133. HL to Edward Bridgen, 29 January 1785, ibid., 16:527–528; HL to Lachlan McIntosh, 10 September 1785, ibid., 16:592; HL to Bridgen, 30 June 1787, ibid., 16:716–717.

134. Ansonborough house: HL to John McQueen, 10 September 1785, ibid., 16:592; HL to John Ettwein, 14 July 1787, ibid., 16:729. Mepkin house: HL to Bridgen & Waller, 19 May 1786, ibid., 16:658; HL to Michael Hillegas, 14 April 1786, ibid., 16:646; HL to James Woodmason, 13 July 1787, ibid., 16:726–727; HL quoted in Wallace, *Life of Laurens,* 424 ("Duke of Richmond"); HL to William Bell, 12 March 1787, in *PHL,* 16:705. HL to James and Catherine Futterell, 4 June 1785, ibid., 16:565 ("old Mansion").

135. "Henry Laurens and the Ratification of the Constitution," 17 April–28 May 1788, in *PHL,* 16:751. On ratification processions, see David Waldstreicher, *In the Midst of Perpetual Fetes: The Making of American Nationalism, 1776–1820* (Chapel Hill: University of North Carolina Press, 1997), chap. 2.

136. HL to Thomas Ridout, 20 February 1786, Letterbook 1785–1787, HL Papers; Keith Wrightson, *Earthly Necessities: Economic Lives in Early Modern Britain* (New Haven, Conn.: Yale University Press, 2000), 30.

137. Carole Shammas, *A History of Household Government in America* (Charlottesville: University of Virginia Press, 2002), 34, 24.

Conclusion

1. Sylvia R. Frey, *Water from the Rock: Black Resistance in a Revolutionary Age* (Princeton, N.J.: Princeton University Press, 1991), 3.

2. Rachel N. Klein, *Unification of a Slave State: The Rise of the Planter Class in the South Carolina Backcountry, 1760–1808* (Chapel Hill: University of North Carolina Press, 1990), 10; Robert L. Meriwether, *The Expansion of South Carolina, 1729–1765* (Kingsport, Tenn.: Southern Publishers, 1940), 73–75.

3. George Ogilvie to Pegie Ogilvie, 25 June 1774, in "The Letters of George Ogilvie," ed. David S. Shields, *Southern Literary Journal,* special issue (1986): 119, 118.

4. Robert Raper to John Colleton, 9 February 1760, Robert Raper Letterbook (photocopy of original in West Sussex Record Office), South Carolina Historical Society, Charleston (hereafter cited as SCHS).

5. Klein, *Slave State,* chaps. 2–4; J. E. Crowley, *This Sheba, Self: The Conceptualization of Economic Life in Eighteenth-Century America* (Baltimore: Johns Hopkins University Press, 1974), 83.

6. Klein, *Slave State,* 9; Peter Manigault to William Blake, [December] 1772, Peter Manigault Letterbook, SCHS.

7. Henry Laurens to Isaac King, 28 October 1769, in *The Papers of Henry Laurens,* ed. Philip M. Hamer et al., 16 vols. (Columbia: University of South

Carolina Press, 1968–2003), 7:181 (hereafter cited as HL and *PHL*); Charles Woodmason, *The Carolina Backcountry on the Eve of Revolution: The Journal and Other Writings of Charles Woodmason, Anglican Itinerant*, ed. Richard J. Hooker (Chapel Hill: University of North Carolina Press, 1953), 6–7, xiii; Pelatiah Webster, "A Journal of a Voiage from Philadelphia to Charlestown in S[outh] Carolina" (1765), SCHS ("vast improvement"); *South-Carolina Gazette* (hereafter cited as *SCG*).

8. Klein, *Slave State*, 36; HL to Richard Grubb, 15 June 1748, in *PHL*, 1:148; quoted in Elise Pinckney, "Indigo," *American Dyestuff Reporter* 65 (1976): 39.

9. J. F. D. Smyth, *A Tour of the United States of America*, 2 vols. (Dublin, 1784), 2:36–37; Klein, *Slave State*, 16, 14n; Tiffort, *SCG*, 7 January 1764.

10. David Ramsay, "David Ramsay, a Selection of His Writings," ed. Robert L. Brunhouse, *Transactions of the American Philosophical Society* 55 (1965): 185–188.

11. Klein, *Slave State*, 15–36; Joseph A. Ernst and H. Roy Merrens, " 'Camden's Turrets Pierce the Skies!': The Urban Process in the Southern Colonies during the Eighteenth Century," *William and Mary Quarterly*, 3rd ser., 30 (1973): 549–574 (hereafter cited as *WMQ*); Peter Manigault to William Blake, [December] 1772, Manigault Letterbook.

12. *American Husbandry*, ed. Harry J. Carman (1775; repr., New York: Columbia University Press, 1939), 315–316, 345; John Drayton, *A View of South-Carolina, as Respects Her Natural and Civil Concerns* (Charleston, S.C., 1802), 113, 120; George C. Rogers Jr., *History of Georgetown County* (Columbia: University of South Carolina Press, 1970), 25–27.

13. James Glen, *A Description of South Carolina* . . . (1761), facsimile repr. in *Colonial South Carolina: Two Contemporary Descriptions*, ed. Chapman J. Milling (Columbia: University of South Carolina Press, 1951), 82–83, 36–37.

14. George D. Terry, " 'Champaign Country': A Social History of an Eighteenth Century Lowcountry Parish in South Carolina, St. Johns Berkeley County" (Ph.D. dissertation, University of South Carolina, Columbia, 1981), 208–216, 227; Robert Gray, "Narrative of Royalist Activities in Charleston, 1780, at Sea" (1782), Misc. Manuscripts Ser. 1, SCHS.

15. HL to Richard Oswald, 7 July 1764, in *PHL*, 4:338; HL to Thomas Bell, 20 July 1764, ibid., 4:348; HL to Andrew Williamson, 20 July 1764, ibid., 4:348; HL to Edward Wilkinson, ibid., 20 July 1764, 4:349.

16. William Henry Drayton, *The Letters of Freeman, Etc.: Essays on the Non-importation Movement in South Carolina*, ed. Robert M. Weir (Columbia: University of South Carolina Press, 1977), 83–84.

17. *The Debates in the Several State Conventions on the Adoption of the Federal Consitution* . . . , ed. Jonathan Elliot, 5 vols. (Philadelphia, 1876), 4:285, 272–273.

18. Jack N. Rakove, *Original Meanings: Politics and Ideas in the Making of the Constitution* (New York: Knopf, 1997), 68–69.

19. *The Records of the Federal Convention of 1787,* ed. Max Farrand, 3 vols. (New Haven, Conn.: Yale University Press, 1911), 1:400; *Debates in State Conventions,* 4:283–284; [David Ramsay], *An Address to the Citizens of South-Carolina* (Charleston, 1788), 7, 9–10; Adam Rothman, *Slave Country: American Expansion and the Origins of the Deep South* (Cambridge, Mass.: Harvard University Press, 2005), 15.

20. Phocion [Henry William DeSaussare], *Letters on the Questions of the Justice and Expediency of Going into Alterations of the Representation in the Legislature of South-Carolina, as Fixed by the Constitution* (Charleston, 1795), 6; Ramsay, "Writings," 195.

21. Robert M. Weir, " 'The Harmony We Were Famous For': An Interpretation of Pre-Revolutionary South Carolina Politics," *WMQ* 26 (1969): 473–501; "Constitution of South Carolina—1778," in *The Federal and State Constitutions, Colonial Charters, and Other Organic Laws . . . ,* ed. Francis Newton Thorpe, 7 vols. (Washington, D.C.: Government Printing Office, 1909), 6: 3248–3257.

22. Appius [Robert Goodloe Harper], *An Address to the People of South-Carolina* (Charleston, 1794), 5, 30–33; Walter Edgar, *South Carolina: A History* (Columbia: University of South Carolina Press, 1998), 254–259.

23. Americanus [Timothy Ford], *The Constitutionalist* (Charleston, 1794), 16, 21, 25.

24. DeSaussare, *Letters on the Questions,* 8–9.

25. Frederick A. Porcher, *The History of the Santee Canal: Dedicated to the South Carolina Historical Society, 1875, With An Appendix by A. S. Salley, Jr.* (Charleston: SCHS, 1903); Ronald E. Shaw, *Canals for a Nation: The Canal Era in the United States, 1790–1860* (Lexington: University Press of Kentucky, 1990), 18.

26. Porcher, *Santee Canal,* 1–7, 14; Frederic Cople Jaher, *The Urban Establishment: Upper Strata in Boston, New York, Charleston, Chicago, and Los Angeles* (Urbana: University of Illinois Press, 1982), 349–350.

27. HL to Richard Oswald, 4 January 1775, in *PHL,* 10:22; James A. McMillin, *The Final Victims: Foreign Slave Trade to North America, 1783–1810* (Columbia: University of South Carolina Press, 2004), 87.

28. Joyce E. Chaplin, "Creating a Cotton South in Georgia and South Carolina, 1760–1815," *Journal of Southern History* 57 (1991): 171–200.

29. Klein, *Slave State,* 251–252 and chap. 8.

30. Drew Gilpin Faust, *James Henry Hammond and the Old South: A Design for Mastery* (Baton Rouge: Louisiana State University Press, 1982), chap. 5.

31. Charles Ball, *Slavery in the United States: A Narrative of the Life and Ad-*

ventures of Charles Ball, a Black Man (New York, 1837), 83, 137, 166–167, 193, 201–202.

32. Ibid., 142; Steven F. Miller, "Plantation Labor Organization and Slave Life on the Cotton Frontier: The Alabama-Mississippi Black Belt, 1815–1840," in *Cultivation and Culture: Labor and the Shaping of Slave Life in the Americas*, ed. Ira Berlin and Philip D. Morgan (Charlottesville: University Press of Virginia, 1993), 166.

33. William Ancrum to Joshua Ferral, 6 February 1779, William Ancrum Letterbook, South Caroliniana Library, University of South Carolina, Columbia; Sam Bowers Hilliard, *Hog Meat and Hoecake: Food Supply in the Old South, 1840–1860* (Carbondale: Southern Illinois University Press, 1974), 104–105; Lewis C. Gray, *History of Agriculture in the Southern United States to 1860*, 2 vols. (1933; repr., Gloucester, Mass.: Peter Smith, 1958), 1:563–564.

34. Charles Joyner, *Down by the Riverside: A South Carolina Slave Community* (Urbana: University of Illinois Press, 1984), 91–92, 104; John Campbell, "As 'A Kind of Freeman'?: Slaves' Market-Related Activities in the South Carolina Up Country, 1800–1860," in *Cultivation and Culture*, 244, 249, 270–271.

35. HL to William Drayton, 23 February 1783, in *PHL*, 16:156; William Dusinberre, *Them Dark Days: Slavery in the American Rice Swamps* (New York: Oxford University Press, 1996); Joan E. Cashin, *A Family Venture: Men and Women on the Southern Frontier* (New York: Oxford University Press, 1991), 112–118.

36. Joyner, *Down by the Riverside*, 19; Dusinberre, *Them Dark Days*, 4, 388–396; Malcolm Bell Jr., *Major Butler's Legacy: Five Generations of a Slaveholding Family* (Athens: University of Georgia Press, 1987), 8–9, 47, 108–109.

37. Michael P. Johnson, "Planters and Patriarchy: Charleston, 1800–1860," *Journal of Southern History* 46 (1980): 55–60; Cashin, *Family Venture*, chap. 2.

38. William Kauffman Scarborough, *Masters of the Big House: Elite Slaveholders of the Mid-Nineteenth-Century South* (Baton Rouge: Louisiana State University Press, 2003), chap. 4, 123, appendices A and B, 1–2.

39. Peter A. Coclanis, *The Shadow of a Dream: Economic Life and Death in the South Carolina Low Country, 1670–1920* (New York: Oxford University Press, 1989), 111–112 and chap. 4.

40. T. A. [Thomas Amy], *Carolina; or, A Description of the Present State of That Country and the Natural Excellencies Thereof* (1682), in *Historical Collections of South Carolina . . .* , ed. B. R. Carroll, 2 vols. (New York, 1836), 2:61; Peter H. Wood, *Black Majority: Negroes in Colonial South Carolina from 1670 through the Stono Rebellion* (New York: W. W. Norton, 1974), 33.

41. Karen Ordahl Kupperman, "Jamestown as the City on a Hill" (conference paper, "Anglo-America in the Transatlantic World," John Carter Brown Library, Brown University, Providence, R.I., 21–23 April 2005).

42. HL to George Washington, 5 May 1778, in *PHL*, 13:257.

43. John Michael Vlach, *The Planter's Prospect: Privilege and Slavery in Plantation Paintings* (Chapel Hill: University of North Carolina Press, 2002); John Norris, *Profitable Advice for Rich and Poor . . .* (1712), in *Selling a New World: Two Colonial South Carolina Promotional Pamphlets,* ed. Jack P. Greene (Columbia: University of South Carolina Press, 1989), 102.

Index